Remembering 1989

Remembering 1989

FUTURE ARCHIVES OF PUBLIC PROTEST

Anke Pinkert

THE UNIVERSITY OF CHICAGO PRESS

CHICAGO AND LONDON

The University of Chicago Press, Chicago 60637
The University of Chicago Press, Ltd., London
© 2024 by The University of Chicago
All rights reserved. No part of this book may be used or reproduced in any
manner whatsoever without written permission, except in the case of brief
quotations in critical articles and reviews. For more information, contact the
University of Chicago Press, 1427 East 60th Street, Chicago, IL 60637.
Published 2024
Printed in the United States of America

33 32 31 30 29 28 27 26 25 24   1 2 3 4 5

ISBN-13: 978-0-226-83532-7 (cloth)
ISBN-13: 978-0-226-83533-4 (paper)
ISBN-13: 978-0-226-83534-1 (e-book)
DOI: https://doi.org/10.7208/chicago/9780226835341.001.0001

The University of Chicago Press gratefully acknowledges the generous
support of the Campus Research Board at the University of Illinois at
Urbana-Champaign toward the publication of this book.

Library of Congress Cataloging-in-Publication Data

Names: Pinkert, Anke, author.
Title: Remembering 1989 : future archives of public protest / Anke Pinkert.
Description: Chicago : The University of Chicago Press, 2024. | Includes
    bibliographical references and index.
Identifiers: LCCN 2024004415 | ISBN 9780226835327 (cloth) | ISBN
    9780226835334 (paperback) | ISBN 9780226835341 (ebook)
Subjects: LCSH: Revolutions—Germany (East)—History. | Protest
    movements—Germany (East)—History. | Collective memory—Germany. |
    Collective memory—Social aspects—Germany. | Germany (East)—Politics
    and government—1989–1990. | Germany—History—Unification, 1990. |
    Germany (East)—History—Historiography. | Germany—History—
    Unification, 1990—Historiography.
Classification: LCC DD289 .P56 2024 | DDC 943.087/8—dc23/eng/20240216
LC record available at https://lccn.loc.gov/2024004415

♾ This paper meets the requirements of ANSI/NISO Z39.48-1992
(Permanence of Paper).

Defeated as we are, we tasted our strength, the power of the crowd. We made a state disappear; we opened the administrative offices. We remembered "the future," for a moment, there it was.

Volker Braun

Contents

List of Figures ix
Preface xi

INTRODUCTION
From Neoliberal Triumph to Protest Memory · 1

CHAPTER ONE
Erasing '89–90 from the Capital · 31

INTERTEXT
Soviet Specters in the Periphery · 72

CHAPTER TWO
Pacifying Memory · 80

CHAPTER THREE
Possible Archives · 127

CHAPTER FOUR
Provisional History · 161

CHAPTER FIVE
Futures of Hope · 200

CODA
Unbound in the Open · 230

Acknowledgments 233
Notes 237
Bibliography 283
Index 311

Figures

0.1. Marx Engels Forum monument (1986) xii

1.1. Map of Central Berlin (ca. 1990s) 32

1.2. 25th anniversary of the fall of the Berlin Wall (2014) 43

1.3. "Window of Remembrance" (2017) 45

1.4. "Leap into Freedom" (1961) 48

1.5. Planned Monument to Freedom and Unity (2014) 54

1.6. Stela at Schlossplatz (2019) 61

1.7. Stela at Schlossplatz (detail) (2019) 62

1.8. Wall separating the US and Mexico (2023) 71

2.1. St. Nicholas Column, Monument to the Peaceful Revolution (2019) 86

2.2. "Peace Prayers at St. Nicholas Church" exhibition (2021) 101

2.3. Sites of the Peaceful Revolution (March 1989) 104

2.4. Sites of the Peaceful Revolution (June 1989) 105

2.5. Sites of the Peaceful Revolution (November 1989) 110

2.6. *white space/ Critical Thinking Needs Time and Space*, Leipzig (aerial, 2014) 118

2.7. *white space/ Critical Thinking Needs Time and Space*, Düsseldorf (2014) 119

2.8. *white space/ Critical Thinking Needs Time and Space*, Leipzig (close-up, 2014) 123

3.1. Stasi Records Agency (still from *Karl Marx City*, 2017) 135

3.2. Aisle in the Stasi Records Agency (still from *Karl Marx City*, 2017) 135

3.3. Archivist of the Stasi Records Agency (still from *Karl Marx City*, 2017) 138

3.4. Epperlein examines archival files (still from *Karl Marx City*, 2017) 140

3.5. GDR police in the fall of 1989 (still from *Karl Marx City*, 2017) 141

3.6. Demonstrators in the fall of 1989 (still from *Karl Marx City*, 2017) 142

3.7. Epperlein and her father at an assembly in 1989 (still from *Karl Marx City*, 2017) 143

3.8.	Clandestine assembly at Luxor-Palast, Karl-Marx-Stadt (still from *Karl Marx City*, 2017) 155
4.1.	Residential area in Halle (Saale) (still from *Material*, 2009) 162
4.2.	*Uncovering the Year 1990* (2019) 166
4.3.	Central Committee building of the Socialist Unity Party (still from *Material*, 2009) 175
4.4.	Rally at Central Committee building of the Socialist Unity Party (still from *Material*, 2009) 176
4.5.	Inmate at Brandenburg-Görden Prison (still from *Material*, 2009) 181
4.6.	"No Violence" armband (still from *Material*, 2009) 181
4.7.	Taped 37th session of the last GDR Volkskammer (still from *Material*, 2009) 189
4.8.	Parliamentarian at the 37th session of the last GDR Volkskammer (still from *Material*, 2009) 189
4.9.	"Wir waren das Volk" (1999) 198
5.1.	Immigrants' first enterprise (1989–1990) 213
5.2.	Kebab sale at the Humboldt-Universität (1989–1990) 215
5.3.	Selling fruit in the canteen (1989–1990) 215
5.4.	Demonstration against xenophobia (April 1990) 222

Preface

This book is about the forgotten inheritance of the East German revolution in 1989. In 1990, the East German playwright Heiner Müller radically mourned the departure of a specter (*Gespenst*) that had long haunted Europe. For Müller, as for many leftist artists and intellectuals in the German Democratic Republic (GDR) and the Soviet Union, the demise of Communism in Eastern Europe did *not* signal the beginning of a new era; instead, it marked the end of a 150-year-old socialist vision. Despite how warped and dictatorial this vision had turned out to be, a sense of sorrow befell the Left once Communism was voted out in 1990. A series of photographs by the East German artist Sibylle Bergemann captures this feeling of loss and defeat.

Taken between 1975 and 1986, the images show that the politics of inheritance was already at stake in the 1970s and 1980s, years before the Marxist state apparatus disappeared. In this respect, the last photograph in the series is especially striking. Shrouded, the Marx Engels Forum monument is being trucked to its final destination during the bleak winter of 1986. It was to be placed in an open square in front of the state's modernist Republic Palace and near the historic Berlin Cathedral, which had survived the Second World War. The GDR often used heroic socialist iconography to celebrate the party's victory. But Bergemann seems more interested in staging a funeral procession across a barren landscape. The austere mechanics of rubber and ropes combine to show hard labor; the forged figures appear forlorn, like exiled ghosts. Although this series is a memorial to the century-long Communist vision in the process of being assembled, these images—looked at from a 2023 vantage point—seem to run history, like film, forward and in reverse. While these photographs unwittingly anticipated the dismantling of the GDR, they also show that by 1986 the bureaucratic Communist dictatorship had already exhausted itself and dug its own grave.

In the coda to Müller's *A Specter Departs from Europe* (Ein Gespenst verlässt Europa), documentary filmmaker Peter Voigt reflects on Bergemann's

FIGURE 0.1. Marx Engels Forum monument (1986), Lustgarten, Berliner Dom, Berlin-Mitte, GDR. Photograph © Nachlass Sibylle Bergemann/OSTKREUZ/Courtesy Loock.

preoccupation with Communist *Untergang* (defeat) and the question of "what remains." Writing in 1990, amid the aftershocks of the revolutionary autumn, Voigt lamented that the lyricism of these images would not stand a chance amid the onslaught of neoliberal triumph. In the last decades, scholars of Eastern Europe have examined the post-1989 conditions in which these laments for the dead were directed at the ruin of twentieth-century socialism. At the same time, in one grand swoop, the Velvet Revolutions of 1989 were dismissed for having frustrated any previous utopian dreams and for having paralyzed cultural production, creating societies obsessed with their national pasts. However, this book aims to shift from defeat and elegy to lived possibility. I argue that both left-wing melancholy over the loss of emancipatory projects in the twentieth century and the neoliberal hubris unleashed in its wake blocked the transmission of an alternative story—namely, that of the political aspirations and tendencies of the abbreviated revolutionary uprising in East Germany in 1989.

For, I believe, the real existing social promise of the autumn of 1989 was hunted down and exorcised in the weeks, months, and years after the revolution. Almost immediately, there was a holy alliance of proponents of Western democracy and unbridled capitalism intent on erasing any aspects of 1989 that didn't fit with the narrative of neoliberalism's global triumph.

Moreover, this book reveals that despite being zealously hunted down and repressed, traces of the hopeful and socialist-inclined people's movements have persisted over the last thirty years. I show how these resilient traces have been expressed on the margins of official public memory. Suppression and exorcism, on the one hand, then, and the stubborn return of these impulses, on the other—this book tells that story and answers three basic questions: What occurred in 1989–90 in the GDR that was so eruptive and radical that it needed to be expunged from the historical record? How has a reunified government, which is invested in remembering 1989 as a moment of neoliberal triumph, used memorials to shape public memory? And how have alternative histories of 1989 resisted this erasure and appropriation?

To explore this contested dynamic of remembering and forgetting in the post-1989 neoliberal era, this book is situated within the field of memory and visual studies. *Remembering 1989* uncovers the limits of what can be known, seen, or represented in the contemporary memory sphere. Amid the tectonic shifts of 1989–90, the late GDR became a social laboratory for leaderless, voluntary, and genuinely democratic self-organizing. These energies of revolutionary unrest circulated in spaces that were commensurable neither with visions of free-market capitalism nor with the centralized governance of socialism. Yet, if acknowledged for the last thirty years by cultural critics and historians such as Timothy Garton Ash, this trend toward basic-democratic, self-governing activism has been dismissed as a mere fantasy of a *third way*. In actuality, however, such activism was the very space of politics, even if only momentarily.

My contention is that we need to unlearn the dominant version of history that governmental agencies and epistemological procedures have perpetually enforced since Germany's unification. And we would do well to also disengage from the recursive melancholic practices of the (old) Left. This process of unlearning will register differently from multiple perspectives (western, eastern, European and American, liberal, leftist, white, nonwhite, and so forth), and the deployment of these categories as stable itself will have to be explored. In this book, I consider how this kind of methodological renovation will allow a reimagining of the unfinalizable impulses of the grassroots political project that flourished in the dying days of the GDR. To that end, *Remembering 1989* brings together film, literature, photography, memoir, and an array of public objects, memorials, and gatherings, including live performances. This counter-archival work reveals the ways in which incongruous memories of the protest movements of '89–90 have often lingered in the last decades in the peripheries of hegemonic memory. I call these spaces of potentiality, borrowing from Jacques Derrida, *archives of the future*.

For the briefest of intervals, life in East German cities was virtually anarchic as people became political subjects and took down an intractable regime. Long forgotten is that for twelve months, an entire country was thrown into a remarkable state of uncertainty, which also carried with it historical possibilities. From Karl Marx City to Rostock, hundreds of thousands of ordinary citizens explored new forms of confrontation *and* cooperation, social protest and solidarity. In September of 1989, when activists of the peace movement gathered in a small town on the outskirts of Berlin to found the New Forum (Neue Forum), they did not call for unification, nor did they envision the capitalist order of the West. Faced with a state of crisis on the brink of violence, they demanded "time and space for open dialogue." The feverish founding of citizens' initiatives, new parties, and oppositional groups in the fall of '89 mobilized society; thousands of community-led councils and roundtables emerged across the GDR later that year. East Germans began improvising and taking up unrehearsed practices of transforming society from below in factories, streets, theatres, libraries, prisons, newspapers, neighborhood centers, and many other public spaces. Nonviolent and self-regulating, the people reorganized and accommodated one another in new political and social networks without imposed or preestablished rules.

At the same time, this book traces how and why any recollections of such collective action in '89–90 disappeared from the national and global memory spheres. These dreams of more collaborative, self-organized publics became buried under the fall of the Berlin Wall, followed by the victorious event of Germany's unification. By the end of the book, I hope to have persuaded the reader that those impulses of an alternative socio-ecological imaginary—which supported plural forms of tending to shared profits and common concerns—can indeed be reactivated. It is important to resituate the revolutionary unrest of 1989 within a longer trajectory of emancipatory history and to connect this uprising and fleeting moment of self-sovereignty to today's emerging global protest movements. After all, in *The Relevance of the Communist Manifesto* (2019), the political theorist Slavoj Žižek declared that "the most famous ghost that has been roaming around in the last 150 years was not a ghost of the past, but the specter of the revolutionary future." This book tells the history of how that specter was hunted down and exorcised immediately after 1989. Much was lost, but not all was lost. And so, this book also tells the story of how the memories of the people's protests of 1989 have persisted in alternative archives.

The five chapters that compose this book excavate the lost revolutionary inheritance of 1989 from different perspectives. Chapter 1, "Erasing '89–90 from the Capital," examines the post-1989 memorial landscape of Berlin to demonstrate how the gatekeeping powers of the State (funding structures, space allocation, Western oversight, etc.) impact practices of commemoration. Tracing the fate of the so-called Peaceful Revolution in Berlin's memorial sphere, I thus pay attention to urban and material spaces as the unreliable inheritors of political "public happiness." In chapter 2, "Pacifying Memory," I take the reader to Leipzig, the city two hours south of Berlin, where the civil uprising began in the fall of 1989. Rather than viewing Germany's unification and (neo)liberal democracy as the culmination of East Germany's civil movements, the local archives in Leipzig provide a particularly compelling story of the unrest and unfinished business that have come to haunt Germany in the era of late neoliberalism. Chapter 3, "Possible Archives," turns to the most powerful official archive in Germany's management of memory, the Stasi Records Agency. Reclaiming the familial and collective memory of the protests in 1989 through the intermedial work of the art documentary *Karl-Marx City* (2017), the chapter shows how to unlearn the existing logic of hegemonic archives centered on perpetrators and victims. Chapter 4, "Provisional History," provides a new, fractured, and open-ended account of the interval year 1989–1990, focusing on how the unfulfilled impulses of a radically democratic future turn up in discarded film footage. Chapter 5, "Futures of Hope," brings the book full circle by pitting protest memories of 1989 against contemporary uprisings, globally and in Germany, on the left and far right. Drawing on the 2018 photography exhibit *BİZİM BERLİN 89/90*, organized by a German-Turkish curator team at a small city museum in the capital, I return to my framing questions regarding how and why we can tell an alternative story of unrest in the late GDR. This chapter concludes by moving the transnational afterlives of 1968 and 1989 into closer proximity to highlight their vital and interlinked political legacies. Fragile, uncommon alliances and more tactical spaces for anti-racist, anti-imperial solidarities emerge. Taken together, the case studies in this book assemble an archive for the future and issue a wide-ranging reminder that neoliberal capitalism and post-democratic political polarization cannot be without alternatives.

[INTRODUCTION]

From Neoliberal Triumph to Protest Memory

The visitor who enters Berlin today will not find any remembrance of the revolutionary uprisings that erupted, over a period of nine weeks, across East Germany thirty years ago. Indeed, when we take issues such as nationalism and unification as a given rather than subjecting them to consideration, we tend to overlook the key element of 1989: its liminal openness. This book reminds us that such an outcome was not a foregone conclusion. The people who initiated and participated in protests in the fall of 1989—when personal risk was the greatest and the outcome most uncertain—saw their future as an open-ended good. *Remembering 1989* deepens our understanding of revolutionary protests and unveils their potent yet often intangible afterlives. In the last thirty years, two interrelated stories—of neoliberal triumph and of leftist melancholia about the downfall of socialism—have worked in tandem to erase the alternative history of the late German Democratic Republic (GDR). Now that Western market-conforming democracy itself appears to be on trial in a hyper-polarized era, where are usable, even hopeful memories for the future? Returning to the politicized interregnum of spontaneous collaborative unrest in '89–90, this book makes a case for political joy and explores the possibilities of vital, open-ended transmissions of revolutionary impulses across space and time.

Memory in the (Post-)Neoliberal Era

The affect of political joy introduces a different beat into the memory of the late twentieth and early twenty-first centuries. In the wake of the collapse of the Soviet Union, the neoliberal turn led to a drastic shift in the dynamics of contemporary memory politics. Once the utopian imaginary disappeared from history, we became engulfed ever further in a culture of retrospection focused on calamity and misfortune. This shift involved the recasting of multiple pasts through expressions of suffering, victimization, and trauma—phenomena that had to varying degrees already defined discourses and practices of memory in the West in the postwar era. In the long aftermath of 1989, it appeared leftist ideas were being absorbed into a black hole: All emancipatory prospects and even the thought of protest were buried by the fall of the Wall; "the idea of a different world order, a different memory, and a different will," Jean Ziegler writes, "fell into disrepute."[1] In this vein, commentators have rightly observed that after 1989, the entire history of Communism was reduced to its totalitarian dimension, and a nationalist return discarded socialism's internationalist paradigm. Perhaps most memorably, this discursive shift was outlined by the cultural historian Enzo Traverso in his seminal 2017 study, *Left-Wing Melancholia*: The memory of Stalinist crimes replaced that of revolution, the remembrance of the Holocaust erased remembrance of antifascism, and the memory of slavery eclipsed that of anti-colonialism. After the Berlin Wall fell, a narrative linking barbarism and revolution disappeared—the dialectic of the twentieth century was broken.[2]

While I agree with Traverso's overall mapping of memory shifts in the neoliberal era, this perspective has absorbed the political potentiality of the 1989 uprising in the late GDR. Overshadowed by the downfall of state socialism, the events in 1989 seemed to have failed to liberate new revolutionary energies. They seemed to have betrayed history, selling out any viable prospects for structural change to come. We are certainly experiencing a reawakening of progressive legacies—a search for visions imagining projects beyond today's ultra-global capitalism, beyond current socioeconomic models and systemic inequalities produced by racist and imperial histories, and beyond complacency with the catastrophic ecological status quo. There are calls to return to the future as a driving force and horizon for evaluating and constructing the past. Even if such calls are not entirely new, they have become louder recently.[3] In this book, I attempt to put into practice this shift toward a future-oriented engagement with memory, illuminating how we can garner radically democratic potentialities from the unrest in East Germany in 1989. Broadly, this study challenges the notion that "failed" revolutions arise and then dissipate without a trace. I hope to make three critical interventions: First, out of disparate memory strands, I assemble an entirely new archive of 1989 in the periphery of the State's historical record. Second, I stress that the activist legacies of late socialist Eastern Europe are often elided from contemporary memory. Third, I demonstrate how natural it is to assume that the present controls the past when we ignore the knowledge that lingers across temporal zones and outside authorized histories, sites, and commemorations. This approach allows new understandings of popular movements that have been forgotten or have been declared failures. My readings illustrate how these pasts, even if effaced from official memory, continue to transgress and fracture the historical record today, compelling us to work for a more livable future.

Indeed, we cannot understand the meanings of events when we do not also consider the processes of forgetting and remembering that have occurred ever since. Therefore, this opening chapter traces the diverging pathways of recalling, erasing, and appropriating the '89 revolution through the last decades, in the official record, in the media, and in the academic arena. I aim to illustrate a dynamic field of discursive, artistic, and historical forces in which 1989 has slipped in and out of sight, even forming a lacuna in recent memory. We begin with twentieth- and twenty-first-century memory regimes that veer toward transcendental teleology and narratives of victory and closure. In the following, I offer a variegated theoretical vocabulary to unsettle the universal perspective of the Peaceful Revolution as the fight for Western freedom and democracy, contouring the book's major argument lines. My focus will be on the spectral revolutionary legacy of '89, the role of nonviolence in the citizens' uprising, and the need to re-politicize the historical interval period. I close the chapter by outlining current research in the fields of memory and visual studies and delineating a method of archival futurity by which to recover what has been lost.

A Western (Neo)liberal Lens: The Official Narrative of 1989

I teach at a public research university in the United States, and when I ask my students how the Berlin Wall fell, they rarely think long before bringing up Ronald Reagan's famous Cold War speech. It is worth recalling the symbolic geopolitical scenario here, even if the reader (as most of my students) will know it was not this speech that made the Iron Curtain crumble. In June of 1987, with the Wall and the iconic Brandenburg Gate as a backdrop, Ronald Reagan declared to a crowd in West Berlin that he knew of one move the Soviets could make that would dramatically advance the cause of freedom and peace. He then spoke directly to his Soviet counterpart: "Mr. Gorbachev, tear down this wall." Although the televised speech received relatively little coverage, Reagan's use of the second person imperative, rarely employed by US presidents in delicate diplomatic contexts, rendered the line particularly memorable.[4] Over time, the popular myth established itself in the US media that the "states of Eastern Europe 'fell to freedom like dominoes' after Reagan's words 'pushed the first one over.'"[5] Especially in conservative networks, Reagan himself appears to have been single-handedly responsible for bringing down the Wall, and for delivering the Soviet Bloc to the freedom and prosperity of the West. Of course, other histories and narratives circulate in academia and the public realm that challenge this dominant interpretation (I will refer to them in the following pages). Yet, it bears repeating that this perspective is one of the most enduring Western universalist frameworks by which the collapse of Eastern Europe has been understood.

Buttressed by this Western (post–) Cold War perspective, a few key events of 1989 have formed into a naturalized, linear narrative in Germany's official history about the so-called *Wende* (literally, "turn" or "change"). The *Wende* describes the turning point in Germany, marked by what is now known as the Peaceful Revolution and leading to the removal of the Berlin Wall, with East and West Germany "reunifying" one year later, eliminating the division "imposed upon Germans more than four decades earlier."[6] This national narrative of the *Wende* is stored in the historical record and recirculated, in reduced form, at each anniversary by global media and official commemorative discourse. It must be noted, though, that forms of mass mediation also shaped the very events of '89. As Jacques Derrida observed, mass media had grown in such an unheard-of fashion and at such a speed that it not only recorded the fall of Marxist regimes but also "contributed mightily."[7] In the interest of outlining this official history briefly, I will attempt to restate the dominant narrative as factually as possible, basing my account on government documents, websites, and newspapers, while selectively tracking how the live-imaging and national and global dissemination of these events structured realities.

In the summer of 1989, thousands of East Germans flee to the West across Hungary's border with Austria, while others escape by storming the West German embassies in Warsaw, Poland, and Prague, Czechoslovakia. Western television cameras are on standby in all locations to catch the risky escapes and celebrations of freedom. On October 7, 1989, the GDR government closes the borders to the CSSR, de facto preventing anyone from leaving, as the Communist state prepares to celebrate its fortieth anniversary with official mass parades on a grand stage in East Berlin. The GDR circulates these hyperbolic images on its official TV channel while the disintegrating relationship between SED (Socialist Unity Party) leaders and Mikhail Gorbachev is displayed. Two days later, the peace prayers at Leipzig's St. Nicholas Church, harking back to the oppositional movements in the 1980s, turn into mass demonstrations. On October 9, an unprecedented crowd of seventy thousand marches in central Leipzig to "demand freedom"—and is broadcast on the West German evening news. The GDR refrains from any military intervention, and on October 9, "negotiations" with the SED, the ruling force of the authoritarian regime, begin. Both West

FROM NEOLIBERAL TRIUMPH TO PROTEST MEMORY › 5

and East German media and international news outlets report in starkly different terms on the event that history books today render as the "peaceful turning point of the revolution."[8] In September, a political alliance known as the New Forum (Neue Forum) is founded by peace movement members Bärbel Bohley, Jens Reich, and others near East Berlin, at the house of late GDR dissident Robert Havemann. The New Forum becomes the first countrywide political movement outside the Protestant Church.

In an effort to squelch the pressure of the population, the Communist leader Erich Honecker resigns on October 18 and is replaced by the SED reform politician Egon Krenz, who speaks the same day on the evening news. The much-cited first legal demonstration (also the largest) takes place in East Berlin on November 4, with artists, intellectuals, and Politburo members giving unrehearsed speeches in front of a crowd of five hundred thousand (including the cameras of Western and international media outlets). Most speakers, such as Christa Wolf, Heiner Müller, Jens Reich, and Stefan Heym, imagine a future of democratic socialism in an independent and sovereign GDR—visions that have been canonized as a "Left out of touch." Under pressure from the mass uprising, the GDR government de facto resigns on November 7, and is officially reconstituted under Krenz. Krenz is affirmed as general secretary of the SED Central Committee and calls for political renewal, aligning the socialist state belatedly with glasnost and perestroika. On November 9, the Berlin Wall falls (images go around the world of the press conference during which a Politburo member accidentally suggests the opening of the border). Two days after the fall of the Wall, the *Bild-Zeitung* (in the West) prints the headline "'We Are the People,' They Cry Today—'We Are One People,' They Will Cry Tomorrow."[9] (Arguably, the slogan "We are one people," retrospectively adopted as a plea for unification, did not originate among East Germans.) Amid celebrations of the fall of the Berlin Wall, political developments happen rapidly: the GDR state erodes as East Germans demand the dismantling of the Stasi, the SED regime's security apparatus. In the winter of 1989, protesters take on the Stasi district offices in several cities, a series of occupations that culminates in early 1990, when the Stasi headquarters in East Berlin is stormed by civil rights activists and by "a crowd of angry citizens who had been spied on for decades." Another hundred thousand East Germans march peacefully in Leipzig, the *Washington Post* reports, "demanding the immediate dissolution of the Stasi and continuing their weekly call for unification with West Germany."[10] Meanwhile, the population continues to flee to the West because the GDR economy is revealed to be bankrupt, and its currency quickly loses value, according to the prevailing story.

As the revolutionary autumn draws to a close before it has even started, the conservative West German chancellor and leader of the Christian Democratic Union (CDU) Helmut Kohl delivers his famous speech on December 19 in Dresden. In it, he speaks of the "unity of our nation" as the remaining goal of the Peaceful Revolution—"should the historical hour permit it"—and thanks the East Germans for "demonstrating in the spirit of peacefulness . . . to build a better future." The ten thousand who gather erupt into thunderous applause as Kohl anticipates his later promise of "flourishing landscapes in the East." Clearly for the benefit of the media, the address takes place near the ruin of the Frauenkirche, destroyed by Allied bombings in 1945, invoking the historical legacy of the Second World War and Germany's division. It is in this place that Kohl realizes that "this regime is finished. Unification is coming!" as millions in East and West, in Europe and across the Atlantic, look on.[11] The trajectory is sealed by the "first free elections," in March of 1990, which the conservative "Alliance for Germany" (Allianz für Deutschland)—an anti-Communist coalition backed by the West German Christian Democratic Party—wins. Alliance 90 (Bündnis 90), a political coalition formed by organizations of the citizens' movement, receives not even 3 percent of the vote.

In May of 1990, the Allied Powers—namely, the United States, France, Great Britain, and the Soviet Union—alongside officials of the FRG (Federal Republic of Germany) and GDR—meet to talk about the future of Germany and Europe, due to "the German people pushing for immediate reunification," according to the narrative provided by the Archive of the US State Department.[12] In reality, plans for the unification of Germany have existed since the fall of 1989 and were shared by Kohl with the FRG Bundestag in November 1989 and with US president George H. W. Bush during an intimate, high-stakes, twenty-four-hour meeting on February 25, 1990, in Washington, DC. The global superpower initially appeared caught off guard but was "relatively quick to overcome its objections and support the Bonn government."[13] The *New York Times* reports on the visit and notes correctly, "Mr. Kohl himself faces elections in West Germany, now scheduled for December 2, 1990. In East Germany, the alliance of conservative parties supported by Mr. Kohl is trailing far behind the Social Democrats and is not expected to win the elections next month."[14] However, the national elections in the GDR lead to the abovementioned victory of the conservative Alliance for Germany and, subsequently, to the constitution of the tenth and final GDR Volkskammer (People's Chamber), which will govern under a Grand Coalition of Christian Democrats and Social Democrats. In quick succession, a handful of FRG and GDR politicians broker the major treaties leading to unification. On July 1, the GDR government ratifies the economic union between the two German states. By midnight, all banks in

East Germany receive West German currency to be handed out at a rate of 1:1. Images of East Germans waving bundles of money go through the international press. The Treuhand, a Trust agency, is created to oversee the (re) privatization of the GDR's state-owned enterprises, which directly involve about 8,500 state-owned companies and four million employees, more than two million hectares of agricultural land, and large parts of the property of the former National People's Army.

On October 3, 1990, with the GDR's accession to the Federal Republic, according to article 23 of the constitution, Germany is "reunified."[15] At midnight, the black, red, and gold flag of West Germany—now the flag of all of Germany—is raised above the Brandenburg Gate, marking the moment of reunification. October 3 has since been named a national holiday, the Day of German Unity. Once all governmental institutions move from Bonn to Berlin and, more importantly, the Memorial to the Murdered Jews of Europe is finally erected, in 2005, the city begins to imagine itself confidently as the new center of Europe. With the formation of the CDU-led government under Chancellor Angela Merkel (CDU) the same year, Germany styles itself as a beacon of Western liberalism, which pronounces that no alternatives exist to the values and structures of a market-conforming democracy. While the atmosphere had not remained celebratory for long after unification—unemployment in the East eventually affects a staggering one-third of the workforce[16]—the axiom of "freedom and unity" forges its own reality in the following decades, as the neoliberal mantra of privatization, deregulation, and liberalization establishes itself.

Ever since, alongside commemorative rituals, official history has harnessed the energies of the Peaceful Revolution directly to these inevitable outcomes of the post–Cold War world in the present. In the era of (neo) liberalism, Germany's ruling narrative eclipsed the unsettled meanings of the abbreviated (or as-yet-unfulfilled, or never-to-be-realized) revolutionary transformation that occurred in 1989. Focusing on protest memory, I critique the perception of 1989 as a historically closed event that aimed at and was inevitably actualized by the West's victory and by Germany's reunification.

But 1989 was not only a national turning point. The nationalization processes by which Germany absorbed 1989 were also a means to (re)constitute a globality that struggled to make itself seen and felt representationally (that is, mediated) until the wall "came down." New forms of the global were being constructed here and made serviceable, among other things, to the erasure of the failed alternative. The Soviet Union and the Eastern European bloc had fostered international relations with African, Southeast Asian, and Latin American countries while being entangled in their (post) colonial histories and anti-colonial struggles. Post-1989, the normative fiction of increasing global interconnectedness centered unabashedly on the expansion of new markets and the ever-rising need for the circulation of capital. After all, this need was legitimized by history itself. As cultural historian Susan Buck-Morss, postcolonial scholar Amitav Ghosh, and others have argued, neoliberalism became the hegemonic structure characterized by the combined forces of global capitalism and nation-state politics.[17] Following the collapse of the Soviet bloc, Western experts, economists, and capitalists went to the countries of Eastern Europe to propagate the seemingly logical and thus inevitable privatization of state assets. Alongside the collapse of existing social networks, political chaos, and the ruthless economic devastation of entire regions with effects felt to this day, this privatization produced the corrupt class of Eastern European oligarchs who are now part of the global elite, implicated in new authoritarian and nationalist structures.[18] In East Germany, rather than producing an oligarchy from within, this capital went nearly exclusively to those private investors from the West. The global is not a new formation emerging from 1989, of course, but at that historical juncture, it becomes a legible and palatable narrative to the East in ways the neoliberal economic policies of the 1970s onward had not. Inevitably, the Velvet Revolutions of '89 were largely forgotten once the new structures of expanded economic global interconnectedness were put in place, while postcommunist memory and commemorations began to produce repackaged cultures of nostalgia.[19]

To my eye, what is most striking in contemporary (Western) post-1989 memory is the continued absence of (Soviet) Eastern Europe.[20] Today, with the rise of nationalist movements in Eastern and Central Europe, awareness of the East has returned, yet often as imagined Other. Intra-European orientalist notions about the East in Europe, for example, have reemerged. This deep-seated prejudice can be traced back to the Enlightenment: the East never belonged to the post-Enlightenment tradition of the West.[21] The more recent, socialist (post–)Cold War histories are also displaced. The Velvet Revolutions—with their obstinate, if ultimately rejected, political legacies of 1968, including the vision of a "socialism with a human face," or the worker-led Solidarność movement in Poland in the 1980s, which influenced civil rights activists in the late GDR—remain obscure. Yet, I suspected in starting this book that it would be important to reclaim some of those remnants and broken traditions of Prague in '68 and '89. After all, I recalled from my own participation in the revolutionary unrest of 1989 that echoes of the Prague Spring were in the air.[22] This refracted double inheritance has become submerged in Western-led narrative orchestrations. Even scholars dedicated to the history and memory of twentieth-century social movements tend to miss the politicized significance of 1989 in the late GDR, if for different reasons. The literary critic Kristin Ross, in her brilliant *May '68 and Its Afterlives*, unwittingly reinforces the liberal thinking that the insurgents of 1989 (unlike those of 1968) viewed their democratic aspirations as incompatible with socialism.[23] Now, historians of Eastern and Central Europe have long advanced this argument about the orientation of '89 toward the Western world order, even if they also usefully examine the different degrees and variations in the transformational post-socialist changes. In what is perhaps the most influential of these works, *A Carnival of Revolution: Central Europe* (2002), Padraic Kenney echoes the approach of Timothy Garton Ash in *The Magic Lantern* (1990) by promising a look behind the scenes at the grassroots movements that toppled Communism. Tracing the liberalizing and democratizing impulses throughout the Soviet empire and across half a dozen countries that changed rapidly after 1989, the study repeats the by-now-familiar argument that mass migration, mainly for economic reasons, played a crucial role in the fall of East Germany. "If the revolution had an imagined end-point," Kenney writes, "it was, for many in Central Europe, the prosperity and economic security of the West."[24] The memory strands recovered in *Remembering 1989* complicate this storyline. Relying solely on the Western lens (no matter how anthropologically embedded) causes us to miss several unforeseeable turning points within the trajectory of the abbreviated, nonviolent revolution in the late GDR. Due to their disinvestment from power and party politics, the citizens' movements may have forfeited a historic chance to carve out an alternative path to remaking the country.[25] Still, the alternative memory work in this book shows that ordinary people certainly practiced a wealth of radically democratic formats in this transient political space.

1989–90: The Gap between Past and Future

In an essay entitled "The Gap between Past and Future," philosopher Hannah Arendt illuminates the limits of transmitting revolutionary histories across historical ruptures. Starting with an aphorism by the French writer and poet Rene Char—"our inheritance was left to us by no testament"—Arendt calls our attention to an impasse to which I'll keep returning throughout this book: once a new order has been established, resistance movements belonging to a different era can no longer be grasped, made legible, or, shall we say, seen within the newly established frameworks of politics and daily life.[26] Although Arendt formulated this insight in 1961, in reference to the postwar era, her thinking can help elucidate the culture of oblivion that emerged in the rapid transition from socialism to a neoliberal free-market economy in the aftermath of 1989.

Abrupt and unexpected, this shift erased not only the German Democratic Republic but also the divergent and often contradictory strands of dissent that had unsettled the socialist East German state. When a monolithic post-1989 framework of the GDR as a "second dictatorship" was swiftly forged and propagated in the post-unification infrastructure, including school curricula, government commissions, museums, award-winning films, archives, and research funding, there no longer seemed to be any institutions or minds capable of asking adequate, meaningful questions about the past.[27] The conservative and national forces emerging from West Germany played a central role in shaping post-1989 memory politics. In 1992, the government appointed a high-profile Enquete Commission with the mandate to "work through the history and consequences of the SED dictatorship in Germany."[28] The commission consisted of mainly conservative historians from the West, with a few former civil rights activists from the East. As cultural historian Paul Cooke aptly notes, the commission's six-hundred-page findings presented an unambiguous line that the majority of the government took, classifying the GDR as "totalitarian system," a term that was crucially important because it allowed "the difference between the whole of Germany's dictatorial legacy and its present democratic system" to be demarcated. The problematic equation of the GDR with the Nazi dictatorship underlined the superiority of the democratic political system in the FRG, and thereby "legitimize[d] the expansion of the West German state."[29] At the same time, the commission's focus on the *Unrechtscharakter* (unjust character) of the SED regime aimed to bring historical justice to the victims of persecution in the GDR whose judicial and material rehabilitations were limited following unification. Given the differentiated political culture in West Germany since the 1970s and 1980s, the force of this normalizing argument after 1989 still surprises. After all, West Germany had officially recognized the GDR as a sovereign state in 1972, and it often described the other Germany in more conciliatory terms as a different political system to foster negotiation and dependable cooperation rather than public criticism.[30] But once the Social Democrats lost power in 1982 and a Christian Democratic government was put in place, the conservative intellectuals' ideal of securing ground for a "healthy" nationalism by laying to rest the ghosts of Nazism (which had after all found its evil twin in Stalinism) gained broader appeal. The continued insistence of the West German Left on coming to terms with the past (*Vergangenheitsbewältigung*) was dismissed as guilt-obsessed. Instead, conservatives advocated moving on, both by embracing Germany's future as dominant power of a united Europe and by reclaiming the positive legacies of the pre-Nazi past. With unification, historian Geoff Eley argues, this emergent German nationalism in West Germany then received an "invigorating boost."[31] While it is important to note that East Germans' participation in Germany's historical success story of "reunification" was acknowledged in the report of the Enquete Commission and the broader public sphere, the conditions and interpretations of that affirmative trajectory toward Western freedom were always already determined in the 1990s.

During that decade, any stable frameworks and infrastructural spaces from within which to question established paradigms had disappeared. In literary and cinematic works, the year 1989 is also often marked as a break or ellipsis, or is simply left out.[32] To borrow from Arendt's essay, what remained hidden were the "small islands of freedom": the instances in the late GDR when people had taken the initiative to become challengers, when they "show[ed] up together" in public spaces in the fall of 1989 and "learnt how to act anew," yet didn't necessarily aim to erode, let alone overturn, the socialist system.

This spontaneous self-gathering, I argue, needs to be understood in and of itself as a political enactment, regardless of the slogans for unity East Germans may have shouted when the chancellor of the Federal Republic visited the city of Dresden by the end of 1989, and regardless of the historical outcome of Germany's unification. In the Archive of the Citizens' Movement, Leipzig, for instance, hundreds of letters written by ordinary citizens in the early fall of 1989 attest to a different historical momentum. The people streaming into the streets of the GDR were motivated by something "irresistible," in Arendt's sense, something akin to a bodily need or sensation.[33] A twenty-nine-year-old woman from Markranstädt writes on October 15, 1989, to one of the newly forming (still clandestine) citizens' organizations, "I've never been so preoccupied with a political situation as at the moment." She had heard a representative of the New Forum on West German television and asks if there are any pamphlets she can hand out in the streets to help "develop activities for the GDR and socialism." As tens of thousands were assembling in the streets of Berlin, Leipzig, Dresden, and Karl-Marx-Stadt, a resident of Borsdorf, a village outside Leipzig, plead in a scribbled note, "I want to partake [teilhaben] in this process. Where can I find members and sympathizers of the New Forum?" A letter written by Lutz L. from Auerbach, a town near the border with the Czech Republic in the southwest corner of Saxony, speaks of a broad support movement in the region of the Vogtland for political and economic transformation in the GDR, "which have only been possible because of the emigration wave and demonstrations in the street." All over the country, citizens sent petitions to the GDR Ministry of the Interior, knowing they risked arrest if the uprising failed. A family living on Käthe Kollwitz Strasse, in Leipzig, gathered with neighbors in their living room to type up an *Eingabe* (a complaint letter, a genre of citizen protest in the GDR). In it, they voiced their anger: "We are outraged," the appeal states, that "thousands of people are at the moment leaving our country. In our opinion, we urgently need a new forum." The New Forum's agenda for improving socialism was to be taken seriously; "things proven should be preserved." Hundreds of collective declarations reveal how East Germans appeared to be "moved by the events during these weeks," even in their places of work. The medical staff at the Poliklinik Leipzig Südwest openly expressed how encouraged they were by "the far-reaching mobilization for renewal from below." Facing state power, they criticized the SED government for its tepid response and urgently noted that "time is running out!" (Die Zeit drängt!).[34]

The sheer upsurge of awe and determination in these archival files suggests a society that was breaking open. Finding oneself naked, "stripped of all masks" (those assigned by society and those fabricated by individuals), Arendt writes, people can experience freedom from officialdom. Most essentially for my argument, she stresses they do so not "because they acted against tyranny" (or dictatorship) but because they have "taken the initiative upon themselves and therefore, without knowing or even noticing it, begin to create that public space between themselves where freedom can appear."[35] It is this sense of public freedom or public happiness that embodies the lost inheritance of the revolution. This loss may have been inevitable in light of political reality, but even the experience of the people who participated was soon consumed by oblivion. In the aftermath of the *Wende*, the failure of memory befell not only the heirs but also those who lived through the interval period.

Today, 1989 has become synonymous with the fall of the Berlin Wall and the ensuing triumph of Western capitalism. The iconic shot of Easterners and Westerners celebrating atop the graffitied Wall (the Western view) under the backlit, triumphant Quadriga, towering over the neoclassical architecture of the Brandenburg Gate, is inextricably linked with the fall of Eastern European socialism and the victory of the history and political system shaped by the West. Materialized in photographic form, the moment of unity entered the global "archive of cultural memory," perpetually reinforcing the dominance of the democratic world. Symbolically, November 9, 1989, marked the teleological endpoint of Germany's national history and the end of the European and transatlantic twentieth-century order. The fall of the Wall constituted a tectonic shift, abolishing the division of East and West Germany and the divided Cold War world. But the Wall did not simply fall, even if this abstract interpretation has established itself as the prevailing narrative. The triumphant images at the Brandenburg Gate documented a national joy and ecstatic, if short-lived, fraternity that played to a global audience.[36] With the global broadcast came the gift—for free, as it were—of releasing the Communist specters once and for all.

In 1992, the editors of Jacques Derrida's *Specters of Marx* (1992) aptly observed, "In the wake of the orgy of self-congratulations which followed the 1989 crumbling of the Berlin Wall, and the subsequent dissolution of the Soviet Union, . . . a wave of optimism engulfed the Western democratic States." This contagious optimism became associated with the popularity of Francis Fukuyama's infamous claim that the end of history was at hand, "that the future—if that word could still be said to have the same meaning—was to become the global triumph of free market economies."[37] Derrida ascribed the euphoria to an already dying (neo)liberalism, its last hurrah. Notably, French intellectuals of his generation rarely lamented the collapse of the Soviet system itself—recalling the atmosphere of the 1950s instead, when they had learned about totalitarian terror in Eastern Europe, from Soviet trials to the defeated uprising in Hungary. Yet the philosophical concerns with legacy and death, survival, mourning, and the trace of the spectral in Derrida's post-1989 works also signaled a geopolitical perspective: a recognition that the reprieve in a world trajectory toward further inequality had come to a close. Thirty years later, we may face the end of neoliberalism (or its monstrous offspring) in the rise of antidemocratic politics both in the East and the West.[38] In my view, this rise is in no small measure related to the politics of forgetting that ensued after the collapse of the Soviet Union and the socialist system in Eastern Europe. I explore this connection in the intertext, "Soviet Specters in the Periphery."

Force of Nonviolence

In this book, I argue that two foundational narratives are linked in the post-1989 memory of the neoliberal era: one centers on the anti-dictatorial uprising for Western freedom, and the other on the revolutions' peacefulness. Perhaps for all the wrong reasons, Germany has celebrated the revolution's peacefulness, honoring at every official anniversary the *sanftmutigen* (gently courageous) East Germans who took on Germany's "second dictatorship," transmitting the discursive linkage between the GDR and the Third Reich.[39] In each official restaging of this origin story, the dynamics of power, mass media, and memory making come into play. To paraphrase the essayist Daniela Dahn, the revolution was so peaceful that all remained the same in the West. (She adds that, in accordance with the foundational logic of the Western system, only private property guarantees security and independence; 95 percent of the East's state-owned, quasi-collective economic wealth was transferred to private hands in the West.)[40] In this historical turn, the existing structures of market-conforming democracy were expanded and affirmed. Thus, it is no surprise that the Peaceful Revolution has been enshrined as a success story in Germany's national memory. In this study, I use "Peaceful Revolution" (initial letters capitalized) to mark official history and its frame of universality and "peaceful revolution" (initial letters lowercase) to signal the event's unfinished quality, its historical contingencies, and its inherent promise. Of course, these discourses also overlap, adapt, and become entangled. Throughout this book, I refer to the events of the early fall of 1989 as *rebellion, revolt, uprising,* and *unrest.*[41] This conflictual space and political forcefield is tamed or pacified in the official notion of the Peaceful Revolution.

Above all else, I argue, this normalizing enshrinement of the Peaceful Revolution has rendered the rupture of '89–90 invisible. To be clear, the peaceful outcome of the events that year is nothing but astonishing if we consider the prevention of bloodshed and the loss of life. Due to the remarkable restraint of protesters *and* military forces, the uprising remained nonviolent for the most part. The truism of the Peaceful Revolutions in Central and Eastern Europe could, however, be challenged on the grounds alone that in Romania nearly a thousand people perished during the overthrow of Nicolae Ceauşescu. Nineteen protesters were killed in Georgia, and in the Yugoslav republics, the peaceful surrender of power by Communist parties was followed by war. Even in the context of East Germany, we could point to numerous cases of police brutality during the early weeks of unrest.[42] In Dresden, Plauen, Leipzig, and Berlin, confrontations erupted between demonstrating crowds and forces of the state. There were incidents of police violence (as well as racist and right-wing attacks on the fringes of the protests, which I return to later in the book).

Arguably, in the neoliberal era, these corporeal, affective encounters are erased from post-unification memory because they convey messy historical potentialities. It is through the medium of literature that important fragmentary forms of alternative post-1989 protest memory can be transmitted and circulated. Ingo Schulze's fictionalized account of 1989, *New Lives* (*Neue Leben*), supplies one of the most visceral impressions of state force on the bodies of subjects who ceased to obey. After the protagonist's mother joins the first protests in Dresden against the GDR regime in early October, he catches a glimpse of the bruises inflicted by police batons on her body. Within this fictional narrative, all the photographs the mother took during the protests turned out blurred (there indeed exists very little visual documentation of confrontations with police in cities across East Germany, as discussed in chapter 3). While the injured mother is in shock and unable to communicate what occurred, the text conjures an alternative archive. She draws on the violent suppression of Salvador Allende's socialist-democratic movement in 1973 in Chile—a learned progressive imaginary in the GDR—as a proxy for narrating her own experience.[43] *New Lives* is perhaps the most poignant literary rebuttal of the invisibility of GDR state violence in the post-1989 media and the official public record. The confrontations with police in the early revolutionary autumn are imagined in this novel as protests against both the orthodox SED regime and the capitalist, globalist, US-led power of the West. Indeed, in both cases, structural violence eludes naming until the police show up. In turn, then, peacefulness is revealed as a hard-won struggle.[44] Far from being given, the nonviolence of the peaceful revolution needed to be continually practiced over weeks and months by ordinary people, by the GDR's oppositional citizens and peace movements, and, yes, for sure, by the police. I turn to this fundamental dynamic in chapter 2, building on Judith Butler's work, which calls this embodied practice the "force of nonviolence" amid a field of violence. I call it an anarchic force of cooperation.[45]

The legacy of these pacifist and nonviolent practices in the late GDR needs to be understood within the broader context of contemporaneous democratic movements in Eastern Europe. These protests were largely nonviolent and deliberately forgoing revolutionary violence, not to speak of terror. Moreover, freedom and political representation appeared to be their only horizon, echoing 1789 rather than 1917, or even 1776 rather than 1789, to borrow Traverso's formulation. The Velvet Revolutions were aimed at negotiating the conditions of freedom rather than at solving social questions. The latter were, Jonathan Schell suggests, unfortunately left on the table in the new world of market globalization.[46] In hindsight, Schell is undoubtedly correct. For nearly three decades, in a post-1989, post-historical world, the critical social question of how to lessen economic inequality was abandoned. Articulated by Marx in the nineteenth century, following the French Revolution's fight for liberty (freedom and representation) at the cost of liberation from poverty (economic equality), the social question seemed to have lost its relevance as socialism collapsed in 1989. And rather than looking to the violence these previous insurgencies entailed, East Germans remained extremely peaceful. Yet they vigorously acted in concert, depriving the repressive SED regime of its legitimacy. While 1989 may not have involved physical blows on a larger scale or a grab of sovereign state power by the citizens' movements,[47] the uprising resulted in violent disruption, shattering the symbolic order. And it was in the resulting fissures, across the politicized interregnum, that a radically democratic, socio-ecological imaginary could temporarily take hold.

Throughout this book, I trace these alternative ideas and ideals in minor, local, and often peripheral memory spaces to signal their survival and elusive promise in the neoliberal era. These alternative memories can be collected, garnered, and recirculated at the "edge of sight"—in the margins of the visible—in the public memorial sphere. Counter-archival readings of mediated, often artistic productions disclose the interregnum of '89–90 as a moment when a future potentiality of political happiness or joy was imbued with the perpetual risk of violence.[48] I approach this cesura through the perspectives of latent temporality deployed by memory studies and through theoretical work by anthropologists and sociologists on liminality and unsettled times in the last decades.[49] But it also proves useful to consider the factual record to grasp the sheer velocity of this historic moment and how relationality and symbolic power became de- and reconstituted and displaced. Significantly, under the regulatory conditions of Stasi surveillance, the formal organization of public space, governing rituals, and linguistic convention were torn open as hundreds of thousands of East Germans marched in the streets to challenge the sovereignty of the SED by nonviolent means.

This dynamic became apparent on several levels: according to estimates, by early November, 250 cities and communities were caught up in demonstrations, with several hundred thousand ordinary citizens occupying public streets and squares. The mobilization of embodied and collective action rapidly spread across the country. More and more people appeared at church services, in theaters, and in concert halls such as the Luxor-Palast in Karl-Marx-Stadt and the Leipzig Gewandhaus, both of which opened up their spaces to democratic debates. After November 9, 1989, when the Berlin Wall fell, the demonstrations doubled, contrary to common perceptions that exist today of that year. Another five or six hundred cities and communities began to hold public conversations among citizens. The oppositional groups began to self-organize more visibly, and the first public forums took place with the goal of launching independent investigations into the SED's defunct regulatory politics. Meanwhile, as hundreds of thousands nonviolently marched in the street each Monday, with increasingly clashing interests, fifty thousand people in Dresden had already called, on October 20, for a "free election." Deploying radically different tactics, the New Forum threatened a general political strike to dismantle the SED's supremacy in early December. Even the state-run factories, companies, and agricultural cooperatives increasingly became spaces for political action and agency. Workers' councils were formed everywhere. By the end of the year, the first local agreement about future cooperation between socialist factory leaders and workers was signed, in the VEB Schwertransport (state-owned heavy transport company) Leipzig. The Eastern German historian Ilko-Sascha Kowalczuk emphasizes rightly, in my view, that privatization and capitalist condition appeared desirable to almost no one, even as all other governing structures—indeed, the whole system—in the GDR, Poland, Hungary, the CSSR, and elsewhere disintegrated at a rapid pace.[50] In December, in this extraordinary and chaotic disintegration of regulatory power, the Central Roundtable assembled for the first time in East Berlin. This self-governing forum harked back to the roundtable that had emerged during the Solidarność movement in Poland in the 1980s. Roundtable talks were also adopted in Hungary during the transition in 1989. Unlike in other countries of Central and Eastern Europe, where this format was limited to the national scale, thousands of local and often informal roundtables sprang up across the unmoored GDR on the state, city, and local community levels.[51]

In this force field of wide-ranging nonviolent collective action that challenged the SED dictatorship, ideas of a socio-ecologically driven society and basic-democratic models circulated in abundance. Opposition groups strove vigorously for a different kind of modern social(ist)-democratic sovereignty. Activists recall that something significant, such as a much-needed third way, might have come of these efforts if only they had been given more time and space. Unlike the Western-backed parties, they often lacked material and financial resources and access to independent media.[52] Even a small catalog of the political language that circulated during the revolutionary unrest can capture the radically democratic, even anti- and postcapitalist orientation of the initial uprising. The various citizens' organizations aimed at a "solidaric community" (*Gemeinwesen*) and the improvement of individual life through freedom of speech and travel, as well as care for the common interests of the country and of humanity as a whole. "Participation in world trade should not lead to the exploitation of economically weaker countries," the New Forum (Neues Forum) declared. According to the citizens' movement Democracy Now (Demokratie Jetzt), a "threatened humanity in search of viable forms of human coexistence needs alternatives to Western consumer society." The initiative, which had roots in the oppositional circles of the Evangelical Church Berlin, demanded "the rejection of uninhibited economic growth" at the cost of the environment. Democratic Awakening (Demokratischer Aufbruch), formed in the fall of 1989 by politically active theologians and cultural practitioners, already signaled an orientation toward a social and ecological agenda in its original name. In December of that year the citizens' initiative became a party, adopting a more conservative program (and eventually joined the national-oriented

Alliance for Germany). But during the revolutionary fall, the group fought most clearly for the "reconciliation of democracy and socialism." Long forgotten today is also the fact that this historical transformation was to center on the handling of social property for the benefit of the common good (Böhlener Platform). As though to echo Hannah Arendt, the newly drafted constitution of the GDR proposed by the Central Roundtable defined "the possibility of self-determined, responsible action as the highest form of freedom" (the plan for a new legal foundation of a sovereign GDR went unrealized). To varying degrees, the citizens' movements warned that capitalist exploitation should not replace polit-bureaucratic oppression. They articulated demands for direct democracy, including the increased influence of factory and citizens' councils, direct referenda, common access to the public sphere, and the creation of new paths toward a participatory society. These multifarious citizens' initiatives reverberated with the anti-capitalist ethos that life is not fulfilled in possession, "but in what I am for others," adopted by grassroots groups in the Evangelical Church.[53] Such was the political ethos that shaped the dissident peace movement in the late GDR.

In light of these longer emancipatory and democratic-liberatory trajectories as well as the astonishing performance of nonviolent and radically democratic conduct by East Germans in '89 amid the unmooring of the GDR, the research findings by the professional class of German historians (many socialized in the West) are somewhat confounding. These findings illuminate one salient reason why the revolutionary unrest could not become more legible in the public arena after Germany's unification. Reinforcing an axiom of supremacy established during the Cold War, the peacefulness of the revolution and subsequent collapse of the SED dictatorship are attributed, at least in part, to a political-cultural value shift in the West. In contrast to the belligerent Soviet regimes, the West embraced a pacific world order following the Second World War.[54] Again, this claim is not false per se. The oppositional peace groups in the GDR were interlinked with the pacifist movements that arose in the 1970s in Northern and Western Europe. Yet this universalizing perspective is noteworthy when considering collective memory and what narratives about the past—or, more specifically, what inheritance of the revolution—become knowable in the public sphere. The East German citizens' movement set a radically democratic project with anti-capitalist inflections into motion. But the open-ended promise of this unfulfilled anti-authoritarian interval is often elided from contemporary memory.

Let us recall Derrida, who posits that inheritance is never a given; it is always a task. In this vein, inheritance has a spectral quality and thus exceeds any historical break and any spatial and temporal binary. We are heirs, "even before wanting or refusing to be."[55] Inheritance relates to the indeterminacy of a political legacy whose unrealized impulses may reach us from the future (I'll come back to this idea). But, like all inheritors, we are also in mourning.

In contrast, German historians have more or less supported a teleological narrative that underscores the victory of Western democracy.[56] Doubtless, they work in a complex, conflictual field, debating the nuances of their positions among each other. But ultimately, the task of these experts is not only to affirm official history—they often work hand in hand with government and funding agencies and as official advisors for memorial projects and museums. They also delimit enunciative possibilities through their involvement in the very institutional structures (universities, professional organizations, media, political parties) that have produced the dominant narrative after 1989.[57] (It is important to note here that this argument is not about identity politics but about a structural impasse, a form of being implicated in a field of power any scholar faces, if in differential ways.) Even as late as the 2010s, official history advanced the thesis that in the decades after 1945, the world experienced a secular trend toward "civilization," entailing a retreat from both "ideology" and "violence." As the British political economist Gareth Dale shows, according to this argument, this civilizing process was pioneered by the West but subtly impacted the Soviet bloc. The discourses of individuality and pluralism (imported from the West) gained traction and eventually "discombobulated the regime," ensuring that the orthodox Communists could no longer deploy violence with authority and had to "relinquish the right to lash out."[58] This approach overlooks the embodied force of the (non)violent radically democratic, socialist-inclined people's movements in the late GDR. Few scholars have openly challenged such a hegemonic discourse from a marginal scholarly perspective. Dale rightly points out that these ideas of the West's civilizing power were projections of the FRG's peculiar experience. At worst, he wrote, this phenomenon calls to mind Cold War propaganda. The East is chastised for its brutishness and backwardness, while the West's own "black book" (that is, France's war in Algeria; British forces in Belfast, Kenya, Iraq, and Afghanistan; the US invasion in Vietnam; and so forth) is ignored. He even ventures to say that New Germany may have prioritized funding for historians tasked "to reveal (again and again, ad nauseam) what a monstrous creature the GDR was" (506). Surely, this approach of relegating the East to an aberrant history, which echoed conservative discussion in Kohl's FRG of the 1980s, is not continuous with neoliberal rationality (based on the spreading of market metrics to all spheres of public and private life) that rapidly expanded into the East after 1989. But, as I will further elaborate in chapter 1, the argument's discarding of any possible historical alternatives to the Western order proved compatible with the ideological presentism pervasive in the neoliberal era. More importantly for my argument in this book, what does not come into view in these contestations, cast through a Western lens—in fact, what is deliberately erased—is the irruptive, mediated performance of the "We, the people" in the streets of the late GDR, including the long-forgotten newly elected parliament during the transitional year '89–90 (examined in chapter 4).

Politicizing 1989

In recent years, scholars in German cultural studies have sifted through the material and ideological remains of state socialism and noted that the GDR disappears in the musealizations that have sprung up since Germany was reunified and Berlin reimagined itself as a global city.[59] One only needs to think of the DDR Museum in Berlin, which has amassed Communist Party paraphernalia, office wares, and mundane household objects, occluding any deeper insight into the project of socialist modernity that failed in 1989. Yet, while excellent studies on the memory of GDR politics, culture, and everyday life abound, scholarship on the role of '89–90 in Germany's official and cultural memory is only emerging.[60] In this context, I urge that we focus more on the temporal and spatial vanishing of 1989–90 itself. How does promoting institutional and public forms of memory link up with a neoliberal rationality that idolizes individual freedom (rather than justice or social equality) and rejects any idea of collective agency?

In public memorial discourse, 1989 as a symbolic break (open-ended and unforeclosed from within its temporality) has remained largely invisible. Eric Santner's brief analysis of 1989 in his study *On the Psychotheology of Everyday Life* proves particularly useful in this context. He picks up, so to speak, where Arendt's reflection on the absent revolutionary inheritance leaves off. Together, their thinking provides the theoretical underpinnings that guide my argument about the unfinalizable impulses of '89–90 protest memory in this book. Simply put, while Arendt is concerned with a gap in temporal transmissions (more closely related to memory, generations, and diachronic dynamics), Santner approaches 1989 as an interval in an established symbolic order on a synchronous historical plane (putting socialist and capitalist society into relation). Following the French philosopher Jacques Rancière, he describes the final days of the GDR, when demonstrators rose against the regime, as "the very space of political dispute."[61] In this conflictual space, or gap, authoritarian forms of socialism were challenged. The distribution of roles and places in this political field and the systems for legitimizing this hierarchical distribution were up for grabs. (Arendt, we saw earlier, calls this fleeting, nameless state "public freedom," where people challenge officialdom and act without masks.)

Rather than solely in reference to parties and politicians in power, I use "the political" in this book to denote the shattering effects of a social and symbolic transformation from below. The revolution may have been blood-less, but it certainly disrupted the naturalized status quo (or what Rancière calls, regarding any modern state and its system of determining of what can be heard, seen, and so forth, "the police order"). Moreover, a radically dis-jointed time, such as '89–90, bears the effects of violent (structural) tear-ing—or, as Derrida put it in *Specters of Marx*, "*disarticulated*, dislocated, dislodged, time is run down, on the run and run down [*traqué et détraqué*], *deranged*, both out of order and mad. Time is off its hinges."[62] However, in the neoliberal era, the political force and potential of this transient disad-justment were buried not only by the various instruments of national and global memory management (closely aligned with the victors) but also by the disappointment, if not shame, among the intellectual Left regarding the historical outcomes of the emancipatory trajectory of the twentieth century.

The degree to which scholars in the transnational academic arena are im-plicated in this amnesiac public memory became clear to me in 2017. When we organized an international conference dedicated to the hundredth anni-versary of the Russian Revolution at the University of Illinois, titled "Work, Inequity, and Protest: 100 Years after 1917," I realized that East Germany's abbreviated revolution, or the revolutions of Eastern and Central Europe in 1989, for that matter, were palpably absent. If those events came up in the lively discussions, they were instantly absorbed by the Left's memory of the cesura as a capitalist tabula rasa. Three decades later, the legacies of the uprisings that "ushered in neoliberalism" have become synonymous with the defeat of history, even a tacitly shared political embarrassment. Given the level of expertise present at this conference, it is safe to say that the revolt in the late GDR had been successfully expelled from any of the emancipatory frameworks newly available today. This moment formed the idea for this book.

As unleashed capitalism rose and crashed, with the global financial crisis 2008, the specters of leftist legacies returned. In the long aftermath of 1989, leftist concerns eventually reassembled in artistic practice and intellectual discourse, in the international arena, during the first decade of the 2000s. On the one hand, this revival was driven by the works of Jacques Rancière, Alain Badiou, Fredric Jameson, and Slavoj Žižek, who recirculated the ideas of Marxism, utopia, and Communism in the fallout of the global financial crisis. On the other hand, the post-Soviet literary scholar Svetlana Boym beautifully rendered this shift from the "no longer" to the future temporality of "not yet" by asking, "So how do we begin again? Let us try to imagine freedom by thinking 'what if' and not only 'what is.'" Boym began to ask whether it is possible to resuscitate a defunct discourse foundational to Western liberalism—a discourse whose progressive version was hijacked in 1989 from the ashes of neoliberal utopias.[63] Around 2011, when the Occupy movement emerged, and public protest movements such as the assemblies in Gezi Park, Istanbul, and the Arab Spring spread around the world in the ensuing decade, we witnessed a new global activist moment and the reinvention of the worldwide left. For the most part, however, that new moment was devoid of any inheritance of 1989.

In fact, now that, thirty years later, the Peaceful Revolution of 1989 is seen as a national uprising that harbored right-wing, anti-statist elements from the start, such critical inquiry may be more important than ever. A few scholars in German studies—among them the historian Frank Biess— have questioned the assumption that 1989, in the German context, was an inevitable historical turning point. He recently acknowledged the outcomes of unification as "the product of particular Western policies, whose consequences, such as the right-wing extremism in East Germany, are with us up to this day." It might be necessary, he urges, "to remember history's open futures."[64] Others, including the UK-based Europeanist Paul Betts, in a recent landmark essay on the role of 1989 in a global geopolitical sphere, have reevaluated this shift at the end of the twentieth century as a seedbed of the resurgent nationalism we see today. Jennifer Allen, a historian of modern Germany, proposed reconsidering the centrality of 1989 as a lens for historical periodization altogether.[65]

In these struggles over memory and more extended arches of temporalization, the narrative that needs to be recirculated is how the interruptive and, as noted earlier, even *anarchic* force of this political moment in 1989 also called into question the legitimacy of Western capitalism itself. During the revolutionary fall and its immediate aftermath, the possibility of intervening precisely in the "perceived necessities of the global market system" emerged in the GDR and was collectively enacted. However, I also agree with Eric Santner: once the slogan turned from "We are *the* people" (Wir sind das Volk) to "We are *one* people" (Wir sind ein Volk), the contingent particularities of politics became officially absorbed into a governmental order of the West that dramatizes itself through principles of universality. Notably, what was lost thereby was not merely some fantasy of a "third path" between market capitalism and state socialism—although, as we have seen, such socio-ecological programs were certainly relevant—but, rather, the very space of contingency (or what Arendt calls "the non-time-space," determined by things that are no longer and not yet). When Germany unified on October 3, 1990, the profoundly upended GDR and the unforeclosed political possibilities disappeared. As Rancière puts it, "politics exists wherever the count of parts and parties of society is disturbed by the inscription of a part of those who have no part . . . Politics ceases wherever this gap no longer has any place, wherever the whole of the community is reduced to the sum of its parts *with nothing left over*" (emphasis added).[66] Throughout the book, we will examine this shift toward foreclosing possibility more closely. Here, at the outset, I will simply note an excess of erasure regarding 1989—or, more aptly, '89–90—in the public realm, or what I approach in this book as the forgotten politicized interval period.

The bulk of the research on 1989 has been conducted under the spell of "the end of history." Since the 1990s, scholars including Charles Maier, Steven Pfaff, and Mary Elise Sarotte have examined the end of socialism and the dissolution of the GDR, while Julia Hell's earlier work and my own were enthralled by the trauma of symbolic collapse, and Alison Lewis aptly analyzed the traumatic effects of unification.[67] When historians and sociologists such as Anne Sa'adah and Andreas Glaeser finally set out to study oppositional movements, they focused on the dismantling of the GDR's surveillance apparatus.[68] And although excellent anthropological studies by Dominic Boyer and Daphne Berdahl have explored the loss of socialism in the ubiquitous practice of *Ostalgie* (nostalgia for the East), they rarely question the inevitability of German unification or the neoliberal course of post-1989 history from the perspective of the uprising in the late GDR.[69] Much official discourse and seminal scholarship in interdisciplinary German studies (my own included) contributed to the disappearance of 1989–90 as a period of heightened contingency, cutting us off from a dynamic historical archive.[70] Although a voluminous body of work by historians, sociologists, and political scientists exists on the collapse of the GDR, Ilko-Sascha Kowalczuk pointed out in 2016 that serious historical investigation into the variegated events and movements of 1989–90 is barely underway.[71]

Two significant historical transitions bracket the book's exploration of post-1989 memory: the collapse of state socialism in Eastern Europe, marked by the fall of the Berlin Wall, and the recent unsettling of liberal democracy in the West. The latter was most viscerally displayed in 2021, when a right-wing attack on the United States Capitol disrupted a joint session of Congress in the process of affirming presidential election results. Accordingly, (post)socialism and (post)democracy can serve as organizing categories for thinking through memory making in the neoliberal era. Indeed, it was on January 6, 2021, watching the storming of the US Capitol by a right-wing populist mob, that I began to reconsider the thrust of the argument developed in this book. I asked myself: Why still examine how a presentist memory had installed itself in dubious neoliberal conditions after socialism's collapse? Whether in the United States, Germany, France, or Eastern Europe, all vectors, at the moment, point toward the fragility of liberal, bourgeois democracy. Scholars such as Wendy Brown and Ann Stoler have argued that the values of neoliberalism (for example, reducing persons to human capital, discarding the welfare state, and empowering large corporations to fashion law and policy to meet their own ends) have undermined any "democratic provisions" in recent decades. For Stoler in particular, the capacity for illiberalism is not the exception to but, rather, part of liberal democracy's central repertoire and its protean principles of inclusion and exclusion. Brown and Stoler agree that as the spread of neoliberal rationality evacuates the content from liberal democracy, there is a risk that the language of freedom and popular sovereignty "disappears or is perverted to signify democracy's opposite."[72]

At the same time, since Russia's imperial attack on Ukraine in the winter of 2022, the ailing democratic imaginary has been revived in the global arena. A transatlantic alliance emerged across various geopolitical regions under the renewed umbrella of a "fight for democracy" and its associated principles of freedom and the rule of law. The echoes of the Cold War are palpable.[73] In turn, in this nationally and globally polarizing climate, it is tempting to give in to pressures to shield democracy—with its rights, constitutions, and institutions—from critique, rather than exposing its limits.[74] I argue, however, that there is no time more urgent than now to return to the late GDR and the geopolitical historical constellations of 1989. The ambitions imposed by the liberal order may have ended self-organized democratization in East Germany, to echo Arendt. However, the year '89–90 constituted a rupture and a suspension of historical time—even if chaotic, it was also a *pause* in the predominant line of historical development.[75] More importantly for today, it was an "unguarded moment," when fighting between two antagonist systems was disrupted.[76] Within this cesura, the meaning of democracy itself was there for the taking, and for a period of a few months, hundreds of thousands of people participated in a process of self-determination. Rather than fearing, today, that democracy is slipping into the past (and securitizing it domestically through walls or in a global showdown with dictatorial forces), we must approach democracy as something that has never existed in a satisfactory way and that remains to come. To be sure, the signifier *democracy* is often abused, but it has not lost its radical potential in the political imaginary (see chapter 5).

Hegemonies and Future Archives

In uncovering an alternative narrative, *Remembering 1989* makes a few specific interventions in the vibrant field of memory studies. By illuminating how individuals and material remains transmit elusive historical alternatives, I join scholars such as Ann Rigney and Michael Rothberg, who are reorienting memory studies to consider the future as well as the past. In conversation with their seminal works, I shine a light on the significant role of activist spaces in the legacies of Eastern Europe, which are often omitted from a current turn toward the memory of "transnational activism beyond the traumatic" in this largely anglophone field.[77] Moreover, although I take inspiration from metaphors of circulation, multidirectionality, and entanglements explored by memory studies in the past decade, I stress the renewed significance of an uneven distribution of power in shaping the differential dynamics of memory work and thus the need for an ongoing struggle for social justice.[78] Accordingly, the importance of shifting the focus of memory studies from the powerful (for example, the nation, governing bodies, experts, museums) to the peripheral (for example, people, performances, art installations, streets, ruins), and revealing their constant state of interaction, is a foundational argument of this book. I pay particular attention to the interrelated dynamics of hegemonic and counter-hegemonic forms of knowing, emphasizing the performative dynamics of memory.[79] Assembling an alternative post-1989 memory requires recognition of how hegemonic historiography and memory making elide certain perspectives and legitimize others, in effect reproducing dominant relations—or how the token stories of East Germans in high-office positions, for instance, are used as a foil to render the victorious '89 transformation. However, the bulk of *Remembering 1989* is devoted to liminal, interstitial, or even counter-hegemonic memory work, in an attempt to recover spaces where East Germans, to a certain degree, become agents or curators of their own history.

Even if the prevailing narrative papers over the lacuna of 1989–90, I argue that a closer look alters that forgetful narrative. Granted, no sustained documentation occurred during those breathless, open-ended weeks of organizing in the fall of 1989. The often-devastating personal and private confrontations that fed the public protests and ultimately dislodged the late socialist regime also went unseen by Western media. *Remembering 1989* reveals how the unforeclosed political energies of the protests were repurposed and put back into circulation. Paying close attention to the fugitive or interstitial memories that flare up in interviews, photographs, manifestos, clandestine video footage, memorials, and archival material, I ask how people who participated in public protests, as well as those representational forms, retain memories of these unrealized futures. I also examine the social and political environments that shaped the revolution that "almost did happen," thus preserving the possibility that it still may. In other words, this study theorizes a shift from memory studies as a critique of power to memory studies as a field where we examine and constitute "archives of the future." My approach can be situated in relation to the kind of archival futurity outlined by Derrida, who considers how archives may not only be driven toward conserving the past but simultaneously open up toward the potential of future rewritings, recasting, and reposing.[80] From within the historical closure of reifying memories, this method allows us to uncover the impulses arising from the "crack of time" when tens of thousands of East Germans showed up in the street and experimented with spontaneous, self-organizing practices.

This book responds to salient questions about the relation of memory, temporality, and mediation that have come into focus since the "archival turn."[81] In the past two decades, the archive as practice, institution, and metaphor has shaped interdisciplinary inquiries across fields in the humanities and arts as well as, more recently, in German cultural studies.[82] Traditionally, German-speaking memory scholars such as Aleida Assmann have focused on questions of storage and classifications of political, historical, or cultural archives and their respective institutional functions. This school of thought is more closely linked to the sociology and cultural history of memory. My thinking around archives in this book, and archival futurity in particular, takes place at the intersection of deconstruction, new materialism, and affect studies, as well as media archeology and urban geography. Given post-1989 memory politics, I am certainly interested in the dynamics of power, rights, and technology that determine the documentation of the past. In chapter 3, I pay attention to the tactile and haptic environments of archives at the Stasi Records Agency and their accentuated claims of authenticity. At the same time, I explore more informal, minor archives, and a kind of (anarchival) feed-forward process produced by visual materials (see chapter 4).[83] "Minor," of course, refers to those intensive, often vernacular forms that may disrupt official or institutional functions and elicit new collective arrangements of affects, materials, histories, and so forth.[84] The emphasis on historicity, afforded by photography and film footage, is particularly salient for this project. Photographic spaces do not just help us understand the afterlives of events; they also allow us to discover an as-yet-unrealized future. The work with images (opening to a future to come) is distinct from the work of the historian, who must look to the past.[85]

Two different traditions then inform my readings of post-1989 archival futurity. On the one hand, I call on Derrida's "spectral messianicity," a force at work in the concept of the archive that ties it, like religion, history, or science, to a singular experience of the promise. In this vein, he writes in *Archive Fever: A Freudian Impression* (1995) that we will only know the meaning of the archive—what it will have meant—"in times to come, later on, or perhaps never."[86] Notably, the book was published in the post-historical era, on the heels of *Specters of Marx* (1993). Still relevant today, the study provides insight into the archive as a space of structural violence and domination. Likewise, Foucault foregrounds the link between power and the archive—the hierarchical and exclusionary, or, more precisely, the superimposed and enunciative nature of archival regimes.[87] The archive, Derrida presses upon us, arises where forgetting—the obliteration of memory—occurs. The very collection of materials leaves only an imprint, an impression. But, harking back to the spectrality of the (Marxist) inheritance, the archive is also associated with an opening to a future, or, as he says, "a future radically to *come*, which is to say indeterminate."[88] In my view, Derrida's rumination is not only a philosophical exercise; it can call us into an activist relationship with the past from the perspective of future possibilities for a more just and livable world. If political legacies are unfulfilled, they are put off until later; they are elsewhere, so to speak. As this sending off "gestures toward the past of an inheritance only by remaining to come," according to Derrida, the inheritance "remains before us," temporally (albeit not chronologically) and spatially.[89] I propose that locating these traces, or material and affective residues in the contemporary public sphere, becomes the task of future-oriented memory scholars.

At the same time, I take my cue from Hal Foster's work on artistic practices, which is more materially oriented. In the seminal 2004 essay "An Archival Impulse," Foster usefully emphasizes archives as an open dynamic structure. He underscores the nature of "all archival materials as found yet constructed, factual yet fictive, public yet private."[90] Perhaps all archives develop in this way, through mutations of connection and disconnection, he reminds us, but art can serve to disclose these processes of rearranging and making meaning out of history. Artistic works may draw on a range of formal and informal archives, but they can also produce them. Thus, this approach lends itself especially well to tracing alternative knowledge, or counter-memories, in the memorial landscape broadly conceived.

Remembering 1989 proposes that an unrealized promise of collaborative action can be released by unlearning the narrative of Germany's inevitable unification. In addition, the book engages a growing body of theoretical work in future-oriented memory studies. This scholarship has important implications for historians who wish to probe the formation of future temporalities in the past. But, I believe, it has not yet altered our understanding of how these unfulfilled pasts become available for perpetual remaking in and by the future. For example, Svetlana Boym and Amir Eshel have sought to free historical pasts of trauma and catastrophe from entrapment by leveraging language's potential for repair. Memory scholars such as David Kazanjian and Ariella Azoulay critique the archive as a pseudoscientific apparatus and try to salvage alternative outcomes and moments of freedom from this institution.[91] While I am in dialogue with their innovative work, my project encourages scholars to consider the critical and transformative value of *self-agentic* memory impulses, which are not contained or recognized by national memory cultures but circulate nevertheless.[92] These fluid "mobile archives" organize memory in ephemeral, contingent, and often intermedial spaces, revealing possible futures of aborted, collective pasts. Consider, for example, the dissident slogan "Critical thinking needs time and space" presumably posted on the door of the Nikolaikirche in Leipzig in the early fall of 1989. Today this slogan proliferates in the Cloud, awaiting anyone who searches for popular protest. By arguing that memories not only chronicle the past but also accumulate their future reception, I move beyond narratives that forget "revolutionary 1989" or dismiss the protests of that fateful fall as failures.

With new social protest movements flaring up in recent years, academics have highlighted the relationship between collective memory and the symbolic environments in which contentious politics occurs. In a 2019 manifesto titled *Revolution Today*, the post-Soviet scholar Susan Buck-Morss argues that "the punctuated interruption of business as usual by ordinary citizens, occupying public spaces," needs to be visible to the world to generate the solidarities required of us today.[93] Reclaiming the memories and visual representations of protest cultures, such as the revolutionary unrest in the late GDR, counters and disrupts public forgetting. In a variety of historical and transnational constellations, this point has also been astutely argued by scholars such as Diana Taylor, Arielle Azoulay, Tina Campt, Ayşe Gül Altınay, Marianne Hirsch, and others.[94] Ultimately, I share their belief that the emergence of such protest scenes in collective and even public memory can have the effect of forming bonds across temporal and spatial distances and across national and historical contexts. However, I stress that we must get better at illuminating the complex histories in which such images and scenes of protest circulate. And we must expose the technological, archival, and ideological conditions in which these scenes of defiance are appropriated, misread, or simply allowed to dull our senses. Protest memory enables us to reactivate the collective pasts of people's embodied actions in the streets, but it also needs to comprise less visible networks of resistance, such as micro-organizing for food security in local communities, artistic improvisation, and giving voice to dissonance among the population. All this activism is vital for new visions of a postcapitalist community today.

A brief word on the shape of the book. Although I have considered a vast amount of material at institutional archives, such as the Archive of the Citizens' Movement Leipzig and the Stasi Records Agency (Bundesbeauftragter für die Stasi-Unterlagen), in the end, I decided to rely primarily on a wide range of published sources for my analysis (for example, government records, printed collections released by the Archives of the Citizens' Movement, published eyewitness accounts, memoirs, photo collections, local histories, and literary works). After all, my focus is on tracing which narratives are endorsed and which are dropped away, left to be retrieved in the publicly sanctioned records that shape the forms of collective, public, and national memory of the Peaceful Revolution. Much of the supporting material I collected over time is placed in the footnotes, which form their own archival pathways. Going beyond mere citation, these notes perform the method of archival futurity I have deployed and examined in this study. This method stresses the role of discontinuities, indeterminacy, and broken lines in producing alternative memory. While the material needs to be managed for readability, the radically disjointed time of 1989 often refuses to be restrained into linear argument arches. Lastly, every academic book is ultimately personal, even if it addresses its subject from a scholarly angle. I open each chapter with a piece of memoir, where I draw from my own experience in the late GDR. This formal choice serves as a commentary on the need for diverse archives to trace potential histories of failed protest movements. I hope it also illuminates how individual and collective histories are permeable and interconnect us with one another across time and space.

In sum, I have written this book on 1989 protest memory to shed light on the open-ended emancipatory possibilities of citizen activism during that decisive year. This year is associated in collective memory today with the defeat of progressive socialist twentieth-century history or the victory of Western democracy and, first and foremost, with the fall of the Berlin Wall. It will be clear by now that this book is not a sociological or historical study but an inquiry into the differential dynamics of memory in the aesthetic, official, and public realms. Accordingly, this book explores the political conditions in which this unsettling interval of basic-democratic organizing in East Germany was rendered obsolete, displaced, and forgotten. It provides methodological tools to garner and reorganize the unfinalizable impulses of earlier uprisings in the mnemonic sphere. I hope these tools will encourage scholars and activists in their respective historical contexts to uncover events excluded from the dominant record or declared failures by later historians, or even by those actors and witnesses who lived through them. Earlier movements may not have left any testament behind for those new generations of protesters who fill the streets around the world today. These younger protesters often unknowingly restage earlier legacies of the progressive struggle for social justice, freedom, and equality and the common investment in public life and public goods. Surely, each new generation and, indeed, every new human being must discover and ploddingly pave anew their own "small non-time space in the very heart of time" as they insert themselves between the past and the future. This interval indeed "may contain the moment of truth," in Arendt's sense.[95]

If there is one collective lesson that I hope reverberates throughout these upcoming pages, it is this: The Cold War world, divided by the Iron Curtain, created an unquestioned reality in which the GDR dictatorship served as a real and imaginary linchpin for a global order of two world powers. In the fall of 1989, the normalized status quo of a seemingly unalterable system was unmoored in just a few days and weeks, and what followed was a brief state of exception. My use of '89 as "brief state of exception" (a rupture in the economic, symbolic, social order; a pause, a gap in the main line of historical development) is different from Georgio Agamben's. He refers to Western nations and "the state of exception," where the unusual extension of power has become the (concealed) norm.[96] In '89–90 history was suspended. In the final analysis, the "treasure of the revolution" was lost, not only because of historical circumstances or the neoliberal adversity that ensued, as critics commonly argue, but because no tradition had foreseen its appearance or its reality, "because no testament had willed it for the future."[97] Two grassroots activists, Gudula Ziemer and Holger Jackisch, who participated in the Peaceful Revolution in Leipzig, described the event in 1989 like this: "All of a sudden, we realized this was it—the sweet revolution we had long yearned for, but since abandoned in our thoughts. We learned it was within our power to topple a regime, and we resolved never to forget that. The first item on the next regime's agenda will be to make us forget again, in the name of stability and the Fatherland, but, in reality, because it is an uncomfortable and arduous task to govern a people with this radical memory: We toppled the regime without a struggle. It was beautiful and very easy. . . ."[98] The chapters that follow uncover and recirculate that political joy——vital not least in emergency contexts. Another cataclysmic era of transition may be on the rise in our (post-)democratic era. This book explores the limits and possibilities of memory as a site of alternative histories in times of crisis.

[CHAPTER ONE]

Erasing '89–90 from the Capital

If Jean Baudrillard once described the death strip (*Todesstreifen*) between East and West Berlin as a *terrain vague*,[1] to this day, it is the absence of the border that confounds me. More than thirty years after the fall of the Berlin Wall, I remain in disbelief each summer when I return to the area near the checkpoint *Sonnenallee*, where I grew up. Sizing up today's lush habitat, I try to recall the three-meter-tall, ashen border panels that once blocked any view to the West. Before 1989, I rarely noticed the looming watchtowers and armed guards as I walked along the Wall that stretched through the neighborhood. This vast, impenetrable barrier appeared as normal as the sunsets it quickened. After the border was built in 1961, the prefabricated modernist tenements that populated the area were nearly enclosed by the Wall architecture. While the German Democratic Republic (GDR) imbued the Wall with sovereign power, those who lived under its shadow were unperturbed.[2] They prepared meals, worked, slept, and dreamt—their everyday lives unfolded, often unremarkably, in remarkable proximity to this militarized zone.

The Wall has truly disappeared into thin air. There is no rubble, no shadow, no trace. Only the rabbits that once scurried across the death strip and set off the blaring alarms at night remain. The winding line that once divided the sky in half is gone. Decades later, I still need to reorient myself in the open space where history has been reclaimed by nature. Devoid of the sense of orientation once afforded by the Wall, a question arises that is as geographical as it is historical: "Where are we?" Walter Benjamin believed that we appropriate reality through sight and touch.[3] Yet residents here in the city's periphery see nothing. They cannot be touched, cannot be moved. Because of this oblivion, memories of the recent past fragment and splinter, as many older inhabitants of this formerly walled-off neighborhood attest. If residents are confronted by anything, they are confronted by their own split memories—broken into a before and after, a GDR past and a bewildering present. The Wall is missing like a *Filmriss* (shredded film/

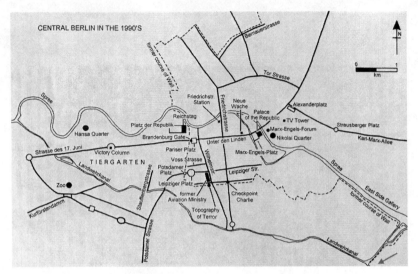

FIGURE 1.1. "Central Berlin in the 1990's," map by Ellen Cesarski. The added arrow (bottom, right) points toward *Sonnenallee*. From Brian Ladd, *The Ghosts of Berlin* (Chicago: University of Chicago Press, 1997). Copyright © 1997 by the University of Chicago. All rights reserved.

amnesia). This chapter examines how the political memories of the fall of the Wall in 1989 were erased with the last traces of the border architecture. I also explore how one might memorialize and even mourn the vanishing of the Wall as a residential space or even as an antifascist monument, however absurdly configured. How does one mourn an absent presence? This chapter attempts to excavate and craft a plausible future vision beyond this post-historical landscape of transformation and forgetting.

Public Memories and Memory of Publics

Cities provide mental and material spaces for personal recollection and the public staging of collective pasts. Visitors who arrive in Berlin today enter a carefully curated memorial terrain. Tourists searching for remnants of the bulwark that once divided Europe find plenty of mementos at which to aim their camera phones. Scattered across the vast urban landscapes of a unified city, some remainders have been remastered for educational purposes, and others have been left to decay on the outskirts of Berlin. Almost every remastered site advertises the triumph of Western democracy. With their simplistic presentations and sweeping narratives, the Wall is invariably cast as an icon of authoritarian oppression.[4] Passing through Germany's capital each day, thousands of spectators unknowingly experience the production of amnesia central to post–Cold War politics. The Wall is its symbol.

At the former Gestapo headquarters near Potsdamer Platz, there is a permanent exhibition titled "Topography of Terror." Established in 2010, the exhibition faces preserved pockmarked panels of the Berlin Wall, which are conserved with a chemical glaze and fenced in for protection. This row of tombstones, eighty meters long, insinuates the spectral proximity of the GDR to the dictatorship of the Third Reich. Moreover, if one peers through the gaps between panels, the austere, angular Nazi architecture of the former Reich Aviation Ministry comes into view in the distance. Housing the Federal Ministry of Finance today, the building served as the seat of the GDR government from its founding in 1949 to its dissolution on October 3, 1990. Glancing down at the building's entrance, a twenty-five-meter-long glass strip exposes a magnified, backlit photograph of workers demonstrating in the national uprising of 1953. The confluence of Nazism, the GDR, and 1953 is central to the triumphal post-1989 narrative of unification.[5] The memorial frames a foundational piece of Germany's post–Cold War memory politics, while nearby, the ultramodern Sony Center at Potsdamer Platz extends skyward, reifying an image of Berlin as a global center of twenty-first-century corporate power.

Only a short walk from here, near the neoclassical architecture of the Brandenburg Gate and adjacent to the government district, one reaches the Memorial to the Murdered Jews of Europe (2005). As the cultural geographer Karen Till put it, the memorial is "hyper-visible."[6] Visitors gradually vanish from sight as they descend lower and lower into the sloping field of nearly three thousand uneven concrete slabs until they finally get to the underground Information Center and its exhibition space devoted to the Holocaust and the persecution of European Jewry. The Memorial to the Murdered Jews of Europe is situated where the Berlin Wall—or what the GDR called the Antifascist Protection Wall—once stood. This exceptional site of remembrance lies at the heart of post-unified Berlin. Unbound from the neat dichotomies of the Cold War, the disparate traumatic pasts of the twentieth century—both its Nazi and Communist legacies—linger in an unsettled, half-buried present. But the authentic, obdurately material remainders of Germany's division are never far away.

The inner border strip once reached one of its narrowest points only a few metro stops to the northeast. Today, a large-scale memorial arena on Bernauer Strasse, the Berlin Wall Memorial (2014), displays remnants of the long-demolished Wall in an increasingly gentrified neighborhood. At the center, a national monument (1998) features the largest restored segment of the inner and outer barriers of the Wall, including a redesigned watchtower and a viewing platform from which many of the one million visitors to the site each year gaze across the simulated no-man's-land. Inadvertently, they recall an emblem of Communist totalitarianism.[7] Mediated and stabilized, Germany's collective memory of the division perpetually links up with a reified notion of the East's pre-1989 dictatorial past.

Absent from this post-reunification memory-scape are the people of the GDR itself, especially those who assembled in the fall of 1989, marched silently in the streets of East Germany, and laid claim to embodied action as a legitimate political mode. Today, it is all too easy to miss the elongated steel pillar dedicated to the Peaceful Revolution passing through East Berlin's former downtown. The pillar was erected where the GDR's Republic Palace (Palast der Republik) once stood and where the monumental Imperial Palace of Prussian Emperors has now been reconstructed (2009–2020). It displays three small, faded photographs of demonstrators who gathered shortly before and after the fall of the Wall. The minimalism of this memorial column may point to a reluctance on the part of designers to represent large crowds in a city tainted by fascist marches. But there was more at work than mere reluctance. The unseen monument to the Peaceful Revolution is a physical manifestation of what has been forcefully evacuated from public memory: the collective force, the "we" of the people, that coalesced in the fall of 1989. Either way, the hundreds of thousands of East Germans who showed up in the streets to fight for civic dialogue and radical reform have been rendered, quite literally, invisible. In today's public sphere, the people of the GDR have been moved out of sight.

In this chapter, I challenge this revisionist narrative, which celebrates the victory of capitalism and the West once and for all, by shifting attention to the social and representational modes in which public memory—or, more precisely, the "memory of publics"—becomes discarded, erased, and reframed. If the concept of public memory invokes the contingent conditions by which a public body, often a nation-state, constitutes itself and deliberates its own existence, then the notion of the "memory of publics" amplifies the contrast between the capacity of certain publics to authorize memories and the struggles of other publics to contest the latter and affirm their own existence and participation in the historical process.[8] Throughout this book, I use "public memory" and "public memories" often interchangeably, but the first stresses the normative regulation and consolidation of meaning, whereas the latter emphasizes the malleability, mediation, and potential plurality of memories that are assembled in the public realm. Moreover, I stress that the "publicness of memory" is often linked to scopic regimes and modes of visibility. In other words, one may not necessarily conceive of public memories in relation to social entities known as publics, especially since publics are unstable from the start and constituted through mediated acts.[9] One might rather think of public memories (in distinction to, say, collective or social memory) as those practices that have been visible to many, that have appeared in view of others.[10] In Hannah Arendt's sense, "something that is being seen and heard by others as well as by ourselves— constitutes reality."[11] Far from being neutral, this "sphere of appearance" is a performative field constituted by often predetermined perceptions and policies, struggles over knowledge, and the exercise of power.

The triumph of (neo)liberal democracy after 1989 has significantly shaped Germany's public discourse and culture of commemoration. Caught in the reified analogy of Nazi Germany with the GDR's Wall regime, the political potentialities of 1989—including the socialist imaginary of the East— have been eliminated from Germany's public and memorial spheres. As a result of national pressure to align the two dictatorial legacies, collective memories associated with these distinct historical periods of victimization and perpetration have reinforced one another. In addition, while "neoliberal shock therapy" dominated the economy of Eastern Europe in the 1990s, the first decade of the 2000s saw the consolidation of neoliberal rationality and politics.[12] Such triumphalist shifts in the economically driven body politic have eclipsed alternative future horizons. Consequently, 1989 is not remembered as the open-ended break with the past that it was for those who took part in it. What was once symbolic of an open future has become, paradoxically, a sign of an absolute end. Recall the literary theorist Eric Santner, who, following Jacques Rancière, describes the final days of the GDR, when demonstrators rose up against the regime, as "the very space of political dispute." In this gap, not only was the calcified, authoritarian form of socialism challenged, but the possibility of intervening in the *perceived necessities* of the global market system also emerged. Alternatives became visible and audible as silent masses protested in the streets. Today, a notable absence looms in the public realm regarding the months leading up to and after November 9, 1989—a period that I refer to in this book as a forgotten, politicized interregnum.

This chapter examines the fate of the so-called Peaceful Revolution in Berlin's memorial sphere to explore how the dynamics of (unsettled) 1989 protest memories can be reactivated. I pay attention to collective memory as the unreliable inheritor of political "public happiness." Public memories appear in places where spectators, historical imaginings, and local geographies interact. Thus, I turn to three official commemorative sites in the capital's center—the Berlin Wall Memorial at Bernauer Strasse, the Monument to Freedom and Unity in the historic downtown of the former East

Berlin, and the Pillar to the Peaceful Revolution in its shadow. Each site highlights a different facet of how and why memories of 1989–90 as an open-ended event of concerted action vanished after unification. It also tracks the enduring myths that have replaced the lived past over the course of three decades. In addition, the conceptual question remains of how to remember assemblies and protests, which are by nature transient and, unlike war or other disasters, do not leave traces in the built environment. Taken together, the memorial spaces showcased here illuminate that the alternative mnemonic strands of 1989 can indeed be wrested from oblivion and reappear in the public sphere.

Mnemonic Shifts in the Neoliberal Era

Following the uprising of GDR citizens in 1989 and the disintegration of the Soviet system, the Berlin Wall disappeared, taking with it the collective memories of the '89–90 liminal period.[13] For nearly a decade, the collapse of the GDR and the vanishing power of Communist Eastern Europe left behind an official memory vacuum. In *1989: The Struggle to Create Post–Cold War Europe*, the historian Mary Elise Sarotte highlights how Western global powers successfully deployed geopolitical strategies and established institutional infrastructures to secure dominance. In so doing, the West "mastered" this new "ordering moment" after the disintegration of the Soviet system in ways that would span decades and are still haunting us today.[14] In Germany, the rearrangements began when the Bundestag voted in 1991 to move the formal capital from Bonn to Berlin. This move marked the symbolic end of the Cold War. Governing authorities, alongside corporate developers, urban planners, media conglomerates, and other institutions, sought to leave the recent past behind and redefine Berlin as the new capital of a unified country and the corporate center of a globalized Europe.[15] Most importantly, in the decade after 1990, Germany's traumatic and violent past was recast in ways that would help foster this expansive global image. During this long post-unification period, Berlin indeed moved forward to confront Germany's Nazi past, facing the country's historical responsibility on an entirely unprecedented scale. An official memory district was built during the first decade of the 2000s near international embassies and the seat of the German government. This district included the Jewish Museum (2001) and the exhibition "Topography of Terror" (2010). Scholars agree that the Memorial to the Murdered Jews of Europe (2005), designed by the American architect Peter Eisenman, reopened a shameful national wound and brought the Germans' past perpetrations out into the open.

To this day, however, what has not come to the forefront in discussions about Germany's legacy of atonement is the extent to which the long-overdue engagement with Germany's Nazi past intersected with the systematic erasure of the traces of the GDR (and its official memory of antifascism).[16] The reflexive engagement with the Nazi past that Reinhart Koselleck calls "negative remembrance" also revitalized memories of a divided Berlin a decade and a half after the fall of the Berlin Wall. Accordingly, I argue that an entangled and often competitive tension between two negative memories, that of the Holocaust and that of state socialism, shaped the politics of memory in post-unification Germany in the first decade of the 2000s. This competitive dynamic is also inextricably bound up with the absence of narratives about the GDR citizens' movements. I contend, however, that what is really at stake in the elision of the GDR's revolutionary unrest is an aversion to the political potential of '89–90 in the neoliberal era.

Now, the workings of neoliberalist valorizations were long masked in Germany's post-1989 rhetoric of democracy's victory, among other things. In the wake of German unification, public money and infrastructure planning played an "all-too-visible role" in aligning the trajectories of two different societies and economies. According to cultural historians Necia Chronister and Lutz Koepnick, this public expenditure obscured that the figure of *homo economicus*—associated with private investment and unfettered self-reliance—had come "to inhabit the center of government post-unification."[17] This oversight was aided by the fact that West Germany during the Kohl era experienced privatization and monetization comparable to those of the Anglo-American world but that the old FRG's inertia and the continued pressure of unions and new social movements placed limits on "the scale of capitalism's transformation."[18] However, the rapid implementation of capitalism post-1989 (a process whereby the logic of urgency led to a sense of inevitability, as Susan Buck-Morss succinctly argued) left the Eastern regions with a devastated social system that had more in common with "Anglo-American" neoliberalism than with the protective social market economy of West Germany. In that sense, the Eastern regions may have anticipated the unraveling of existing social networks set in motion by globalization that would affect Germany as a whole.[19] With a focus on discarding the socialist past of the GDR in post-1989 memory politics, these experiences of exposure and loss in the Eastern regions—the prevalence and afterlives of neoliberalism in post-unification Eastern Germany—came rarely into view. In turn, framing the GDR as a second dictatorship helped absolve Western Germany of any responsibilities related to the legacies of the Nazi era.

It's clear that the forces of history, memory, and politics are deeply intertwined in shaping national identity. Indeed, the significance of the tectonic shift in Germany's national memory politics that occurred as the official Holocaust memorial was built cannot be overstated. The sheer number of post–Cold War memorial projects alone illustrates this point. In the first decade of the 2000s, many institutional memorial sites appeared rapidly. The Cold War past was once more taken up. It was redeployed in the sphere of public memory by federal and state governing authorities, private consultants, and experts, as we will see in more detail later in this chapter. This redeployment included the spectacular removal of the GDR's Republic Palace (2006–2008), the Master Plan for the Commemoration of the Berlin Wall (2006), the federal authorization of the Monument to Freedom and Unity (2007), and the founding of the Berlin Wall Foundation under public law (2008), all followed by the open-air exhibit "Revolution and Fall of the Wall" at the former Stasi Headquarters/BStU (2016). Granted, these post–Cold War memorials did not follow entirely predictable ideological lines—the sphere of public memory, after all, is not only contested, but able to accommodate clashing party politics in a normative effort to stake out distances from an undesirable past.

This shift in commemorative politics in the middle of the first decade of the 2000s initially occurred for incongruous reasons and on multiple scales: on the one hand, the city of Berlin moved toward the official re-memorialization of the Wall under the leadership of a center-left government, which also propelled the Party of Democratic Socialism (PDS) to provide evidence for its notoriously reluctant acknowledgment of the GDR as SED dictatorship; on the other hand, the federal governing body turned conservative in 2005 under the chancellorship of Angela Merkel. The combined effect, however, was that the (monolithic) notions of the GDR as *Unrechtsstaat*, an unlawful regime, and "second dictatorship" recirculated widely across a range of societal and discursive domains, echoing the relentless Stasi debates and parliamentary battles over the meaning of the GDR as totalitarian system and the illegitimacy of the PDS in the early post-unification years.[20] Meanwhile, the revival of Cold War clichés of Communism and concepts of totalitarianism affected the reorganization of sovereignty in the European Union in the neoliberal era. The entry of Eastern European countries into the European Union during the first decade of the 2000s relied on the central role of state socialism as a failed experiment with nothing worth recuperating. The EU also turned to history and memory to solidify its legitimacy after the Cold War. According to historians Paul Betts and James Mark, Eastern Europeans' experiences were incorporated into "a tale of European integration produced through a continental struggle against the horrors of fascism and Communism."[21] Embracing the memory of the Holocaust, and acknowledging the participation of their own societies in the genocide against the Jews, were seen as nonnegotiable commitments for Eastern European countries to enter the EU.[22] But these equivalencies between fascism and Communism, the GDR and the Third Reich, were also resuscitated in the international realms of academia. For instance, a special 2006 issue of *Telos*, originally a journal of the New Left, was dedicated to the "two evil twins," Nazi Germany and Communism. The editors revisited the theories Hannah Arendt first put forward in *The Origins of Totalitarianism* (1951). In hindsight, one wonders why the language was so overdrawn, even in these liberal circles in the West. The interlocutors concluded that "Germany was the undisputed center of the Nazi world . . . while East Germany was merely a provincial satellite, a colony of a world power headquartered elsewhere."[23] Taken together, these shifts render legible the pervasiveness of efforts to discard the socialist Eastern European past. The parallels between the two systems were reinforced across diverse political, public, and scholarly spaces in the long post-1989 era.

Although, naturally, the realignments that I have outlined are never as clear-cut (power and epistemic closures must perpetually establish themselves), what stands out is this: first, memory discourses about Communism as the embodiment of evil reemphasized a need to break with the past. The sociologist Andreas Glaeser has remarked that the demonization of the Stasi in the 1990s "allow[ed] Westerners an incredible economy of judgment in a grandiose synecdochical swoop," as East Germans were cast— wholesale—as perpetrators. In part, Easterners rejected this fetishization of the Stasi past; in part, they willfully participated since, at least initially, this practice offered tempting ways to discard the shadows of the past.[24] Second, the negative memory discourses of state socialism repropagating in the middle of the first decade of the 2000s also have a significantly different and twofold function. On the one hand, the notion of the GDR as an authoritarian state or "Wall regime" certainly allows the FRG to continually distance itself from Germany's dictatorial legacies, thereby affirming its democratic credentials, as Paul Cooke has noted.[25] In this view, the notion is reaffirmed that confronting the atrocities of the Nazi era was solely a project of the postwar Western society, an argument that I challenged in *Film and Memory in East Germany* (2008). On the other hand, unlike in the 1990s, the shift in public remembrance during the first decade of the 2000s produced a mnemonic culture focused on multiple, and often conflated, histories of victimization.

By the mid-2000s, the realms of Holocaust memory and a negative memory of state socialism began to overlap uneasily, in the process leveling further fundamental differences between the two ideological projects of Nazism and Communism; their consequences became equated and a depoliticized victimhood began to circulate as a shared narrative. If the Stasi debates of the early 1990s promulgated a discourse by which East Germans were inscribed into the illegitimate or abject trajectory of German history and thus tainted by its legacies of perpetration, the first decade of the 2000s—with a public shift toward those murdered at the Berlin Wall—offered narratives of authoritarian oppression and victimization. This new public remembrance has systematically erased recollections of hope, activist struggle, or political projects based on collective solidarities. The historian Cristian Cercel makes a similar point in his seminal essay "Whither Politics? Whither Memory?" He aptly notes that Cold War memory discourses about Communism were "redeployed in order to delegitimize attempts to critically engage with contemporary neoliberal policies and their attendant body of thought," which constituted the main paradigm informing the post-1989 social, economic, and political evolutions in the Eastern European regions.[26] The principle of TINA (There Is No Alternative [to capitalism]), with its perpetual absence of a future horizon, had settled in by the end of the decade (but, as I explained above, in Germany, was rarely legible as such). Around 2009, however, the neoliberal discourse that had started out with Margaret Thatcher's conservative ideology of TINA in the 1980s became openly prevalent in Germany's government discourse.[27] Thus, an enduring shift occurred in the first decade of the 2000s, whereby neoliberal rationality was undergirded by a renewed celebration of unbridled individual freedom staged also in the arena of memory politics. This shift toward a neoliberal, hegemonic memory politics continuously risked arresting the variegated, indeterminate public discursive, social, and mnemonic fields. When I use the term "neoliberal" to qualify memory making in the post-1989 era, I refer to the kinds of memorial procedures that are funded and reproduced by the German state, private donors, foundations, juries, experts, consultants, and other governmental and institutional structures for enhancing, if not "discursively appropriating," self-serving notions of freedom and democracy, in an era in which politics increasingly conforms to the logic of the market.[28] Nevertheless, the public arena remains the ground for struggles over the meaning of democracy: the site where contested memories preserve the possibility for contested futures. In the following section, I outline how these multidirectional dynamics and normative pressures affected the official re-curating of the Berlin Wall Memorial at Bernauer Strasse.

Re-Curating the Berlin Wall at Bernauer Strasse

The first highly visible private wall memorialization appeared in 2004. Although the story is well known, it warrants repeating here to illustrate the competitive tension between Holocaust memory and the post–Cold War memory of Communism. The privatization process culminated in the sensational installation of more than a thousand black crosses by the artist Alexandra Hildebrandt on a privately leased lot near Checkpoint Charlie.[29] The center-left city government eventually removed all the crosses and cleared the site, at least partly because Hildebrandt envisioned the "Freedom Memorial" in direct relation to the Holocaust Memorial. After Hildebrandt had claimed that the temporary memorial represented all the victims of the Communist regime, the city also recognized the lack of any broader and integrative public commemoration of the Wall in the decades since unification and responded with a newly developed "Comprehensive Plan" (*Gesamtkonzept*) for Berlin. Overseen by the senator for cultural affairs, Thomas Flierl (PDS), the carefully crafted plan outlined deficits in Berlin's politics of memory and proposed to establish a modular, highly distributive commemorative network stretching across the city's downtown and through many of its formerly divided neighborhoods.[30] The plan also stipulated that Bernauer Strasse—the site of spectacular escapes during the building of the Wall—was to be developed into Berlin's central post–Cold War memory location. This location was the site of one of the longest remaining stretches of concrete panels, including the Wall monument (designed by Kohlhoff and Kohlhoff in 1998). Further legitimizing the plan, supportive positions of official experts were circulated. These experts were historical consultants associated with the federally funded History Consortium "Reappraisal of the SED Dictatorship" and the Potsdam Center for Contemporary History, which since its founding in 1992 focused on comparative research of communism and dictatorship, including recent German history in an international context. Flierl's plan invoked the historical distance to the fall of the wall and noted a growing willingness among the city's inhabitants to deal with the recent history of the SED-rule (*Herrschaft*) in the GDR. In addition, the experts anticipated a surge of domestic and international visitors to Berlin in search of authentic traces of the GDR Wall regime and its "monstrous border barrier," thus supplying interpretive frameworks for the extensive re-memorialization.[31]

Arguably, the exercise of mnemonic power over the GDR's memory perpetually veered toward finality. But it is worth noting that other significant public voices could still be heard when the debate over the Wall resurfaced two decades later. One of those voices was Axel Klausmeier, the director of the Berlin Wall Foundation. In 2011, Klausmeier suggested that only the presence of such a material testimony would be able to make palpable how "the people in the GDR fought for their rights through a peaceful revolution."[32] Manfred Fischer, the pastor of the Church of Reconciliation in West

Berlin, which had been blown up by the GDR government in 1985 to expand the border strip, had also long advocated for a memorial. Under a poetic title borrowed from Manfred Fischer, "'To Grasp Something, There Must Be Something to Grasp,'" Klausmeier wrote movingly about the Berlin Wall as an object of monument preservation. Initially, there was no authoritative conservation method. Yet, Klausmeier explains that following the findings of a scholarly conference and expert commission, it was agreed that "the special historical significance of the existing structural remnants of the border fortification lay not only in their sheer existence but also in their fragmentation."[33]

In 2009, engineers determined that it was impossible to verify the solidity of various segments of the Berlin Wall along Bernauer Strasse. Hence, during the process of expanding this central location of Wall memory, the remnants were to be cautiously repaired using a method of minimal intervention in order to "allow the fragile condition of the Wall at the moment of its defeat to be preserved."[34] In other words, the re-curated Wall in its tangible but fragmentary form would become a memorial to its own overcoming during the Peaceful Revolution. Yet, what is also revealed in the debate over the memorial site's material form is the tension between the institutionalization of Wall memory in the capital and the challenges of curating the difficult knowledge of violent pasts in public places.[35] Similar to other national or transnational post-conflict situations, we can observe here what happens when such knowledge is reinserted into the public domain and how in this process, certain ideas of the past propagate or fossilize while the residual presence of other historical experiences disappears. This tension took place, of course, in the conservative, neoliberal atmosphere of the post-unification era. According to cultural historian Marion Detjen, the emerging bureaucratization and nationalization of Wall memory signaled a systemic change in memorial institutions and infrastructures. This fundamental shift went hand in hand with an all-pervasive professionalization. The official memory of the Wall, she argues, was largely curated by experts trained in the West and not by those who were most affected by the removal of the physical border Wall in 1990. The result was that "nearly all material documentation of the GDR as living world had disappeared." Moreover, the historical subjects who were most connected to the Wall were, at best, assigned the role of exhibition guide or interviewed subject.[36] This large-scale shift can hardly be addressed without raising questions about the differential nature of the public realm: Who has the power to appropriate the past? Who should have the sovereignty to reinterpret the inner Berlin border?[37]

The exhibition at Bernauer Strasse examines the traumatic wounds inflicted by the city's Cold War division. But it also functions—flexibly and

FIGURE 1.2. Official ceremony at the Berlin Wall Memorial, Bernauer Strasse, commemorating the twenty-fifth anniversary of the fall of the Berlin Wall, November 9, 2014. Photograph: © Curt Nickisch.

prosthetically—as a postwar mourning ground, where disparate pasts are brought into contact and linger in an unsettled present.[38] We see in a moment that what is at stake at the former border of the "GDR Wall regime" is a kind of performative necrology. This "call of the dead" relates to and ultimately ministers to Germany's perpetual project of dealing with the Second World War and the Third Reich.[39] This obsession overshadows and erases the significance of 1989, especially its politico-emancipatory potential.Surely, set in the lively contemporary neighborhood of Berlin-Mitte, the Wall Memorial offers multiple access points for public use. The Wall Memorial is a place for personal reflection, official pedagogy, archival preservation, and State ceremonies. In every case, the iconography and ritualized setting of Cold War divisions is used for political purposes and mediated effects. While permeable to some degree, the official Wall memory that emerged in Berlin's memorial topography late in the first decade of the 2000s aligned most closely with the hegemonic, governmental forms of Germany's renewed post–Cold War imaginary. In this way, the symbolic location of Bernauer Strasse morphed into a "crime site" and a national monument to the victims of the Wall, while "1989" was forgotten or narrowly refashioned into a historicized narrative about the "triumph of freedom" from "communist tyranny."[40]

PERFORMING FLIGHT AND DEATH

An aesthetics of remnants and ruins is at work in the national Wall Memorial. This aesthetics can appropriate multiple histories of trauma and has the effect of enhancing the normalized narrative about the terror of the Communist regime. The Visitor Center across from the Nordbahnhof metro station is the starting point for registered groups and guests to the Berlin Wall Memorial. Nordbahnhof is one of the so-called ghost stations that became defunct in the GDR after the Wall was built. The station only reopened in the early 1990s. The massive one-and-a-half-kilometer-long memorial area at Nordbahnhof exposes an empty expanse punctuated by stretches of Wall panels, heaps of Wall debris, and rust-coated information stations. Hence, the site possesses a document-like character while suggesting the authenticity of archeological excavations. Overall, the site epitomizes an "archival impulse" that is, as Hal Foster shows, both flexible and institutionalizing, rhizomatic and instrumentalizing.[41] In the present study, this archival impulse is tantamount to the performative force of an alternative post-1989 memory, which manifests itself, especially in art or peripheral memorial arrangements. Still, we see here that it also nourishes highly visible public, official, and even hegemonic projects in the early twenty-first century.

At Bernauer Strasse, this archival principle accentuates the porousness of the site to other histories and temporalities, a porousness that is underscored by the liminal language of the memorial design. Foster suggests that the incomplete nature of archival aesthetics may offer several "points of departure," that is, openings to new interpretations. While I agree this may be the case in much contemporary art, and to a certain extent at Bernauer Strasse, I wish to foreground the risks of such an approach in the context of post-unification, post-1989 memory production. To start, echoes of Holocaust remembrance elsewhere in the city are palpable in the Wall Memorial park. Passing through the large, open terrain, thousands of visitors will stumble over the former metal tracks of the Wall that zigzag across the area. The same is true in the downtown Jewish Museum, which was opened in 2001 and designed by Daniel Libeskind in his signature postmodern style.[42] Like the Jewish Museum, the Berlin Wall Memorial is attentive to the grammar of voids. Amid border remnants, the memorial draws on an aesthetics of vacancy and erasure that uses, if not appropriates, the figurative language associated with the global and national memory of the Holocaust. For example, the site features minimalist outlines on the ground of the vanished border houses that the GDR demolished to build the Wall in 1961. Palm-sized metal plates, also in the ground, bear the stamps of a number and the name of a person who escaped from the

East to the West (resembling the memorial principle of the *Stolpersteine* [stumbling blocks or stones]). This aesthetics is concerned with victimization in the context of "extreme and abyssal violence."[43] Such a narrative confuses the significance and chronology at the Wall Memorial and keeps both triumph over Communism and borrowed trauma at the center of the visible mnemonic field.

Moreover, the site entangles the Nazi era, postwar death, and the Cold War into an elegiac field. The relationship between major and minor memorial objects at the site helps organize these disparate and entangled meanings. In the "Comprehensive Plan," Flierl had already emphasized that the memorial should give a "face" to the victims who died at the Wall.[44] The "Window of Remembrance" constitutes the focal point of the largely empty expanse on one side of a massive steel divider (which conceals the hybrid monument of an actual stretch of the Wall, including a watchtower, outer and inner barriers, and no-man's-land). In keeping with the exhibit's aesthetics of consciously produced authenticity, to recall Jonathan Bach's insightful reading,[45] the installation features black-and-white headshots of some of the at least 140 people who died at the Berlin Wall between 1961 and 1989. These instrumentalized images of Wall victims perform a kind

FIGURE 1.3. "Window of Remembrance" (2017), Berlin Wall Memorial Park, Bernauer Strasse. Author's private collection.

of double poetics: they function both as a testimony to history and as a "cipher" of it. They are both eloquent and obstinately silent (which also makes them permeable to other temporalities and histories).[46] For the most part, however, these photos are ghostly; they are decontextualized and unencumbered by any specific life narrative. Once the natural light no longer falls through the spectral images, they appear to dim and fall silent until the entire length of the rusty contraption turns impenetrably dark. In many ways, the heterogenous circumstances and political and personal motivations of the people who escaped the GDR remain undisclosed here at the Window of Remembrance. The iconic master signifier of "flight and death" ultimately engulfs the open-air exhibit.

In contrast, the sprawling site that winds alongside the Sophien Parish cemetery spurs a web of associations around Germany's traumatic national history. Near the Window of Remembrance, a minimalist white cross recalls the approximately one thousand World War II bombing victims who might have been exhumed when the border grounds were built by the GDR government. Even if infinitely understated, it is a shoulder-high gravestone off center that holds together the disparate meanings of loss at the Wall Memorial park. The gravestone faces the cemetery and carries the inscription: "Monument to the victims of the Second World War and the division of Germany." This message amplifies the discourse of victimization by combining distinct groups into one legible, commemorative space. The association of death and loss with the Wall is called upon, so to speak, converging with a public discourse about Germans who died in the war, a discourse that in the aftermath of the debate about W. G. Sebald's 1999 essay "Air War and Literature" (and the anxiety around revisionism) continues to look for a space. In this way, post-1989 Wall memory is repurposed at the Wall Memorial park, including for reparative reasons.

The phantom photographic design dedicated to the GDR fugitives also serves as a commemorative stand-in for the casualties of the Allied air raids and the millions of nameless Germans who perished in military combat. The design commemorates those who remain faceless—the unburied, reburied, or never-buried victims of the Second World War. In turn, the losses of nearly one hundred fifty victims at the Wall obtain historical gravity by being visibly and discursively resituated within the West's conventional framework of national memory (where that memory of the Wall dead has been stored all along).

Relying on familiar notions of victimization, any meaningful interrogation of antifascism or the failed project of social modernity is absent. The possibilities asserted during the liminal period of '89–90 have been pushed beyond the margins of this ruinous, traumatic memorial space. Here, Germany's national memorial site underscores a unique perspective of crime and violence that, according to the post-Soviet scholar Alexander Etkind, has dominated the understanding of post–Cold War, post-socialist Europe in the field of contemporary memory studies itself.[47] Imperceptibly, spectators passing through the open terrain of the exhibit become aligned with an instrumental (Western) gaze. Such scopic relations are indeed emphasized throughout the vast Wall Memorial arena, where the visual choreography centers on spectacular escapes from the East to the West. This emphasis is created through a series of dynamic photographic scenes placed in the built environment that index the forcible motions of climbing, crawling, running, and digging at the original site. Here the performative authenticity played out at the memorial site as a whole gets enacted and stabilized through the central role of photographs, an issue I take up throughout the book. In light of the dramatic escapes from the "terror of the border regime," the erasure of the interval '89–90 and the collective memory of the GDR goes entirely unnoticed.

LEAP INTO FREEDOM

Today, only a handful of readily available border photographs shape the cultural and political memory of Germany's postwar division. Peter Leibing's August 1961 photograph "Leap into Freedom" is showcased at the Wall Memorial Bernauer Strasse. Selected by UNESCO's Memory of the World program in 2011 as one of the hundred most significant historical images, it also been archived by the Unites States Library of Congress. The iconic image serves as shorthand for authoritarian oppression behind the Iron Curtain in the GDR and Eastern Europe. Meanwhile, the iconography of the Antifascist Protection Wall that circulated in the East abruptly disappeared from the official image archive of the unified FRG. The socialist iconography was designed to portray the border patrol groups (*Kampfgruppen*) in a humanizing and collective translation with open faces, shoulder to shoulder, bonded.[48] Instead, Peter Leibing's widely distributed photograph has dominated the contemporary imaginary as historical evidence of the violence inflicted by the Cold War. Leibing's photograph captures the moment when Conrad Schumann, a nineteen-year-old GDR border guard, jumped over barbed wire from the East into the West. Schumann took his famous leap on August 15, 1961, in the midst of official orders by SED authorities to erect the Berlin Wall. (Here, too, a closer examination of the photograph and further research would reveal a different, appropriative, and mediated storyline. Once taken, of course, photographers rarely promise their subjects anything about the future of an image.)[49]

FIGURE 1.4. Peter Leibing, "Leap into Freedom" (August 15, 1961), Berlin Wall Memorial, Bernauer Strasse. Author's private collection.

Today, just as distinct historical periods merge with the passage of time, the "Leap into Freedom" is on course to become the sole metonymy for 1989. Continuously reproduced, the photograph has been disconnected from the social and affective fabric of everyday life in the GDR. Of course, images can exist outside their communities of production, as any museum makes clear. But this iconic image circulates and forms perceptions of both the Cold War era and the post–Cold War era in a way that structures historical contingencies into a teleological story.

This epistemological narrowing in a delineated, public field of knowledge and memory can already be witnessed at the Wall Memorial Park's Documentation Center. Reopened in 2014, the Documentation Center has further stabilized any reflexive or multivalent historical meaning that linger at the overall site. As visitors pass from the open-air memorial arena to the new permanent indoor exhibit, they enter into a foyer where postwar national history is displayed at its normalized beginning point: "1953." This national origin story is signaled by a life-size photograph of a Soviet tank facing off with protesting workers in East Berlin. Predictably, the exhibit then moves via "1961" and a chapter on the "dictatorship of borders" toward the back room of the modular space, which is dedicated to "the Peaceful Revolution and the fall of the Wall." The exhibit thus eliminates the disparate elements of a radically "disjointed time." The twists and turns of '89–90 disappear through an act of *consignation* (consignment) that condenses the liminal period into a linear and unified narrative in Derrida's sense.[50] At the end of the exhibit, visitors create their own "portable monument" and hang it up near a video of the peaceful demonstrations. In 2017, I saw a memory-mobile spinning in the air, making this dynamic of conjoining Cold War Wall memory and '89 legible. Below a sketch of the soldier jumping across the barbed wire, an English-language display read, "FREEDOM, the borders are only in the mind." As a medial emblem or index of "individual overcoming," the familiar image of the Wall jumper compresses the contingent and collective drama of revolutionary protests into a universal affirmation of individual liberties. However, signed by a visitor from Columbia, the piece also repeated and expanded the meaning of the Berlin Wall on the scale of transnational, global memory and called to mind the US-Mexico wall and other border fortifications. It inadvertently exposes how Germany's post-unification public memory aligns with neoliberal rationality. I discuss later in the chapter how the plane of the visible can be reorganized when the category of "authentic documentation" is refused as the sole criterion for determining the borders of what can or cannot show up in the public memorial experience.

Suffice it to say, rather than de- and recontextualizing the unrest of 1989, the Wall Memorial at Bernauer Strasse insists on the familiar histories of Communism's victims and operates under the Cold War sign of "dictatorial suffering," albeit poetically rendered.[51] In '89–90 the grassroots citizens' movements in the GDR, if for the briefest of intervals, believed it was possible to claim freedom *and* equality as the signature of a basic-democratic revolution. But it is precisely the emphasis on freedom—decoupled from the social-as-political question—in the dominant visual language of the Wall Memorial park, and Germany's official memory more broadly, that perpetually helps stage democracy as the crown jewel of the West. In the process of re-curating the Berlin Wall that had already vanished twenty years earlier, the emancipatory memory of 1989 that had "belonged" to the East was ever so subtly appropriated by the existing discourse and institutional forces of the West. Germany's complex postwar division, failed Communism, the defeat of the Soviet system, and ultimately the peaceful revolution were concealed in the assumedly transparent, knowable space where public memory is shaped and controlled. Lost is the fact that the Wall was once a lived reality for East and West German inhabitants of the city as well as a piece of the GDR's antifascist socialist vision.[52] The Italian cultural historian Enzo Traverso makes a similar point about a global perspective on memory in the neoliberal era. Focused almost exclusively on victims (of the Holocaust, Communism, and colonial atrocities), any idea of collective agency, such as antifascism, revolution, and anti-imperialism, has disappeared from the history of the last two centuries.[53] However, these (disfigured) histories of resistance did not simply vanish with the collapse of Eastern Europe; their disappearance had to be perpetually enacted.

Built on Erasure: The Monument to Freedom and Unity at Berlin Palace

Twenty years after the forgotten revolt of 1989, its political meanings were ever further evacuated. In the first decade of the 2000s, Berlin's memorial politics increasingly converged with market-driven efforts to reinvent the city center as a global model of preserving cultural heritage.[54] Although these efforts were often promoted as citizens' initiatives, they were largely driven by managerial strategies and neoliberal agendas in the era of corporate globalization. The notion that neoliberal urban policies led to a heightened commercialization of public space in Berlin is well established. However, the urban development of Berlin's historic city center, which gained momentum with the demolition of the former GDR parliament building in 2006, showed how deeply neoliberal rationality—a privileged, normalized way of thinking about what is valued and valuable—became embedded in the capital's politics of memory. This embedding raises questions about who actually has the right to develop the city's public memorial spaces. Where and how is the public constituted under the differential conditions of politics in a market-conforming democracy?[55]

Scholars have compellingly told the story of the protracted dismantling of the Republic Palace. With a keen eye toward the instrumentalized redeployment of the public sphere, they have shown how the collective memory of the GDR has been erased in the process of reconstructing the Royal Berlin Palace.[56] My focus is related but different: the reinvention of a narrative and central mnemonic space for the Peaceful Revolution—a process that unfolded simultaneously to the neoliberal, presentist execution of what cultural critic Friedrich Dieckmann called a "second tabula rasa." Plans to establish the Monument to Freedom and Unity in front of the Berlin Palace/Humboldt Forum powerfully illustrate how government-controlled collective memory in the neoliberal era also systematically fostered the forgetting of the 1989 revolt's disruptive, emancipatory pathos. Three dilemmas emerged from debates surrounding the construction of a national monument at the center of the new Berlin: First, discussions revealed the risk of normalizing the legacies of the Nazi era—a predicament that echoed the 1980s Historians' Debate in West Germany. Second, questions arose about the authority of governmental bodies to determine memorial discourses without significant public support. And third, many socialized in the East were concerned with transforming the peaceful revolution into an ostentatious national commodity.

In 2007, the Bundestag initiated the development of the monument in Berlin-Mitte with parliamentary approval.[57] If the arena of the Wall Memorial supplied the visual and narrative dramaturgy to make 1989 legible as a fight for freedom from "the tyranny of the Wall regime," then this parallel monument sought to conjoin the public memory of 1989 with perceptions about the inevitability of German unification. Taken up at the highest levels of administration, plans for the monument had been disseminated through a variety of public and private channels and across a range of governing bodies, bureaucratic associations, civil spaces, and media platforms in the preceding years. Lawmakers were convinced that they were backing a civic initiative with broad popular support.[58] Yet, the monument in Berlin-Mitte was a niche idea. Plans for the monument were similar to the neoconservative project of the Berlin Palace. The fundamental, atmospheric shifts in memory politics during the mid-2000s were necessary for the idea to become a public thing, even if this process was commonly perceived to be led by ruling elites from above.

However, memorial meanings do not gain legitimacy simply through top-down regulations. Instead, the Peaceful Revolution as a commemorable event took hold over a decade in a dynamic field where conflicting political agendas and normative ideas about the past converged or failed to converge. Within a national economy of memory, where the resources and impacts were breathtakingly uneven, a depoliticized interpretation of the 1989 uprising emerged. In 1998, four high-profile conservative officials with lobbying access to the Bundestag approached the CDU chancellor Helmut Kohl and Berlin's mayor. Their proposal, titled "Monument German Unity," outlined the need for a monument dedicated to the Peaceful Revolution that would honor "the courageous protesters who took to the streets in the GDR to challenge the oppression of the SED-dictatorship with peaceful means."[59] Compare this statement to the alternative affective language of collective force, rendering citizens who were "fearless" or "disobedient" and events that were "unlawful," "violence-free," or "anarchic." Such irruptive accounts would surely shake existing representations to their core. This destabilization would expose the FRG's post-political structures as neither neutral nor self-transparent and reveal the urgency of restoring the agonistic dynamics that is the very condition of a vibrant democracy.[60] In considering the historical ramifications of the national imaginings set in motion by the Monument to Freedom and Unity, however, we should note the dominant discourse of sublation. Resorting to the Hegelian language of *Aufhebung*, the initiators conceived of the monument as representing both the victory over the dictatorial history of the twentieth century and the completion of the trajectory of democratic revolutions that began in 1848. The parliament rejected the initiative in 2000 with the reasoning that unity between East and West had not yet been achieved. Yet the proposal supplied a new narrative of continuity and renewal (understood as internally self-sufficient and self-standing). Therefore, even without initial parliamentary backing, the project gained the support of the powerful Federal Foundation for the Reappraisal of the SED Dictatorship, founded in 1998, and was ultimately managed by the German Society e.V., a central instrument of political education in the FRG. By 2007, the conservative advocates requested support from the government for what they now called an "idea from the middle of society."[61]

It is tempting to argue that this affirmative preoccupation with Germany's past interlinked quite comfortably with the disappearance of future-oriented, emancipatory politics in the long aftermath of the collapse of Communism across Europe. By the middle of the first decade of the 2000s, the Nazi past seemed visibly institutionalized and integrated in Berlin's and Germany's official self-images. On the one hand, this institutionalization prompted both conservative and liberal supporters to openly endorse (albeit for different reasons) a new master narrative of German history with positive, if not heroic, strands as an overdue shift in an official politics of memory focused on mourning and shame.[62] Critics, on the other hand, feared that the agenda promoted by a handful of influential planners and governmental officials would not only add to the capital's memorial topography but also create a counterweight to Holocaust commemoration and thus indelibly change it.[63] After all, the planned memorial site was just one mile from the Memorial to the Murdered Jews of Europe. At the same time, the curators of the Berlin Wall Memorial wrestled with multiple specters and entangled temporalities associated with victimizations inflicted during the twentieth century, as pointed out in the previous section. Thus, the high-profile debate around the national monument risked veering toward what Dominick LaCapra once called a "harmonizing mode of narration."[64] In a 2009 treatise, the most ardent defender of the monument, Florian Mausbach, then president of the Federal Office for Construction and Spatial Planning, envisioned the ensemble of the reconstructed Berlin Palace/Humboldt Forum and the Monument to Freedom and Unity as the "triumphant endpoint" (*Höhepunkt und Schlusspointe*) of national history. His ardent defense attests to the legitimacy of end-of-history thinking and to a universalizing, presentist interpretation of the past in the sphere of governance.[65]

NATIONAL SOCIAL SCULPTURE

Even if the debates in the political arena perpetually foreclosed competing interpretations of 1989 under the axiom of "freedom and unity," the designs submitted for the monument competition were not as easily contained by such an instrumentalizing logic. In 2011, Sasha Waltz, the well-known artistic director of the dance company, and the Stuttgart design office Milla and Partner won the second round of the monument competition with their project entitled "Citizens on the Move." The curatorial team proposed erecting a fifty-meter-long, 330-ton glittering steel wing in front of the reconstructed Berlin City Palace. In its original conception, the monument was designed to engage with the multi-scaled, historical environment of the restored Schlossplatz. At the vast open site, the dynamic opticality and interplay of sculptural work with space and time would be investigated and set into motion. The jury noted that the form of the monument, which elongates upward from the historic pedestal, seemed to sublate the past toward the future.[66] Waltz hoped the sculpture would become a symbol of how civic movements occupied public space and changed it in the process. In its "expanded field," this *Denkort/Denkmal* (thinking space/monument) was to transform into a performance where the notion of the monumental monument (as a site where "one remains in prayer") would be questioned, deconstructed, and transformed.[67] Initially, '89 protest scenes were to appear on the undersurface of the suspended golden sheet, illuminating the power of photography to function as a self-reflexive cipher of history in visual form. Thus, the contemporary meanings of the uprising in the GDR would also be investigated.

In 2012, however, Waltz withdrew from the project over differences regarding aesthetic questions and practical concerns about the monument's construction. In an early defense of the single, curved design, she said, "There is no swing, no seesaw and nothing loud at all. It's an elongated sheet that breaks free from the ground, separates itself from history."[68] The sculpture would render the rhythms that challenge established orders. The architectural effect suggested a kind of weightlessness—which, to my mind, evoked the provisional assembly of the populace in 1989. But Waltz's concept was overruled by Milla's literal plan for a more robust bowl or swing. Plunked onto the remaining pedestal of the once grandiose statue of Kaiser Wilhelm I, the memorial bowl corresponded to the colossal style of the original figure monument of the emperor. In 1950, the SED had demolished the national monument to the first emperor of the unified Germany and the ruined Royal Berlin Palace to make room for official demonstrations at Marx-Engels Square (renamed Schlossplatz in 1994). Sixty years later, critics argued that yet another gigantic national monument would only further emphasize the logic of teleology, centered on triumphant illusion. Devoid of any poetic interplay or historical specificity, Milla's proposal risked reducing the memorial design for the Peaceful Revolution to an unequivocal icon, in McLuhan's sense, where any ambiguity is stamped out to enforce a singular, reified interpretation of the event.[69] Taking up the original plans for the Monument to Freedom and Unity, put forward in 1998, the goal appeared now, ever more forcibly, to be to "'complete' the national memory-

FIGURE 1.5. Planned Monument to Freedom and Unity (2014), Berlin. Photograph © Milla & Partner.

scape by 'closing' it with a monument that embodied the happy ending of German history," thereby transcending any contentious, contingent, or "negative parts."[70]

The choice of a bowl in particular, and its elevation into a memorial form, trivializes the jagged, on-the-ground memories of 1989. Art historians have indicated the broader challenges of finding a suitable language for commemorating transformative historical events that have no legible victors or individual heroes to celebrate. The winning design of the bowl, traditionally used only as an accessory, stood in a long history of victory monuments and material and symbolic representations dedicated to state foundational events.[71] Arguably, the design agency Milla and Partner promoted the monument in more dynamic terms than such decorative commemorative art and called the monument a kinetic object, or "social sculpture," a concept drawn from the postwar West German artist Joseph Beuys. It is worth noting, however, that Milla's literalization was either done without awareness or was a purposeful adjustment of Beuys's antiestablishment notion of social sculpture. The political impulses of the artist's vision were certainly expunged. This problem is precisely the same one that befell the legacies of the GDR activists. The grassroots networks in East Germany dismissed the orthodox socialist and capitalist orders as viable paths, and yet only their fight for freedom was culled from that history for the hegemonic post-1989 memory politics. Beuys's political vision emerged in the 1980s from a fundamental critique of the central role played by private corporate capital in global inequality and injustice. In his view, unleashed market growth led to irreversible ecological devastation that endangered the planet's future. Faced with the nuclear arms race of the Cold War, Beuys formulated the idea of "social sculpture" as an alternative to the centralized economies in Soviet regimes in the East and the professed democratic order of market capitalism in the West. Contemplating the future at the end of the twentieth century, he asked, "How can all the planet's inhabitants cooperate economically for the benefit of all?"[72] Such fundamental concern with the political interrelation of *freedom* and *equality*, and shared ownership and property in particular, was echoed in the ideals of oppositional figures, peace and environmental groups, and basic-democratic movements in the late GDR that rose up in the fall of 1989. We only need to recall the highly mediatized statement by Bärbel Bohley, the co-founder of the New Forum, released on November 9, 1989, warning forces in the West to intervene in the *Umbruch* (radical change) of the GDR. Activists in street demonstrations called for the political work of self-organizing from below to prevent the sellout of the property and land (*Grund und Boden*) to "Western monopolies with the help of the SED."[73] It is potential histories such as these that the national monument and Germany's post-unification politics of memory in the neo-liberal era have disavowed and erased.

Although scholars working across the humanities have long observed that national memory is managed through institutions such as museums, libraries, archives, and formal commemorations, more work needs to be done on the ways that public memorial objects and the tangible, embodied practices they enlist can help stabilize hegemonic meanings about the past. By distributing surfaces and assembling words or forms, certain configurations of what can be seen and what can be thought are established in the material world, giving rise to modes and spheres of publicity. These configurations obviously change over time; monuments have the capacity to adopt new and unexpected interpretations.[74] However, the publicness of memory cannot be separated from things and power in the dominant post-1989 public sphere. According to the planned design of the national monument, tourists physically enter a very large rocking dish (1,400 people can be accommodated). Once at least twenty or thirty visitors move from side to side, the structure tilts in one direction or the other. Across the bottom of the steel bowl is a large inscription: "We are the people. We are one people" ("Wir sind das Volk. Wir sind ein Volk"), condensing all the disparate slogans and meanings from the Peaceful Revolution.[75] When participants set the gigantic contraption in motion, they thereby animate only a basic understanding of democracy as majority rule rather than democracy as an unending process of negotiating for freedom and equality. Surely, 1989 as a "polemical scene," as an interruption of the "natural" order of domination by "the part of those who have no part," to echo Rancière, also fails to come into view. The definitional contestation of democracy itself is rarely at stake in the official focus on freedom and unity.[76] Yet, this contestation was at the crux of the spontaneous citizens' movements in '89–90, as we see in a later chapter. Instead, a teleological understanding of historical upheaval culminating in national victory is made fully visible. A neoconservative, revisionist imaginary would be performed at this symbolic site, at least for the foreseeable future, as in the rest of Berlin.

Divorced from its historical context, the specific political meanings of the monumental inscriptions will be lost on most visitors to the capital. This loss is one reason why the Linke Party repeatedly argued against remembering the demonstrations of 1989 together with the event of unification. The choice to use the slogans reminds audiences only of the "contraction," the shrinking of temporalities that saw the shift from "Wir sind das Volk" to "Wir sind ein Volk" in the end. As Anna Saunders compellingly explains, a monument that promotes a myth of such immutable linkage would suggest, at least to future generations, "that the desire for unity was one of the principal aims of the demonstrators in 1989," thus refashioning history "to fit a nationally oriented agenda."[77] Yet the refashioning of 1989 memory also reveals, more broadly, how grave the distortion or blockage of East Germans' access to the state-sanctioned governmental sphere of memory politics could be. As Michael Warner has argued, externally organized frameworks of participation may be a poor substitute for self-organized publics. When denied, however, such blockages can lead people to feel powerless and frustrated, or worse, the result can be a kind of "disintegration of politics toward isolation, frustration, anomie, and forgetfulness."[78] (All these cumulative, systemic humiliations should be considered when we are faced, as we are today, with a real or perceived sense of disenfranchisement in the East.) Not only did a member of the GDR citizen movement circulate a protest petition in the parliament early on, in 2001, but even with the passing of time, many who had participated in 1989 resisted the idea of erecting a memorial while the active historical agents of the Peaceful Revolution were still alive.[79] After all, revolutions topple the existing order and often their statues; why would their agents want a monument? The year 2007 saw the failure of two significant counterproposals: the Alliance 90/the Greens demanded a broader public debate about the monument, echoing a concern that those who participated in the fall of 1989 should be involved in the process; and the Linke Party requested to establish a documentation center for the remembrance of the Peaceful Revolution. Here the political and civil agency of ecumenical and peace movements in the late GDR—movements that had set the transformational change in motion—would be displayed.[80] But these histories of the alternative publics that formed in 1989 were disregarded; their collective action was absent in the performative field of a national, public memory in the neoliberal era, where a perpetual sense of the present absorbs the past and the future.

Delayed, aborted, and reinitiated over the span of a decade, the plan to build the monument was once more pushed through by the CDU in the Bundestag in 2017, with backing from the Federal Foundation for the Reappraisal of the SED Dictatorship, which revealed that—unlike the purported design—public spheres in late capitalist societies, in Nancy Fraser's sense, denude "public opinion" of any practical force.[81] Many lamented the monument's ahistorical, triumphalist message in light of the aftermath of the dramatic events in 2015, the year in which one million refugees arrived from Syria and other war-torn countries and populist grievances led to the rise of PEGIDA and the right-wing AfD (Alternative for Germany). At the same time, for different reasons, in 2017 only 16 percent of Germans supported the national monument, which they viewed to be cumbersome, politically motivated, and—at a price tag of 17 million euros—simply wasteful.[82] When

W. J. T. Mitchell asks, "What does an image, or even a sculpture want?" he ensures we understand this question is not just metaphorical. He assigns a kind of vital agency to such things or objects. "Sculpture wants a place to be *and* to be a place," he writes.[83] What if we surmise, then, that the inverse can also hold true, namely, that the National Monument to Freedom and Unity—if it wants, or desires, anything—wants *not* to be launched into being, not to be built (even a colony of rare bats nesting underground would lose their habitat)? Unrealized, it appears to insist on the *Lücke*, the gap, on the receding rhythms and transitoriness of movements. Waltz compares freedom to a blank white sheet. For Hannah Arendt, freedom is ephemeral; only "for a fleeting moment" were the political actors able to hold "the treasure [of revolution] in the palms of their hands."[84]

Such a poetics of absence notwithstanding, by the end of 2023, the national "Monument to Freedom and Unity" will complete the neo-traditionalist tableau of the Berlin Palace/Humboldt Forum. As the construction of the monument began, a cross, the symbol of Christianity financed by a private donor, was hoisted up onto the dome of the Berlin Palace/Humboldt Forum. The Berlin Palace/Humboldt Forum houses the much-embattled collection of non-European art that is itself mired in histories of racial and colonial theft.[85] In an astounding culmination of post-1989 memory politics, postcolonial hubris of conquest and disregard, the cross atop the castle was lauded by conservative governing authorities as a symbol of cultural reconciliation. This final architectural ensemble at the heart of the German capital includes a restored band of text compiled by Friedrich Wilhelm IV, King of Prussia, in 1840 that calls for the submission of all men to Christianity. If the conservative supporters of the Berlin Palace/Humboldt Forum had often rebuked any criticism with the claim that the reconstruction of the Royal Palace was not an authentic replica, now in 2020, at the height of their control over the built environment and Berlin's image, they argued in favor of absolute originality.[86]

The vanished interval of '89–90 may not be recoverable as long as western narratives of progress hold sway. But we can retrain ourselves to notice the slippages, residues, and gaps in the visual memorial plane. Doing so is the first step to reimagining and recapturing a future-oriented memory of past emancipatory struggles. Over the last two decades, legal governing bodies have quietly empowered private interests and expert knowledge alongside privileged artistic forms. These forces have been foundational in producing a dominant post-unification imaginary that has displaced and erased other histories. Once we recognize these differential memory dynamics, we can also learn to unlearn such hegemonic emplacement of memorial power in the sphere of appearance. Below, I will attempt to rehearse the practice that Arielle Azoulay calls "potential history" and which I refer to in this book as "future archives."

The Edge of Sight: The Peaceful Revolution Pillar in the Shadow of the Berlin Palace

Networks of dominant publics become constituted by performing a vital link between memory, knowledge, and power. Paying attention to these procedures reveals how alternative histories become displaced, submerged, and even blocked from transmission. But the implicated role of alternative memory curators should also be considered. To start, in her essay "The Gap between Past and Future," Hannah Arendt illuminates the limits to transmitting the histories of revolutions across historical ruptures. When those who rose up in 1989 pass through the unified capital of Germany today, the disappearance of "the revolutionary treasure" is not an abstract or philosophical matter. Arendt was right: only on the rarest of occasions is the human mind "capable of retaining something which is altogether unconnected. Thus, the first who failed to remember what the treasure was like were precisely those who had possessed it and found it so strange that they did not even know how to name it."[87] The Peaceful Revolution has been enshrined in Germany's national imaginary as foundational myth for "freedom and unity," and, as we have seen, only a few material mnemonic residues of the radical upheaval can be found in Berlin today.

Downtown, a memorial Pillar to the Peaceful Revolution demonstrates what the post-1989 public sphere continues to elide: the plural political performativity of the '89–90 uprising and the political dimension of its corporeal, nonviolent street politics. Walking through the restored historic section of Berlin, it is easy to miss the red stainless-steel column. Placed in between the massive Berlin Cathedral Church, which was built in the late nineteenth century in the exuberant forms of high Neo-Renaissance style, and the Berlin Palace/Humboldt Forum, the reconstructed center of Prussian imperial power, the mnemonic object submerges into the accelerated urban rhythms of the modern, global city. In the summer of 2019, the twelve-foot-high narrow structure was plastered with stickers. It could easily have been mistaken for a lamppost amid the four-lane traffic of "Under den Linden," a grand historic boulevard that runs east-west to the Brandenburg Gate. The steel column belongs to a memorial information system called "Sites of the Peaceful Revolution in Berlin" (*Orte der Friedlichen Revolution in Berlin*), commissioned by the Robert Havemann Society in 2010, and connects to the open-air exhibit *Revolution and Fall of the Wall*.[88] This exhibit was established in Berlin-Lichtenberg, the Eastern district at the periphery of the capital, on the grounds of the former Stasi Headquarters (today BStU), linking the legacy of the peaceful revolution to the GDR's oppressive state apparatus. The memorial network consists of eighteen information stelae installed in different parts of the city, including one near the Press Office at the GDR Council of Ministers, where the Politburo member Günter Schabowski announced a new travel ruling on November 9, 1989, which led to the fall of the Wall, and one at the Zion Church, where local dissident activities began in the 1980s. Situated at the edge of sight, these interactive memorial columns raise questions about how memory takes place and space and about the function of "appearance" and visibility itself. Though a crowd comes together in shared visibility, the self-organizing publics that came together in the 1989 peaceful revolution struggle to be visible in the representational realm of the stelae. Representations of the past that are "seen by many," I have argued, delineate the sphere of public memory.

Few scholars dispute that photography is among the most apt media to capture an instant in time and also to transmit the passing of time. Difficulties arise, however, when we think about which images survive a socio-symbolic rupture and how they survive. Zooming in, for a moment, on the three vertically arranged black-and-white photographs on the stele, we see how, even on the smallest of scales, the national imaginings privileged by governmental, if not hegemonic, memory dynamics are configured into memorial sites, including those commissioned by activist groups who were there in 1989. Each of the palm-sized images shows small crowds demonstrating near the Republic Palace, the former GDR parliament building that was demolished in 2006. The wording of the captions is important: "7 October 1989. *Peaceful Revolution in the GDR. The first major protest demonstration in the GDR since the uprising of 1953*," followed by "24 October 1989 protest in front of the State Council building against the newly appointed state and party leader Egon Krenz." The last reads, "11 January 1990 *East Berlin construction workers* marched to the Palace of the Republic and demanded the *total dissolution of the Stasi*" (emphasis mine). The focus on construction workers in this montage links the protests in the late GDR even more closely to the uprising on June 17, 1953, where they were indeed the central historical agents. Accordingly, a teleological narrative of historical inevitability emerges from the grouping and captions. The mediated form anchors the Peaceful Revolution in the GDR in the 1953 uprising (until 1990, June 17 was a national commemorative "Day of German Unity" in the West) and authorizes a historical trajectory that culminates in the demand for the "total dissolution of the Stasi," the GDR's secret surveillance apparatus.

FIGURE 1.6. Stela at Schlossplatz, Sites of the Peaceful Revolution (2019), Berlin. Author's private collection.

This foundational formula of conjoining 1953 and 1989 in Germany's collective memory is as remarkable for its enduring power as for what it omits. The Robert Havemann Society was founded in 1990 as a political association of the New Forum, the civil organization that emerged during the revolutionary autumn. Former opposition leaders, including Katja Havemann, Bärbel Bohley, and Jürgen Fuchs, focused on the inheritance of the Stasi and the FRG's initial reluctance to deal with secret-service documents and former personnel. After 1990, they were bereft of the revolutionary trea-

FIGURE 1.7. Stela at Schlossplatz (detail), Sites of the Peaceful Revolution (2019), Berlin. Author's private collection.

sure, so to speak: the chance of society's basic-democratic reorganization. The initial avoidance of the Stasi issue in the early 1990s was perceived by the former dissidents as a final confirmation that the revolution had not been realized.[89] Consequently, the Stasi legacy—rather than the spontaneous mass protests—took over in Germany's collective memory, a trend that soon aligned with the FRG's own self-serving efforts to recall the GDR as a socialist dictatorship (alongside, as we saw earlier, Cold War division and an imaginary of death and flight). Yet here I wish to make a different point: Even in its minimalist form, the play with frames on the slim red stainless-steel pillar, recalling the "Peaceful Revolution," organizes a visual experience in the urban periphery that can further illuminate how public memory is not neutral but, rather, subject to the influence of certain conditions that render or limit the recognizability of certain historical actors. The small protest pictures are framed, of course, as any photographic image is: by their edges, within which the past moment is captured—and yet the three photographs on this stele appear to hover over empty space, seemingly cut out of the metal pillar. On the right side, however, they are abruptly cut off, giving the impression of dropping away into the unbound space of today's city. I read this as a commentary on framing as a way to make sense of the past. The frame itself is called into question on this pillar.[90] The memorial shows that a picture never quite contains the scene it was meant to limn and that, with regard to the Peaceful Revolution (bound up today with the fall of the Berlin Wall and Germany's "reunification"), something may have occurred that does not conform to our established understanding and that under current conditions of memory politics cannot come into view.

CRAFTING PROTEST ARCHIVES FROM THE UNSEEN

If something in these photographs exceeds the frame that still may have the potential to trouble our sense of presentist reality, what is the story that perpetually dissipates and slips back into oblivion? To find out, one only needs to investigate the date "January 11, 1990," mentioned in the caption of the third image. This image stabilizes the interpretive possibilities of the demonstrations in national meanings by showing a crowd of construction workers (incidentally, the professional group marching against the GDR regime in 1953). Recall that the montage aligns the protests in 1953 and 1989, creating an interpretation that supports Germany's master narrative and ignores other possible international constellations (for example, 1956 in Hungary, 1968 in Czechoslovakia, or the Gdansk movement of Solidarność in 1980s Poland). What also falls outside the officially legitimated memory frames are the differentiated rhythms, multiple agendas, and heterogeneity of the protests in the late GDR—and the violability of those in the streets involved in the citizens' movement. Not only did a group of construction workers show up in the streets on January 11, 1990 (linking '89 to 1953 in the memorial's national narrative strand), but later that evening, a motley crowd of twenty thousand East Berliners gathered to demonstrate against the GDR government's plans to establish a "new" intelligence service. In the sense of political outrage, these people were "beside themselves," uncertain and decentered (and far from the self-owning, freedom- and unity-seeking individuals the national public memorial discourse often evokes). Moved by the others in the crowd, these subjects transposed themselves into new forms of political and civic participation, refusing the established norms of governance. Together, they occupied and claimed public space by exposing their bodies to the incalculable powers of the state. For instance, they formed a human solidarity chain around the Republic Palace, where the proto-parliament of the GDR, the Volkskammer, had been in session. New Forum and other oppositional groups organized these mass protests. Over the course of the revolutionary fall, they had become active in the radically democratic, extra-parliamentary networks of the so-called roundtables. In the next two days, thousands entered the square to protest the supremacy of the SED Party.

But perhaps what is most important is that on January 11, unification was not the issue at hand in the East German public sphere. Reestablishing this fact in the post-historical era serves to dislodge the revolution from the teleology that is now part and parcel of the narrative about the end of the GDR. On that Thursday, the GDR parliament convened in the Republic Palace, and in a ninety-minute-long government declaration, the interim premier, Hans Modrow, emphasized that "the reunification of the two German states is not on the agenda; the relation between the FRG and the GDR needs to be integrated into a European path." He called on the citizens not to barter away "the historical chance of a democratic revolution."[91] Now, Modrow was a longtime SED official from Dresden who became the de facto reform leader of East Germany (supported by Mikhail Gorbachev). He may have had his own agenda and used the assembly to stabilize the regime's power under the waning control of the SED-PDS.[92] Faced with the erosion of its legitimacy, the SED had been attempting since the fall of 1989 to recast itself as a party of democratic socialism while retaining many of its material resources and advantages.[93] However, in an interview with West German filmmaker and cultural theorist Alexander Kluge, Gregor Gysi of the PDS expressed a less cynical view. He stressed Modrow's tactical role during a time of "all-pervasive chaos and uncertainty" in early 1990 to ensure the interval continued to be bloodless.[94] In other words, far from being foreclosed, this time was "radically disjointed," a formulation Derrida, in his 1992 book *Specter of Marx*, attributes to 1989.

It is true that the task of memorial sites and discourse is not to bring all of history into view. My wager here is not to cram more in the frame but rather to examine those conditions in the post-1989 public sphere by which certain exclusions related to the so-called Peaceful Revolution are put into play. I am also not seeking to expand the authentic records of the largely forgotten 1989–90 protest movements, erased in a perceptual field that is dominated by normative remembrance of the unification and the Wall regime. After all, memory itself is inevitably selective and mediated, and even as the interactive memorial pillars are placed at historic sites around the city "to recall the events surrounding the fall of the Wall," authenticity and indexicality decades later become more of an effect rather than an achieved ontological certainty. As I will elaborate more fully throughout the book, photographs that circulate in the memorial sphere are a particularly useful tool not only for analyzing the dynamics of memory transmissions but also for starting the work of reorganizing archives and knowledge surrounding the historical rupture of 1989. Visual theorists remind us that photography brushes against the unseen and, residing on the brink of the visible world, draws awareness to what lies beyond visibility. The miniature snapshots of '89 protests displayed on the memorial pillar near the Berlin Royal Palace are more casual than this high artistic register suggests—and yet one demonstrator captured in the first image, who carries a "New Forum" sign, points incidentally toward the field of vision outside the frame, as though compelling us to not only question the conditions that limned the scenes in the first place but also to search beyond them. If we follow the image's directive to look at what is at the edge of sight in these historic scenes, we can craft what is left out and imagine anew what has thus far remained invisible.[95]

UNREST IN 1990

The workers' public appearance in Berlin on January 11, 1990, was part of a rather disorderly countrywide upsurge of protests earlier that year. During the week of January 7–14 alone, a dizzying number of mass demonstrations, warning strikes, and smaller assemblies flared up all across the GDR. Far from focusing solely on the Stasi or toppling the GDR, each of these heterogeneous public gatherings had different and often conflicting aims. The demonstrators' aims ranged from demanding participation in factory councils, calling for transparent democratic elections, and supporting German unification *to* urging socialist reforms, advocating price control for children's clothing, and fighting against neo-Nazis.[96]

66 ‹ CHAPTER ONE

Unexpectedly and despite political rifts, new, unforeseeable, temporary alliances were formed early that year. On February 5, 1990, for instance, opposition groups relinquished their initial politics of resistance and joined the GDR government under Modrow's leadership while keeping the Stasi issue central and continuing to voice their skepticism about the SED-PDS efforts at political "renewal." Notably, even if the leaders of the citizens' movement were often reluctant to define themselves in left-right terms, they regularly expressed their loyalties to some kind of anti-capitalist and anti-consumerist, if not socialist, agenda. The historian Ann Sa'adah argues that between November 1989 and March 18, 1990, "a pluralistic landscape hesitantly took shape in the DDR, important organizational options were considered, coalition patterns were established, and programmatic decisions were made."[97] Civil unrest gave rise to unconventional coalitions. In other words, Germany's official channels of national memory today have forgotten that in the relatively fluid, open public sphere of the interval period, the very ambiguity and dispute generated by direct, participatory, and even radical conceptions of democracy were most exhilaratingly at play.

As we pass through Germany's capital, what lingers outside the perceptual and epistemological sphere today is history's openness. Not only did the upsurge of revolutionary energy in 1989–90 challenge the status quo and mobilize multitudes of various excluded sectors in the GDR, it also revealed potentiality. History, for the briefest of moments, broke apart and became unfixed. From within this unfinished temporality, the final moment of suture (Peaceful Revolution/unification) was not graspable; rather, it was deferred indefinitely, never to arrive. Not unlike members of the various citizens' movements in the GDR, the Argentinian and Belgian political theorists Ernesto Laclau and Chantal Mouffe posited in 1985 that both liberal democracy and orthodox Marxism were the problems and a variable left-wing alternative the solution. In their formulation, democracy (radically mediated, performed, and non-self-identical) was only to be achieved by introducing conflictual forces into politics—different antagonisms and points of rupture—so that political operations could always be open to future revision.[98]

In Germany's commemorative discourse, however, this intense heterotopian opening recedes and perpetually disappears. Wherever the 1989 revolution emerges in the circumscribed frameworks of the public realm nowadays, it is through the endlessly repeated emphasis on its peacefulness. In the miniature black-and-white photographs of the memorial pillar hidden in the shadows of the reconstructed Royal Palace, the protesting crowds look civil, well-organized, and friendly. In one of them, two policemen, who are captured from the back, casually stand by. According to the Robert Havemann Society, the memorial network was funded by the German Lottery Foundation Berlin and by the Federal Government Commissioner for Culture and the Media, based on the federal ruling by the Bundestag. Thus, it's unsurprising that the columns were designed to capture "the peaceful course of the first successful revolution in Germany." Yet the information system (a collaboration between two designers, Dagmar Wilcken and Helga Lieser, both trained in the West) also aimed at leaving material traces of the "joy" involved in occupying the streets and organizing social change and at showing the wide support for the Peaceful Revolution in West Berlin (another rarely told story). Recall Arendt, who defines the lost revolutionary treasure as public happiness, by which she means the interruptive "freedom from officialdom." Public happiness arises when people assemble and free themselves from officialdom through collective action. Although some critics detect in Arendt's interest in public freedom a liberal universalist sense, I agree with those scholars who stress her view of the public as a political, agonistic scene of world-making, self-disclosure, and interaction.[99]

This performative political dimension of 1989–90—a memory of plural publics—remains largely beyond the visual, mnemonic field in Germany's capital. In contrast, neoliberal forms of governmentality depend on a public memory that galvanizes a neater and more linear story (and evacuates more complex historical plotlines to liminal spaces). The narrative of the *Peaceful* Revolution served the neoliberally oriented national post-1989 order perfectly. As Wendy Brown points out, neoliberalism dreads the political mobilization of the citizenry and looks to "market and moral discipline and a severely leashed democracy to pacify and contain it."[100] Chapter 2 takes up this normative fiction of Western victory *qua peacefulness* and focuses on the local memorial landscape of Leipzig, where the revolutionary uprising began. Suffice it to say that this teleological, mono-focal interpretation of the Peaceful Revolution was indispensable for a post-1989 national discourse, by which the West to this day legitimizes itself as emerging victoriously from the large-scale shifts in Central and Eastern Europe. During the long post–Cold War era, nearly all other memories of these ordinary and extraordinary forces of resistance were drowned out (to such a degree that even those dissidents and citizens who participated appear no longer to remember the plurality of views, positions, and collectives).

Coda: Memory Activism

In 1989, when Germans danced on the Brandenburg Gate almost overnight, Cold War Berlin became an image of a vanished past. This past was often only recoverable in the form of *Ostalgie* (nostalgia for the East), accompanied by a material and medial investment in prehistoric GDR kitsch. But scholars such as Daphne Berdahl have also shown how *Ostalgie* could take on reflexive counter-memorial forms (or what I have delineated here as memory of publics) and be mobilized by local communities to contest the new order.[101] Clearly, these yearnings for the previous era were also "appropriated by neoliberal entrepreneurship, repackaged accordingly and sold to the public."[102] But despite these nuanced scholarly engagements with the GDR's material past in everyday encounters and practices, too many historians consider post-unification public memory as if it literally espoused some truth of collective identity, or critically trained memory scholars turn toward multidirectional transnational configurations where East Germany risks falling out of view.[103] In either case, nationalist presumptions of closure and continuity are undergirded. The memory of the late GDR is absorbed by national frameworks or lacks the malleable, unsettled nature of other memory forms that warrant closer attention.

In contrast, the performative public memory dynamics that I have put forward here reemphasize the differential distribution of power and knowledge. Access to the memorial sphere is regulated by policies, discourse, and political capital and by the performative effects of self-legitimizing, often exclusionary networks formed by legal and governmental bodies. I argue that these governmental bodies and their myriad extensions often imperceptibly control what historical imagination is valued in the public field. When I speak of performative effects, I refer to the intangible, normalizing practices that establish certain institutional domains and not others as the obvious custodians of collective memory in the aftermath of a society's collapse. The chapter also considers the role of professional experts, consultants, artists, victim groups, and so forth in a city such as Berlin, where the politics of memory emerges from multiple tectonic regime shifts.

In post-unification Germany, these differential dynamics matter because they construe the past of the GDR and 1989 in ways that erase historical contingency. As Arendt submitted, faced with the new status quo, future generations may no longer know what questions to ask of the past and how to undo the epistemologies of the established order. A performative approach foregrounds how these variegated forces of power, knowledge, and policies work to stabilize a dominant memorial sphere over time and never linearly. Refusing closure, the liminal, interstitial, and, for that matter, minor memory spaces are certainly implicated in this conflictual hegemonic sphere of memory, but they can also serve to contest commemorative norms and even break with them.[104] Concurrently, the three sites examined in this chapter produce narratives of German history and the Peaceful Revolution that may be described as reflexive-global, neoliberal-nationalist-triumphalist, and activist-political. To varying degrees, these narratives sustain, enforce, and challenge the mnemonic depoliticizing of the 1989 past.

Finally, liminal mnemonic spaces, as I have shown in the case of the Peaceful Revolution pillar in the shadow of the Berlin Royal Palace, tell us much about the unstable stabilizing of hegemonic meanings and authoritative discourses related to the past. But, more importantly, I have stressed the potentially emancipatory role of such liminal sites, and their power to prompt interrogation, if not demand activist reorganization of the visual memorial field. As it stands, the handful of red stainless-steel pillars commemorating the Peaceful Revolution, scattered across Berlin, appear like lone survivors in a post-historical, neoconservative terrain. They release what Hal Foster calls "promissory notes for future elaboration."[105] Accordingly, retrieving the agonistic, grassroots impulses of '89–90 at the edge of sight in the memorial sphere of Germany's capital today is not "merely" a matter of reorganizing narratives about national history but also of uncovering the contradictions of global market-conforming democracy in the present.

Crafting '89–90 from unseen realms, a future-oriented approach to memory bears out incongruous narratives and historical paradoxes. To start, such a project of unlearning and relearning would relinquish antifascism as a mere ideology of dictatorial power, upheld far too long in the official memorial landscape of Berlin but also perpetuated by professional academics. It would investigate, for instance, how young collectives have recently reactivated the memory of antifascism to organize for a shift from a neoliberal ethos that is devoid of any future *to* horizons of future-oriented, transnational politics.[106] An activist approach would practice a performative disengagement from the immutable, frozen images of the socialist and antifascist pasts while taking an un-nostalgic look at former East Germany, including the role of racism and anti-Semitism in the GDR.[107] Memory activists would issue a call to dismantle the stronghold of neoliberal memory politics through forms of mobilization and alliance in the street, on-site, at government-sponsored events, and in the discursive arena of academia. In 2019, I attended a public reading of the book *Fenster zur Freiheit* (Window to Freedom) by the West German author Peter Wensierski about a GDR dissident group, held at the Federal Foundation for the Reappraisal of the SED Dictatorship, Berlin. Introduced by the co-chair of the Green Party/Alliance '90, Robert Habeck, also socialized in the West and by his own admission unfamiliar with the East German oppositional movements until recently, the former dissidents in the room, who had illegally printed the *Radix-Blätter* in the 1980s, remained silent all evening. In the end, some of their young adult children rose from their seats to disrupt the self-serving event in protest of a liberal narrative that fused the GDR opposition—heterogeneous and fractured—to affirmations of the contemporary Western order.

It is finally also time to collaboratively rehearse why the Berlin Wall was erected in the first place in a war-torn, post-fascist era of deeply divided economic geopolitics.[108] It is time to give up easy answers and to reengage with the complex, incommensurable rationale behind erecting the Wall to safeguard a twentieth-century social vision in 1961, while also acknowledging the illegitimacy of trapping an entire population and the pernicious effects of authoritarian power in people's everyday lives. Indeed, the Berlin Wall can and should be read as an icon of authoritarian oppression, as the capital's official memorial landscape suggests. But, in my view, it is a mistake to turn this into the only framework to understand the history of Germany's division. On a local scale, I indicated at the outset of this chapter that the Wall was an architectural structure that shaped the everyday reality of East Germans who lived in its shadow. Even if this truth is difficult to acknowledge with a Western-centric gaze, a walled environment can become an everyday reality that is not (only) experienced as oppressive. East Germans had diverse responses to the border and its symbolism, depending on their generational or political stance or where they lived in the GDR. The GDR argued that building the wall was necessary to stop the "drain" of the professional class. Education was free in the socialist GDR, and the state-run economy depended on a viable, modern workforce. In light of the ever-increasing disparities in Western democracies, the original (and failed) vision of a society with less inequality can be instructive. The Wall kept out the West, whose consumerism was desirable for many in the East. But the Wall also kept out unemployment, poverty, and crime (all of which became pervasive after 1989, especially in the Eastern regions, with effects felt to this day).

Needless to say, walls are structures of sovereignty imbued with power. The Berlin Wall was held up by two superpowers during the Cold War. The East and the West had to invest the Wall with material, symbolic, and psychic meaning to stabilize a Cold War world order. If the Berlin Wall is read exclusively as an "icon of authoritarian oppression," what does this reading say about the (visible and invisible) walls currently erected in other parts of the world? Democracies in the Northern hemisphere fence off people from the Global South. The Cold War rhetoric of the dictatorial GDR (and its Wall) obfuscates how histories of inequality interconnect across time and national contexts. Of course, this is not a numbers game, and yet: The Berlin Wall was a site of authoritarian oppression where at least 140 people were killed between 1961 and 1989. More than twenty thousand migrant deaths and disappearances have been recorded on the central Mediterranean route since 2014. Since 1998, at least eight thousand undocumented migrants have died attempting to cross the border from Mexico to the United States. And what about the walled-in cities in the US, the gated communities of the hyper-wealthy? What about the prisons and their intimate connection to the past of slavery and Jim Crow in this country? Of course, these examples are all differently situated histories and forms of systemic entrapment. Still, we must expose these entanglements between "Western" and socialist "Eastern" histories to develop more viable social visions for the future. As the US government built its last stretches of the border wall in August 2023, the city of Tijuana in Mexico made its own statement by laying remains of the Berlin Wall a few steps away.

In sum, I am not arguing the Berlin Wall was a legitimate political enterprise. However, this book wishes to offer alternative perspectives by discussing the downfall of Eastern European socialism in conjunction with Western democracy's promises and deficits. Only then will the radical potential of 1989—including the principles of greater equality, liberty, and social welfare it embodied—be exposed in the public field of the visible.

FIGURE 1.8. People walk along the wall that separates the United States from Mexico near a slab of the Berlin Wall in Tijuana, Mexico, on August 25, 2023. Photograph: AP Photo/Gregory Bull.

[INTERTEXT]

Soviet Specters in the Periphery

Specters (*lat. Spectrum*, an image, figure, or ghost), spectator (*lat. Spectare* to view, watch).[1] I am aware that the notion of public memory that insists on publicity—or that which becomes visible to many—risks perpetuating a status of spectatorship as a socially and historically dissociated "hovering act of looking." A stable kind of agency is assumed, as though there is a singular, immersive standpoint from which public memory as a form of knowledge is produced and negotiated (or can be critiqued).[2] However, it will become clearer that agencies regarding a post-1989 politics of memory are redistributed across an array of memorial sites, available frameworks, and different participants or viewers. Memorial sites indeed enable relations that are situated and contingent, temporary and dispersive, where memory is *assembled* across time and space rather than merely revealed. Those dynamics, however, are not free of forms of control that delineate the limits of commemorative space, publics, and discourse. Rhythms of restoration and decay, which shape the built environment over time, are also relevant for remembering and disremembering multiple pasts in the post-unification memorial sphere. In the public reorganization of memory, the spectral, material, and affective realms come into play.

A closer look at how the Soviet War Memorial, a socialist leftover space in Berlin's periphery, is used for improvised assemblies can be instructive for the dynamics of public memories in the long aftermath of 1989. Although normalizing notions of the public sphere persist in Germany's liberal democratic imaginary—as though equal participation and reasoned discussion are possible in some homogenous meta-public sphere—such countercultural or provisional dissenting publics occupy a differentiated field of asymmetrical powers. By definition, these counter-discursive domains are situated within and alongside the performative, hegemonic forces of the post-unification order, where pasts are transformed in the process of being interpreted. In this brief intertext, I want to probe further the global perspective of memory in the neoliberal era, according to which, after 1989, any viable emancipatory histories of collectivity became erased. More aptly, I suggest that the (unnamable) specters of antifascism and Stalinist socialism disappeared and reappeared in the peripheries of public memorial spaces after the end of history was declared.

THE ANTIFASCIST VOID

Scholars have surely attended to a post-unification, post-1989 memory vacuum in recent years. The established critical interpretations propose either that the centrality of Holocaust memory occluded the GDR past, which sets these legacies against one another, as though to endorse a model of memory competition where the confrontation of the Nazi atrocities was solely undertaken by the West. I have challenged this argument in a previous book. Or there is the astute analytical view of the GDR's obsolescence itself in post-1989 official memory, which may espouse a critique of the FRG's hegemony, but also more or less situates the political project of the GDR in the vanishing point of the twentieth century.[3] I believe none of these interpretations identifies what this disconnection of past and present, this breaking apart of temporal continuity *in* 1989 entailed. What is forgotten is a radical heterogeneity of negotiated historical culpabilities of the twentieth century during the politicized interval period of '89–90.

To put it bluntly, even during the weeks now known as the Peaceful Revolution, the GDR's affective attachment to antifascism and its orientation toward the Soviet Union was not dead, but most of our ideas about 1989 still cling to that model, as if the "myth" had completely lost legitimacy among the East German populace and politically exhausted itself. The arrest of (antifascist) futurity has turned into an axiom that only few scholars have challenged so far.[4] In fact, current re-examinations of 1989, in light of the upsurge of right-wing movements thirty years later, stress the seeds of nationalism rather than alternative history (I will return to this point in the final chapter). We may no longer believe that the GDR's display of antifascist virtue on the official stage can be redressed for a progressive political imaginary, but we should certainly pay more attention to why the historical victors deemed those antifascist legacies to be dangerous or disposable, with consequences we are still feeling today. These incommensurable memories became evacuated through a series of displacements and transfers.

At first sight, the Soviet War memorial in Berlin's periphery appears to offset any claims about a post-historical landscape of erasure, which, I argue, emerged from the collapse of Eastern European Communism in 1989 and the dissolution of the GDR. After all, the arena's sheer size alone suggests an excess of memory regarding this charged legacy. The monumental architecture of the enormous burial ground also works against any critical aesthetics of belated temporality, afterness, or the spectral. Stepping out of the *S-Bahn* station Treptower Park, thirty minutes southeast of the city's center, one faces quite literally a historical junction. The visitor may walk further into this former East Berlin neighborhood alongside a large municipal park with a military cemetery and the massive Soviet War Memorial. The site opened in 1949 to commemorate seven thousand of the eighty thousand Soviet soldiers who died in the battle of Berlin in May 1945. Alternatively, one can move toward Kreuzberg's artsy, multiethnic area in the former West, passing by a small, neglected neighborhood park at Schlesischer Busch, where one of the two remaining watchtowers of the Berlin Wall appears to have been left to decay. Not visible from the streets of the capital, one enters the Soviet War Memorial through a triumphal arch bearing Soviet iconography and an inscription honoring those who died liberating the socialist *Родина/Heimat*. Other elements of the memorial park near the entrance include the statue of the grieving "Mother homeland." Turning into a broad passageway, the site showcases two statues of kneeling soldiers, flanked by stone flags, until the design opens into the central square, which is lined on both sides by eight sarcophagi with bas-relief renditions of the Soviet liberation narrative and citations by Stalin in Russian and German. The iconic soldier carrying a child looms atop a massive kurgan, at the end of the enormous memorial and burial grounds, in the distance. The gigantic, twelve-meter-high, seventy-ton bronze sculpture of the Soviet soldier with the sinking sword over the destroyed swastika was intended as a heightened symbol of the Soviet Union's efforts in defeating fascism.

After 1989, only the claims of Soviet hegemony and the self-stylization of the Red Army as savior came into view; the site was reduced to its central role in the GDR's sacralization of politics and antifascist iconolatry by official, academic, and media discourses.[5] Then, as Berlin reinvented itself as a unified global capital in the 1990s, the memorial park at the periphery, farther to the east, fell into disrepair. Left to decay, the site began occupying the slippage between ruin and debris. Unlike mere rubble, the state of ruin still relates to a future or futures, even as it falls back into a time past.[6] Unrealized histories and their interpretations are not (yet) erased. A resident of Berlin-Treptow recalls the dilapidated burial ground in the 1990s: at the sight of disrepair, they were befallen by a sense of melancholia, of grief—not for the GDR itself but for a failed socialist utopia, and for the discarded antifascist East German–Soviet imaginary the site now symbolized. Post-1989, half-erased, half-there, the Stalin quotations once etched into the stone sarcophagi echoed not only the millions of lives lost in the "Great

War," they also haunted the grounds with the Soviet histories of violence and the countless people murdered for the sake of those ideas.

We may say, then, that in this diminishing state the memorial site was able to take on the more indeterminate function of double mourning, associated with the defeat of socialism in the GDR, the Soviet Union, and Eastern Europe, more broadly. Examining post-1989 memorial politics in the Soviet Union, Alexander Etkind writes in *Warped Mourning*: "Whether socialism inescapably led to Stalinism or whether the latter was a result of unique and unfortunate choice and circumstances, there is no doubt that the Soviet regime compromised the ideas of socialism gravely, and maybe irreversibly. As a result, mourning for the human victims of the Soviet experiment coexists with mourning for the ideas and ideals that were also buried by this experiment."[7] It is notably this dual role of mourning that Germany's hegemonic memory of the late GDR in 1989 tends to foreclose. In that official incantation of freedom and unity, the legacies of earlier twentieth-century emancipatory struggles—including the Russian revolution, the failed vision of "socialism with a human face" espoused by the Prague Spring, and global social movements in the 1960s—have become invisible. Amid the post–Cold War rhetoric of the FRG, the turn of 1989 offered to the vanquished nothing but the memory of a disfigured socialism, "the totalitarian caricature of an emancipated society." Traverso puts it this way: in the age of neoliberalism, "not only was the prognostic memory of socialism paralyzed, but the mourning itself of the defeat was censored."[8]

Arguably, the monumental Soviet War memorial in Berlin-Treptow has facilitated this collective form of censorship and erasure of viable socialist pasts. By 1998, when the site had fallen victim to vandalism and disrepair, the liberal-conservative newspaper *Frankfurter Allgemeine Zeitung* observed that the vast complex was pervaded by a sense of melancholic irony, exposing the "bloated triumph of the Soviets as defeat" in the postcommunist era.[9] Those specters of twentieth-century sorrow, even legible to the ideological victors of the Cold War, disappeared when the monument park was restored. In fact, one may wonder why the Soviet memorial in Treptow outlasted the demolition of socialist monuments, such as the nineteen-meter-high figure of Lenin designed by the Soviet artist Nikolai Tomski in Berlin-Friedrichshain, which was torn down in 1991, and similar highly symbolic and politically charged sites across Eastern and Central Europe that were rejected as "dissonant heritage."[10] After all, Berlin's former secretary of interior affairs, the CDU politician Heinrich Lummer, had reportedly stated in 1998: "We don't need the Soviet Army junk at all." Other critics, referring to the inscriptions of quotes by Stalin, lamented the site's "monstrous pathos."[11] In 1992, Germany and Russia signed a treaty that obligated both countries to maintain the other's war memorials and burial sites on their respective territory. If the neglected monument arena had to be restored, this restoration would at least allow a reframing of twentieth-century history and Germany's role in it. By 2006 (once more the year of a drastic shift in memorial politics), with the help of federal funds, the large-scale arena was renovated and recontextualized. New signage was added, and any specific reference to the GDR and its engagement with antifascism was erased in the post-unification mnemonic field, delineated by the performative relations of knowledge and power.

Indeed, this elision may go unnoticed today, which is precisely the logic by which new ideological truths become established. The absence of any viable (or even official) antifascist past of the GDR reveals the fundamental workings of institutions, such as museums, archives, memorials, and official exhibitions in the post-1989 era, which often relied, if more imperceptibly, on hegemonic frameworks and "imperial" forms of thinking. Throughout the postwar Cold War era, the burial site at the Soviet War Memorial was not only used for official purposes, such as ritualized antifascist commemorations of the GDR state that recalled and staged the role of the Soviet Union as a liberator of fascist Germany, or ceremonies of the SED youth organizations that performed the mass spectacles that interpolated adolescent East Germans into the antifascist project of the state. This site was not only deployed for the public orchestration of a postwar political commitment, a commitment that historians after the *Wende* cast enduringly in terms of a cleansed "antifascist myth."[12]

In the GDR, East Berlin citizens and often young people adopted this highly stylized public arena of the dominant sphere as a gathering spot and neighborhood park. I agree with those scholars who recognize that the site had been embraced in the GDR as a positive stand-in for liberation, hope, and antifascist tradition. To a degree, even East Berliners subscribed to this reading of history.[13] Here, they showed up for everyday leisure activities alongside visitors from Russia and other Soviet states, who were there to place commemorative wreaths, or they encountered personnel from the Soviet military forces and their families taking walks. This mixed scene transformed the burial site de facto into an affiliative, even semi-countercultural space, where many East Berliners appeared precisely because the hollowed-out antifascist, socialist ideals of the SED state rang most true in recognition of the innumerable losses of Soviet lives. The performative and socially cohesive power of monuments, animated for multiple and often contradictory purposes, even in more outwardly repressive systems, is certainly underexplored.[14] At the same time, since 1968, various incongruous pasts that were associated with Eastern Europe's legacy of Communism worked themselves into popular consciousness, often through unofficial circuits (literature smuggled in from the West) or liminal references in the cultural realm, such as DEFA films of the 1960s. Even Gulag-related memory—a warped concept in itself—began to permeate underhanded discussions.[15] The totalitarian mass violence committed in the name of socialism under Stalin or the rapes of German women by Russian soldiers in 1945 were two distinct histories of violence that were repressed in the GDR's official antifascist discourse until the 1980s, yet the unspoken knowledge circulated widely. These various ambiguous, entangled pasts are invisible today; they are expunged from the recontextualized memorial arena in Berlin-Treptow.

As the cultural historian Courtney Glore Crimmins observes, the reconfigured site allows the visitor to experience the narrative produced by the memorial as one connected to a pre-and post-GDR.[16] The added information boards only refer to the post-1989 treaties (signed in 1990, 1992) and thus emphasize the FRG's governmental obligation, not including any reference to East Germany, to the memorial's long history under the GDR, or to those atrocities committed by members of the Red Army in 1945 for that matter. Consequently, and most important for our concern with the vanishing of 1989–90, the SED-PDS-supported mass protests against neo-Nazis on January 3, 1990, organized by the Spartacist Workers Party (SpAD), also fail to come into view in the resituated reframing of public memory. The interval year's leftist "protest publics" do not appear in this memorial sphere. To this day, what has been incessantly repeated in the circuits of collective memory about this time period are images of nationally oriented East German crowds (and the racist hunts of 1991–92). These images and narratives are the dominant ones that need to be situated, historicized, and un- and relearnt, and from which a counter-memorial discourse of publics would have to disengage. While established narratives highlight Antifa groups from West Berlin fighting East Berlin neo-Nazi cells (reportedly 6 percent of youth in the late GDR), the spontaneous antifascist mass assembly of East Berliners in response to the devastation of the Soviet War Memorial, when recorded at all, is instantaneously reduced to a Stasi maneuver (which is not implausible, even if no evidence has been found).[17] No less than 250,000 GDR citizens participated during that transitional period, in early January 1990 and notably weeks after the fall of the Berlin Wall and after the SED had lost its supremacy, to take a stance against the defacing of the memorial with anti-Soviet graffiti.

This scene is captured in a haunting photograph included in the 2020 archival collection of rarely seen images, *Uncovering the Year 1990 (Das Jahr 1990 Freilegen)*.[18] In a gesture of alternative knowledge, this belated mediated protest memory is recirculated across history, reengaging an unforeclosed relation between past, present, and future. In the illuminated night, the monumental Soviet soldier looms like a ghost, while the glimpse of a red flag is visible in the distant margins. At the edge of sight, the "double mourning" for the victims of Soviet violence *and* for the ideals killed by that violence is also reanimated. Both the defeat of utopia and an antifascist inheritance are unreliably transmitted, across "1989," by the photographic scene. Regardless of Germany's national memory project where such foundered socialist, collective ideals were exorcised, the specter of antifascism here permeates any temporal binary, and any boundaries between the global imaginaries of the "East" and "West."

STATE OF DEBT—THE WORK OF MOURNING

These past struggles over the monument's meaning and the discontinuous twentieth-century legacies of East and Western Europe have left no mark at the recontextualized site, nor does this knowledge circulate in official channels in any form. There are no traces of the (failed) liberatory, antifascist legacies associated with the foundational project of the GDR. Today, the gigantic architecture of the large-scale area appears polished, unmovable, and permanent (some of the building materials used after 1945 were long rumored to have come from the demolished new Reich Chancellery, completed by Albert Speer in 1939 and damaged during WWII), stressing links between totalitarian, nationalist cults of fallen soldiers.[19] To be sure, the massive monument park preserved in the periphery of the urban environment evokes a debt to the Soviet Union/Russia that, according to the center-left *Berliner Zeitung*, even in 2020, is otherwise "shamefully absent" in Germany's national discourse.[20] Rarely named, twenty-seven million Soviets lost their lives in the war that Nazi Germany started. For the seventy-fifth anniversary of the end of the Second World War, no official ceremony was planned by the German government to commemorate the liberation of Berlin by the Soviet Army. A grassroots initiative called on citizens in social media and the press to leave flowers at the monument. Spontaneously, a fleeting counter-public formed, involving a wide range of the population, including those of the former East who are structurally excluded from the neoliberal order by some combination of ideology and class and not attracted to the right-wing grievance politics of the AfD (Alternative for Germany). Through mediated acts of memory, provisional mnemonic communities or publics were formed. Most prominently and devoid of that lived history, however, situated within Germany's post-1989 memorial sphere, the enduring, extraterritorial mausoleum to the Soviet dead ends up serving as a crypt, a tomb that merges and enshrines twentieth-century history under the sign of (fascist and Stalinist) totalitarianism. In official circuits, the entire history of Communism can be reduced to its totalitarian dimension, which appears in the performative field of memory as a monumental and easily legible past, imported from a (defeated) "world power headquartered elsewhere."[21] Russia's invasion of Ukraine in 2022 confirms the narrative of Russia as the threatening imperial Other in its most simplistic form. However, the impact of current Russian military imperialism on memory of the GDR will have to be a topic for a future book.[22]

At the Soviet *Ehrenmal* in the periphery of Berlin, nothing appears unsettled about the post-historical commemorative culture. In a story titled "Pushkin Allee," and in reference to the monument, Yoko Tawada writes: "For a scene of carnage everything was awfully well-ordered."[23] In "Thoughts on May 8, 1995," Zafer Şenocak observes: "Word of normalcy is making the rounds. History again becomes an instrument of power politics and attains its original significance for the future of the nation."[24] In this vein, the antifascist burial ground is a stark reminder of *all the memory work that was not done in post-unified Germany or globally, in the neoliberal era,* regarding the entangled legacies of the Second World War, the Nazi era, and the GDR's antifascist commitments. This undone memory work also involves the FRG's NATO alliance, the expanded influence of the United States with its own "black book," the atrocities of Stalinism, and Germany's unmourned responsibilities for the deaths of millions of Russians and Ukrainians and hundreds of thousands of Georgians, Armenians, Kazakhs, Belarusians, and inhabitants of nine other states in the Soviet Union. In an effort to delineate a changed map of Europe after 1989, those histories were erased, distorted, and forgotten, and Russia was always already imagined to be the (potentially threatening) imperial Other as which it unleashes itself once more in the present. The Other may serve as a foil against which (ailing) Western values of freedom and democracy can be limned and perpetually stabilized. But those spectators of a global conflict who look only to affirm their views are often not in the most competent position to "speak to the specter," to recall Derrida—the specter of implicated histories of violence, of erasure, forgetting, disregard—a specter that haunts out of a need to be heard.

[CHAPTER TWO]

Pacifying Memory

In *Oblivion,* French philosopher Marc Augé illuminates the middle spaces between living in history and telling it, between systematizing culture and constituting it. He proposes that forgetting plays a crucial role in memory itself. He muses, "One must forget the recent past in order to find the ancient past again."[1] Augé promises truer knowledge that can only be gained when we release recent injurious histories within longer temporal trajectories.

However, what if we can never really forget anything on our way to remembering something else? What if all we ever remember is cast in light of everything we already knew? Like countless protagonists in postcommunist literature and film, I left East Germany in the aftermath of the fall of the Berlin Wall. Following my reluctant departure for the United States, nothing drew me back to where it had all come apart.[2] I had no reason to return to Leipzig, where I had lived during the revolutionary autumn and where the mass uprising of GDR citizens against the calcified socialist regime in 1989 began. When the evaluators arrived from the West, colleagues and friends at the university lost their positions and were scattered around the world.[3] Neighbors working at the cotton spinning mill nearby were laid off, like thousands of others in the early 1990s, at schools, newspapers, breweries, cement plants, and the S. M. Kirow factories in Leipzig-Plagwitz. *Dreamworlds and catastrophe,* all over again. *A glimpse into the abyss of freedom.* The long-forgotten 1992 series of photographs *Luxus Arbeit* (Luxury Labor) remains a testimony to this disappearing world.[4]

Coming back to a place one abandoned is hard. Curators Jan Wenzel and Anna König are right about the impact of the *Wende*: "Losing jobs, being torn out of familiar social contexts, was a traumatic event for individuals. Identities were destroyed, lives devalued."[5] In June 2009, I took a crowded Intercity train from Berlin, two hours south, to visit local archives, and have returned many times since to study the city's lived engagement with the past. In this chapter, I explore how the memorial architecture of Leipzig (what is preserved and what is forgotten) has been shaped by hegemonic forces and regional and global articulations, and how the resistant repertoires of multiple publics intersect and come into play. I pay close attention to the spatial and temporal meanings invoked by memorial movements across Leipzig's cityscape, such as resiting, reappearing, reverberating, and resonance. I deliberately trace the ambiguity opened up by the connotations of both repeating and renewing such situated memorial processes afford.

Counter-Hegemonic Limits: Revolutionary Recall in Leipzig

In Berlin's political and built environments, the memory of 1989—especially the utopian social impulses of the late GDR—nearly vanished over three decades. The governing forces of the FRG played a significant role in determining which elements of this period were preserved in Berlin's built environment and in the sphere of public memory and which were not. In contrast to Berlin, whose landscape evinces the palpable absence and even state-orchestrated erasure of 1989–90, Leipzig has encouraged visitors and residents to engage with the uprising as a vibrant, commercial, civic, and critical memory domain. Since the first demonstrations started here in September 1989, Leipzig has leveraged the role and significance of being the original location of the revolution to build a legacy as the "city of heroes."[6] According to this narrative, seventy thousand inhabitants marched around the inner-city ring road on October 9, 1989, and, due to this rising popular pressure, the SED dictatorship crumbled. At the same time, the city has managed to integrate the events of 1989 into the narrative of a long-standing humanist heritage and a centuries-old national and European history of occupation and international trade. Notably, celebrating Leipzig's recent past relies largely on the ubiquitous trope of the revolution's peacefulness, which is rather compatible with memory politics in the neoliberal era. The selfsame narrative of brave and peaceful East German heroes allows us to cast unification and thus the expanded Western order continually into a redemptive historical arch. In Germany's public memory, the pacifism of '89 tends to work prescriptively as an individualizing, moral argument and as a normative fiction underlining the "natural" downfall of the GDR, even if this form of resistance has a complicated social and political history.[7]

In Leipzig's official story, the exposure of the "political" performed by the nonviolent revolution is also anxiously guarded. A socio-symbolic disarrangement such as the upheaval in '89–90 always involves structural forms of violence. Put simply, a potentially disruptive force exists within (though is rarely recognized by) any police order, in Rancière's sense. The police order is not, as commonly understood, the state apparatus of order keeping and repression, but rather the name for everything that concerns the distribution of places and functions, as well as the system that legitimates that hierarchical distribution. A political act not only disrupts this order (exposing its arbitrariness), it disrupts in such a way that it radically changes what people can see and hear; it overthrows "the regime of the perceptible."[8] Leipzig's official memory sphere erases these shattering effects of a transformation from below. Instead, October 9, 1989, figures not only as the "deciding day" of the Peaceful Revolution in a way that "naturalizes" cause and effect but also as the date of a new beginning that ignited a return to historical normalcy.

Most historians agree that it was no coincidence that the revolutionary unrest began in Leipzig. The city was home to semipublic spaces of dissent organized by the "church from below." The idea that people wanted to "break out of a closed-off society" retrospectively serves as a frame to galvanize the heterogenous activities of alternative, civil rights, and basic-democratic groups. But a decade of oppositional organizing within the Church, an arterial road suitable for mass rallies, and the annual influx of Western journalists with their international currencies and cameras are the manifold reasons why Leipzig became the city where it all began. Moreover, the colossal devastation of the ecological and built environment and, last but not least, the intellectual and cultural legacies of a defiant mentality among the Saxon people are often cited as explanations. Arguably, the practiced self-perception among the Saxon inhabitants of being more defiant than other East Germans reached back at least to the 1950s. Fostering a local image of Leipzig as "the real capital of the GDR," the population positioned itself against the party-administrative system in Berlin. The continued influence of political philosophers such as Ernst Bloch, Werner Krauss, and Hans Maier, who taught at the University of Leipzig during the early Cold War period, should also not be ignored. Marxist in orientation, their legacies were imbued in a (failed) project of socialist modernity and echoed across the second half of the twentieth century in some of the dissident movements in Eastern Europe. In the wake of the uprising in Hungary in 1956 and the building of the Berlin Wall in 1961, Bloch and Maier left for the West. According to Leipzig-based social historian Hartmut Zwahr, all these factors contributed to the society's ineluctable *self-destruction*, culminating in the protests of 1989.[9] These public protests, in turn, led inadvertently— and not by design and certainly not in any linear fashion—to the eventual demise of the GDR.

After 1989, this complex storyline disappeared from official memory. It was replaced by the dominant incantations "Long live capitalism" and "Here is to the survival of economic and political liberalism," to recall Derrida.[10] But two hours south of Germany's capital, Leipzig provides an alternative, regional site that allows us to think through the contingent "memory of publics." As outlined in the previous chapter, this concept refers to the contrast between the capacity of certain publics to authorize memories and the struggles of other publics to contest them. This distinction is limited in that the presumed unity of each of these publics depends on notions of selfsame transparency and arbitrary social closure, whereas power is unevenly distributed in this field.[11] Still, without the insistence on this difference, I have argued, emancipatory impulses of the peaceful revolution can also not come into view. Given the performative role of both publics and memory, a set of questions arises: how do the embodied, collaborative action of citizens in 1989 become visible or disappear within the frameworks of collective memory that scholars suggest are also relatively mutable and change over time?[12] To what extent is the memorialization of the protests that challenged governing power during the era of the (late) GDR once more shaped by hegemonic, neoliberal forces or by grassroots efforts from below? Can these gatekeeping dispositifs and frameworks be confronted or even deliberately exploded?

We have also seen—concerning the public memory of the Berlin Wall and 1989 in the capital—that not all projects enabled by these forces are tendentious, instrumentalizing, or totalizing as such. Indeed, cultural and governmental structures engaged in producing collective memory are dynamic. After all, memories do not exist in closed systems, as they are always already inflected, strengthened, modified, and "polarized by other memories and impulses to forget within the context of a given social reality."[13] Especially in Leipzig, the cultural legacy of 1989 has emerged on multiple scales. It is shaped not only by the influence of state and city politicians (that is, SPD lord mayor Burkhard Jung, who moved to Leipzig in 1991 from the West and has been in office since 2006) but also by a broad network of regional stakeholders, including GDR dissident organizations, church leaders, civic groups, and local historians, who may not usually (and certainly did not in the GDR) associate with established forms of state authority.[14]

Moreover, local artists, designers, and architects participate in animating a memorial infrastructure, as does the public when it chooses to accept, opt out, protest, or reject particular memorials and memorial plans. Yet, as the historian Anna Saunders correctly states, commemorative politics in Leipzig need to be understood as an integral part of the national memory dynamics of unified Germany.[15] What remains rarely acknowledged in this context, however, is that localized mnemonic practices are often susceptible to the pressures of a complex field of differential, institutionalized power (on a local, regional, and national scale).[16] These pressures reward the aggregation of hyperlocal forms of recall into a universal, more holistic memory architecture. In other words, we must investigate the paradoxical ways local remembrance can help reproduce and reinforce national memories and nation-state institutions of memory, or how it may slip away from those normative constraints.

My discussion of Leipzig's memorial politics invokes the twofold sense of the word "pacifying" that titles this chapter and the productive tension created by these meanings: first, I attend to the revolution's *pacifist* legacy, exemplified in the grassroots movement for peace emerging from the peace prayers held at Nikolaikirche (St. Nicholas Church) Leipzig in the 1980s. While led by pacifist (that is, passive, peacemaking) principles, these movements are better understood as disruptive, nonviolent, and thus temporally displaced political energies that provide directives for future change today. Rather than viewing Germany's unification and (neo)liberal democracy as the culmination of these civil movements, the local archives in Leipzig provide a particularly compelling story of the unrest, multiplicity, and unfinished business that has come to haunt Germany in the era of late neoliberalism. Second, I examine pacifying as allayment, as an act of calming or quieting dissent. By quelling disruptive elements and mythologizing peaceful demonstrators, national and commercial interests in Leipzig have *pacified* how the revolution of 1989 is remembered in memorials and exhibits. Unlike Berlin, Leipzig has managed to keep alive the memory of the spontaneous street protests of 1989. Still, the influence of the Church to this day has also ultimately pacified the revolution's more radical elements.

The glossing over of such incongruous pasts may lead to forgetfulness. However, these opposing forms of memory must be vital to recollecting revolutionary histories and the "disjunctive experience" of '89–90. The city only peripherally recalls the radical implications of the democratic self-organization that dismantled the GDR state during the peaceful revolution. But those gaps in the ever-shifting memorial networks are significant for the possible reordering of knowledge. The following pages work out a tension between what is official and enshrined and what is local and unbound in the recollection of the collective protests in 1989—while tracking the kind of open-ended, future-oriented memorial spaces I celebrate in this book. Taking the reader from the colossal white column near St. Nicholas Church (1999) to the amorphous light installation *white space* (2014) at Wilhelm-Leuschner-Platz, I perform the movement and analytical practice toward what I have called in this book "archives of the future." Framed this way, this chapter about the Saxon and Eastern German city of Leipzig also tells the story of two different symbols created fifteen years apart: a single classical column and a series of light-emitting diodes. One quite literally set in stone, the other floating away seemingly without limits. Just as unbound memory can become so diffuse that narratives can no longer be articulated, the boundedness of memorials can accentuate forgetting and stifle future imaginations of the past. Situated in this dynamic field, Leipzig's memorial landscape of the Peaceful Revolution reminds us that public space is shaped by the perception and interplay of subjects. The city engages us in considering the conditions of how public space is made through political or collective action.

Appeasing the Past: The St. Nicholas Church Column and the Peace-Prayer Exhibition

Efforts to absorb localized, often ad hoc, and variegated projects into a master narrative of unified Germany follow a similar temporal trajectory in Leipzig as in Berlin. While the 1990s were characterized by instituting small, targeted memorials that blended into the restored downtown area of the burgeoning trade center, Leipzig shifted its focus toward a large-scale, more centrally guided public memory plan around 2008, twenty years after the *Wende*. However, those efforts will not be apparent to Leipzig's visitors today because the citizens ultimately resisted the unifying mnemonic tendencies of national memory production. Walking out of the enormous railway station (Europe's largest and a local treasure in its own right), one passes through a narrow, busy store-lined street and, in only ten minutes, reaches the St. Nicholas Church, where the clandestine assemblies began in 1989. Surrounded by medieval *Fachwerk* buildings and shops, tourists often start here to search for the authentic location of the first illegal gatherings in the public square and set foot on the historic cobblestones, or what the regional press has dubbed the city's "Revolutionspflaster" (revolutionary cobbles).[17] Amid the array of vendor booths, it may be easy to miss the actual memorial at the site, even if for different reasons than in Berlin, where the scarce minimalist information pillars "Sites of the Peaceful Revolution" are almost too narrow, too liminal to see. A colossal white column commemorating the uprising, crowned by light-green palm leaves extending toward the sky, presides over the square. This design points to a vexed relation between the publicness of memory, visibility, and scale.

Drawing from the city's deep-rooted cultural heritage, the memorial in Leipzig's historic downtown area fulfills an integrative historical role. In 1994, the site-specific proposal by local artist Andreas Stötzner won the international competition for the artistic design of the courtyard at the

FIGURE 2.1. St. Nicholas Column, Monument to the Peaceful Revolution (2019), Leipzig. Author's private collection.

St. Nicholas Church, awarded by the Cultural Foundation and the City of Leipzig (Kulturstiftung und der Stadt Leipzig); the memorial was officially inaugurated in 1999. Stötzner recreated one of the eight original pillars from the church's interior nave and placed it outside in the courtyard to symbolically transport the idea of departure (*Aufbruch*) out of the church and into the open square.[18] The victory column signals that the protest, ignited by the peace prayers in the St. Nicholas Church, had conquered the public space in the early fall of 1989 as a church-based, essentially pacifist citizen movement. Performing a literal translation of this process of conquering the streets as a unifying force, the symbolic vertical sculpture is accompanied by a bronze plaque reading: "October 9, 1989." Set in the ground, the plaque shows a dozen footprints of various sizes, all aligned in the same direction, rendering not only the demonstrations in Leipzig but also the role of people, who fled in the summer of 1989 to the West via Hungary, in effecting change. Historians have applauded this process of "voting with one's feet" in a demographic plebiscite. In contrast, the activists of the New Forum Leipzig in 1989 called it—more poignantly—a citizen exodus.[19] For these various movements need to be distinguished. The dramatically increasing flow of GDR refugees to neighboring East European countries in 1989 revealed that many people had given up hope that the GDR's gerontocracy could change; yet the spilling-out of citizens from the church into the Leipzig streets took more decidedly the form of political experiments. This new kind of spontaneous reorganizing consisted of numerous rearrangements and displacements, where the normalized "partition of the perceptible" in GDR society was disrupted. With thousands of people on the move, the boundaries of classified and state-administered spaces became permeable. By word of mouth about the tumult downtown, more and more ordinary citizens were drawn each Monday during the peace prayers to St. Nicholas Square. Many were reportedly afraid to be openly seen as they resisted their state-assigned roles. Believing their views and dreams had been hitherto unaccounted for, these people now catalyzed visibly into targets and began to constitute provisional publics by showing up. Inversely, the upheavals took official state representatives, including Stasi and SED members, out of their bureaucratic enclosures. Thanks to a secret audio recording of an ad hoc SED Party assembly held in the City Hall on October 9, we know today that the comrades of the local political units received detailed instructions to blend in with the crowds in Leipzig's churches. The audio recording surfaced from the archive only twenty-six years later.[20] Likewise, eyewitness accounts attest that SED members at Karl Marx University were ordered by their superiors to go to St. Nicholas Church on the afternoon of October 9 and take up all seats in the pews—so that those same seats could not be filled by rallying citizens. The unintended effect of these orders was that some SED members reported that the spontaneous speeches at the prayers had challenged their established beliefs that the unrest was organized by "counter-revolutionary elements" and had moved them.[21] The SED had two faces, opportunists and hopeless idealists; many of the latter signed the petition of the New Forum.[22] As chaos erupted on several Monday nights in Leipzig's downtown in September, a host of strangers, neighbors, coworkers, and their superiors came into contact unintentionally while undercover

Stasi agents, reserve army battalions, and police fractured the crowd pushing their way through the throng. Those physical dislocations also dislocated the very idea of politics—moving it out of its "proper" place, the State party, and into the streets.[23] By showing up, people disrupted the natural state-controlled "givenness" of public places and how they were used, and thus they helped destabilize the classifications of the police order.

And yet, this discontinuous reordering of society had vanished in the rearview mirror of history by the 1990s. The proposal for the elegant St. Nicholas Church columns found broad community support: two-thirds of the funds needed to build the public memorial were donated by citizens, businesses, institutions, and significant public figures.[24] While devoid of any traditional, monumental language of heroic enshrinement, the design also eschews any contemporary sense of political particularities. Such particularities trouble the established normative frameworks of a Peaceful Revolution by activating the fractured agendas of multifarious activism or the performative corporeality of the crowd. The absence of such political configurations may explain why a reviewer praised the successful outcome of the site by referring to the artist's transhistorical ability to "set the prayers for peace to a monument."[25]

Indeed, most visitors entering the charming, historic cobblestone courtyard at St. Nicholas Church will find the memorial space (*Erinnerungsraum*) uplifting and pleasing. Despite its unexpected placement and stunning, slightly surrealist play with scale, the pillar ultimately underscores the universalism of history in the overall memorial arrangement. Rather than animate fracture, tension, and discontinuity (meanings also signaled by the iconic '89 slogan of revolutionary *Auf-bruch*), the design relies on harmonious lines.[26] The original pillar replicated here resulted from the neoclassical renovation of the gothic church in the late eighteenth century, inspired by French enlightenment architecture (albeit, rather than being cut in marble, as Stötzner initially intended, it is now made of concrete to reflect the mass demonstrations of ordinary citizens). Classicism in the eighteenth century defined itself through the ruins of antiquity (the stand-alone victory pillar, for example). Still, it aimed at symbolic representation achieved through harmony of forms and totality of style.[27] Due to this aesthetic choice, East German citizens' disruptive, (non)violent intervention into "so-called historical necessity" gets absorbed into the edifying, classical design commemorating the clandestine uprising. Far from inciting visitors to interrogate the perplexity of how nonviolent resistance to (repressive) state violence in 1989 became possible, the contingency of this historic moment—the tectonic changes, the rupture, the unknowable risk and effects of violence and violation—is erased. After all, to show up in an assembly and to be short of protection is a concrete form of political exposure and inherent struggle. Such subjects are, to borrow from Judith Butler, "at once concretely vulnerable, even breakable, and potentially and actively defiant, even revolutionary."[28] Those protesters are not composed or self-possessed.

Stötzner defended his use of classicist forms for the memorial against a critique of regression, arguing that "the timeless is the most explosive [*brisant*] in every moment." For him, it was about "creating a place" and the promise of "return and homecoming."[29] Today, according to residents, Stötzner's column, together with a water fountain and light installation added in 2003, has been embraced by the citizens of Leipzig and lauded as a significant memorial of the political *Wende*.[30] What is less reliably passed on is the role of the church as an inherently fissured, disjunctive space where dissent and conflict played out. According to historians, the GDR church is often seen as an essential protagonist in civil society. Yet the civil realm took on a political function in the countries of Eastern Europe. Organizing dissent is, for thinkers such as Rancière, the meaning of politics. In the GDR, the church formed a constitutive force field of the public and private spheres shaped by radically disparate, often clashing interests. In a recent book titled *At the Edge of the Wall*, Hanno Hochmuth makes a similar argument. The difference between his and my thinking, however, is that for him, "the state essentially assured the existence of churches [and] the church for its part helped hold together the state."[31] This mutually beneficial, if not complicitous, relationship between church and state, as I see it, was always precarious in that the church, especially throughout the 1980s, increasingly lost control to more fundamental political groups and thus turned into a radical political space. These conflicts played out in the spaces of the church and precipitated the undoing of compliance among the larger population. The Stasi District Office in Leipzig certainly framed the tensional forces in the sphere of the church as "activities of the political underground" that deserved the surveillance state's "utmost priority." Reporting back to the Ministry of Security in Berlin in late August of 1989, the city's local lieutenant general, Manfred Hummitzsch, was so confounded by the uncontrollable shift of realities that he rendered the truth. "The 'peace prayer' no longer needs to be organized," he stated in a secret meeting with Minister of State Security Erich Mielke. "The gathering has established itself over weeks, garnering a broad following; not even leaflets are necessary, no other activities. The people go there completely on their own accord [*Die Leute gehen völlig selbständig dorthin*]."[32] This overwhelming, collective force of spontaneous self-gathering—the now-derelict GDR had always coveted such a thing as a sign of popular support for its socialist agenda in divided postwar, Cold War Europe.

PRECARIOUS PEACE PRAYERS

The legacy of the Peaceful Revolution and its connection to the Protestant Church is particularly enduring in Leipzig. This endurance is visibly embodied by the gigantic victory column, elevating the symbolic meaning of '89 in the historic square. To this day, the shock provided by the "explosive social atmosphere" and "sheer threat of disorder"—at the moment people first mobilized inside churches and then took to the streets—is not transmitted in national circuits of collective memory.[33] Because of the dominant fixation on East German courage, it appears all too often as though GDR citizens rose up against the Communist dictatorship to peacefully hand the GDR to the victorious Western order. According to post-unification memorial discourse, it is as though this world-historical event had a clearly delineated plotline and an air of inevitability. The protagonists of the "revolution," too, were deemed to have a defined moral character based in their "heroic daring."[34] The media soon decried the peaceful restraint that enabled reunification as dictatorial docility once Western companies had established their power in the East and the new elites expected individual initiative in light of a restructured labor market. Inversely, when East Germans expressed their dissatisfaction with the new system and the inequalities it produced, these articulations were rejected as lacking the right tone or as indicative of individuals who complain too much. The label *Jammer-Ossi* has had a silencing, resistance-quelching effect over the last three decades since unification.[35] As a descriptive and official mnemonic category, "Peaceful Revolution" revolves around an imperative to contain the complex social, economic, and political displacements of 1989.

However, it is the local recall of the revolutionary fall within the institutional, non-secular contexts of the church today that reveals some of the political undercurrents of the citizens' movements in the GDR—even if here, too, those radical, unfulfilled impulses are tamed by frameworks related to the exegesis of the Christian gospel. Any political vision shared with contemporary translocal protest movements in the fight for social justice is cautiously disclosed by the legacies of the GDR's oppositional organizations. Far removed from the city's commercial memory infrastructure, including many souvenir stores, a small exhibit opened in 2015 at St. Nicholas Church, a decade and a half after the unrest occurred in Leipzig. Secluded inside the south chapel, the modest exhibit entitled "Peace Prayers at St. Nicholas Church: Service in the Everyday World" ("Friedensgebete in der Nikolaikirche: Gottesdienst im Alltag der Welt") appears hidden in the recess of the gothic cathedral.[36] Each time I visited, the exhibit attracted only the occasional postrevolutionary flâneur, although the numbers have reportedly increased in recent years. In this hallowed sanctuary, the dominant national narrative of East Germans yearning solely for the Western order is unsettled. At the same time, the transhistorical pacifist mission of the centuries-old religious institution is safeguarded and preserved.

Today, historians rightly view the peace prayers as the seed (*Keimzelle*) from which the Monday demonstrations in the streets of Leipzig were eventually born, crediting the significance of pacifist practices to the revolution's peaceful outcome.[37] (The actual story is not as linear as the historians would have it or as neat as the exhibit reveals.) The practice of peace prayers began at St. Nicholas Church in September 1982. The weekly gatherings initially served a small group of nonconformist youth rejected by the state. As the end of the decade approached, the prayers for peace attracted more and more citizens, such as those who sought refuge after having lost state protection when they applied for an exit visa to the West or those who had become furtively involved with any of the alternative, oppositional groups that organized under the GDR church's roof to address environmental protection, global disarmament, world hunger, justice, or human rights. These groups self-organized, in all major cities since the 1980s, around various local agendas intended to improve society radically. Since there was no freedom of the press or of assembly in the GDR, they formed widespread networks dependent on the physical spaces, printing resources, and protection of the church. As local historians often mention at St. Nicholas Church in Leipzig, internal tensions developed between those who wanted to leave the GDR for the West, those who pursued the political agendas of basic-democratic oppositional groups, and those who tried to reform socialism—whose mantra by 1989 became "We will stay" ("Wir bleiben hier").

To be sure, the peace prayers were not only a parochial affair, something lost in contemporary collective memory. The dominant narrative privileges the image of a walled-in state whose "barriers had only fallen away with the collapse of Communist regimes and the spread of liberal capitalism" rather than a world-oriented GDR.[38] The practice of peace prayers in East German churches—which was legal, after all—evolved in the geopolitical context of pacifist legacies in East and West Germany, as well as that of the peace movements garnering momentum across Western and Northern Europe during the Cold War arms race between the Soviet Union and the United States. Since the 1960s, the global struggle for world peace had turned Leipzig's annual International Documentary and Short Film Week into a political stage for celebrity activists, such as Jane Fonda, who aligned some of their politics with the anti-imperialist, internationalist agenda of the Soviet bloc. The film festival also became the site for small-scale local protests. Illegally, young people gathered, for instance, in November of 1983 in front of the cinema, illuminating the night with traditional peace candles to challenge the antidemocratic GDR. Pablo Picasso's white dove, designed for the Paris World Peace Congress in 1947, served as the festival logo. In a parallel yet interrelated sphere, the peace prayers in Leipzig emerged from the ecumenical peace decades, which originated in the Netherlands in the late 1970s and were taken up by the Protestant Church in both the GDR and FRG in 1980. The gatherings were held ten days before the Day of Prayer and Repentance (Buß- und Bettag) in November and were soon after established as weekly practice in churches across the GDR. At St. Nicholas Church in Leipzig and other religious spaces in East Germany, peace prayers were conducted on Mondays at 5:00 p.m. (making them run parallel to the ritualized meetings of the SED, the Communist Party, also held each week on that day). Inadvertently, then, the church in the GDR became a training ground for civil resistance and nonviolent practice, all while the clerical administration adhered to the ameliorative formula "Church in Socialism"—which since its inception in 1971 maintained the GDR's order. This legacy of dissent is captured inside St. Nicholas Church today. Mounted at the entrance near the parish's bulletin board, a colorful handmade symbol reminds visitors that since 1982 the local peace prayers have been organized under the biblical symbol of swords to plowshares, attracting disparate strands of the population throughout the 1980s and developing into a movement that combined religious practices with political and social hope.[39] (The sign with the symbol of swords to plowshares is easy to miss amid crowds of tourists photographing the spectacular church nave.)

In the GDR, this proclamation of peacebuilding—and the pacifist role of the peace prayer—were perpetually tested. Without a legitimate public sphere, the peace prayer turned into a space where internal conflicts disordered the affective alliance among interest groups. By the late 1980s, however, the situation escalated. A more radical subset of counter-publics emerged that was delineated as such by the Evangelical church itself, stigmatized, and finally pushed out. Once the peaceful revolution broke through, this narrative was largely forgotten (or its circumstances unknown).[40] For instance, eyewitnesses in Leipzig recall how repeated fights broke out in February 1988 over speaking time at the microphone in the central aisle of St. Nicholas Church. Activists claimed the platform to articulate their divergent complaints against the undemocratic, inhumane SED regime. Protesters occupied the nave in August, leading to a tumultuous state of affairs.[41] This history is not directly mentioned in the exhibit, nor are there any images of the sensationalist fights of more militant factions that began forming among the alternative groups. In *Sanfte Revolution* (Gentle

Revolution), the Protestant pastor Klaus Kaden remembers the turmoil in September of 1988. Fundamentalists wore bandages over their mouths to make visible the repression of free speech by the church itself. Then they wrangled over the most visible spaces in the balcony of the church nave to garner the attention of the West German press present in the Church during the Leipzig trade fair. But the narrative that can be pieced together locally by the yellowed, typewritten documents in the small peace-prayer exhibit is no less astonishing.

In the summer of 1988, regional clergy and the Evangelical church administration of Leipzig faced increasing dissent, even if they had supported the critical *Offene Arbeit* (open work) of the alternative groups.[42] After St. Nicholas Church pastor Christian Führer gave a sermon entitled "Living and Staying in the GDR" in February of 1988, the crowd swelled every Monday at the peace prayers from a small gathering of fifty regulars to about six hundred people. In an open letter to the congregation, the pastor later lamented that oppositional fringe groups were appropriating the peace prayers for their political purposes of confronting the SED regime more directly.[43] The narrative assembled at the small exhibit sidesteps the complexity of the role played by regional church officials in navigating this inner tension with the GDR state. Documents held by the Archive of the Citizens' Movement Leipzig reveal that for years the politicization of Church space was not only discussed at the highest governmental level of the SED state and the GDR's Evangelical Church Synod but also regionally, putting the Church of Leipzig de facto under (self-) surveillance. Already in 1988, the SED District Office of Leipzig warned regional church leaders of grave consequences in light of the Church's political dissident role. A transcript of a meeting in August 1988 between Leipzig's SED Secretary for Church Affairs, H. Reitmann, and two representatives of the Regional Church Office (Landeskirchenamt) shows the strategies by which regional church leaders were trying to rid themselves of radicalized secular forces in the Church. B. (blackened according to StUG) urged, "*We do not initiate groups; they spring up like mushrooms.* Those who come to church have the right to speak out, but then they discuss anonymous letters *to overthrow the government.* It cannot be the task of the church to support oppositional groups. The state should give them space to discuss."[44] Arguably, this language indicates that the regional Church had long lost control and even accentuated the anti-hegemonic challenges of oppositional groups. In an effort to reestablish normalcy in the Church, religious leaders had long refrained from asking the state to intervene, expand public discourse, or avoid escalation. Shortly before Germany's unification, Bishop Leich recommended dropping the official designation of "Church in Socialism" and replacing it with "Evangelical Church in the GDR." By 1990 the axiom rang with meanings about the more dubious practices by which the religious apparatus had contributed to maintaining a repressive order. The small exhibit at the South Chapel of St. Nicholas Church, with its paper scraps and faded black-and-white photographs as evidence, delineates a more mediated protest history and reveals how tactics were shaped on the ground.

Like many evangelical ministers, Führer advocated that Christians in the GDR engage in a kind of "cooperative protest" and strike a balance between "resistance and refusal." Given the all-pervasive state surveillance, some activists recall that the Church provided the only protection for local dissident groups on the margin of society, without which they would have "become fair game."[45] Once under the auspices of the local church, however, some protesters drew attention to their agendas on the fringe of the prayers for peace in ways that angered clerical leaders. When *Basisgruppen* (grassroots groups) continued to turn the service at St. Nicholas Church into a spectacle, a "reified political forum," Führer condemned the "de-Christianizing of the peace prayers" and "disregard for the Gospel's message of reconciliation." Those embodied performances appeared to him more like "carnival" than spiritual edification. Furthermore, he noted, it was not clear "who these unknown instigators are."[46] On November 10, 1988, for instance, members of the "AK Gerechtigkeit" (Justice) intensified their actions around questions about who could lay claim to public space in the church by disrupting the service dedicated to the commemoration of Jewish victims of the pogroms in 1938. The exhibit stresses that by heckling the audience, the activists instrumentalized the church's space for political purposes by distributing leaflets that compared the SED regime with the Third Reich. However, documents in the Archive of the Citizens' Movement Leipzig reveal the extent of the inner friction across the heterogeneous spaces of dissent. While the church administration claimed people who wanted to leave the GDR and surrender their citizenship had taken over the "AK Gerechtigkeit," the group pushed back and insisted that the perception that the activity was aimed to further the exit visa of individual applicants was simply wrong. Nevertheless, they circulated a statement urging the church to address the root causes of the waves of exit visas in the society of the GDR.[47] Yet, that discursive space was rapidly disappearing. The junior pastor of St. Lucas Church, Christoph Wonneberger, in charge of the peace prayers and affiliated with the so-called Leipzig Opposition since 1986, had already been suspended in the summer of 1988, and the diverse oppositional groups had been de facto excluded and censored.

It is worth noting that tensions between local clergy and civil rights groups escalated over the degree of force and methods of resistance. In a 2015 interview, Wonneberger explained that he had envisioned peace prayers across the GDR churches as an organizing format. He was one of the activist priests, a small minority in Leipzig's Protestant Church. This format allowed the political agendas of the alternative groups to become visible and for activists to "build translocal networks and stay tactically mobile."[48] According to Führer, however, even if he supported the political engagement of the ecological, human rights, and justice groups, their increasingly aggressive tone and strategy were incompatible with the church's sacred setting and pacifist orientation. Facing enormous pressures from the state and regional Church Boards, the Superintendent of the Evangelical Church Leipzig-East, Friedrich Magirius, determined that "the worship character of the peace prayer had to be preserved."[49] Saxony's church administration communicated this strategy in letters to citizens who organized in the oppositional groups.[50] In the spring of 1989, the church council allowed the alternative groups to attend the peace prayers again, but only under the condition that they submitted their speeches for approval and refrained from any of their guerrilla tactics. But instead of submitting to these constraints, the groups took the tactics they had honed in the Church into the streets.

By acknowledging these variegated practices of nonviolence in 1989, we rediscover the importance of social bonds and interdependency, however fraught those relations may be. Clearly, the subjects of the revolution were not merely spiritual, self-possessed, or peaceful as such. Their agencies were constituted in a conflictual field of discursive, social, and state power. The tension between the growing congregation of St. Nicholas Church and the GDR police mounted in the early fall of 1989. In time, the pacifist impulses of the original peace prayers turned into a force wherein nonviolence was performed in spontaneous, perilous actions. In the wake of protests outside St. Nicholas Church (filmed by West German cameras on September 4th), a massive concern with public order and its breakdown ensued. The SED government's fear of the population taking to the street manifested itself in a dramatic increase of police and Stasi at street corners, side streets, the train station, tram stops, and St. Nicholas Square. Although the local press branded the protesters as dangerous, it was the police presence itself that escalated the situation into violence.[51]

By mid-September of 1989, Christian Führer took a political stance of nonviolent resistance at significant personal risk. Although he usually dressed casually to lead the peace prayers, the Protestant pastor began appearing at the altar in a black suit and tie, announcing to the church assembly (and, thus, to all Stasi officials present) that he would only lay down this "mourning attire" (*Trauerkleidung*) when the "bludgeoning" (*Knüppelei*) ceased and there were no more arrests. He also instructed everyone facing arrest outside in the church courtyard to shout out their names, "and of you who hear those names, write them down, so we can pray for those people."[52] This foreboding atmosphere is brought to life in the exhibit in the St. Nicholas Church south chapel today in all its temporal incongruity (when I visited last, the adjacent sanctuary filled up with majestic music, as the organist happened to be playing Bach). In a videotaped interview, Beate Tischer, then a thirty-year-old mother and member of the *Basisgruppe* Women for Peace (Frauen für den Frieden), recalls the police mobilization (as the visitor hovers over a small audiovisual plywood box). Her perception of the acute threat in the early fall of 1989 changed once she could look from Führer's rooftop apartment down into the Nicholas Church courtyard and the surrounding area. She states, "It was strange, you were waiting for something, but you couldn't tell what that was. . . . If you came here [to Nicholas Church courtyard], you didn't know if you ever came back."[53] The corporeal revolt against culturally sanctioned violence resulted in arbitrary punishment. Those forms of state power remain invisible in any modern state until the empirical police show up.

The sense of chaos can also be felt in an eyewitness report by Gabriele Schmidt, a night-shift worker who was downtown on October 7. The Neue Forum recorded her account. In the afternoon, she bought flowers at the farmers' market to leave outside St. Nicholas Church. There she ran into a few colleagues, and they stopped for a chat, noticing security forces. She stated, "Nothing unusual; all was peaceful and quiet, and nothing indicated any unrest. Suddenly one of them yelled 'Action,' and panic ensued. In seconds the entire square was filled with police, armed with batons [*Schlagstöcke*] and police Humvees [*Mannschaftswagen*]. Then the police beat wildly and aimlessly onto the citizens. They pulled us on our hair over the square. When we were pushed onto the truck, an officer in civilian clothing yanked us up. You couldn't trust anybody. He shouted, 'You swine,' and grabbed our jackets; we were pulled on our cloth to the benches."[54] The women were transported to the horse stables at the Agra arena, where dozens of arrested citizens were detained overnight in brutal condition.[55] Recall that Führer wore a black suit to demonstrate dissent. The bodily display of the pastor during the peace prayers is significant. It marked the disappearance of East German citizens who lacked legal protection outside this sacred semipublic space. Notably, his stance of nonviolent resistance is embodied and not reliant on speech. Violence and nonviolence are revealed here most poignantly as interdependent, albeit not equal, forces, where the latter takes on, as it were, a negative form. These volatile assemblies recalled by eyewitnesses also highlight that the refusal to cooperate with governmentality or to strike out was not a given in the late GDR. Finding peaceful-ness in the upper reaches of a clear sky is easy. But these nonviolent actions had to be perpetually practiced in the church and then on the street. Indeed, the peacefulness in the demonstrations was not found in either location. This situated grassroots tactic continued into the mass gatherings during the following weeks, including those on October 9, 1989, which would be-come the "deciding day" and the focal point of Leipzig's local management of the past in the present.[56] The narrative that downtown was besieged by police and paramilitary units of the SED regime and that armed personnel carriers moved into place near St. Nicholas Church, as well as the petition of the six leading figures of the city broadcast over the city radio, have nearly mythological status, even in Germany's anemic collective memory of 1989.

But more disjunctive strands of history rarely take hold. Messy corporeal affects and enactments fall outside established frames. Unsettled temporal-ities are contained by linear narratives. Most confoundingly, how could the direction of violence be inverted in a force field of violence? I argue that whatever "doing the right thing" meant retrospectively had to be negoti-ated in a vexed and ambivalent field of relational responsibility and in the face of a persistent, destructive potential. A teacher may have locked arms in the demonstrations with her school principal, confronting the police, but what if the uprising turned out to be unsuccessful? More importantly, the meanings of the revolt's success were not yet formed. Butler makes a similar point about the interrelated, open-ended dynamics of violent and nonvio-lent modes at moments of historical crises. They write that when the world presents as a force field of violence, *the task of nonviolence is to find ways* of living and acting in that world that check or ameliorate this violence. The direction of violence may be turned precisely at moments when it seems that the violence has spread and saturated that world and *offers no way out.*[57] The body can be the vector of that turn, but so can discourse, collective practices, infrastructures, and institutions. Let us illustrate this inversion of violence with only one of the myriad ad hoc strategies deployed by the oppositional groups: organizing the distribution of pamphlets. A thirty-seven-year-old teacher recalls that the atmosphere in St. Nicholas Church on the evening of October 9 was stretched to the breaking point (*zum Zer-reißen gespannt*). At two thousand people, the church nave was filled to the last seat, "from outside through the church walls penetrated the enormous chanting . . . the loudest was No Violence! . . . somehow, we all appeared to duck down, expecting a terrible blow. Even the SED members ordered to attend the service seemed extremely reserved; they must have also seen the military vehicles on their way in."[58] The peace prayers concluded with the "deeply moving words of solidarity" by Saxony's regional bishop, Johannes Hempel, and an appeal to absolute nonviolence that he delivered in all four overcrowded churches that evening.[59] Then, the two thousand people inside the church moved outside into the square, where the crowd was so massive that they had to fear being crushed. Any provocations from the crowd were matched with chants of "No Violence." In just three days, the pastor of the St. Lucas Church, Christoph Wonneberger, and a handful of activists from the *Basisgruppen* "AK Justice," "AK Human Rights," and "AK Environment" had illegally printed thirty thousand copies of an urgent appeal to refrain from any force, using a simple manual press in the church basement. The leaflet was addressed not only to "all people," but also to the State's and city's "operational forces," that is, police, army, and paramilitary troops. It read: "WIR SIND EIN VOLK! Gewalt unter uns hinterlässt ewig blutende Wunden!" (WE ARE ONE PEOPLE. Violence leaves wounds that bleed forever).[60] Here, the collective meaning of the slogan was first articulated, and the call for UNITY did not have any national meaning directed at the West.

A sense of collectivity was provisionally performed not only through acts of solidarity among ordinary citizens. The police and military forces on the ground also had to refuse the State's justification to defend against this violent threat of demonstrators.[61] The official GDR media, police training instructors, and bureaucrats cast those assembled in the streets as "a mob" (rowdies). Thus, the state signaled that the revolting citizens were a chaotic and destructive threat to the social order. They were named and figured as potentially or actually violent. This logic of violence had to be disarticulated. The leaflets were distributed all over the city to the tens of thousands of non-Church-affiliated citizens of Leipzig who showed up in the "space of appearance" while fearing that the police and military troops waiting in the wings would crack down on the demonstrators, as in June of 1989 on Peking's Tiananmen Square. Indeed, being seen and heard by others constituted a new reality, where a public formed in the presence of others as a political act. This self-gathering also occurred under heightened conditions of surveillance. Today's church bulletin board displays a faded article about Christian Führer, the late pastor of St. Nicholas Church, featuring recollections of the transformative fall under the title "Power of Nonviolence" ("Macht der Gewaltlosigkeit"). The activist theologian described the spontaneous nonviolent breaking down of barriers as a miracle: "The spirit of Christ, HIS peace accompanied the people out of the church and into the streets" (Der Segen Gottes mit SEINEM Frieden begleitete die Menschen aus der Kirche auf die Strasse und Plätze). From a secular perspective, however, violence and nonviolence are intimately linked. The peaceful revolution was then not so much a "miracle" after all, not some divine intervention (versions of which have formed into legends). Instead, this nonviolent unrest actualized relations of partnership, solidarity, and sharing that come into being at the expense of sovereign power. This revolt sought out the political ontology of a "civil imagination," where citizens display an interest in themselves, in others, and in their form of coexistence, as well as in the world *that they create and nurture*.[62] Furthermore, given the defunct ideologies, such as socialism or Marxism, in East European societies, political spirituality becomes a new transformational force. In Foucault's sense, this practice involves "risking no longer being oneself," accepting that one may be transmuted, abolished, and transformed in relation to others, objects, truths, death, and so on.[63] Rising up needs to be practiced, and nonviolence in the late GDR played itself out as a social, ethical, and political force.

The uprisings in Eastern and Central Europe have been cast as "Velvet Revolutions" in global memory, accentuating a sense that they occurred nearly effortlessly (a sentiment shared by many who participated). However, the mandate was that state violence had to be challenged without reproducing its terms—hence the use of nonviolent force. As Arendt anticipated, repressive governments collapse when deprived of legitimacy. In *On Revolution*, she wrote: "That all authority in the last analysis rests on opinion is never more forcefully demonstrated than when, suddenly and unexpectedly, a universal refusal to obey initiates what then turns into a revolution."[64] But those who believe that the GDR merely collapsed miss the force of the demonstrations. Although the official discourse mythologizes the peaceful, ordinary East German citizen, the fine-grained exposure of the past in the local exhibit shows that the practice of nonviolence was not predicated on a moral choice or on individualism. It is not a matter of self-same virtue (that is, a superior character trait that some have and others fall short on): in Leipzig, the fracturing relations between the administration of the Saxon Church, local pastors, and the political demonstrations improvised by oppositional groups "ignited" the revolution. These local struggles over tactics illustrate how a contemporary, alternative reading of 1989 needs to account for the ethics and politics of nonviolence rather than fetishize the role of peacefulness in the transformation. This approach highlights that "selves are implicated in each other's lives, bound by a set of relations that can be as destructive as they can be sustaining."[65] The eyewitness Hartmut Zwahr puts it most poignantly: "The demonstrations intersected with the impact [*Wucht*] of the critical system destabilization and eventually system change. This led to the peaceful but by no means violence-free [*gewaltlose*] revolution of autumn 1989."[66] Unforeseeably, the departure (*Aufbruch*) into the better GDR, which started in Leipzig, led to its demise and downfall.

Naturally, the echoes of the protesters' shouting out their names in the face of state-police brutality in the early autumn of 1989 can no longer be heard today in the historic courtyard of St. Nicholas Church. Much like the symbol of "swords into plowshares" in the nave, their echoes are drowned out by international tourist groups and telephone vendors. Strikingly, the relationship of the contemporary site to '89 appears rather understated, despite the memorial column in the public square. Further evidence of Leipzig's protest history can be found in the recesses of the church, in the south chapel. Astute observers who take their time will be able to parse out the complex, conflictual dynamics of the unrest in 1989 that I just outlined. Yet ultimately, the small exhibit is framed to recall the peace prayers, accentuating the timeless message of pacifist, ecumenical work rather than the forcibly political dimension of nonviolence.

A simple discursive linkage of peace prayer and Peaceful Revolution ensures that any jarring, discontinuous meanings associated with the messiness and potentiality of nonviolence are evacuated. (The tension, conflicts, betrayal, falling-apart of coalitions, and the basic-democratic attempts to restructure the political sphere in late autumn of 1989 drop out of the purview of the localized narrative in the Church. The account ends on the peaceful turning point of October 9; this is where the highly localized performance of the Peaceful Revolution that visitors can see in the back of St. Nicholas church leaves off.) According to the exhibit and the slim, locally produced catalog available at the church bookstore, "the prayers for peace and the Peaceful Revolution of 1989 are inextricably linked" in local memory. More importantly, the text states, "The names of both already refer to what connects them in their innermost being. But it would not be enough to reduce the prayers for peace to this historical climax, albeit a dramatic one."[67] To that end, the modest permanent exhibit, which includes analog materials such as newspaper clippings, eyewitness reports, and an audio station, is interlinked with a detailed account of how the sanctuary was restored from 2011 to 2015 to shelter and arrange the documents. While working on the chapel, conservationists uncovered some of the material sediments left behind by repeated remodeling since the fourteenth century. The exhibit itself underscores the pacifist and religious (*geistlich*) dimension of the Peaceful Revolution by displaying information banners that all begin with a verse from the "Sermon on Mount Sinai" and end with a programmatic slogan from the Peaceful Revolution.

This arrangement also amounts to a deliberate rendering of the revolt, deploying a series of memory frames associated with centuries-old religious practice. The small exhibit aims to emphasize that the peace prayers transported traditional Christian principles, making them a "crystallization point of the Peaceful Revolution" by "enabling and encouraging

FIGURE 2.2. "Peace Prayers at St. Nicholas Church: Service in the Everyday World" exhibition (2021), St. Nicholas Church, Leipzig. Author's private collection.

people to risk, as it were, to walk upright and to engage in a peaceful commitment for democracy and human dignity."[68] Centering on the spiritual role of the peace prayers, the exhibit connects the past to the universal, holistic role of the Gospel in work against hunger and poverty today. (Even in the GDR, the local church sought to protect its most sacred principles and resisted notions of corruption by political ideology). To this day, peace prayers are held at St. Nicholas Church at 5:00 p.m. every Monday. The continuity of such an ecumenical mission also aligns with the projects of the Peaceful Revolution Foundation (Stiftung Friedliche Revolution), which was established on the twentieth anniversary of the "deciding day," October 9, 1989, by citizens from East and West, church people, and peace activists under the leadership of Evangelical minister Christian Führer (1943–2014). The Foundation aims to "transfer the basic values of the people who stood up for peaceful change in the churches and on the streets to the present day."[69] This localized inheritance of the revolution notwithstanding, visitors who enter the St. Nicholas Church will not encounter any commemorative signage or images of 1989 unless they move on to the south chapel, where unobtrusive information sheets are suspended from a nearly invisible wire. Far more prominent is the sign at the imposing oak entrance gate reminding tourists of the institution's more than 850-year history and asking them to respect the contemplative space for prayer. This choice embeds, if not diffuses, the memory associated with 1989 into a much longer temporal trajectory—a wholeness and continuity afforded by two millennia of Christianity. In fact, in rather poetic (and pacifying) terms, the curators hoped to signal that the exhibit about the peace prayers, while informative and rich in history, should be seen as "a guest in the church's dignified, hallowed halls."[70]

Traumatic Memory Grid: The Peaceful Revolution in Leipzig's Urban Space

Although the mnemonic ensemble at the St. Nicholas Church ultimately pacifies the radical political dimension of 1989, some disruptive leftovers of the revolutionary fall are found in the peripheral spaces of Leipzig's larger downtown area. Since the 1990s, Leipzig has attempted to integrate the local remembrance of peaceful transformative change in the late GDR into a universalizing narrative. The uplifting, even heroic, victory column in the St. Nicholas Church courtyard symbolizes these public, highly visible efforts to erect a tranquil past. The fractured history of the revolution is confined to the deepest recess of the Evangelical church's Gothic interior. However, a more provisional, self-reflexive archival memory network is also in place today. Equipped with a map, anyone can locate an ad hoc grouping, a set of slim metal grid installations, each featuring a historic black-and-white photograph and app-friendly multilingual descriptions stretching across the city. Scholars in museum studies describe this interactive engagement with discursive spaces outside or on the boundary zones of museums as "civic seeing." They highlight how such viewing experiences contribute to remembering as a form of "refracted memory."[71] The uneven, horizontal topography of the photographic installations creates multiple points of access, from Grimmaische Strasse, near the university, where the police lined up in the early fall of 1989; to Augustusplatz, the site of the mass demonstration on October 9; to the former Stasi headquarters between St. Thomas Church and the New Town Hall, which Leipzig citizens stormed in December of that year. Located in the transitional contexts of park entries, tram stops, through roads, and busy intersections, the pillars appear incidental rather than chronologically organized. Although barely visible today, I argue that these scattered remnants form a kind of traumatic memory grid from below and demonstrate how the haunting impulses of photographs can unsettle fixed historical meanings.

In her seminal book *On Photography*, Susan Sontag linked image production and traumatic shattering through metaphorical language. For Sontag, the force of photographic images comes from the fact that they are material realities in their own right, "richly informative deposits left in the wake of whatever emitted them, potent means for turning the tables on reality—for turning *it* into a shadow."[72] To my eye, the black-and-white photographs of revolutionary scenes in Leipzig's open-air exhibit generate such shadows by delineating the memorial sphere's perceptual (and counter-hegemonic) limits. As the distant protest images appear spectral in the urban space, they exceed any temporal binary and remain linked to an experience of the possible that may be yet to come. Thus, the installation has the potential to function as an "archive of the future," albeit a particularly tenuous one. First, let me elaborate on how the exhibit works as an architectural structure in urban space and how the archival forms of storage and transmission signal the unfulfilled legacies of the citizens' movement elided in the national memory of 1989. What comes to bear here is a tension between a hopeful, recuperative reading of social activism and a reading of historical trauma related to the late GDR and the interval year. This tension is also indicative of current shifts in memory studies.

As the historical photographs are hosted by a locally situated and dispersive memorial architecture, this *siting* in urban space warrants closer attention. The team from Studio Kw. Kommunikations-design, based in Frankfurt, envisioned the three-meter-tall porous metal structures to form an open memorial topography across the city where the pillars blend into the urban space. The idea for the memorial was influenced by the design philosophy of their commercial work, where they specialize in orientation and guidance systems for buildings, offices, corporate spaces, and urban infrastructures. Such integrative systems provide a communication and graphic interface between architecture and the user, where "in the best-case scenario, everyone knows them, but hardly anyone notices them."[73] Once applied to memorial design, however, this logic creates a peculiar status of (in)visibility. Starting at Augustusplatz near the Gewandhaus, for instance, one may or may not catch sight of the memorial columns featuring a faded image of a mass assembly on October 9. The ultramodern trams, however, with their advertisements flashing by—here in one of the city's largest and most crowded intersections—are impossible to miss. Echoing the memorial design in Berlin, each pillar is an appellation of all the others in the series, and the visitor has to walk through the city to gather their interrelated meanings. Taken together, the pillars are arranged according to a quasi-archival logic, that is, into a barely visible matrix of citation and juxtaposition related to events in '89–90, a logic that also uses a nonhierarchical

FIGURE 2.3. Sites of the Peaceful Revolution (March 13, 1989), Leipzig. Prayers for peace and demonstrations for freedom to travel, coinciding with the Spring Fair. Author's private collection.

spatiality across the urban environment to advantage.[74] The installations in urban space serve as critical conduits for transmitting the revolutionary impulses of 1989—or, at minimum, they shape and provisionally institutionalize the memories of publics.

In Leipzig, we see how this institutionalization unfolds when grassroots organizations work hand in hand with established governmental power. In 2004, the Citizens' Committee (Bürgerkomitee Leipzig e.V.) provided tem-

FIGURE 2.4. Sites of the Peaceful Revolution (June 10, 1989), Leipzig. Street-music festival for the freedom of art. Author's private collection.

porary text-image panels that, in 2010, became the permanent exhibition "Sites of the Peaceful Revolution in Leipzig's Urban Space," drawing on financial support from the Federal Foundation for the Reappraisal of the SED Dictatorship, the state of Saxony, and the city of Leipzig.[75] Similar to the Robert Havemann Foundation in Berlin, the Citizens' Committee was formed by local activists in 1989 and sees itself today as "custodian of the Stasi legacy and its successor bodies." Accordingly, the exhibit showcases East Germans' "self-liberation from dictatorship" in more normative terms.

At the same time, the twenty thematic pillars also mark a range of particular locations and differently scaled events in Leipzig that are considered relevant to the uprising. These memorial pillars span from January 1989, the date of the first unauthorized public gathering for basic-democratic rights in honor of Karl Liebknecht and Rosa Luxemburg at the Leipzig marketplace, *to* March 18, 1990, the date of the first free parliamentary elections in the GDR, which set the country on course to unification. On this trajectory, the exhibit does not only feature the iconic, historical cornerstones on which the national narrative in the neoliberal era would come to depend, such as Deciding Day (October 9, 1989), the occupation of the Stasi headquarters (at the end of the year), or the elections (as a referendum for the rapid introduction of the D-mark and German unification). A handful of pillars also display information about less well-recognized actions the GDR opposition took, including the Pleiße pilgrimage in June 1989, a political protest against heavy pollution in the city's canalized underground river, and, more broadly, against the destruction of the environment.

Barely legible in national memory today, this recall of the environmental protests is a salient example of the translocal and transnational orientation of resistance movements in the GDR.[76] The church-based environmental groups founded small libraries that became nodal points for the decentralized and heterogenous GDR opposition.[77] (These spaces were modeled on the tactical strategy of the so-called Flying Universities in Poland, an "underground" network where "mobile" educational experiences arose in private apartments before the declaration of martial law in 1981.) In the 1980s, such makeshift archives sprang up in churches across East Germany, in Berlin, Wismar, Grosshennersdorf, Halle, Karl-Marx-Stadt, and Leipzig (in 1988). The activists not only collected and distributed samizdat materials from the various oppositional groups that organized around the issues of peace, human rights, women's struggle, and so-called third-world solidarities in the GDR, they also turned to the catastrophic state of the environment "kept secret" by the SED regime. Local records show, for instance, that the air and soil in Leipzig's south were so highly contaminated that a cattle farmer asked, according to a university newspaper in 1989, "Who thinks of us, of our health of which we lose an irretrievable piece every day?" After the GDR collapsed, the country's ravaged ecology was recorded by a Greenpeace team that traveled from the German-Czech border to Cuxhaven on the river Elbe. They measured such a high level of toxic pollutants in the East that they determined the Elbe was the "dirtiest body of water in Europe."[78] Evidently, hardly any NGO or government agency of the FRG was interested in the local counter-knowledge spaces of the GDR's oppositional movement. An activist in Leipzig recalls that in 1989 the change of power took place in only a few weeks. The contact offices of the opposition, the environmental libraries, and the samizdat, which had been criminalized under dictatorship, were mere history in a very short time.[79]

Yet, from these clandestine environmental libraries (often literally tucked away in church basement rooms, such as at Leipzig's *Markusgemeinde*), activist groups had initiated translocal collaborations with ecological movements in Poland, Hungary, and the Baltic states of the Soviet Union as well as close contacts to the Green Party and media in the FRG. For sure, the potential of environmental approaches to connect the delineated East and West European pasts in a relational memory framework remains underutilized. In search of new narratives for the FRG more than thirty years later, historians such as Frank Uekötter are correct, in my view, to point to the entangled significance of environmental movements.[80]

In Leipzig, mountains of documents gathered at the local Archive of the Citizens' Movement disclose the widespread underground knowledge among citizens and oppositional groups that Saxony was one of the most devastated regions in the GDR. The silence in the state-run media was especially preposterous in light of the all-pervasive ruination. I still recall taking the train through the industrial area of central Saxony, Borna-Espenhain, in the late GDR. All passengers had to gasp for air as houses and factories behind the window disappeared behind a ghastly toxic glare. Once social transformations were underway in 1989, the city suddenly promoted measures to reduce pollution under the slogan "Environmental protection concerns us all."[81] For the first time, the level of smog was also announced by local radio stations. The oppositional movement, however, had already garnered such momentum that many ordinary citizens demonstrated in the street. Far from the cries for freedom and unity to which we have become accustomed in Germany's hegemonic memory, these protests against the GDR regime reached back to the alternative agendas of oppositional groups, including freedom of speech and assembly, free media, protection of the environment, the release of political prisoners, and the investigation of abuse of power and SED corruption. Another such event forgotten in Germany's collective memory and marked by the local memorial network in the city's geography is the Alternative Church Congress (Alternativer Kirchentag), held during the official meeting of the Protestant Church of Saxony in July 1989. Over 2,500 activists of various oppositional groups defied orders to remain within the horse racing arena located at Leipzig's periphery. They took their protest into the streets, visibly marching toward the city. For a few days, Leipzig became the center of the GDR opposition movement and civil rights initiatives—well before the seminal and by-now-iconic mass demonstration of October 9, 1989.

These localized, clandestine events emerging in the late GDR and leading up to the revolutionary fall are elided in the central channels of Germany's public memory—not least because the dispersive impulses of such activist movements often misalign with the historical agenda and epochal outcome of the country's unification. But we also must pay attention to what the locally situated narrative in Leipzig leaves out. Suppose the city as a spatial form can be regarded as both cause and consequence of social relations. In that case, spatial layout and scales, and flows of people, goods, money, and information also imperceptibly shape the dynamics of memory production in the built environment. Reliant on authentic locality, the memorial pillars in Leipzig have to be "found," and whether or not their open-ended meanings become transmissible memory depends, among other things, on the social regulation of who has access to the commercial and governing districts of the city, who manages the public spaces for tourism, and so forth.

FUGITIVE MEMORY

Although we have recovered some of the missing storylines in Germany's national memory, the material information panels in Leipzig's downtown area today tell a less hopeful, more elegiac story. As one resident put it, the pillars themselves look abandoned and sad. The Citizens' Committee Leipzig e.V. views its educational mission as using local museum practices to reappraise a repressive past. Outwardly, this memorial translation of the revolutionary events in 1989 follows the ubiquitous (national, unified) memory politics centered on the master trope of the SED dictatorship, with the Stasi and the massive militarized entrapment, the Berlin Wall and closed borders to the West, as its most important instruments of power. To that end, the installation's designers harnessed the symbolic meaning of state oppression by using metal mesh (*Streckmetall*) repurposed from the border fortification of the GDR regime (even though Leipzig itself was not near any dividing structure between the East and West). The association of metal with strength or dead-thingness persists today; we only need to think of a long line of tropes, including "the iron cage, brass tacks, steely glares, iron wills," the Iron Curtain, etc. Because the hardest metals, such as iron or steel, do not seem to vary in texture or ductility, metallic materiality can act as an absolute boundary.[82] Yet these porous metal panels used for the local exhibit in Leipzig do more than evoke material and symbolic references to totalitarian power. Arranged in lattice spaces, they are also full of holes, vacancies, and certain defects. Although the grid-like structures are, in one sense, an allusion to the order of things, to control,[83] they also indicate that something is missing, even mourned.

After all, the idea for these memorial objects was drawn from a global commemorative sphere of loss and violence. If nationalizing cultures of memory tend to take the borders of the mnemonic community as a given, the localized approach in Leipzig indicates that publics and their recollections can be created "prosthetically" through mediated acts of remembrance, as memory scholar Alison Landsberg poignantly put it. Such improvised acts of transcultural borrowing place the exposure of East Germans to state violence into an international terrain where power asymmetries and forms of oppression stretch into the present. Ann Rigney and Chiara De Cesari make a similar point when they show how the borders between imagined communities, which are implicated in different histories of political violence, become "reconfigured through the agency of cultural remembrance itself."[84] The design for the peaceful revolution panels is based on practices of cultural memory frequently performed at sites of traumatic (*einschneidend*) events: hanging flyers, for example, or leaving flowers, candles, and other mementos on fences to give voice to one's feelings. We need only think of the shrines and walls of remembrance in the streets of New York after September 11.

Such improvised remembrance happened in September 1989, when Leipzig's citizens demanded the release of political prisoners, as pastor Christian Führer showed up at the church service in black mourning attire. The citizens placed cards with the names of protesters who had been arrested in the early days of the uprising behind the metal struts in the windows at St. Nicholas Church. The memorial form recalls the nonviolent resistance cultivated by East Germans in the ecological, civil rights, and social-justice grassroots movements, often associated with the church, as we saw earlier. Today, the mournful temporality, the sense of *afterness* evoked by such memorial fences for the dead or disappeared, may belong as much to the victims of the GDR state as to the vanishing memory of the radical uprising transmitted by the Peaceful Revolution exhibit in public space. Protest gatherings are necessarily transient. Such transience is linked to their critical function, which means these assemblies could happen again at any time, as Arendt and Butler remind us. Such political gatherings serve, therefore, as one of "democracy's incipient or fugitive moments."[85] Yet, in Leipzig's urban geography, one cannot help but wonder if the traces of democratic unrest will disappear. With the memorial pillars, the temporal and spatial dimensions of the revolutionary event are intended to come alive, as the city's transformation since 1989 is palpably enhanced and documented through those historical black-and-white photographs. Photographic images can create a form of mediated perception that makes it possible to see and experience the unseeable, lost across space and time. Given their emphasis on temporality, photographs also allow us to project ourselves into a future from which to look back. The materiality of the archival installation likewise shifts our sense of time. The memorial stations have eroded as the metal frames are tainted and dulled. I am struck by the material impermanence, the motility of the metal, and its relation to much larger geo-affects and geological time arches. Stuck or residual memory impulses linger at the edge of consciousness.

FIGURE 2.5. Sites of the Peaceful Revolution (November 18, 1989), Leipzig. First approved rally of the New Forum. Author's private collection.

Unwittingly, the exhibit assembles a haunting meta-commentary on post-1989 "protest memories" themselves and, more specifically, on their forgetting.[86] What happened in 1989, to this day, appears to be (traumatically) split off from recent memory. Perhaps because the protest images present themselves without taking much hold of the passersby, they seem to haunt; the black-and-white pictures are small, unheroic, and disaggregated—there is nothing about the photographs to catch our gaze. The information panel "October 7, 1989—40th anniversary of the GDR, nationwide protest against the regime" is particularly instructive. The pillar is located on the busy main street Grimmaische Strasse, across from Leipzig University, right next to the entrance of a lively café. When I approached students who hung out there with their laptops, they confessed to having never noticed the slim installation. The archival network submerges into the commercial downtown area as crowds of shoppers move by. Rather than storing the past, the shadowy image in the periphery illustrates both temporal traces and memory's elusiveness. The photograph reveals nothing of the police power and the violent arrests of more than two hundred demonstrators in Leipzig that day. As we learned earlier, they were held under inhuman conditions in the horse stables at the Agra exhibition grounds, Markkleeberg. The images do not transpose the sense of danger when eight thousand security forces were waiting in the wings, ready to strike out on what would later be reified as Deciding Day.[87] The handful of police lined up with shields and batons in the black-and-white photograph—if spotted in the perceptual margins of this urban, commercial space—appear forlorn. Likewise, in the courtyard of St. Nicholas Church, the memorial panel "September 4, 1989"—showing the iconic photo of civil rights activists unfurling a banner reading "For an Open Land with Free People" (Für ein offenes Land mit freien Menschen)—languishes in a dim corner, literally and figuratively in the shadow of the presiding Victory Column. As such, these are protest "images in withdrawal," images of '89 preoccupied with their own leave-taking, to draw on the critical theorist Gerhard Richter, who links figurations of *afterness* to the limits of representability.[88]

Importantly, Richter's approach allows us to understand that the predicament of the "memory of publics" is not that there is a past reality of the revolutionary fall that in some form of mimetic belonging can or cannot be represented (after all, the memorial pillars refer to the relevant information). Rather, the relation between textual discourse and image fragment in the transitional context of the present everyday stages the dynamics of public memory politics as the very scene in which there is no longer a stable memory image of something. Put differently, the (dis)placed floating black-and-white photographs of revolutionary assemblies, in retreat, claim our attention precisely at those sites in Leipzig where they linger and refuse to leave "our own experience of this appearance, untouched."[89] The metal grids stand out for their peripheral status, their invisibility, suspending the stark black-and-white images of revolutionary organizing (which often took place at night) like undead melancholy ghosts. In turn, the radical political signification of the Peaceful Revolution appears to be unclaimed, up for grabs.

However, the past can also form an underground memory, so to speak, accruing unfinalized impulses for concerted action. Unfulfilled, we may say, these protest impulses are in search of addressees and in limbo in the neoliberal era. This suspended uptake in attention and activity garners its significance not only from the past but also from a future promise. In Leipzig, each singular metal lattice flashes a small yellow sign with a bright red "'89," as though to maintain—for or from the future—"an energetic pulse, slightly 'off' from that of the [memorial] assemblage," and certainly off from the city's historical and urban memory architecture.[90] Working together, these scattered memorials may signal that a non-reified, open-ended understanding of the GDR's socio-ecological protest histories is indeed vital. Yet, as in Germany's capital, in Leipzig, an institutionalized desire to create more-permanent structures to memorialize 1989 as the springboard toward "freedom and unity" had also emerged twenty years after the fall of Wall.

National Schema and Unwanted Gifts:
The Freedom and Unity Monument

If local memory has a greater capacity to be prismatic, permeable, and heterogeneous, as we have seen, then what are some of the processes that can help secure national meanings of the Peaceful Revolution from these more particular regional constellations? In Berlin, such efforts became increasingly entrenched in a central reorganization and restoration of historically significant space in the built environment. In Leipzig, this form of mnemonic and social governmentality depended on practices of "performative consensus," wherein the city's inhabitants participate in the production and transmission of knowledge and have a measure of agency. Yet, even though official domains and spheres of citizen engagements may exist in constant interaction, these procedures in liberal democracies are not performed in a neutral vacuum. These forms of "civic representativity" are also shaped by the media. They are embedded in digital circuits deployed by federal and local bureaucratic bodies, their rhythms of information and communication, and the modes of appropriation they put to work. Leipzig's governmental sphere has attempted to banish the complex embodied and incongruous memories of 1989 to the past. In this section, I will briefly outline the relatively familiar story of Leipzig's official nationalizing memorial efforts and insist we rethink our analytical methods. As memory studies expands the range of material, transcultural mobilities and formats under consideration, the field has turned too far away, I believe, from the significant role played by normative relations of knowledge and power in transmitting memory.

Two decades after the *Wende*, the shift toward a more triumphant national memorialization of the Peaceful Revolution in Germany's capital impacted Leipzig's locally situated memory politics. In 2008, the plan for a national monument for "Freedom and Unity" in Berlin was promoted by the CDU/CSU and ratified by a parliamentary decision. At the same time, the federal government passed a resolution to fund the contested "Freedom and Unity Monument" (Freiheits- und Einheitsdenkmal) in Leipzig, where the revolution began. Arguably, this resolution resulted from local resistance to hegemonic memory politics. The plan for a monument in Leipzig was initially spearheaded by prominent figures of the former citizens' movement. They conceived the idea as a counterproposal to the sole focus of Germany's government on a National Monument to Freedom and Unity in Berlin. A year after the federal decision to authorize the memorial plans in the capital, on June 17, 2009, the Leipzig city council commissioned the mayor, Burkhard Jung (SPD), to initiate a competition to design the "Freedom and Unity Monument," invoking the symbolically relevant anniversary of the national uprising on June 17, 1953. (Ironically, archival documents show that in October of 1989, the unrest of June 17, 1953, was referenced by the SED's political officers in Leipzig to train police, whereas the demonstrators reportedly sang left-wing anthems and US civil rights songs.)[91] In 2011, after a survey enlisting three thousand participants, as well as a round of workshops involving citizens, civil rights activists, experts, and young people from Hanover, Krakow, and Houston (all sister cities), the city council determined that the future monument would be placed on Wilhelm-Leuschner-Platz rather than on Augustusplatz (formerly Karl-Marx-Platz) where the main assembly of protesters on October 9, 1989, had taken place. At this location, near the New Town Hall, the monument could leverage national symbolism by redeveloping the public square (to be officially renamed Platz der Friedlichen Revolution) across from the seat of the city government; it could also form an endpoint of a central axis through the city, starting at the Völkerschlachtdenkmal (Monument to the Battle of the Nations, in remembrance of the Battle of Leipzig, in 1813). As Anna Saunders astutely points out, this site was also considered to provide the optimal conditions to enhance an affirmative national dimension of the Peaceful Revolution and Leipzig's connection to Central and Eastern Europe.[92] However, we need to carry this point further. A closer look at the memorial competition shows how official procedures in service of public memory dynamics install a historical schema of intelligibility—a normative ideal as a preexisting condition for analysis. Such general historical schemas establish domains of the knowable and constitute a dynamic field, at least initially understood as a priori.[93] While the competition announcement, issued by the city in 2011, indeed deployed a relatively open, non-bureaucratic language grounded in the methodologies of museum pedagogy (for example, "the Freedom and Unity Monument should be a work of art that inspires reflection and engagement"), it also set the national and liberal parameters of the memorial project in advance. The announcement casts the Peaceful Revolution in 1989 as "self-liberation [*Selbstbefreiung*]," a "recovery [*Wiedergewinnung*] of freedom," and as an event during which "GDR citizens stood up to dictatorship"[94] rather than requiring contestants to interrogate these historical constellations, let alone challenge the present conditions that produce these interpretations.

By now, attention to this reified governmental terminology may strike the reader as pedantic if it were not for the fact that in the public realm, speech is indeed powerful. Of course, meanings about the past are not established by language alone, but it is precisely the seemingly self-evident repetition of specific terms in official discourse that performs semantic transfers across local, national, and international scales. Induced and reproduced, this language establishes itself as the dominant norm and acclimatizes public discourse over time to the logic of the inevitable course of history. Put differently, "self-liberation," "dictatorship," "recovery of freedom," and not least, "freedom and unity" and "reunification"—this is all familiar material. Certainly, Roland Barthes's mythical speech comes up regarding reified post-1989 discourse, for instance, in Jonathan Bach's excellent book *What Remains*, but I find Diana Taylor's reference to Barthes particularly useful. In *Archive and the Repertoire*, she writes about "portable frameworks" that bear the weight of accumulative repetitions.[95] This approach reminds us that language works its way into our bodies, shaping corporeal behaviors such as gestures, attitudes, or tones that may promote certain views while helping to occlude others. For instance, retrospective notions of a GDR dictatorship inscribe themselves into docile bodies, while the incessant repetitions of, say, "self-liberation" produce subjects that comport themselves in measured confidence. In turn, Leipzig's local memorialization makes clear that reified language can become recognizable as such within epistemic fields opened up by more provisional, even counter-hegemonic practices and forms of knowing.

The official project for the Freedom and Unity Monument faced such resistance from various publics that the competition was broken off in 2014 due to disagreement over the name, location, and legal proceedings.[96] In light of the foundered plans for the Freedom and Unity Monument, local dissent had exposed the limits of national, hegemonic schemes to disseminate interpretive (and, thus, real) power and seemed to have won out in the contestation over collective public memory. Notably, when confronted with waning popular support for the Monument to Freedom and Unity in Berlin in 2018, Johannes Milla, the Stuttgart-based co-designer, believed that popular majorities should never decide on memorial art.[97] However, Leipzig's city government had another monument plan in its back pocket. Since 2014, the only proposal still in the running for Leipzig's commemoration of the Peaceful Revolution was a massive sculpture, sponsored by a private donor, the American sculptor Miley Tucker-Frost, to be placed at the corner of the Stasi Museum downtown, the central location where civil and governmental-official strands of post-dictatorial memory productions intersect. The citizens of Leipzig, however, continued to push back on the offer. The US artist had made a name for herself with a patriotic and religious kind of public art that displayed arrangements of wild running mustangs and triumphant symbols of eagles, including the seal of the president, at the George W. Bush Presidential Center in Dallas, Texas.[98] Nine meters wide, the proposed monument rendered a group of life-size protesters holding candles in their hands, along with other figures displaying a sash reading, "No Violence" (*keine Gewalt*) across their chests, forming into a bulwark of revolution. Ironically, Tucker-Frost's iconic sculpture representing the unrest in the GDR echoed the overdrawn aesthetics of socialist realism, which had undergirded the ideology of a state that the East German populace decided to openly resist. The people may have also apprehended that the gift of the bronze monument was not a gift at all but a debt to be returned.[99] According to the local newspaper *Leipziger Volkszeitung*, while the memorial was an aesthetic embarrassment, private interests and profitable political connections between Leipzig and the US state of Texas were at stake.[100] The plan revealed a desire for a peaceful and brave revolutionary hero, a stock figure from a limited number of narratives with innumerable variations.[101] This substitute proposal for the contested Monument of Freedom and Unity reified the revolutionary victory of the East—in barely concealed fashion—as a geopolitical success story of the global West.

In the following, we will continue to see that, without ever being purely one thing or the other, the shaping and organizing of collective memory combines various trends of remembering. Memory is conjured through the senses and thus embodied; it links the deeply private with social and even official practices. Memory is often difficult to evoke and always operates in conjunction with other memories.[102] Cultural memory is a practice, an act of imagination and interconnection; communicative memory focuses on the transmissions of narratives about the past between and across generations; public memory relies on more circumscribed ritualized performances that may (or may not) garner the population's support, and it often interacts with commercial practices. In the debates over the appropriate local forms of commemorating the Peaceful Revolution in Leipzig, neither a federally sponsored nor privately funded monument materialized, which put Leipzig's annual Light Festival (Lichtfest) front and center as a memorial space. Since 2007, the Leipzig Tourism and Marketing GmbH, with assistance from the city of Leipzig, has cooperated with local businesses, regional media, and the civic initiative "Day of the Peaceful Revolution-Leipzig, October 9, 1989" to stage a spectacular annual Light Festival.[103] Even if official plans for a Monument of Freedom and Unity repeatedly stalled, the city came to rely on an arsenal of entrepreneurial commemorative practices that continually engaged the public at the intersection of local and national memory.

Public Preposition: *white space/ Critical Thinking Needs Time and Space*

In the present book, I challenge the false universalizing of 1989 in contemporary memory discourse. Small-scale and liminal memorial spaces in the urban periphery, such as the installation "The Peaceful Revolution in Leipzig's Urban Space," indicate how this dominant narrative breaks down, is never cohesive in the first place, or can be unlearned, releasing new impulses for a protest memory in fugitive spaces. But, even highly visible, commercially driven events, such as the Light Festival in Leipzig held since 2007, have the capacity for interventions where the publicness of memory can itself be interrogated. The Düsseldorf-based concept artist Mischa Kuball calls such interventions "public prepositions." This format brings together various and indeed competing terms for space and publicity, explores what public space and the political might be, and what relationship artworks have to this space. Notably, while drawing on knowledge of locality, his art projects emerge from and move in international circuits. One project in particular shall serve here to illustrate how contemporary public art can create a realm where the critical role of publics in securing, structuring, and circulating the memory of '89–90 can be acknowledged and performed.[104]

Curators have noted that Kuball's 2014 light installation *white space/ Critical Thinking Needs Time and Space* works in the liminal area where experimentation and mainstream cultural pressure meet. Across the board, these pressures have led in recent years to what Susan Ingram calls a "feel-good tactical radicalism," where practitioners create spectacular productions designed to get audiences to inform themselves about useful aspects of history and to engage with possibilities for more socially equitable futures.[105] But, I argue, Kuball's self-reflexive public prepositions have something different to offer; they investigate the very conditions that limit and enable the reordering of public memory. The multimedia project *white space* does not only draw from the commercial parameters of the Lichtfest; the Leipzig-based curator Barbara Steiner suggests that it also intervenes in and challenges the overtly event-based, marketed memorial culture that allowed Leipzig to turn the 1989 Peaceful Revolution into "a product, a brand, and an institution, in equal measures."[106] In turn, this local investigation of 1989 protest memory can be placed in the context of art's critical capacity to engage with global conflict and activism in the twenty-first century.[107]

For the past three decades, Kuball has collaborated with the (neo)conceptual American artists Jenny Holzer and Lawrence Wiener, as well as with other internationally known practitioners, installing light sculptures and performance pieces in cities across the globe. For him, such public interventions provide, in essence, "a tool that makes it possible to observe both the present and the past status quo of the public sphere," a status quo that is constantly changing. In 2014, Kuball placed the slogan "Critical Thinking Needs Time and Space—Here and Everywhere" at public education and media institutions in various cities across Germany, including Düsseldorf, Cologne, Munich, Hanover, Leipzig, and Berlin, to transform the demand into an invitation independent of time and place. The installation harkened back to a small banner that, according to the artist, had appeared, at significant risk, in the early fall of 1989, in the St. Nicholas Church courtyard (even if I have not been able to confirm this specific occurrence, which enhances the performative element). According to Kuball's website, "the inaccessible 'white space,' a 70,000-watt LED light field, brought to mind the citizens' movement of the time and anchored the reflection in need for critical thinking in current events."[108]

While the civic and softly political intention of the project works rather well within the parameters of the "eventification" championed by the Leipzig Light Festival, the fact that Kuball executed his project at

FIGURE 2.6. *white space/ Critical Thinking Needs Time and Space*, Leipzig (aerial, 2014). Photograph © Archive Mischa Kuball.

Wilhelm-Leuschner-Platz is significant, even provocative, and points to rifts in the memorial cultures of cities driven by neoliberal (or post-1989 national) agendas. Wilhelm-Leuschner-Platz is the vast site, on the periphery of the Leipzig ring road, where the Monument to Freedom and Unity was to be built. The public's resistance had focused on challenging budget models and the Leuschner-Platz as an appropriate location for commemorating the mass protests in '89, overlooking that even such "inauthentic" sites can be repurposed to reactivate memories, especially when artists deploy conscious strategies of display. Aside from the city government building, the planned monument site is also adjacent to the city library, theatre and music schools, and a large community park named after Clara Zetkin, the Marxist theorist, activist, and early advocate for women's rights in the Socialist Democratic Party. Arguably, Kuball's resiting of the project here also reinvestigates the social parameters of the built environment and communal use of public space. His works are steeped in Western 1960s theories of the public—a lighter, more relatable inflection of Habermas and Negt/Kluge, with elements of phenomenology, media theory, and Latin American radical art activism (he was influenced by Vilém Flusser, the Czech-born philosopher who moved to Brazil). Even if Kuball is primarily concerned with the role of art in the public sphere, his piece in Leipzig also needs to be situated within the city's changing field

FIGURE 2.7. *white space/ Critical Thinking Needs Time and Space*, Düsseldorf (2014). Photograph © Archive Mischa Kuball.

of memorial culture specifically and of memorial form in the twenty-first century more generally.

British museum scholar Chloe Paver has pointed out that the conventional boundaries between exhibitions and memorials have become increasingly blurred in the past two decades. We certainly saw this cross-fertilization happen in Berlin's Wall Memorial Park. While memorials traditionally have been fixed in place, made of lasting materials, executed in one primary medium, and addressed mainly to our sight, exhibitions, by contrast, are constructed of multiple materials and media, are not designed to last forever, and have the potential to be mobile (at least when limited to simple displays).[109] In 2010, for instance, a multipronged exhibit entitled *Europe '89* opened in Dresden, Prag, Wroclaw, and Bratislava/ Žilina.[110] One meeting point for the two creative modes is the art installation. Kuball's *white space*, a "light installation of architectonic dimension,"[111] sits at this intersection between memorial and exhibitional forms: The projection sculpture is transient; its scope requires movement and addresses the whole body (and sensory capacity) rather than just relying on optical contemplation. At the same time, it constitutes a commemorative site.

The artist relied on the material and metaphorical properties of technology to curate this transitory memory space. The blazing effect of the LED light field was reinforced by artificially produced fog, which was intended to translate the notion that collective memory requires space and the passage of time. One visitor to the Leipzig Light Festival praised the capacity of the temporary light installations to bring back the charged atmosphere of the street assemblies in the fall of 1989. The ability to relive this experience, albeit in mediated form, is deemed more valuable than any physical monument. To be moved, we see with public memory, as with personal memory, something always needs to be *unverfügbar* (undisclosed)—the site literally constitutes an inaccessible space where meaning is not immediately assigned or grasped.[112] Rather than eliciting a commemorative post-1989 image—say, of marching crowds or East Germans at the toppled Berlin Wall—the public installation makes space for perpetual thinking and recalling, for future-oriented impulses on the most intimate and public scale. History's taillight (*Endlicht*) in the post-Soviet era is turned into a space of possibility.[113] Kuball's spherical light project simultaneously engages with salient questions about the relation between the impermanence of events (and of assemblies in particular) and the conventional need for the permanence of memorial objects.

EPHEMERAL PUBLICS

When asked to articulate the particular political structure and sensation associated with the mass gatherings in 1989, those interviewed often lack a language. At its most compelling, Kuball's *white space* creates an immaterial public thing, to draw on Bonnie Honig's work on D. W. Winnicott, that functions as a transitional object or holding environment. Here, individuals are charmed into collecting themselves together for the world—specifically, for recalling past assemblies and protests.[114] As I argue throughout this book, this memory of collaborative revolt is both particularly elusive (assemblies disappear with the arrest of the activities) and, on the level of the national imaginary, inconvenient and thus rarely shared. While the light space aids remembering and forgetting, the massive field of effervescent energy bursts open any rigidly defined, established frames by which Germany's national memory of the recent past has been institutionally safeguarded. The massive field of LED lights Kuball assembled at the Leuschner-Platz in 2014 may be the most visceral translation of the uprisings in 1989, taking place as open space. Following the sociologist Hartmut Rosa, my term of choice to describe this event-space is a "relational field of resonance." Rosa theorizes resonance as a sense of *being-related-to-the-world*—in which the world, or at least some segment of it, is experienced as responsive or energetically charged. Resonance is a workable conception of alienation's other. It involves difference and transformation; it bridges the gap between identity and difference and has no reifying implications.[115] Eyewitnesses remember this dynamic charge. When asked whether the revolution created heroes, activists Gudula Ziemer and Holger Jackisch said no: it was a "People's Festival" (Volksfest). On October 9, "it was simply beautiful to be in this crowd of people, to laugh under the tension, to sense one's neighbor, to agree with them—for the first time without boredom."[116]

Arguably, the political particularities of the 1989 unrest dissipate in *white space*, given the persistent presence of energies. But we should note that even theorists such as Rancière, whom I repeatedly elicit to delineate '89–90 as a disjunctive space, have considered the political force of such a "vibratory vitality." Compared to Rosa, Rancière is less interested in how a public emerges than in the means by which its apparent coherence can be interrupted. And still, Rancière's model leaves room for imagining the being of the *demos* not as a fixed thing or fixed entity "but [as] an unruly activity or indeterminate wave of energy."[117] Similarly, Foucault introduces the idea of the incorporeal as a strange kind of matter that is unrepresentable within frameworks of fixity, but that is shed from the thicker compounds of bodies and hits our senses to give notice of an outside, beyond the discrete individual. He speaks of emissions that rise like "wisps of a fog."[118] How can this ontological imaginary square with the politicized understanding of embodied action—of subjects appearing in, claiming, and constituting public space—explored in the present book?

To answer this question, I turn to Ingo Schulze's 2005 novel *New Lives*, one of the few fictional accounts set during the Monday demonstrations in Leipzig. The writer animates a scene of vibratory effluence where the normalized conditions of a policed environment break down. Conjuring the demonstrations in Leipzig on October 2, 1989, the main protagonist recalls a kind of protean force that propelled the bodies into action: "All of it—the people, the twilight, the warm air, the underground current that flowed from the group—seems like a dream or a vision to me now. Instead of registering each detail, each vibration, I felt less and less. All the same, I was convinced I was experiencing a historical moment . . . As the crowds pressed tighter together in the twilight, the chants spread more quickly."[119] Later on in the novel, the disappearance of this capacity for resonance is associated with the fall of the Berlin Wall. Those who study crowds have shown that an immaterial energy can traverse the bodies of such improvised assemblies.[120] For Rosa, resonance is a more specific way of relating to the world that occurs when we feel truly moved by something or someone we encounter. If we answer this call, we experience self-efficacy; we transform ourselves in the sense of a coproduction; we are being (un)done, and the other side is also changed.

Needless to say, there are particular political risks to this reordering of relations. There are risks, especially, in highly polarizing situations of large-scale unrest where protests and State violence clash, altering the sphere of the perceptible. Consider, for example, Uwe Ch., a twenty-six-year-old recruit of the Leipzig police force (*Bereitschaftspolizei*). He was recorded by one of the surveillance cameras installed on rooftops downtown during the police operation on October 7 that led to the aforementioned wave of arrests. As the explosive social atmosphere was palpable in the streets on the eve of the GDR's official fortieth-anniversary celebration, he became caught up with a throng of demonstrators in front of the pharmacy on Grimmaische Strasse. Rather than pushing the rioters back, he broke ranks by trying to reason with the crowd about the unpopular forced presence of police. Inspecting the surveillance footage, his officers caught this act of treason. Amid the chaos, the shield belonging to the recruit's riot gear leaned unattended against the building wall nearby. In the fall of 1989, police personnel who refused to follow orders during these demonstrations (reportedly about 10 percent of the force) were suspended from the operations and threatened with severe military punishment proceedings.[121] And yet, some, such as Uwe Ch., shed their assigned roles and were drawn into the energy of collective action, unable to anticipate what this spontaneous intersubjective transformation would result in.

Just as Rosa situates the phenomenological concept of resonance in the sociological and political arena, Kuball has been credited for disclosing light's political and social position like no other artist. Rather than implying that light is an aesthetically alluring medium, one of interacting colors (akin to music), Kuball insists that "light is sociology; light is politics."[122] In an interview during the Light Festival, Kuball stated at the sight of the luminous field, "I like standing here anonymously and listening to the viewer's remarks. A basin? An aquarium? Hour zero? An iceless skating rink? Lots of associations. First, it is a space bereft of purpose and intention. It can contain our thoughts, worries, wishes or ideas, anything we want to project. That's an ideal situation for me. Like a three-dimensional piece of paper. A blank that you can fill yourself."[123] At minimum the spectators are drawn into a collectively shared contemplative mood. For the visitors of Leipzig's Light festival, the empty space could also become an invitation to reflect on the absence of "1989" in Germany's larger, nationally oriented public memorial culture.[124]

Moreover, the poetry of this haunting site in the night shows that assemblies do not have to involve language or linguistic modes of confrontation and persuasion. Such gatherings may occur through stillness or silent embodied action. Recall that Arendt assumed that the production of public space, in the political sense, requires a space of appearance where people negotiate their shared concerns through acting and speaking together.[125] In contrast, Butler insists on the affective and bodily dimension of collective action, especially in a space that undergoes a historical transformation. Both thinkers agree (and Kuball's ephemeral field renders it) that the alliance between people is not tied to location; it is highly transposable and

FIGURE 2.8. *white space/ Critical Thinking Needs Time and Space*, Leipzig (close-up, 2014). Photograph © Archive Mischa Kuball.

"'can find its proper location almost anywhere and anytime.'"[126] In November 1989, East German writer Volker Braun described how in that open interval—after the iron *Kommandos* (orders) were gone—the people were faced with figuring out new solidarities and flexible forms of governance.[127] In 2014, these disruptive potentialities of nonviolent action in the St. Nicholas Church courtyard in 1989 (and in the GDR church as a constitutive sphere) finally come into view, albeit as a liminal, negative space of history.

The light installation/performance *white space/ Critical Thinking Needs Time and Space—Here and Everywhere* marked the twenty-fifth anniversary of the mass assemblies and protests in the churches and streets of Leipzig on a scale and level of memorial intervention no other city had achieved. Today, transient and often decontextualized, the digital images capturing the performance proliferate on the World Wide Web, far removed from the recalcitrant material fragments and rubble of the Berlin Wall in Germany's capital. Depending on the search terms, these images pop up alongside Kuball's public prepositions worldwide, including *Solidarity Grid* (2013) in Christchurch, New Zealand, or *Private Light/Public Light* (1998) in São Paulo, Brazil. These online collages form new, unsettling relations with fundamentally Christian book covers in what Hal Foster calls the mega-archive of the internet.[128] Variably, the power of the '89 Leipzig installation to call others who are distant in time and space into critical thinking and collective action dissipates or is retained in altered form. These local meanings may translate into concerns with the future of publics that have begun to unfold in the twenty-first century on both translocal and global scales. As the revolutionary recall in Leipzig shows today, the memories of these radically democratic assemblies also risk being appropriated by post-democratic hegemonies for their right-wing agendas (I turn to this concern in chapter 5).

Coda: Forgetting

I opened this chapter by asking: What if all we remember is cast in light of everything we already knew and have since come to learn? This notion of a mnemonic inevitability is certainly bleaker than what I advocate for the present book, devoted as I am here to considering the creation of future archives of protest and collaboration. My wager has been that what has been erased or nearly forgotten can be productively called upon. Such memories are unbound, so to speak, and can be released, reorganized, or harnessed. We witness these scattered memories in Leipzig today with the memorial exhibit about the Peaceful Revolution in urban space, which I likened to a "traumatic memory grid." In 2009, activist Christian Führer urged, "We do not want to put the Peaceful Revolution into a museum; we want to go further and encourage action today. The peaceful revolution must intervene in the *economy*."[129] I believe this point is the most crucial future-oriented lesson of this unfinished local legacy. Neoliberal forms of governmentality and hyper-capitalism are not a given. The editorial newspaper *Broken Bonds: Remontage of Time* (*Zerrissene Gesellschaft: Remontage der Zeit*), organized by an artist collective in Leipzig in 2018 to celebrate the eighth year of the f/stop Festival for Photography, began to anticipate such a shift toward assembling 1989–90 as an archive of the future. An ad-hoc photographic installation appeared at Wilhelm-Leuschner-Platz. Images recalled the long-forgotten citizens' protests in the spring of 1990 against the planned 1:3 currency union alongside the postindustrial devastation of Leipzig's region in the aftermath of the democratically ratified Treuhand takeover.

Leipzig shows that even thirty years after the *Wende*, unfinalized, alternative memories of the so-called Peaceful Revolution are still at play. Rather than exclusively enshrining existing legacies, the cultural, public, and collective memories of the peaceful revolution in the "city of heroes" work on multiple scales. Localized acts of memory labor, such as the small exhibit on the peace prayers in the St. Nicholas Church, are crafted independently from the official public memory dynamics. The city capitalizes on the legacy of 1989 while privileging national, global, and commercial interests. In the previous chapter, I demonstrated that Berlin's memorial politics ultimately absorbed the revolutionary impulses that unseated the GDR into a dominant, official language of "freedom and unity." Leipzig, however, has attempted to keep the remembrance of the street protests and uprising alive while various religious, civic, governmental, and entrepreneurial strategies have ultimately tamed its disruptive potential. In the local public memorial sphere, any recollection of the revolutionary break tearing a naturalized order apart is glossed over. The focus rests instead on the continuous role of the Protestant Church in the Peaceful Revolution and the significance of the Stasi's defeat—a narrative fostered by former GDR dissident groups, such as Leipzig's Citizens' Committee, in conjunction with the regional and governmental representatives of the FRG's national memory apparatus. Each of these stakeholders inevitably deploys frameworks that reproduce the past from within their respective ideologies, historical experiences, and biographies (even if these frameworks need to be stabilized and become entangled). All converge more or less around the shared goal of fusing the local story of Leipzig's decisive role in the peaceful transition with an affective economy of uplift and a sequential narrative of democratic renewal. Conversely, mnemonic counter-publics would make more substantial claims regarding exclusions from the hegemonic public sphere.

To be sure, the gigantic victory column in the courtyard of St. Nicholas Church is arresting, but the emotions it arouses come from the harmony of forms and the spectacle of standing at attention. Our gaze is pulled toward the pillar's crown leaves extending into the sky. Older visitors may associate the column with a jubilant possibility or even the "miracle" of concerted action. This spontaneous collective sense seems to have disappeared after Germany's official unification was achieved. But this prominent symbolic representation fails to evoke the force field of the activist movements in the late GDR (let alone the internal conflicts of the Protestant Church's rupture, on the local scale, into revolutionary unrest). The public sculpture renders neither the volatile interrelations of violence and nonviolence negotiated in the fall uprising of 1989, nor the hopes and fears of those who lived through it, nor the defeat of activists disappointed with the ineluctable results. Decades later, Leipzig offers its visitors a recall of the revolution's pacifist legacy, organized from below, while participating in the public construction of a pacifying post-1989 memory in the neoliberal era.

In conclusion, forgetting can also be vital, especially if involving defeat. Mischa Kuball's public light work in Leipzig gestures in that direction, playing with phenomenological notions of an incandescent field. At the outset, I enlisted Marc Augé, for whom our concern with recent histories obscures the insights gained from a *longue durée*. Although in the final analysis, I agree that memory and oblivion are both "necessary for the full use of time," the case study of Leipzig illustrates that we must examine the historical and political conditions shaping collective forgetfulness. Cultural forgetfulness occurs when there are no larger frameworks of significance into which a past way of life could fit.[130] The next chapter explores this dynamic of memory withdrawal or atrophy by taking up an intergenerational narrative. We will see that forgetting can be a matter of survival for those who lived through a tumultuous, if not traumatic, event—just as the openness formed by collective oblivion may offer the promise of a brand-new start.

[CHAPTER THREE]

Possible Archives

In an essay entitled "Ephemeral Archives," Susan Buck-Morss writes that what survives in the archives does so by chance; "disappearance is the rule."[1] In July 2019, my father handed me a thick, yellowed folder with a faded stamp bearing the seal of the Stasi Records Agency (BStU). His aging voice seemed strained: "Why don't you read this!" We had performed this ritual every few years over the last two decades, and, like so many times before, I was about to put the material back on his desk. In the 1990s, I had spent weeks reading the voluminous files of GDR writers such as Jurek Becker and Christa Wolf, which brimmed with meticulously collected half-information. After that, I consciously decided not to let the Stasi shape my family's story.

That July, however, with the thirtieth anniversary of the fall of the Wall approaching, I opened the folder. I scattered a bunch of notecards, forms, resumés, self-evaluations, ID images, and handwritten letters on the table. Sitting across from my father in the cookie-cutter apartment in East Berlin where I grew up, I began sorting them by date: 1955, 1957, a long stretch of nothing, then 1969, and then a cluster of documents from 1978. Thinking back to the seventies—I was a teenager then—there had been a period when he seemed uncharacteristically stressed. But the source of that stress could not be discussed by my family. I'd felt a sense of insecurity that seemed to have no referent. Looking at his file decades later, I noticed a copy of the recruitment form in the pile, prepared for signing to confirm my father's collaboration as IM (*Inoffizieller Mitarbeiter*, unofficial collaborator). But the signature box is blank. According to *Führungsoffizier* K., several conspiratorial meetings had occurred. When I looked up at my father, he shook his head: he did not recall such a series of events. Another note, added later by the officer to the record, stated that, in fact, only a single meeting took place in which the "target" (my father) declared that he was not suited to the work of a *Geheimmann* (informant). What if that note had gone missing in the archive? I thought about the pressures he must have faced. The possible threats of reprisals. And why had it taken me so long to look at the files? Of course, in retrospect, the reason is clear; everything about the GDR after 1989 rendered a person's proximity to the socialist state as nefarious and improper. In the memory management of post-reunification Germany there existed no framework for my father's actual outcome: the paradoxical stance of someone who maintained an (implicated) utopian political loyalty and also refused to comply with the Stasi.

Farther down in the file were notes from "IM Erich," the unofficial informant who had reported on my father (later revealed to be a colleague and friend). He'd preserved only the pieces that accorded with the GDR's cause, praising my family as "harmonious," "culture-loving," and "decent citizens." I felt an unexpected twitch of pride, but then I remembered that this person had been made the executor of our private memory estate. The notes continued with descriptions of our family attending the classical concert season of '78 in the newly opened GDR parliament building, the *Palast der Republik*—which, by the time I sat reading those notes, had long since been demolished. Banal details flashed through my mind. The purple polyester jumpsuit I'd worn to accompany my parents for the first time to an evening event, the plush seats in marigold velvet lining the assembly, long since discarded in a damp storage unit on the outskirts of Berlin. Secret files, it seemed, make marvelous memory aids. Or were the recollections prompted by the Stasi record illegitimate, desecrated, and best left untouched?

Intermedial Contingencies in *Karl Marx City* (2016)

Thirty years after the collapse of Communism and the fall of the Berlin Wall, the public memory of the postwar era is more closely linked than ever with the legacy of the Stasi, the secret-service apparatus of the GDR.[2] With nearly fifteen hundred employees, the Stasi Records Agency (BStU) was among the best-funded agencies in the Federal Republic of Germany (FRG). The BStU was located in Berlin but had numerous regional branches across the former East territory. In 2019, the BStU announced that all its holdings would be transferred to the Federal Archives (Bundesarchiv) within the next two years. Ironically, this decision led to a public outcry among the parliamentary representatives of the right-wing party Alternative for Germany (AfD), who accused the FRG government of denying the crimes of the SED regime by closing this chapter of the past. In actuality, the transfer was designed to protect Stasi documents permanently and only involved a new structure of oversight and no physical relocation of the files.[3]

The Stasi Records Archive, in Berlin-Lichtenberg, will continue to house over a hundred kilometers of shelved records of GDR citizens, including a total of about forty-one million index cards—organized into more than four thousand subsystems—and countless amounts of surveillance footage, photographs, and microfiche. According to the BStU, the stream of applicants, who were either researchers or former GDR citizens wishing to gain access to their own Stasi files or those of deceased relatives, had remained steady since 1989. In addition to the BStU's dominant administrative role spanning three decades post-unification, Germany's public memorial culture manages the history of the Stasi and keeps it alive. The former Stasi prison in Berlin-Hohenschönhausen is a focal point for obligatory school trips, during which high school students also visit Checkpoint Charlie and pass through the city's Wall Memorial Park at Bernauer Strasse. In these spaces, as I have shown in chapter 1, the GDR perpetually emerges in public and national memory as the second dictatorship in the aftermath of the Third Reich.

As of 2018, anyone can experience the weight of all the conspiratorial evidence collected by the GDR regime. That year the Stasi Records Agency in Berlin opened a new exhibit entitled *Access to Secrecy* (*Einblick ins Geheime*), which is billed as a "Monument to Surveillance" ("Monument der Überwachung") and takes tourists and visitors inside the stacks.[4] After leaving their belongings with a guard, visitors are led through the narrow basement hallways of the institution and then into one of the archive wings. While most of the hundreds of movable shelves in the archival stacks are shut, forming a grey wall, one open section reveals mountains of records. It is easy to get distracted by the sheer number of carefully bundled files, the piles of faded Marxism books, and row upon row of thick, black, old-fashioned leather satchels or to stumble on the giant sacks, filled with millions of shredded paper snippets, that sit on the floor. According to the guide, the satchels were taken directly from the Stasi archive in the GDR and are the most effective way (even in this technological age) to preserve the evidence of people's lives under total surveillance.

In this chapter, I turn to the low-budget film *Karl Marx City* (2016), directed by the German-American artist team Petra Epperlein and Michael Tucker. A relatively unknown film, *Karl Marx City* tells the story of an East German family in the interstices of public and personal memory, and of the role played by visual records and archival technologies in the trans- and post-generational transmissions of the past. After numerous long takes through the iconic BStU stacks in Berlin, a pivotal scene in the film takes the viewer into the quiet space of an archival reading room. Surrounded by large industrial shelves lined with document folders, we see the filmmaker

Petra Epperlein poring over countless meticulously cataloged photographs, which were taken by the Stasi during the street protests in the fall of 1989. Inspecting these photographs with a magnifying glass, Epperlein attempts to glean evidence of a personal and collective past that has slipped away over the course of more than two decades. What is at stake amid these innumerable anonymous sources is the past of Epperlein's family—especially her father's suicide in 1998—as well as the vanishing of the German Democratic Republic, the country in which the filmmaker grew up. After a brief pause, her focus falls on an oversized file containing key photographic documents, which Epperlein, wearing white gloves, handles with care; she wishes to exculpate her father from suspicions that he may have collaborated with the Stasi. She locates a 1989 protest photograph showing her father and announces her find, incredulously, to the camera. Her discovery and her reaction emphasize the role of photographic images and archives in shaping personal and public memory—the topic the film sets out to investigate.

Throughout this book, I have noted the capacity of minor archives to retrieve and remodulate memories of the transitional year 1989–90. These provisional archives release unfulfilled impulses of a more collectively oriented future. I have shown how this subterranean knowledge often lingers on the periphery of official memory circuits, outside the stabilizing post–Cold War narrative that positions the FRG as national victor. The previous chapters touched on the significance of the Stasi for Germany's official memory politics, in particular the government's ability to delegitimize the history of the GDR and to subjugate East Germans, in Heiner Müller's words, to a sense of collective guilt.[5] *Karl Marx City* enters this contested field of post-1989 memory politics but does so on its own self-reflexive terms. While the West German director Florian Henckel von Donnersmarck's successful melodrama *The Lives of Others* (*Das Leben der Anderen*) (2006) ultimately does not question the status of the Stasi Records Agency as a permanent repository of truth,[6] Epperlein and Tucker's *Karl Marx City* probes the archive as an institution bound up with state power and violence. Marketed solely for an international, English-speaking audience, the documentary has been praised by the *New York Times* as a highly personal addition to the growing corpus of distressingly relevant tales about the relationship between government and private life, a corpus that includes George Orwell's *1984* and Hannah Arendt's works on totalitarianism.[7]

At first, the film appears to support a conclusive, evidentiary reading of the GDR as a totalizing surveillance state. Portions of the documentary consist of seamlessly intercut surveillance footage, propaganda films, and Stasi snapshots (which contribute to the viewer's own sense of being watched) and an extensive sequence shot in the BStU archive in Berlin. These scenes illustrate the Stasi's efforts to document every aspect of people's lives in search of conspiratorial activities. Yet, the film is also invested in self-reflexive artistic modes of performativity and mediation, as were West German feminist documentarians such as Helke Sanders and Ulrike Ottinger decades earlier.[8] For example, throughout the film, we see Epperlein ostentatiously carrying large headphones and an oversized microphone. Perhaps because Epperlein, who is not only the filmmaker but the film's protagonist, is so close to the story the production team portrays, the film is marked by a mix of sincerity and heightened artifice. Peppered with pop-cultural sensibilities, the film has a camp style similar to the pair's earlier documentaries like *The Prisoner or: How I Planned to Kill Tony Blair* (2006).[9] Early on, we see Epperlein with her audio equipment standing at the shores of the Atlantic coast in the United States, gazing over the water into the horizon. A fast-paced montage invokes a reflexive longing for East Germany (*Ostalgie*), a feeling that is questioned the moment it arises. Across the screen flicker the shards and remains of that vanished past, including family photographs of Epperlein's socialist youth ceremony, a newsreel about the 1971 erection in her hometown of the Marx monument designed by Soviet sculptor Lev Kerbel, and footage of DEFA *Indianerfilme*. Meanwhile, a voice-over by the co-directors' daughter narrates this sequence with just enough irony to resonate with both socialism's failure and, arguably, its historical possibility.

Intermedial spaces, I contend, are particularly well suited as performative loci of alternative knowledge and counter-memory. Self-constituting and unstable, they have the potential to open up the epistemic foreclosures that have contributed to preserving the neoliberal status quo in Germany's public memory politics. I have termed these alternative spaces "future archives," or "archives of the future," by which I refer to open-ended, unfinalizable, and often subterranean channels of memory and knowledge production. The post-1989 mnemonic sites and events I have explored so far perform, self-theorize, or, in the case of the Berlin Wall Memorial (Gedenkstätte Berliner Mauer), adopt and institutionalize a kind of archival impulse. Hal Foster defines this impulse as ramifying practices that "seek to make historical information, often lost or displaced, physically present."[10] I have noted both the ephemeral and material dimensions of these minor and official transmissions. More than anything, and perhaps paradoxically, the concept of the archive has served as a useful analogy to track discarded, unformed, and fugitive memories. In this chapter, I turn to institutionalized archival collections—the "real" archives, so to speak. I examine the BStU archive as an official repository where institutionalized forms of national memory are controlled.[11] With these reified grand palaces of historical information in mind, I return to the disjunctive minor key of interstitial practices and to this book's claim that such practices produce and circulate an alternative post-1989 memory.

Given the global publicity for *Karl Marx City*, it must appear that Epperlein and Tucker cater to the market's desire for retrograde Stasi films. But the art documentary is more interested in exploring the complex role that photography plays in mediating personal and public memory than it is in exposing the GDR as a surveillance state per se (an interpretation championed by the film's press kit and by reviewers).[12] In this regard, the film's handling of photographs as intermedial spaces is vital. As David Campany and others have suggested, if we were to survey all moments in which cinema deploys photos—and they are countless—we would find that most evoke the complex status of the photograph as evidence.[13] We saw that photographic images are often enlisted as historical records in the sphere of public memory, even if these images rarely disclose any of the volatility and open-ended promise of '89–90. Challenging the evidentiary role of these photographs used by memorial installations in Germany today, I have argued that photographic images are a particularly suitable medium for delineating a future-oriented memory. These memorial photographs function as archival records and as cipher. They elicit spectators who collectively assemble public memories and who are called equally to interrogate what is shown in public space about the peaceful revolution in the late GDR and what is left out. More importantly, once sited (and sighted) in the situated urban geographies, these modular image archives in Leipzig and Berlin, we saw, can force us both to recognize and resist the very conditions of the uneven distribution of the visible produced by hegemonic memory regimes. In *Archive Fever*, Derrida calls on photographic images, in particular, to delineate the notion of an "archive of the future" and describes the work with images (opening to a future to come) as distinct from the work of the historian who must look to the past. This delineation prompts him to ask, "Is there a historian of the promise, a historian of the first door?" Most memorably, Derrida speaks of the decision to step aside and let the photographic specter "speak" as a "sign of respect before the future to come of the future to come."[14] This activist, poetic, and epistemological practice, I have argued, can orient viewers, curators, and scholars toward the unfinalizing impulses of the revolutionary '89 past. Such practice is especially viable when we augment these alternative image archives by uncovering memories in a myriad of other minor artistic, textual, urban, digital, and so forth archives. What I have in mind is less a nudge or a nuance than a paradigm shift in (collective) memory making, a different way of thinking about the crafting of counter-memory. Photographs in film are there to "make us see" and to make us believe. A film essentially comes to a halt while we look at the photograph, register it as different from the flow of cinema (and of narrative), and give it the status of ontological truth. Whether in mainstream or avant-garde, modern or postmodern film, Campany points out, the "proof" of photography as memory or history is nearly always at stake.

However, when stripped of their institutionalized context or any clearly circumscribed relation to an origin, still photographs within the cinematic medium begin to undo what tames them; they begin to produce meanings of their own. In other words, the evidentiary status of still photographs in moving images quickly becomes slippery. This protean nature is amplified when photographs are circulated to work out the incongruous relation between national memory and familial postmemory.[15] In what follows, I first show how the indeterminacy of the photographic image in *Karl Marx City* destabilizes the status of the Stasi Records Agency (BStU) as the sole legitimate proprietor of East German life. Pensive, self-reflexive photographs put the evidentiary status of the archive in a different light. I then turn to the surveillance photo of Epperlein's father at the 1989 protests to discuss the risks of excessive investment in mediation in the current age of false content and "fake news." Here, the decontextualized, found image needs to be touched, quite literally, to secure its ontological index, its foundational truth.[16] This touch, in turn, connects to the other haptics at play in the archive: the dust, the endless rows of paper files, and the feeling of material as evidence that authenticates historical truth.

Finally, through a close examination of the handling and placement of this archival photograph in the concluding scene, I consider how photography can move beyond the evidentiary and help us produce alternative personal and public memories. The photograph Epperlein uncovers offers a provisional resolution of her father's rumored status as Stasi collaborator— and, consequently, some resolution regarding his death in the late 1990s— but it also points to a historic moment that destabilizes established narratives about the GDR and the transition in 1989. Rather than a finalized and stored-away past—the Stasi version of the GDR's dictatorial history the BStU is designed to administer—the film camera scans the photograph for unexposed "spaces of possibility" and future temporalities within a history of revolutionary failure. What strikes me as remarkable is that in both Epperlein's family story and my own, the fear of finding out about one's father's Stasi activity overshadowed all other concerns during this period of upheaval. In the end, I learned that my father had refused to collaborate and did so at great risk. Epperlein also realized that her father did not work for the Stasi and instead was spied upon. In fact, he participated in the uprising of 1989 (which she seemed to have forgotten). Astonishingly, the post-1989

Western logic of interpreting history had worked its way into the minds of the heirs. Rather than remembering the political revolt of 1989, families were caught in the mediated legacy of the GDR as a surveillance state and the frameworks imported by the new order.

Unlearning the Archive

Karl Marx City investigates the possibilities of recovering truth in a vanished past. Although the premise of a daughter tracing the story of her father's suicide might promise an intimate look at her family, this expectation remains unfulfilled. Even the family photographs used in *Karl Marx City* (snapshots of Petra's socialist confirmation ceremony, a photo album with pictures of the parents at a workplace party, or an image of the parents' weekend home) give little texture to the Epperleins' private past. They mainly serve as stand-ins for knowledge and life experience in the GDR. Because these family photos yield no insight into the father's decision to take his own life, the official BStU/Stasi archive is called upon to disclose the truth by supplying clandestinely collected information. More than anything, Epperlein's journey through these archival institutions shapes the film's storyline of discovery and holds the promise of eventually exculpating her father from rumors of his participation in East Germany's oppressive past.

In light of an incomplete familial memory, *Karl Marx City* starts out privileging archives as evidentiary domains above all others. While Petra and her family wait for weeks to receive word on the Stasi file of her father, which could clarify whether he was an informant, Epperlein visits the BStU in Berlin-Lichtenberg. The collection of the former Stasi archive, we learn, includes not only millions of records, images, and strips of surveillance footage but also thousands of miscellaneous files, ranging from interrogation transcripts and intercepted mail to internal documents on espionage and the GDR's business connections with the West. Throughout this segment, placed toward the middle of the film, Epperlein maintains the documentarian's slightly performative, self-conscious pose. Carrying her signature oversized headphones and microphone, she roams the stacks and interviews various experts in the field. However, as we begin to follow her through the stark, barren halls of the archival institution, populated by millions of paper files, the film takes on a somber tonality that exposes the GDR as an undead surveillance machine. Framed in long shots down the archival aisles, Epperlein points her microphone toward the paper folders on the shelves while we hear hundreds of muffled (presumably clandestinely recorded) voices of East Germans in their workplaces and living rooms. Here the film animates the GDR state as a totalizing apparatus that administered the lives of its citizens by harvesting their interior worlds and forcing an institutional passage of their thoughts from the private realm into a secret archival domain.

Certainly, this place is one where the specters of people's dreams of a different GDR were cataloged and processed into an archival logic that almost

FIGURE 3.1. Stasi Records Agency, Berlin. Still from *Karl Marx City* (2017), directed by Peter Epperlein and Michael Tucker.

FIGURE 3.2. Aisle in the Stasi Records Agency, Berlin. Still from *Karl Marx City* (2017), directed by Peter Epperlein and Michael Tucker.

no one could escape. As the soundtrack of diffuse voices slips in and out, we become aware that these archival taxonomies destroyed cultural and social fabrics, silencing people and leaving them wordless. According to memory theorist Aleida Assmann, such secret collections compiled under dictatorships are political archives that function as instruments of domination, utilizing forms of punitive forgetting (*damnatio memoriae*) to eradicate the enemy.[17] Governed by the surveillance regimes of the Stasi, East Germans expected that what they said might be recorded and transcribed into an anonymous filing system. Therefore, many of them learned to censor their speech, until they no longer knew how to speak up. We see Epperlein pass through the stacks of the BStU where voices appear to emanate as whispers from out of archival memory, allowing us to hear "the spectral echo of what they silence."[18] And when a rapidly cut montage of Polaroids captures the work of Stasi staff with the audible click of a camera shutter, we are further reminded that the Stasi's laborious investment in the archive would not have been possible without the technologies of photographic recording and the labor of memorization, repetition, and reproduction—work which was conducted not just by machines but by human beings in mailrooms, in darkrooms, and at the copying bench.

While focused on the historical violence of the Stasi, Epperlein and Tucker's film also exposes the violence of the archive itself. In *Archive Fever* (1995), Jacques Derrida calls our attention to the "politics of the archive"—that is, to the structures and enactments of governmental authority and to the excessive and ultimately gratuitous investment in technologies and procedures involved in mass document collection. Likening the archive to the accumulation of capital, he writes that there is no political power without control of the archive, if not of memory.[19] Performance scholar Diana Taylor also concludes that "the archival, from the beginning, sustains power."[20] Archiving itself, then, must involve forms of selection and forgetting. *Karl Marx City* navigates the taxonomic aisles where the imperial power structure of the BStU comes into full view. The performative interviews with experts who are authorized to represent the institution illuminate how the archive that inherited the GDR's Stasi records was established as a "neutral threshold" separating the past and the present, history and politics.[21] In reality, the BStU performed a central role in the FRG's management of public memory, which was considerably invested in rendering the GDR a totalitarian surveillance state and a successor to the Third Reich.[22] According to its website, the Stasi Records Agency branded its own political efforts in hegemonic and binary fashion: "The better we understand dictatorship, the better we can shape democracy."[23] This kind of branding is characteristic of post-unification memory politics in general, where notions of democracy, dictatorship, and revolution are deployed as though they are transparent terms or self-evident concepts rather than practices, institutions, and systems to be negotiated.

But the violence of the archive is also mitigated by the contents of the collections and their relationship to the lives of the people involved. When protesters stormed the Stasi headquarters in all major East German cities in 1989, Stasi employees left behind tens of thousands of sacks containing an estimated six hundred million pieces of torn-up documents (some of which are displayed today at the permanent museum exhibit *Access to Secrecy*).[24] In 2013, the German government funded a comprehensive archival project to reassemble the shredded documents digitally. These material remnants enabled a fantasy of paper-based history, to draw on Ariella Azoulay's formulation, and the emergence of "historical value" from these leftovers inspired the BStU to accumulate and preserve other people's pasts.[25] Notably, deputy head archivist Johanna Schütterle, whom Epperlein also interviews, interprets the reconstruction of the mangled files as repaying an unsettled debt to society. When we see a female staff member using actual stones as archival tools to flatten the scraps of shredded paper, the fragmented documents become visible as the archive's cherished objects. Although archivists often claim neutrality, and the archive is commonly "envisaged as driven by invisible hands of abstract guardians,"[26] Schütterle announces here—with a sense of responsibility and pride—that "we reconstruct records so that at some indefinite point in the future people will have access to their own files or to those of relatives, and learn something they would have otherwise never known." In searching through the archive for evidence of her father's involvement in the Stasi, Epperlein can also access a past (and, therefore, a future) that, in a world without institutionalized locations of document collection, she would have never encountered.

The palpability of the collections also demonstrates the fraught relationship between the constructions of historical and personal memory. This relationship is demonstrated during an interview between Epperlein and head spokesperson of the Stasi Records Agency, Dagmar Hovestädt, who carefully pulls a set of microfiche out from transparent envelopes. When she runs her fingers over the film, wearing white, oversized gloves, she performs the crucial touch that enhances the material's believability as proof of the Stasi's surveillance activity—even if this touch of a filmstrip already seems to take place at a greater remove than a viewing does, on the Stasi Records Archive's website, of thick, yellowed paper Stasi folders. Those photos used on the website and in the museum exhibit have such an indexical, haptic quality that it is as though, just in looking

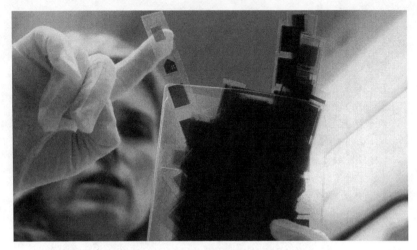

FIGURE 3.3. Archivist of the Stasi Records Agency, Berlin. Still from *Karl Marx City* (2017), directed by Peter Epperlein and Michael Tucker.

at them, one can feel the weight, dust, and smell that authenticate the Stasi records as historical depositories of truth. After picking up the microfiche, Hovestädt explains to Epperlein that the Stasi photographed the envelopes of intercepted mail—which, laid out flat with their flaps open, look like miniature houses. In a kind of poetic double reflection, these negative filmstrips of thumbnail-size houses allegorize the archive as a domicile for the files.[27]

The clinical interior contributes to the archives' perceived scientific objectivity. But cast against the largely white mise-en-scène, these shadow images also suggest that this place has become an eerie, ghostly new residence for the indefatigable post-1989 archival administrators and possibly for the displaced filmmaker. At the beginning of *Karl Marx City*, we learned that Epperlein had left for California after 1989 to release herself from the "voodoo of nostalgia"—the sense that East Germany was a viable home.

If the multivalent meaning and indeterminacy of photographic images remind us that archives are institutions of mediated, assembled evidence at best and hegemonic institutions at worst, then any indexical, trustworthy handling of the Stasi documents is forfeited.[28] Yet what if there is something important to be found amid the reconfigured and revived wreckage of the files? Having unlearned the archive and exposed its artifice in the first half of the film, Epperlein roams the abandoned halls of this temple of truth in an attempt to encounter her own hidden past.

Photographic Contact

Karl Marx City ultimately rejects any simple claim that it is possible to recover truth from a vanished past. If anything, the film's heightened artifice (Epperlein's mobile recording equipment, the austere black-and-white cinematography, the graphic intertitles) underscores a focus on mediation that echoes Benjamin's notion of memory work,[29] where any sifting through the past and its residues will also involve random, fruitless searching. Rather than gaining clarity about her father's past through recall and remembrance, Petra Epperlein appears to become increasingly caught up in the all-encompassing scopic strictures of the Stasi and the surveillance mechanisms the agency once employed. The spectator is drawn with Petra into a kind of "spherical dramaturgy," in which the assemblage of multiple cinematic streams creates a kinetic flow.[30] This assemblage includes surveillance footage recorded by the Stasi, GDR propaganda film, rapidly sequenced Polaroid freeze-frames of the Stasi's clandestine activities, and an array of more personal records such as a home video, documentary-style expert interviews, and narrative sequences of Epperlein visiting her family or roaming the ghostly streets of her hometown. The sheer abundance of visual material creates the sense of a larger structure or presence, where presumably nothing escapes an all-seeing eye.

In the final segment, however, devoted to determining whether we can or should trust any claims about the father's brush with the Stasi, we seem to break through this web of mediation and remediation and arrive at the archive's evidentiary core.[31] The Stasi emerges as a vital recordkeeper under the purview of the BStU, when, right after the last expert interview with Johanna Schütterle, the viewer learns that the father's file has turned up and his reputation is restored. Cutting from the interior of the archive to an exterior street scene, we see Epperlein receive a phone call and then announce to the camera, stunned and visibly relieved, that her father did not work as an informant. In a conspicuous affirmation of binaries (which is at odds with the film's performative artistic style), the documentarian later implies, "Good, he was not one of the bad guys." While we do not hear the voice on the other end (presumably an archivist), the next sequence shows Epperlein, her brothers, and her mother in their apartments poring over copies of the file. Testifying to the Stasi's method of intimate betrayal—or what the politician Wolfgang Thierse has described as the banality of a network in which informers were "friends, neighbors, and even relatives"—a secret is revealed.[32] Not only was the father not a Stasi informer, but he was denounced and spied upon by a family acquaintance, his former boss.

Notably, however, the parsing of the written record dramatized in these scenes (the camera pans over typed and handwritten documents, and the mother reads the denunciation letter aloud) leaves Epperlein with more questions than answers, especially regarding her father's death—an impasse I will take up in a moment. Only by highlighting the discovery of a photograph in the archive and enlisting its evidentiary power as indisputable proof does the film achieve the emotional closure demanded by the family plotline, allowing for a reassertion of the father's moral integrity. As Epperlein returns to the BStU archive, the voice-over (Tucker and Epperlein's daughter) rather lyrically announces, "The last Stasi report on her father was filed in October 1989, a month before the regime fell. What happened in Karl Marx City in those final weeks? Driven by a nagging sense of the familiar, a misplaced memory, a gap between her own recollection and history, she seeks solace in the files." When the film cuts to the spacious interior of what looks like a public office or reading room in the archive, we see Epperlein equipped with a professional, compound-lens magnifying glass. She is bent over a large industrial desk, closely inspecting a contact sheet of photographic images taken during the protests in the streets of Karl Marx City.

At this moment, the film most effectively dramatizes the shifting evidentiary and disclosive capacities of photography in the production of memory.[33] Given pause by a kind of "tactile looking," Epperlein herself takes on the role of the (positivist) archivist, ever so closely tied to the production of the original, indexical meaning.[34] Following Epperlein as she grasps the meaning of images through her ocular and manual touch, the film enlists the

FIGURE 3.4. Petra Epperlein examines archival files. Still from *Karl Marx City* (2017), directed by Peter Epperlein and Michael Tucker.

photographs in a process of haptic authentication, highlighting the ability of visual imagery to activate senses other than sight.[35] Once the still photographs expand and fill the frame of view, the tactile material creases in the visual records (photographic objects) become visible. They bear the indexical traces of the archivist's handling—or, more likely, of the Stasi's attempt at destruction. At this point, the film slips back into a self-reflexive, mediated register. A rapid montage animates archival stills of the unrest in Karl-Marx-Stadt's public square (photos taken by the Stasi in 1989) and brings the mood of risk and danger palpably alive through a sound mix that includes snippets of an approaching helicopter, muffled street chanting, and dramatic music swelling in and out. Unlike light, sound does not leave an imprint on the photograph.[36] Yet here, the photographs' silence is filled with the distant noises of motors and streetcars and the chatter of organizing crowds. Especially when pictures show the GDR's paramilitary troops lining up in front of demonstrators, our minds insist we are watching a fragment of a lived and potentially volatile historic moment.

This segment also echoes an earlier nighttime sequence of grainy Stasi surveillance footage capturing the violent response by state security forces to the mass riots near Dresden's main train station in early October, when some of the nineteen designated trains carrying East Germans who had escaped to the FRG embassy in Prague and Warsaw were expected to pass through the GDR to the West.[37] This leaderless unrest soon escalated into violent and uncontrollable confrontations. As with any mass frenzy, clear lines between protesters, bystanders, police, and paramilitary troops

FIGURE 3.5. GDR police in the fall of 1989. Still from *Karl Marx City* (2017), directed by Peter Epperlein and Michael Tucker.

FIGURE 3.6. Demonstrators in the fall of 1989. Still from *Karl Marx City* (2017), directed by Peter Epperlein and Michael Tucker.

quickly eroded. 1,300 people were arrested, and hundreds of citizens went missing without a trace in the ensuing days.[38] *Karl Marx City* reminds us, once more, that raw, eruptive, and bodily events, such as this one in Dresden, tend to be eclipsed by the FRG's public memory, which depends on a tamer, pacifying narrative of the so-called Peaceful Revolution and culminates in the nonviolent *Wende* in Leipzig on October 9.

Not only does the animated still-photo sequence of the public protests in Karl-Marx-Stadt, together with the surveillance footage of Dresden, remind the viewer that hardly any film footage existed of these early protests against the regime until October 9; it also explores the complex relationship between photography and film—between the still and the moving image. Together with the mimetic clicks of the camera shutter, which signal the role of the informers in the demonstrating crowd, *Karl Marx City* creates a sequence of moving images that resembles a photo story. Equally anchored in historical reality and cast through multiple distinct perspectives—that of the Stasi, the archival collection, and the third-generation voice-over—this animated scene of protest memory, we come to realize, is also constructed.

TOUCHING PROOF

Despite the film's emphasis on the instability of memory transmission, the documentary ends with an arresting scene that makes strong claims to authenticity. In the final two minutes, the entire visual, haptic, and spatial choreography of Epperlein's archival work comes to a standstill. With our attention focused on a single still image, we witness a "process of becoming"[39] that belongs as much to memory as to photography and the magical power ascribed to still images to stand in for the past. The relationship between the perceived authenticity of photography and personal and public memory managed by the archive is crucial here. In the final scene, Epperlein reveals two mid-size sheets of paper with faded color photographs from a large archive folder. With magnifying glass in hand, she carefully handles the contents with the iconic white gloves previously shown worn by archival BStU administrator Dagmar Hovestädt and also by the Stasi. We see the sheets first from their blank backs, and then—in a nearly full-frame, over-the-shoulder shot—we realize that these images were taken at one of the clandestine citizen assemblies that occurred inside churches and theaters in the early fall of 1989. Looking up from the file, Epperlein halts in silence (over barely perceptible sounds) and tells the camera, "That's me . . . and my father." With the photo in hand, the autobiographical documentarian invites the viewer to become a pensive spectator, as it were. Epperlein wants to affirm her father's innocence through the existence and veracity of the photograph and the truth afforded to the archive, but this moment of recognition also illustrates the fraught relationship between the archive, photography, and memory.

In this final scene, the role of photographs in film as intermedial thinking space comes into full effect. Building on Roland Barthes, film theorist Raymond Bellour describes as "pensive" the "response of the spectator

FIGURE 3.7. Petra Epperlein and her father at an assembly in 1989. Still from *Karl Marx City* (2017), directed by Peter Epperlein and Michael Tucker.

faced with a photograph or freeze frame in a film. Pensiveness is a suspension, a moment of anticipation when things hang in the balance. Literally and psychologically, the still image causes a pause."[40] This suspension, this gap, this space between (forgotten) memory and history, snaps into place, so to speak, once Epperlein recognizes herself and her father. The over-the-shoulder shot, showing them together at a protest meeting in early October 1989, enhances the photo's status as a piece of evidence for what is presumed to be the father's innocence and integrity—as he ultimately resisted the GDR regime. David Campany writes, "Viewing a photograph in a film is very different from viewing it directly. Film tends to overstate the photograph's difference while presenting that difference as if it were its essence."[41] There are varying accounts of time at work in the moving and in the still image. And it is the qualities that distinguish photograph from film that are exaggerated here: its stillness, its temporal fixity, its objecthood, its silence—even its deathliness, as if it were turned to stone.

To a large degree, what we witness in this scene is media and photographic theory in reverse. The closure of the Stasi's narrative of the Epperlein family and the intersubjective encounter between the father and the daughter require the photograph to be imbued with the status of a record—that is, with strong indexical certainty and relevance as evidence, and with a physical relation to its original. From Barthes to Sontag, photography theory has increasingly distanced itself from such an approach since the 1970s.[42] And given Epperlein and Tucker's previous work in contexts rich with media technology, it is safe to assume they are aware of this distancing as well.[43] Although we watch the film in a digital format (which enables us to construct new associative networks of meaning by skipping from scene to scene), the final segment reminds us that contact with the father, across time, is enabled by an analog photograph that attests to his physical presence and the idea that something or someone, in that past moment depicted by the photograph, was indeed there. In *Death 24x a Second: Stillness and the Moving Image*, Laura Mulvey explains this power of the evidentiary: "Whatever their limitations, photographic machines register the image inscribed by light on photosensitive paper, leaving the trace of whatever comes in front of the lens."[44] The irony of discovering the truth about the father in the very archive of the oppressive regime that placed him under surveillance is not lost on the filmmakers. As the camera holds the photograph in full frame, the voice-over concludes that now she remembered what she knew all along. She was there in the theater that day, next to her father. "Of all the things the Stasi recorded, this moment is surely true. The picture was taken as evidence. In another version of history, it would have been used against them. Instead, the Stasi unwittingly captured the father she always knew." Then, as if to echo the "violent shutter of the archive" itself, the film promptly cuts to a final, black intertitle, with the dedication "For my father."

At the end of this chapter, I return to the enigmatic protest image in *Karl Marx City* to show how this visual object, the photograph of Petra and her father, functions as a portable, unforeclosed "archive of the future" situated in the interstices of Germany's contemporary memory politics. Thus far, I have focused on intermedial relations of still photography and moving images—and especially the sensory, indexical register of touch—to explore the slippages of personal and public memory embedded in the BStU's hegemonic archival control in the aftermath of the GDR's historical erasure. Before I take up this final archival photograph of Petra and her father one more time, I turn to the film's elegiac inquiry into the father's suicide. Attention to a lower frequency of mourning running through the film reveals a different line of narrative and psychic reasoning for the father's death—one that is not associated with the reach of the Stasi but with the politics of revolutionary failure and the neoliberal absorption of the demolished GDR.

Memory and Death: A Post-1989 Elegy

At first sight, Epperlein's speculation that her father's suicide may have been related to a (wrongful) revelation of his Stasi complicity appears plausible. Especially when we consider the grave concern—if not hysteria—that initially surrounded the confrontation with the Stasi legacy in the volatile post-Wall public sphere.[45] In "Memories and Fantasies about and by the Stasi," critical theorist David Bathrick pointed out that starting in the spring of 1990, the cultural industry began to shift away from a focus on redemptive revolutionary events and toward a punitive discourse—likening the Stasi, for example, to a sea monster whose tentacles had enveloped every aspect of East German public and private life. On March 26, 1990, the liberal weekly news magazine *Der Spiegel* ran a cover story titled "The Long Arm of the Stasi," showing a picture of such a giant cartoonish creature.[46] Soon after, the political and cultural life of the GDR—and of the many who intentionally or unwittingly contributed to its peaceful revolution—would be presented as nearly synonymous with the Stasi. Together with the frenzy of post-Wall allegations, this phantasm helped sustain a turbulent period when a wave of verbal aggression was directed toward those who had worked with the Ministry of State Security (MfS). A stream of sensational revelations about Stasi collaborations hit the headlines in the tabloid press

146 ‹ CHAPTER THREE

nearly every day. A mixture of fact and fiction, these headlines fueled the public's anger and bolstered a culture of stigmatization.

Karl Marx City amplifies this heightened atmosphere of denunciation following the demise of a socialist dictatorship that fostered spying on one's neighbor. Close-ups of a series of anonymous, typewritten mailings that accuse Epperlein's father of having worked as a Stasi informer are crosscut with footage of Nazi rallies and thus situate the post-1989 culture of (false) allegations within a longer temporal trajectory.[47] While the voice-over comments that "they say every family has a secret," we learn these letters were sent to the father (presumably, to his new boss) in the fall of 1990. Only now, fifteen or so years later, interviewing her mother, Epperlein appears to find out that her parents kept from their children that he had first attempted suicide in the spring of 1991. Epperlein herself expresses regret that it had never occurred to her to ask about her father's past in the wake of the GDR's unmooring. Yet, even taking these familial and historical contexts into consideration, the father's suicide in 1998 remains the unresolvable secret of the film. For it is worth noting that Stasi accusations were not uncommon and that the truth about someone's collaboration could rarely be established beyond any reasonable doubt. Even those prominent figures accused early on of having worked as secret informants could not be convicted or suspended from public office. Defining the relative guilt of unofficial employees of the Stasi in a legal context often proved difficult. Perhaps because these allegations could not be settled in judicial terms, the official memory discourse around the thirtieth anniversary of the fall of the Wall in 2019 was still haunted by these high-profile cases.[48] But in the 1990s, the public's initial outrage after the opening of the files gradually subsided, superseded by the considerable material and social concerns resulting from unification and colored by the revelation that the majority of people had not, in fact, ever been under direct surveillance.[49]

While the enigma of the father's decision to take his own life is never dispelled (if anything, the film's poetic language accentuates the irresolvable ambiguity around this event), the directors do appear to lay some tracks for us to follow. In contrast to the mythmaking of *The Lives of Others* regarding the link between suicide and the repressive regime of the GDR, *Karl Marx City* subtly orients the viewer toward the larger political and socioeconomic (and perhaps symbolic) significance of the father's suicide in the aftermath of 1989.[50] The documentary hints at an alternative understanding situated outside the dominant frameworks of the Stasi pre- and post-1989. During a dimly lit night scene, we see how Epperlein removes the father's suicide note (which he sent only to her) from her personal archive (an old-fashioned suitcase stuffed with paper folders, functions as a mini-depository of the past, a portable, mobile archive emphasizing the haptic). First, Epperlein opens the envelope (placed next to a large heap of coins) and reads out loud the brief handwritten note it contains, while we hear in the background the muted track of a haunting microtonal chamber piece. "Indeed, it would be time to emigrate from Germany, forever! But because you are still so young—not like me! Warm regards, December 22, 1998." The envelope also contains a postcard that Epperlein had sent her parents "after the first and last free election in the GDR," which took place on March 18, 1990, and the father remarks in the suicide note that he kept this card all those years. Looking at the camera, the daughter comments that her father may have been unhappy with the state of Germany, and adds, in disbelief, "But you don't kill yourself because you are unhappy with your country, do you?" Next, like a detective, the camera takes in the elusive postcard image—an open door, revealing a blank space of diffuse light, which enhances the poetic, metaphorical quality of the connection between memory and death, and the tenuous link between fact and fiction accentuated by the film. However, in one of the post-screening interviews the directors gave to a college audience in the United States, in 2017, Epperlein appeared more direct when she explained that after the Wall fell, East Germans, especially of her parents' generation, "were basically like immigrants, without having left the place where they were living."[51]

The film project, shown and advertised on the international film and academic circuits, begins to circulate a post-1989 collective memory at the periphery of the German public sphere. Nearly thirty years after the GDR collapsed, East Germans' internal displacement and perceived disenfranchisement becomes figurable in a borrowed language of migration. I will turn to this silent discourse and imperceptible sense of a quasi-migrant status in the last chapter of this book. Suffice it to say that a closer inspection of the postcard object resituates the father's death more palpably in relation to the failure of the so-called Peaceful Revolution. Such reframing is only possible with the digital technology of stopping the DVD on the computer and thus turning the scholar herself, uncomfortably, into a kind of spy. The postcard included in the father's suicide note in 1998 functions both as unreliable evidence and palimpsest. For a second, we see that attached to the card the daughter had mailed to her parents a decade earlier is a small local newspaper clipping of an excerpt from Wolf Biermann's obituary (*Nachruf*) for the GDR that was originally published in the West German newspaper *Die Zeit* in early March 1990.[52] The political songwriter had been famously expelled by the GDR in 1976. Shortly before the election on March 18, 1990 (where the CDU, as part of the Alliance for Germany would win the majority of votes), Biermann castigated the rise of a national spirit among the masses who demanded the "total and immediate annexation [*Anschluss*] of the East by the West" after the collapse of the Iron Curtain, and he ridiculed the Left in East and West for "look[ing] on from the sidelines, dumbly smiling." Scribbled in the margins of the newspaper snippet are Epperlein's barely legible handwritten words, which have faded over time, appealing to her parents not to feel too despondent (*geknickt*).

THE TRAUMA OF *ABBRUCH* (TERMINATION)

There is a pattern in post-1989 literature of symbolically associating a father's suicide with the failure of an alternative social(ist) vision.[53] Not only did the GDR fail in 1989–90, but so did the oppositional civil rights movements that emerged from the disintegrating East German society (see chapter 4). Adding insult to injury, by the mid-1990s leading figures of the New Forum had either been erased from public memory or aligned themselves with the new order. Although I'm not suggesting the film necessarily ties the father's historical disappointment to this strand of history, the postcard with the suicide note certainly invites speculations. After the election defeat in March 1990, and particularly after Germany's unification, civil rights activists seemed to have lost their progressive visions. A small independent faction of the New Forum continued to exist after forming Alliance '90 in February 1990 (which gained only a handful of seats in the transitional GDR parliament and subsequently in the Bundestag). In the mid-1990s, however, the New Forum appeared to be at an endpoint when discussions took place about whether the organization should be dissolved. Critics argued that the relevance of the New Forum was kept alive, however, through the media-effective trial of Gregor Gysi, which was initiated by Bärbel Bohley and Katja Havemann in 1994. In August 1995, the former activists also met at a high-profile event in Bohley's Berlin apartment with Germany's chancellor, Helmut Kohl. The sidelined activists intended to recenter their concern with the *Aufarbeitung* (reappraisal) of the GDR as *Unrechtsstaat* (illegitimate state), including the SED crimes and the Stasi, in Germany's official public discourse. In response, some of their former compatriots argued that, rather than organizing resistance against the new injustices of the *Wende*, such as the Treuhand (Trust Agency) or a social politics that fostered drastic inequality, these activists had finally sold out for good and betrayed the values of the dissident movement.[54] The critics lamented that the inheritance of the East German civil rights movement in hegemonic and collective memory was deformed, if not erased.[55] The testament of the revolution was recast as the legacy of the Stasi. There existed no stable frameworks whereby the revolutionary unrest and its radically democratic politics could become legible, I have argued in this book. Of course, civil rights activism and leftism were not necessarily synonymous in the post-1989 political realm. By the late 1990s, some former civil activists who played central roles in the revolutionary fall had aligned themselves with the centrist, conservative politics of unified Germany, and taken on key positions in the FRG state apparatus.[56] While officially this trend was lauded as sign of the East's successful integration, progressive civil rights activists viewed it as cooptation. This narrative of cooptation, if not betrayal, can be traced back to December 1989, when the citizens' group Democratic Awakening (of which Angela Merkel incidentally was a member) transformed itself into a political party and joined the conservative Alliance for Germany, which won the last elections in the GDR and set the country on the inevitable course toward "reunification." This victory is the one that—on the postcard included in the father's suicide note of 1998—is remembered as defeat.

Now, sociologists drawing from Émile Durkheim have argued that larger political undercurrents related to the *Wende* did not lead to increased suicide rates in East Germany.[57] They also surmise that sudden historical events (in contrast to a gradual breakdown of society) are not affectively interlinked with the intimate decision to end one's own life—even if, in Epperlein's case, uncovering such undercurrents provides new contexts and frameworks in which to shed light on the father's self-erasure in 1998, at the age of fifty-seven. Needless to say, I'm not talking about Epperlein's real father but about the "character" constructed in the film. Before 1989, the father emerging here did not exactly traffic in the cultural-dissident milieu that shaped the *Wende*. In the nighttime scene in which Epperlein tries to decipher the suicide note, the carefully placed GDR identification photo—a utilitarian image created for bureaucratic purposes—reminds the viewer that Epperlein's father was caught in the official strictures of the GDR. "He worked at the Heckert Kombinat, where he was the assistant to the director," the voice-over later states. According to theorists of institutional photography such as Tina Campt and Ariella Azoulay, quotidian portraiture used for administrative purposes involves a certain form of indirect violence. At the same time as the repressive genre of identification images reduces those photographed to state subjects, these utilitarian pictures also signal an opportunity. Often showing the person dressed in official attire (as is the case with Epperlein's father), this type of headshot strives to enunciate aspiration and respectability, albeit within the regulated regimes of social and geographic mobility.[58]

Listening to the lower frequencies of the documentary film, one can detect another barely articulated narrative, which belongs not to the violent oppression of the GDR regime or the defeat of the civil rights movement but to the forceful collapse of people's lives during the *Wende*. Asked about the fall of the Berlin Wall, Epperlein's mother replies, "Well, then we were unemployed. Dad too. In his VEB Mechanisierung [a tool-manufacturing company] they didn't want him anymore. So, he sold watchbands. And I sold newspapers." With 40 percent of all employees in the GDR tool-manufacturing industry working in the district of Karl-Marx-Stadt, the privatization of industries by the Treuhand (Trust Agency) hit that area particularly hard.[59] Overall, a third of all jobs vanished in East Germany within three years of unification. She struggles to speak about how the life they were used to was suddenly terminated (*brach ab*). Pausing often, she strains to explain that "what one had acquired in all these years . . . the knowledge . . . and the careers . . . there was suddenly nothing left. . . . That is difficult for some and easier for others," she adds. "I adjusted to the new life, I think, relatively easily. I enjoyed doing something new. "[60] Then the interview suddenly breaks off, Epperlein's mother says almost inaudibly, "I can't do this anymore," and the narrative of how these abrupt changes affected her husband remains unarticulated and falls into a silent void.

Indeed, there is a statistical link between the rise of a precarious sense of masculinity and self-destruction. *Karl Marx City* recognizes this link and stitches together snippets of fictional and real narratives of suicide by men in crisis.[61] Historian Udo Grashoff, an expert in suicide studies, is also interviewed by Epperlein for this personal and collective memory project. In 2006, Grashoff commented for the centrist news magazine *Focus* on the so-called post-*Wende* suicide phenomenon, which disproportionally affected men aged forty-five to sixty-five between 1989 and 1991 (the same period in which the father attempted suicide for the first time).[62] The tender, almost intimate conversation between Epperlein and Grashoff on camera, however, does not turn to the historical studies specific to the post-unification East. Instead, they focus on the universal and personal grammar of suicide letters, looking for traces of love expressed to the daughter in the enigmatic note the father left behind in 1998.

The traumatic undoing of people's lives in the aftermath of the *Wende* reverberates in the representational and mnemonic archives assembled in this book. For Epperlein's parents, the economic fallout appears to have been compacted to the year 1990, when the "Arbeitsgesellschaft DDR" (work society of the GDR) collapsed overnight. The collapse can be graphed and registered in statistics, but its long-lasting effects on people's livelihoods can hardly be grasped.[63] Consider Ingo Schulze's 2005 novel *Neue Leben*, which provides a fictionalized account of the privatization of GDR industries, such as newspaper and book publishing. The narrative shows how divergent material conditions almost instantly cut through post-1989 society.

West German cars had turned into icons of moderate post-unification success, available to East Germans who blanketed the new states in mid-level sales jobs for Western-run conglomerates (often until those companies had established themselves in the Eastern territory and those intermediary jobs became superfluous). Indeed, Epperlein's father appears to have been employed and reportedly drove a company car. Sociologists have shown, however, that the dissatisfaction with the new institutional order was not predominantly of an economic nature, even if the discontent in the East was first attributed to the shocks imposed by the economic and monetary union of July 1990. After all, the introduction of an open-market economy in East Germany was accompanied by massive deindustrialization and double-digit unemployment rates. Yet, according to these studies, the older generation tended to be more dissatisfied with the outcomes of systematic change than younger ones, a trend researchers related to the probable experience of discrimination and West German paternalism after unification and to the persistence of socialist values and aspirations.[64]

Thus, the peril of postcommunist life belatedly became the spectral, almost secret (shameful) subject of Tucker and Epperlein's 2016 film, which focuses on the complex memory of Stasi surveillance. Two and a half decades after Germany's reunification, Epperlein's return to her deserted hometown may have seemed highly stylized, if not misplaced at first sight. The haunting scenes of the deserted city were filmed in 2016, and they seem to belong as much to the present as to the early post-1989 past.[65] But as the filmmaker roams the desolate streets, passing by decaying prewar buildings, cemeteries, vacant stores, and dimly lit sex shops, it becomes clear: the inhabitants left the region not only because Communism was over but because the postcommunist capitalist city failed to sustain the economic livelihood of the people who dwelled there. The voice-over comments, "Karl Marx City was famous for manufacturing precision tools; thousands worked in the factories. After the Wall fell, the highest bidder purchased the factories with the promise of a future that never arrived! A quarter of the population moved away, whole neighborhoods abandoned, slated for demolition. The suicide rate of middle-aged men peaked in 1991; in 2006, Chemnitz [formerly Karl-Marx-Stadt] had the lowest recorded birthrate in the world." In a performative, ironic posture, the filmmaker herself may have crossed the deserted city and eventually walked through a dark underpass, so to speak, into the post-socialist light. Yet the flat voice-over emphasizes the precarious conditions of a postindustrial era, which Karl Marx-Stadt would come to share with cities such as Manchester, Lyon, Flint, and Detroit. Repeated shots of Lev Kerbel's colossal Marx monument signal that the abandoned Soviet Eastern European legacies of greater social equality persist in the East German city after unification. As the modern patron saint of capitalist critique is worshipped by the filmmaker traversing the bleak downtown, the histories of economic decline and stagnation experienced by Western manufacturing cities, resulting in massive job loss, social unrest, and urban devastation in the 1970s and 1980s are also recalled. Literally too heavy to be removed, the Marx sculpture remained as intransigent memorial object amid ruins. In this post-1989 space, multiple failed histories of struggle for better labor conditions in the neoliberal era are invoked.

Unforeclosed Futures

Considering these lingering tonalities of individual and collective loss in the long aftermath of the *Wende*, the contemporary significance of recovering the meaning of the 1989 protest memory at the end of the film becomes all the clearer. In this image, the viewer sees Epperlein and her father inside a church or theater. Although *Karl Marx City* reinvests in an indexical ontology of the photographic image, there is more at stake in this final contact than meets the eye. In fact, by using cinema to think about the medium from which it ultimately evolved (and by doing so in the mediating context of the archive), Epperlein and Tucker steer the spectator in the direction of interpretive work and toward an open-ended encounter with the protest image. For what is referenced but not mentioned here is the citizens' assembly on October 7, 1989, at Karl-Marx-Stadt's Luxor-Palast. Undoing the transcendent teleology of reunification, the film directs us toward the historical interval of 1989—the early fall unrest, when people gathered and acted in concert in the streets of Karl-Marx-Stadt, Leipzig, and Berlin, with no intention of toppling the Wall or ushering in the capitalist democracy of the West. That the film keeps the historical importance of the Luxor-Palast scene effectively secret, and only apparent to those in the know, shows how distant and deeply buried these memories became.

The narrative of Germany's inevitable reunification is well established in public discourse today, while the revolutionary fall is often forgotten. The cinematic tendency to dwell on the photograph as a mute and intransigent object from the past is also present in *Karl Marx City*. The scenes caught by the Stasi photographers in the theater nearly three decades ago are rendered on faded color prints, which are, quite literally, trapped under the magnifying glass Petra uses to inspect the images. But Epperlein and Tucker's film moves this photographic moment (and the particular history of early 1989 protest it represents) out from underneath the temporality of

POSSIBLE ARCHIVES › 153

these selfsame archival taxonomies (of what *did* happen) and into the more inchoate, open-ended realm of the future.

Let us recall that the index has a privileged relation to time, to the moment and duration of its inscription, and that it also has a physical relation to its original, for which it is the sign. Yet even as the index is a record of a fraction of time fixed in the photograph, the moment when rays of light record an object's presence (remember, father and daughter were actually there in the theater), "they also inscribe that moment of time, henceforth suspended."[66] The film's final frames show in blurry close-up the photograph of Epperlein and her father on the upper balcony of the theater. As the material support amplified throughout the scene (lens, magnifying glass, paper, folders, etc.) appears to drop away, the soft tip of the white glove and the now barely perceptible frame of the magnifier stretch into a diffuse outer boundary of the image. The transition recalls the representational subjectivity of a vignetting effect. And with this gesture, the image is eerily brought to life. Stripped of its material scaffolding, the spectral nature of the image and the scene itself is palpable: the figures in the photograph are still, of course, and the eyes of a younger Petra have turned into empty dots in the magnification. The viewer has time to think as the image hangs in the balance.

Rather than revealing evidence, the final image becomes a space for interpretation. By cutting to the poignant dedication intertitle "For my father," the film calls upon the spectator to assign the image meaning. Bound up in structures of trauma, the photograph resonates with the metaphors of erasure and self-erasure that are emphasized in earlier chapters of the film—the fall of the Wall ("within weeks every trace of Karl Marx and the communist past was erased") and the father's suicide ("In 1998, much like Karl Marx City, her father set out to erase himself . . . he then secretly collected and burned all of his papers and photographs"). Almost like a "floating flash," the picture of Epperlein and her father suspends meaning across time, hovering in the gap between "an abandoned past and an unredeemed future"—a language used by the narrative voice early on in the film, as Petra wanders through the gloomy streets of post-1989 Chemnitz, a place she refers to as a "city of ghosts."

Yet, despite the photograph's uncanny quality, the enlarged close-up of Petra and her father alongside protesters appears placid and undersignified in some way. Once Epperlein places the magnifying glass over the image and the extreme close-up simulates the aforementioned vignetting effect, we see only Petra and her father in a kind of contemplative pose in the front row of the balcony. The photograph becomes magnified and pixelated to a point that the affective power of the *punctum* of the *that was* is nearly dispersed. It is precisely because this scene is inward and quiet, I suggest, that the image needs to be heard.[67] Given this amplified stillness, we wonder "what the picture wants from us." W. J. T. Mitchell addresses this question when he describes the capacity of an image to enthrall and transfix its beholders by renouncing direct signs of desire. The power of the picture to call us to contemplate its meaning, he argues, comes from "its indirectness, its seeming indifference . . , its anti-theatrical 'absorption' in its own internal drama."[68] We know what motivates the photograph's appearance (in the archive and in Epperlein and Tucker's film), but what actually motivated the appearance of the attendees in the theater is less clear. If we let the spectral image speak, as it were, it orients us toward the inaudible and unseen realm beyond the film. In a gesture that invites the viewer into a dialogue, we are drawn into a search for other possible archives.

LUXOR-PALAST, KARL-MARX-STADT—OCTOBER 7, 1989

What is elided from the public memory record? What happened in the theater that day and outside in the streets that Germany's narrative of Western neoliberal victory conceals? The first color photograph that Epperlein removed from the transparent sheets of the archive folder might help orient us toward the undisclosed spaces within a history of revolutionary failure. The picture is of a handmade banner on display in the upper balcony of the theater. It reads "Freedom to Travel instead of Mass Flight" (Reisefreiheit statt Massenflucht) and recalls the illegal slogans produced on old fabric and sheets at great personal risk in the early fall of 1989.[69] Those signs were suddenly unfurled by protesters in state-controlled public spaces and in churches. The historian Ilko-Sascha Kowalczuk notes that aside from churches, theatres all across the GDR took on the new role of self-constituting a public sphere during the revolutionary unrest. Starting out in Dresden, where actors from several theatres interrupted their protocols by opening discussions with audiences, many other stages in the GDR followed this initiative. After October 3, dozens of theatres passed resolutions signed by thousands of actors and theatre employees. Actors in many places read these declarations night after night at the beginning of the performance; some theatres changed their programs at short notice and offered plays that directly referenced the tense social situation in the country. Many other institutions, such as the Leipzig Gewandhaus under Kurt Masur, released their stages for public discussions, and countless citizens showed up. Finally, by mid-October, prominent artists began to attend more and more frequently the opposition events in the churches, giving those spaces further legitimacy and leading to a cross-fertilization of the improvised activist movements.[70]

FIGURE 3.8. A clandestine assembly at Luxor-Palast, Karl-Marx-Stadt (October 7, 1989). Still from *Karl Marx City* (2017), directed by Peter Epperlein and Michael Tucker.

The situation was similar in Karl-Marx-Stadt. According to eyewitness accounts, the organizers of the sold-out morning gathering at the Luxor-Palast on October 7, 1989, hoped to read the political resolutions of newly formed (but still illegal) civic activist organizations to diffuse any provocations and establish a civic grassroots dialogue among the activists and between the populace and the state. The organizers also knew the gathering had been infiltrated by the Stasi.[71] Initiated by members of the New Forum and representatives of civil and church groups, citizens assembled at this regional theater located at the periphery of the GDR. This grassroots meeting took place on the same day that state officials in Berlin, accompanied by the Communist Party leader and Soviet Union head of state Mikhail Gorbachev, orchestrated mass parades to celebrate the fortieth anniversary of the founding of the GDR. As in Leipzig on that morning, trucks with state security forces (*Kampfgruppen*) in civilian attire and ostentatious construction helmets had been positioned in the side streets of the theater building in Karl-Marx-Stadt. According to eyewitnesses, the ad-hoc event—silent, foreboding, and tense—led to altercations provoked most likely by the Stasi and was quickly aborted before the resolutions of the clandestine activist groups could be read. Just as in Berlin, Potsdam, Leipzig, Dresden, Plauen, Jena, Magdeburg, Arnstadt, and Ilmenau that day, this illegal impromptu assembly of about four hundred people spilling out of the Luxor-Palast into the public square led to street protests and confrontations with state security forces and police, as animated in Tucker and Epperlein's archival photo story.[72]

156 ‹ CHAPTER THREE

In historical hindsight, the characterization of the GDR as a second dictatorship in Germany's public post-1989 memory discourse foregrounds Stasi terror, the oppression of the GDR regime, and the tearing down of the Berlin Wall (which is often invoked with the iconic footage of East Germans breaking through fences at the Hungarian-Austrian border that opened on September 11, 1989). However, *Karl Marx City*'s final photograph of the assembly at the Luxor-Palast in early fall incites, albeit fleetingly, an alternative memory and reading—one in which people constituted themselves as political subjects through the performance of collaborative, embodied action. Rather than a call for toppling the GDR state, these were provisional, heterogeneous gatherings where people acted in concert, not knowing how things would turn out—or, for that matter, what kind of radical shift one could even ask for. The political resolution of the Städtische Theater (City Theatres) Karl-Marx-Stadt, supported by three hundred signatories, was read to the public later that evening at the small Spielstätte Elisenstrasse and, shortly thereafter, at the Schauspielhaus, both filled to the last seat. The petition characterized the goals of the newly emerging civil movement as follows: "The all-pervasive, fear-induced silence in this society needs to be broken.... The dogmas and taboos in our society have to be dismantled through critical dialogue between society and state so that new potentialities can be set free to provide new perspectives for the development of our country."[73] Of course, the stiff, bureaucratic tone of the State's official language still resonates in this first protest resolution, as though radically new epistemologies have not yet formed. But those who attended the event that night, such as the actor and director Hasko Weber, registered the all-encompassing, persistent force of nonviolence.

Throughout this book, I argue that the nonviolence that ultimately prevailed should not be understood as a *moral* position chosen by individuals in a field of possible action (a meaning adopted by the national narrative of the Peaceful Revolution aiming at Western democracy). Rather, what I attempt to bring into view is nonviolence as a social and political practice that was undertaken in concert and that culminated in resistance to systemic forms of destruction (GDR/Stasi). Nonviolent resistance and cooperation were coupled with a commitment to a world built upon social, economic, and political freedom *and* equality—ideals that challenge the foundational principles of the West.[74] Similar to the unauthorized events that erupted in spaces of the nascent (disobedient) civil sphere in Leipzig, Dresden, Halle, and Berlin that early fall, those in the assembly in Karl-Marx-Stadt's Luxor-Palast "demonstrated their commitment to work together to actualize the radically democratic renewal and transformation of our socialist society" and "to open the theater as a space for a confrontation and engagement with the citizens." An insistence on truth, and on embodying the force of that truth, armed "the people" with matchless power. "The audience," Hasko writes, "rose from its seats and applauded for minutes on end—an unforgettable experience for all involved."[75]

Karl Marx City's final photographic reference to an open-ended, unfinalized story of emerging dialogue and spontaneous collaborative action (not aimed, from within its own temporality, at the fall of the Berlin Wall or the ushering in of neoliberal capitalism) may slip through the selfsame taxonomies established by an archival lens. We must keep in mind that the frames, circuits, and official channels available in the post-1989 public sphere were the outcomes of tacit understandings and wholesale structural shifts in politics and media, fostering new regimes of power. Social institutions, including the FRG's Stasi Record Agency (BStU), the Federal Foundation for the Reappraisal of the SED Dictatorship (Bundesstiftung zur Aufarbeitung der SED-Diktatur), and, of course, the Stasi itself, require far-reaching processes of self-stabilization. To shape the understanding of personal and collective pasts, they privilege certain interpretations over others, forming self-reinforcing dynamics and feedback loops.[76] Taking their cue from Epperlein's personal family story, the directors of *Karl Marx City* invite us to ponder how historical memory is constituted in the course of time and how it is influenced by the successes and failures of our actions, by the ways in which we perceive the relationship between the past and the present, by archives and photography, by our conversations with others, and by the institutional networks in which we move.

Although the film was celebrated for portraying the everyday terror of dictatorship and, at least on the surface, catered to such binaries of totalitarian East Europe and the victorious democratic West, *Karl Marx City*, much like the directors' earlier works—such as *The Last Cowboy* (1998) and *Gunner Palace* (2004)—refuses to give any easy answers. This refusal is most evident where meditations on photography, memory, and the archive intersect. The documentary moves beyond blockbusters such as *The Lives of Others*, which offers a much simpler vision of the archive as a place where the past is found rather than a place where an understanding of the past is shaped amid asymmetrical relations of power. Like *Karl Marx City*, the conclusion of Henckel von Donnersmarck's movie features an iconic scene in the reading room of the BStU. The protagonist, Dreymann, a playwright from former East Germany, is waiting for his victim file. The camera cuts away, and we see the colossal stacks with endless rows of tightly packed filing shelves. Eventually, from the recesses of this archive, the attendant produces a cart piled high with folders, nearly collapsing under their weight. As a voice-over reads the reports in the files out loud, the protagonist discovers the code of his informer, HWH XX/7, and finds next to it a red ink print left behind by the informer's finger—a touch, an index, a haptic sign of truth. Dreymann approaches the archivist in the room, and from an index catalog, the informer's identity is revealed. To be sure, Donnersmarck's tracking of the archival procedure and technology, while cinematically enhanced, is not inaccurate; *Karl Marx City* also includes the naming of the informer who spied on Epperlein's father.

However, ever so powerfully insisting on a kind of performative indexicality of a still photograph, *Karl Marx City* loosens the archive's claims to knowledge, opening into new and possible spaces where the amassing of information has not yet produced its full ideological truth effect.[77] The larger question of "how we know what we know about the past" is at stake in the film. Restoring the interpretive authenticity of the photograph, Epperlein and Tucker remind us of the medium's capacity to refer to an original event while also linking personal memory and collective history, however incompletely. This claim to an indexical ontology may appear out of step with the digital age, where images countlessly proliferate or are altered to produce fake news and false content. But in the end, it is precisely because of this new digital reality and the culture of "post-truth" it fosters that the final analog print of a protest image in Epperlein and Tucker's documentary enacts almost poetically such an emancipatory move. The photograph's tangibility provides an anchor and a strategy for coming to terms with ever-proliferating information; it provides a space for finding meaning and for constructing personal and collective memory. Released from indexicality and context, images may generate multitudinous perspectives and narratives on ever-shifting terrains. The capacity to touch a photograph, however, may allow for the photograph to touch us and, in the process, liberate a memory of the future—here, of a collaborative, radically democratic society that Epperlein, her father, and the East Germans in the theater in 1989 stood for—that had become stuck in the past, or been erased.

Coda: Surveillance Capitalism

In this chapter, I have shown how the self-reflexive, intermedial aesthetic of *Karl Marx City* unsettles a transparent, sociological documentation of (socialist) surveillance. The boundaries between private and public records, legitimate and secret surveillance accounts left behind by the GDR and administered by the BStU archive, are perpetually blurred. Epperlein and Tucker explore how the documentation of socialism turns into remediated post-socialist memory and how this process is hindered or facilitated

POSSIBLE ARCHIVES › 159

through stranded visual objects and vast compilations of files and data. But what ultimately concerns them even more are the much broader, formal, and political questions about the liminal space between surveillance and documentary truth-making in the socialist past and in the neoliberal present.

Karl Marx City's final moment moves these questions about surveillance structures and technologies most poignantly into the contemporary realm inhabited by the viewer. Here, the film appears to ask why we incessantly document everything online in an era in which democracy is perpetually undermined by digital data proliferation and social media has crept into every aspect of our public and private lives. Following the dedication "For my father," an ever-changing collage of thumbnail-size Stasi surveillance videos overwhelms the screen. Yes, *Karl Marx City* certainly compels us to recall the totalizing practices of the Stasi, yet the film goes even further than that, prompting us to consider the role of government monitoring and illegal wiretapping practices today. This post-1989 East German documentary remains relevant in an age when oversight has shifted from a totalitarian Big Brother to a digital "Big Other" operating in the interests of surveillance capital.[78]

Karl Marx City functions as a contemporary memory project in the digital age, but the film also advances a commentary on digital culture. What drives Epperlein and Tucker is not only the history of surveillance in the GDR and its post-1989 aftermath but also more topical questions about how the nexus of private and public life is mediated through photography, film technology, new media, and unfettered government surveillance. Imprinted in the documentary is modernity's enduring fascination with visibility and with the capacity of analog media, such as film and photography, to track their own shadows and recognize that something has been lost, in contrast to digital recordings, where nothing can hide.[79] Mixing quiet, elliptical tonalities with an absurd number of images (snapshots, family portraits, official ID pictures, etc.), the film poses timely questions about the possibility of knowing the truth about others, or oneself, as this truth is remediated and distributed across our personal, collective, and technological lives. Ultimately, in the era of fake news and digital selves, *Karl Marx City* makes the claim for the performative value of an indexical anchor. If it matters more today that a picture is truer than real life, then we must come to a better understanding of our own epistemological frames; we must devise strategies for learning to read the endless stream of images and information (the politics of truth and factuality) in virtual space, in a post-truth era.[80]

At the end of the documentary, film and photography converge as the aforementioned projections of multiple surveillance clips, crammed into thumbnail-size frames, stream over the screen. Since moving images emerged in the late nineteenth century, photography and cinema have often had a strained, even "incestuous" relationship.[81] Both media have been caught up in questions of the evidentiary and of secrecy and surveillance. Yes, the mechanically reproduced copies of Stasi surveillance footage, showing countless East Germans going about their lives, seem interchangeable, as they are continuously switched in and out in a series of rows and columns. The visual grid transitions to a final scene of a Stasi officer who watches multiple television screens, reminding the viewer of the film's opening, where we saw a secret agent setting up conspiratorial equipment. It feels as though we are trapped once more in the surveillance logic of the GDR state, which forced Epperlein to rearrange the postmemory of her father's life and death. But the film actually offers an invitation to zoom out much farther into an expansive, ontological large-scale view and take in the spectacular impassiveness of these running images and their insistence on repeating the same message (or no message at all).

In the final analysis, the film echoes the claim of cultural criticism that today, in the age of hyper-capitalism and democracy, we still live in a society of spectacle, simulacra, and surveillance. The distant street-surveillance scenes appear fabricated and devoid of content, and it is as though the perpetually proliferating images held within the miniature frames turn into screens themselves, akin to those of cunning machines such as smartphones. While new media may have made communication seem more transparent and democratic than ever before, their algorithms also facilitate commercial and governmental data collection.[82] Moreover, mobile devices can accelerate the rapid advance of biotechnological surveillance in the service of health security or be used to record and combat police violence. At a minimum, digital culture enmeshes us in labyrinths of endless image cycles and networked relations, and, just like the computer technology and virtual reality on which they rely, these new media race simultaneously toward the future and the past.[83] Both anchored and mobile, the infinite loops of the surveillance footage in the small frames at the end of *Karl Marx City* appear to move across time and space; they also seem obdurately indestructible, and, as with any idol, any attempt to destroy them would be in vain.[84] While Epperlein and Tucker inch toward a dystopian vision, the violence of the archive (embodied in the archive fever of both the Stasi and the BStU, if not of today's internet) strikes back. We no longer have the agency to house the material in some remote storage place to access it for our review and contemplation; instead, the digital data freely and possibly of its own volition recombines and accumulates, directing us, watching us, and, eventually, closing us in. We become the archive then; the archive is turned inside out.

[CHAPTER FOUR]

Provisional History

Something's always left over. Remnants that don't work out. Some images lie around waiting for a history/a story [*Geschichte*].

Thomas Heise, *Material*

The 2009 archival documentary *Material* by Thomas Heise opens with a single panning shot over a deserted neighborhood, taken a year after the collapse of the GDR. We see a fallow in an East German urban landscape: a field of half-tidied ruins somewhere in Halle, where children play. Past the abandoned shell of a *Trabant*, an East German car, the kids begin working together to drag long pipes over scree, building bridges that lead nowhere and maybe everywhere.[1] Barren trees among the war-torn houses stretch into an open sky; the children's voices, while barely audible, echo across the derelict expanse. These stranded dwellers appear sedulous, unaware they may be transporting last belongings or discarded bits and pieces into an uncertain future. The scene seems to have been shot for *Material* when, in fact, all the segments in the film are found footage and were recorded for other narrative purposes in Heise's earlier works. In incidental images, the film reflects, we may say, on a forced withdrawal of history—on the vanishing of a country—while not succumbing to melancholy.

With the official unification of Germany on October 3, 1990, the GDR disappeared. A year or so after the mass demonstrations in the GDR, Heise's urban wasteland accumulates the residues of the socialist past, serving as a metaphor for the long aftermath of the Second World War.[2] Heise himself worked as an assistant director at the GDR's DEFA film studio in Potsdam-Babelsberg in the 1970s; subsequently, his documentary films were prohibited from screening by the SED government. All his works went straight to the archive shelf. DEFA, in turn, was dissolved in 1992 by the Treuhand (Trust Agency), which de facto eliminated any East German control over the images and narratives of the *Wende*.[3] Twenty years after the fall of the Wall, Heise compiled unseen footage from some of his earlier films for *Material*, which was screened to a niche audience in the late-night program of *Arte*, a European public-service channel based in Germany and France.

161

FIGURE 4.1. A residential area in Halle (Saale) in the early 1990s. Still from *Material* (2009), directed by Thomas Heise.

As I rewatched the film for this book, I recalled the summer of 1990, when *Stadtreinigung* (city sanitation) containers lined Leipzig's streets. Piled onto the garbage trucks were masses of outdated Marxist books that had once been mandated by the now-vanishing state to prop up its Communist Party. Soon after, shells of GDR cars, stripped of their tires like the ones in Heise's opening, were abandoned in the streets.

I remember the frantic purging of the past. However, I am rarely able to conjure the street protests in Leipzig that had taken place months earlier in 1989, which ended up bringing down the GDR. Later images are superimposed on earlier ones—the fall of the Wall, the opulent state ceremony of unification under the Brandenburg Gate, or even the recently rediscovered images of the first mass demonstrations.[4] Collective and personal memory eventually converge, registering only the historical outcomes. In the early fall of 1989, most people were not yet aware that they were making history. Indeed, "there was almost no way to tell where the demonstrations ended, and everyday life began. It was equally unclear in what direction the demonstrations were going to move."[5] Some, at least, were frightened by the specter of impending violence. When I returned to Leipzig on the evening of October 9, the square outside the train station was deserted.

Only the voice of Kurt Masur, the music director (who later went on to the New York Philharmonic), echoed through the city radio: "We urgently ask the people of Leipzig to be calm so that peaceful dialogue becomes possible." A handful of officials and cultural leaders had signed off on this public appeal to force a political negotiation with the SED government. Mikhail Gorbachev had just been in East Berlin to celebrate the fortieth anniversary of the GDR with party dignitaries in front of mass parades. From the historical record, we know that seventy thousand demonstrators had amassed in front of the *Gewandhaus* at the Karl-Marx-Platz that night while thousands of police officers, combat groups, and NVA soldiers descended on Leipzig. Later, I rode my bike back downtown. By then, the crowd had marched straight ahead, pushing its front rows practically into the arms of the police cordon. The overflow of visitors at St. Nicholas Church had also formed into a procession through the streets. A bird's-eye view could have captured how the roads filled up—thousands of people turning into political subjects quietly while the armed police retreated and watched on. Within the crowd, the arm of the person next to me was touching mine; our bodies smashed together. There were no signs, no slogans, no shouts. Just a sea of candles, which people silently held in their hands, lighting up the city loop, the *Ring*, in the dark. The "beating in unison" of hearts was no longer a mere turn of phrase but unforgettable, implanted in my memory.

At least, that is the tale I have settled on over time. As though "the mind has ceased, for some mysterious reasons, to function properly,"[6] every return to the evening of Monday, October 9, 1989, has to pass through the only grainy black-and-white images available on the internet today. Shot illegally from a rooftop by two amateur filmmakers, the footage was smuggled through the closed border to the West on a VHS tape. Thirty years later, the crowd in the blurry filmstrip appears otherworldly. When West German photojournalist Martin Gross arrived in the East German city of Magdeburg a few weeks after the uprising in the winter of '89, he would speak of a palpable vacuum. In a notebook entry from January 16, 1990, Gross writes: "In addition, God knows, there is nothing revolutionary to report: no street battles, no military action, no resistance, no eruption, no drama. Everything slides along, dissolves, smiles a little. . . . And how should you research here, take photos, all these things that you have to be awake for. . . . You walk around between these discarded things like a shadow, a ghost."[7] Gross's observation of disarray in the late GDR reflects that after a brief surge of political energy, history had exhausted itself, that "after this, nothing happened."[8] According to the philosopher Jonathan Lear, this statement is a retroactive declaration of the moment when history comes to an end.

But even while I pick up this melancholic thread suffusing the images and reflections in the aftermath of 1989, I take my cue from Heise's *Material* to steer the recall of that time in a different direction: to move beyond the point where the end of the twentieth century appears solely as victory or defeat. This chapter offers a provisional account of 1989–90—one that delineates a configuration of possibilities to challenge the so-called historical necessity of the neoliberal capitalist status quo. Revolutions, in Arendt's sense, are not the cause but the consequence of the downfall of political authority. They always succeed with amazing ease in their initial stages because those who supposedly "make" revolutions do not "seize power" but rather pick it up where it lies in the streets. Later, many revolutions become doomed, deformed, or simply fade out. And restoration, the consequence of an interrupted course, usually provides no more than the normalized cover under which disintegration continues unchecked.[9] In what follows, I am interested in exposing '89–90 further as a historical juncture, an odd in-between period when the actors and witnesses—the living themselves— became aware of an interval in time that was altogether determined by "things that are no longer and by things that are not yet."[10]

Rendering History as Dead Past or Active Force

In '89–90, the East German people became for a moment self-sovereign: *das Volk erhob seine Stimme(n)*, a people raised its voice(s). Soon after, however, the story of the East's revolt in '89–90 was absorbed into the official history of the West. Critics observe that even decades later, the view of the GDR, its downfall and its settlement (*Abwicklung*), is distorted through nostalgia for the East (*Ostalgie*), transfiguration (*Verklärung*), or sheer negation. This morphing, if not deforming, of post-1989 memory in Germany's public sphere was fueled by the various failures of social utopia since the mid-twentieth century.

After the failure of May '68 in Western Europe and certainly after the collapse of Communism in Central and Eastern Europe, a loss of faith in progress became pervasive. Several other crises resulted from this loss of faith—in history, narrative, memory, representation, and image. More recently, scholars in several fields, including memory and visual studies, have responded to these crises by reconfiguring the relations of the past and future. They have challenged established, often amnesiac, histories by giving space to an interplay of relationships between these two temporal orientations.[11] The work in media archeology is particularly suitable for disrupting, troubling, or abandoning the hegemonic narrative about the Peaceful

Revolution in 1989. Media-archeological practices are not only deconstructive, nonnormative, and potentially subversive but also invested in old and new materialities and technologies of memory. As Heise's work reminds us, these technologies have agency over what gets preserved or discarded. In turn, this approach can help dislodge historical processes stymied in the official record and disclose new pathways for a revolutionary protest memory. Rather than historical outcomes, what we see and re-envision in *Material* are outtakes from old VHS tapes recording the myriad communal improvisations across the late GDR during that revolutionary year.

Accordingly, my thinking in this chapter is guided by the term "prospective archeology," a term that works against the tendency toward global synchronizing of universal (Western) memory and the forgetting of particular histories to echo its most ardent proponent, the media theorist Siegfried Zielinski. Developed within the framework of media archeology, prospective archeology is a field of research and practice that contributes more broadly to those who engage with artistic processes based on technology in the context of academic collections, archives, and exhibition spaces. Zielinski looks at media phenomena in their material-technical manifestation as fragments of physical and imaginary worlds no longer available. At the same time, he makes even stronger political claims for not only excavating forgotten, suppressed, or largely neglected histories but also providing a constructive intervention in existing temporal relations. As a tactic, prospective archeology aims to "generate knowledge through the past and into the potential space of the future."[12] It thus helps contour what I develop in *Remembering 1989* as future archives.

Arguably, we cannot uncover '89–90 self-sovereignty without exposing how this memory gets blocked, transmitted, or erased. Moreover, here I am not only thinking of hegemonic pressures. Equally important is the gravitational pull of historical ruptures. Despite brave calls for going against the grain, for digging into the past, in order to discover there an as—yet-unrealized future, film historian Thomas Elsaesser reminds us that we cannot escape culture's tendency to preserve the past, "to fetishize 'memory' and 'materiality' in the form of trauma and loss."[13] In other words, media-archeological practices bring into play the relationships between feelings of hope (or Arendt's temporality of *no longer* and *not yet*) and history's exhaustion, its remains.

The 2019 art object *Uncovering the Year 1990* (*Das Jahr 1990 Freilegen*), curated by Jan Wenzel—with thirty-two mini-essays by West German media philosopher and filmmaker Alexander Kluge—embodies and performs this tension between erasure and potentiality. The book, as an archival art object, is a material desideratum of a forgotten history. At two pounds and more than six hundred pages, it appears like a stranded object on post-historical shores. After only a few months on my desk, the pages of the massive book have yellowed, and (surely as intended) it has begun to resemble a pile of *Altstoffe* (recyclable paper) once collected in the GDR. The book contains hundreds of photographic records, word montages, and narrative traces. It appears to disappear even as I write this book. A small note on the cover reads: "In comparing the years 1989 and 1990, it is remarkable that they have been recorded so differently by the collective memory." Almost everyone in Germany still vividly recalls some version of the year 1989. "It's much more difficult to describe 1990 in a few words: The events roll over [*überschlagen sich*] or stop suddenly. Such a year is hard to remember."[14] The curators argue that 1990 is like a blind spot in our memories. Across the front page sprawls a massive photograph of a torn-up Ernst Thälmann Strasse in Leipzig at the end of May 1990, which unmistakably renders '89–90 as a traumatic event. Every single cement segment of this main traffic artery is turned upside down.

In his 2019 archival film *Heimat Is a Space in Time* (*Heimat ist ein Raum aus Zeit*), released nearly thirty years after the fall of the Wall (and a decade after *Material*), Thomas Heise also relies on such traumatic visual imagery. In this multigenerational story of his family—spanning Nazi persecution, the rise of socialism, and the Cold War—Heise intersplices extensive sequences where the camera silently pans over entire highway stretches that look as though an earthquake has shifted them out of their architectural cas-

FIGURE 4.2. Jan Wenzel, ed., *Uncovering the Year 1990: With 32 Stories by Alexander Kluge* (Leipzig: Spector Books, 2019). Photograph courtesy of diepluralisten.

ings. These unsettled images of disarray belong as much to the derailment of socialist utopian dreams in the 1960s as to the dislocated history of 1989.[15]

Wenzel opens *Uncovering the Year 1990* with two pages printed entirely in black, as though the archival record brings the year back from oblivion. Likewise, Thomas Heise's *Heimat Is a Space in Time* explores the gaps in collective memory. In this conceptual documentary, the moment of unrest in the fall of 1989 drops nearly into a fade to black. Over panning shots of the *Ostkreuz* train station in East Berlin—the moving of freight trains in the dark of night—the disembodied voice-over (Heise himself) reads one of the infamous eyewitness accounts of the violent arrest and beating of demonstrators by GDR police near Gethsemane Church in Prenzlauer Berg on October 7, 1989.[16] In this work, the filmmaker recounts his own arrest, a story originally published in the 1990 anthology *The Gentle Revolution* but absent from the 2009 *Material*. For Heise, the trains function as a metaphor of history. The rendering of 1989 as a violent rupture remains invisible, marking the limits of the relation between history, memory, and representational form. After his release, Heise returned to the often-discussed rehearsals of Heiner Müller's *Germania Tod in Berlin* at the Berlin Ensemble, which itself became an ad hoc stage of the disintegrating country and the revolutionary rise.

In this chapter, I examine '89–90 from the perspective of its material and visual afterlives to reclaim the crux of the lost inheritance of the peaceful revolution—a performative play with radically democratic change, where people occupied and reorganized public realms for responsible political action. To that end, I first explore images and various archival records of the people's self-constitution (*Selbstermächtigung*) in the early fall of 1989 to highlight that the performance of "We, the people" is itself an irruptive act. After all, this revolution was not televised (and if it was, then it was televised mainly through a Western lens that showed East Germans as a homogenous mass rising from the shadows).[17] Heise's dynamic films provide mediated glimpses into these irruptive acts by which, it appears, an entire population self-organized into vast nationwide grassroots networks until and even after the revolution failed. In this context, the lost footage of the thirty-seventh session of the GDR's last parliament recovered in *Material* is worth revisiting. It provides a timely reflection on the limits (and possibly the potential for recovery) of representative democracy. Even if Heise may deny that this survival of material and visual, photographic forms can give us "common ground to tread upon,"[18] he is interested in depicting utopian images of that interval period.

Rather than revolution or unification, the year '89–90 can reveal a story about power and failure, promises, and the fragility of dreams about structural reorganizing from below. These memories have disappeared from the official historical record, which has, in effect, merged the fall of the Wall with Germany's unification. Troubling this normalized narrative, I propose a more provisional history, assembled through the recirculation of minor footage and photographic discharges of society and through unseen and unheard archival remnants. Animated by the practice of media archeology, this provisional history focuses on unfulfilled potentiality. The point is to insert useful grains into the media archive, rewriting the revolution from the sentient ground of being there.

Archival Release

Linking seemingly contradictory events and images, happening independently of each other, into a single whole is a way, Heise states, "to make history as a process into a sensory experience."[19] Bound up with the material conditions of memory, archiving, and mediation, Heise's film about '89–90 sets out not to tell a story but to preserve the disintegrating material (some of which he shot together with cameramen Sebastian Richter, Peter Badel, and others). The material included 35mm segments of the demolition of the Republic Palace in 2008 and original VHS tapes with footage upon footage capturing the spontaneous self-organizing in the streets of Berlin in 1989. We see, for instance, how the party base rallies in front of the building of the Central Committee of the SED on November 8 to interrupt an official meeting where the SED Politburo reshuffled its leadership. No one today recalls this event, one day before the fall of the Berlin Wall. Heise's material also draws from footage of theatre rehearsals under Fritz Marquardt at the Berlin ensemble in 1988–89, a neighborhood meeting in Berlin-Hessenwinkel in December 1988, and scenes of a 1992 screening of Heise's documentary film *Jammed: Let's Get Moving* (*Stau. Jetzt Geht's los*). In addition, the archival collection integrates the television broadcast of the thirty-seventh parliamentary session of the transitional GDR government, newly formed in April 1990 under the governing power of a grand coalition, in order to think through the relationship between spontaneous and formalized political assemblies in constituting viable public spheres.

Deconstructing conventional forms of the historical documentary, Heise presents these disparate visual remnants nonchronologically and underscores a sense of polyrhythm with a discordant soundtrack by the American musician Charles Ives. Heise's film reflects the belief that "one can think of history as linear, but really, it's a heap." This credo is announced by Heise's poetic voice-over an hour into the film (dated November 10, 1989), one day after the opening of the Berlin Wall. *Material* is a film about the end of the GDR without images of the fall of the Wall. Accordingly, the film refuses to supply any retrospective meta-historical storyline. Aside from the occasional intertitle with citations, poetic commentary, or announced dates, spectators can barely orient themselves. Neither an official narrative nor fixed counter-images are produced. Instead, *Material* derives its multiple and heterogenous meanings about the disintegrating GDR from ever-shifting peripheries or the side-stages of historical action: prison cells, coffee shops, train carts, urban wastelands, and local community centers. The grain of the film stock of each segment varies widely, marking them as differentiated archival records; the images also range from black-and-white and grayscale to faded color. Some shots are so blurry that history itself appears to have faded out; these images hover at the limits of being comprehensible. Most viewers, for example, will not understand that the frightening night sequence placed second in *Material* is associated with the riots in November of 1990 when squatters were evicted from *Mainzer Strasse* in East Berlin's district of Berlin-Friedrichshain by the (new) FRG police force. Symbolically, East German civil rights activists perceived this event, long forgotten in the present, as the first act of neoliberal governmental powers post-unification.

According to Heise, he used these leftover pictures from the late '80s to 2008 Germany so that present, past, and future temporalities could reflect each other. As a witness and activist, he also stresses, "it is [his] picture," formed from his experience there. Heise's impulse to repurpose his own film scraps echoes theoretical works by media archeologists. This echoing includes an emphasis on incidental and sensory materialities, an interest in the transfer of analog and digital media, a concern with the temporality of the interval, and a focus on projective or prospective genealogies. In his media-archeological manifesto, Siegfried Zielinski highlights that in this type of practice, "elements are reassembled in a different order than before."[20] Notably, when Heise digitized the 16 and 35mm analog remnants of otherwise lost recordings of street protests, parliamentary sessions, and so forth, new interpretations of these recordings were created. Things that had been suspended in the medial memory yet were inaccessible— for example, affects, images, and meanings of the revolts in '89–90—now became updated through modern technological devices. They went into a "captivating state of tension with history."[21] Here, it is worth recalling that the hegemonic post-1989 narrative absorbs these indeterminate elements by reproducing iconic images: for example, the GDR NVA soldier stepping through the wall, or the fireworks over the Quadriga at the Brandenburg Gate. Works such as Heise's explore how histories are unevenly transmitted by an artistic practice that fundamentally occurs with and through ever-changing technical means. Such projects uncover the role of specific technologies, rather than content, in shaping contemporary culture and collective memory.

These different technologies are important for thinking about collective memory and signal the material conditions by which archival regimes are produced. Together with *Material,* Heise released a DVD with two other films, *The House (Das Haus,* 1984), about the day-to-day operation of a welfare office in Berlin-Mitte, and *People's Police Force (Volkspolizei,* 1985). He had shot these pieces when he worked for the State Film Documentation (SFD) at the GDR Film Archive. Both films were quarried material, footage shot for later use in "real" DEFA films. Since the raw material produced by the SFD was not intended for the current public (*Öffentlichkeit*), future viewers became the proxy addressee.[22]

There is extensive scholarship on Heise's involvement with the SFD. Still, I want to briefly highlight how the artist's various experiences with the differential dynamics of archive, power, and memory inform his thinking about regimes of visibility in *Material.* Heise (born in 1955) studied at the Academy of Film and Television (HFF) in Potsdam-Babelsberg between 1978 and 1982. His early documentary work as a film student was confiscated by the SED. His student film, the documentary *Why a Film about These People (Warum einen Film über diese Leute,* 1980), shot on 16mm black-and-white reversal film, was entirely produced with materials bought on the black market. Heise broke off his studies when the film was banned from public screening and he was de facto kicked out of film school. All the works he then produced—three scripts; four films, including those shot for the SFD; and three original radio features, as well as drafts, fragments, and video protocols—were accessible to the public only after the collapse of the GDR. Unvarnished observations of people on the margins of society characterized all his documentary works. Film scholar Claus Löser writes that Heise as an artist practiced essentially "outside of general perception."[23] The early films were either blocked or destroyed and remained in storage until the end of the GDR in 1989.

However, when Heise tried to gain access to his material after the collapse of the SED regime in 1989, the FRG archive also denied his request. The German Federal Archives-Film Department (Bundesarchiv-Abteilung Filmarchiv) now oversees the archival records of the GDR. After being mired in an unsuccessful legal dispute with the German government about the film rights to *House* and *Police,* the artist managed to digitally reconstruct the films on his own initiative by 2001 ("there never was and still isn't a positive print of the edited negative").[24] He could also not legally prevent the Federal Archives and its distribution arm from selling clips for use in other post-1989 television productions about the GDR. Completely stripped of context, they were deployed to buttress the normalizing, hegemonic (Western) vision of the dictatorial SED regime. As far as I can tell, no fragments from these two earlier pieces are edited into *Material*; they only form companions in the DVD set, released in 2010, twenty years after Germany's unification. However, Heise's concern with the limits of what is openly visible and audible across space and time informs *Material*'s visual archeology of the unrest in '89–90.

Performing the People Is an Irruptive Act

Thomas Heise's art documentary *Material* unsettles any official efforts at foreclosing the history of 1989 in Germany's public memory. According to Heise, the nearly three-hour montage of unused footage from previous films, including unfinished pieces, is "an attempt to create an open picture of history, a public thought process in images."[25] In the fall of 1989, Heise freelanced as a directorial assistant at the rehearsals of Heiner Müller's *Germania Tod in Berlin* under Fritz Marquart at the Berlin Ensemble, where he had also started the year before to shoot footage with a video camera, a Panasonic MV 5, obtained from the West. Interested in visibly reflecting connections between historical events and his own life experiences, Heise took the camera out into the streets in early November, after the uprising in Leipzig on October 9, 1989, led to a nonviolent unsettling of the SED regime. The protests were spurred by the nationwide clandestine oppositional movements active in the Church since the 1980s (see chapter 2).

Filmmaking's logistic, institutional, and technological conditions in the GDR have significantly impacted the limited visual archive and collective memory of 1989. To start, hardly anyone had access to such portable equipment. Documentary directors employed by the DEFA film studio had to navigate a complicated bureaucratic procedure to receive official approval from the State Ministry of Culture and to access recording technology and rationed stockpiles of photographic film. In October 1989, Andreas Voigt, Gerd Kroske, Petra Tschörtner, and others were still waiting to take their heavy 35mm equipment into the streets. By the end of the month, three DEFA teams finally arrived in Leipzig, Dresden, and Berlin, where they produced a series of films that are forgotten, rarely screened, or difficult to access today.[26] Despite conditions of censorship, an underground Super-8 film scene existed in the GDR. Artists and curators began to organize semiclandestine screenings and film festivals throughout East Germany in the

1980s. These events were often oriented toward abstract, nonrepresentational films, influenced by French poststructuralist theorists and the most experimental strands of the Nouvelle Vague. Amateur film clubs, sponsored by the State's Cultural Association, were also quite active in the GDR: about two hundred such clubs existed nationwide, some well-equipped with 16mm technology, but because these hobby cineastes were in the grip of a centralized structure, their visual repertoire was rather conformist, often focusing on factory production, nature, or official celebrations of the socialist state.[27] In other words, these technological-ideological conditions are partly responsible for the absence of images of the radical democratic movement in 1989. When the revolutionary unrest began, however, Heise went out into the city and doggedly kept filming—all he wanted, he recalls, was the material.[28] Amid the chaos, he was rarely stopped by police or asked if he had official permission to be filming. The images of street assemblies and protests he hastily captured disaggregate the calcified narratives about the *Wende*. Pictures of the fall of the Berlin Wall or Germany's unification are omitted. The rift between the intellectual elite and populace, responsible for the democratic direction of the revolution according to the post-1989 master narrative, is also ignored.

Therefore, the documentary compilation is as interesting for what it shows as for what it leaves out. Without any commentary to direct the viewer's understanding of what is unfolding on the screen, *Material* captures an unforeclosed interval period of radically discontinuous self-organizing. Most of the time, people run somewhere, assembling in front of a GDR government building, in community centers, or cafeterias—debating, arguing, cajoling. We see East Germans of many social, cultural, and political strata gathering in public spaces in the fall of 1989. And then, as though to mark the revolutionary interregnum as a gap, a pause, we repeatedly witness how historical momentum slows down as those coming together suddenly fall still, fall silent, into waiting. The digitized VHS recordings, akin to an archeological source, are interspliced with brief 35mm color segments of the city, shot at a later time. This unsettled technique undermines established visual regimes that structure dominant historical narratives.

For instance, when theatre practitioners co-organized the first legal mass demonstration in East Berlin on November 4, 1989, Heise filmed with his portable camera from within the assembly, recording "situated alliances" in flux. Official Western television cameras broadcast the event at high platforms from above, thus creating hierarchies in the visual field between the speakers on the stage and the amorphous crowd in the square. In these official images, as film scholar Simon Rothöhler astutely observes, the direction of the historical movement is already fixed toward unification.[29]

On that day, artists and intellectuals such as Christa Wolf, Heiner Müller, and Stefan Heym called for a "democratic socialism where no one wants to leave."[30] The (always already foreclosed) hegemonic narrative of 1989 soon became that the new (counter) elite was entirely out of step with the population. According to official memory, East Germans revolted against the SED regime to aim for national unification and to fulfill the failed efforts of the 1953 uprising that took place in the aftermath of the Second World War and Germany's division. In contrast, *Material*'s provisional recollection of '89–90 refuses any such narrative closure. Following a vacant intertitle (and the date November 10), we sense that the Berlin Wall must have fallen, yet no border crossing or reified images of reunifying celebrations come into view, only deserted streets shot from a moving city train. However, the montage of localized, spontaneous debates among East Germans in public spaces instantly draws the viewer back into the pulsating rhythms of open-ended history.

Heise points out that the technological limitations of the video camera shaped his images of the street assemblies, clandestinely recorded from amid the demonstrators. The video camera had a slow focus, equipped to work on one automatic setting; therefore, it was only possible to pan over the photographed subjects very slowly until the focus would inevitably be lost and the shaky images blurred.[31] This limitation had consequences for the visual language recording this historic moment of collective self-organization. The images have a certain self-reflexive aura of ad hoc documentation, snatched amid an unstoppable temporality, as though history is cleaved, a continuum is broken open. Amid the unrehearsed crowds, Heise finds the unseen glances, faces, words, and silences—the revolutionary gestures of *Selbstermächtigung* (self-sovereignty from below)—where historical outcomes were not yet determined. When the portable camera catches a woman at the November 4 assembly push through the silent crowd, a handful of citizens nearby anxiously study her handmade sign protesting "Stalinist terror." Any such discourse was taboo in the GDR. Here, one has the distinct sense that East Germans are trying out new roles.

It is important to note that cultural historians such as Matt Cornish and Jonathan Bach have compellingly elaborated on the historical change in 1989 at the intersection of popular unrest, institutional space, and theatrical practice. Readers of Heise's *Material* likewise rarely fail to acknowledge the many meanings of political spectacle and theatricality explored by the documentary. To different degrees, these scholarly works adopt an interpretation that foregrounds the power and effect of public demonstrations— the staging of the people—rather than, say, the expressive nature of such events.[32] In turn, literary works such as Ingo Schulze's *New Lives* (2005) and Christa Wolf's *City of Angels* (2010) have deployed a performative, cinematic language to represent the unrest and grassroots organization in the late GDR, whereas films such as Andreas Dresen's *Silent Country* (1992) observe the revolutionary uprising from the peripheries of a small-town theatre. In my view, a provisional recasting of '89–90 needs to expose more forcefully the irruptive heterogeneity of self-sovereignty exercised by the East German population during the interval year.

The large-scale uproar in the fall of 1989 did not only play out in theatres, universities, factories, or city governments—the historic shifts were felt even more dramatically between oppositional church and civil rights groups, in the party base of the SED, and in the margin of society, for instance among correctional staff and inmates in local State prisons. Let me briefly turn to two localized revolts (I use the term loosely), also interspliced in Heise's *Material*: One erupted in the East Berlin chapter of the Communist Party in early November; the other was staged a month later in the Brandenburg-Görden Prison, an hour north of the GDR capital. Both uprisings are animated by *Material*. These two interrelated sites can illustrate how the seemingly raw, incidental visual choreography in Heise's reclaimed video footage accentuates the sheer range of East Germans' ad hoc participation in renegotiating the visible limits of public spheres. I argue that the unfulfilled historical potentialities of the '89–90 interregnum hover in these incongruent spaces involving protests and new radically democratic, participatory modes. From here, the film supplies a sensible imaginary of people coming together as an irruptive political force.

EXPOSING PROXIMITIES

In early November of 1989, Heise collected footage of a spontaneous rally of SED rank and file. Even a cursory examination of these visual and sonic fragments can show how the orthodox Communist Party's shattered remains reassemble into disparate visions. A lengthy set of archival footage, recorded with an unsteady camera, recalls the urgent presence of fired-up speakers and their clashing views on how to proceed in the wake of the Politburo's loss of legitimacy. Alongside party officials who briefly show up, a range of party members—a factory worker from the Kabelwerk-Adlershof, the party secretary of the Berlin-Mitte fire station, a mother, a female chemist from the Academy of Science, a district officer, a law professor from Humboldt University, and so forth—grab the microphone in quick succession. They occupy the space near the GDR's Republic Palace, with the iconic Marx-Engels monument in sight. Amid the chaos, the footage preserves only a few of the speakers' words; complete lines of thought are sparse as people speak over one another. A multivocal, unfinished sound emerges from the concerted action. One woman shouts, "Comrades, I am unprepared. But I was compelled to come to this rally and speak to you. Because—" Then the attention abruptly shifts back to Egon Krenz (who had just reinvented himself as a reformist SED leader). When another party member steps up, a voice from the crowd intermittently rises: "Who are you, comrade?" Unflustered, the speaker identifies himself as a university teacher before warning that the party's Central Committee "may have resigned, but just to be reincarnated in virtually the same form. Neither comrades nor people trust the Politburo." The unrehearsed public exchanges draw on improvisation and a repertoire of stylistic affectation, similar to the verbal jousts and outbidding seen in mass assemblies in early antifascist films. Each speaker is interrupted by booing, clapping, and cajoling. The scientist reporting from her party unit, which has "thoroughly and carefully discussed the political situation in our country," reads her declaration so fast that she is stopped by the crowd and then instructs herself, "More slowly. The time is racing!" We are instantly drawn into a "moving history," with a feverish sense of acceleration where time itself is dislocated.

FIGURE 4.3. Citizens walking to the Central Committee building of the Socialist Unity Party (SED), Berlin, November 8, 1989. Still from *Material* (2009), directed by Thomas Heise.

FIGURE 4.4. Rally at the Central Committee building of the Socialist Unity Party (SED), Berlin, November 8, 1989. Still from *Material* (2009), directed by Thomas Heise.

In this historic moment suspended between the past and the future, the party gerontocracy may, as Arendt knew, grasp for legitimacy by attempting to reform itself. Yet the power of the old order had already eroded before the rise of the people and was now to be had in the streets. Faced with the new selection of the Politburo in East Berlin, the party base in Heise's archival footage assembles itself without yet knowing how to step into this open space where power is up for grabs. The official symbol of the SED Party on the exterior of the building recedes further into the shadows as the night falls. The speeches become shorter and more rapidly cut as political thought splinters. Not yet formed into new agendas, clashing ideas overwhelm and displace one another. The extempore proposals range from a university student's call for discipline and calm to a tired-looking Politburo member's sudden support of perestroika. With a Rosa Luxemburg–inspired pathos, a female comrade observes that this moment is nothing less than the first historical chance to "legitimize real socialism before the rest of the world." At the same time, demonstrators implore the crowd that only exposing Stalinist structures would move the country forward. A factory worker pleads to directly influence the elected SED apparatus while other comrades passionately call for a nationwide party conference from below that would de facto dissolve the GDR government. Each speaker is looking for the right measure, rhythm, or word as a post-production sound mix is cast over the protest, blending distant street noise with the mournful screams of crows and the swelling of foreboding orchestral music.

However, the incidental visual work of Heise's video camera fractures the revolutionary scene even further, as though to amplify the heterogeneity of the people's embodied action. At first, we follow the group of people rushing across a large field toward the improvised meeting spot as though they are moving into a space of heightened exposure. What looks like a crowd of curious onlookers turns into a scene of spontaneous mobilization. The unsteady movement of the camera creates a state of alarm, signaling that this small-scale collective upsurge is taking place in a localized margin of the country's revolutionary events. Once in front of the headquarters of the SED Central Committee, the camera pans over the crowd's shoulders to catch a glimpse of the speakers at the microphone. The scene is dynamic and often tightly framed: we rarely see a single face or person, always a motley collective—a people on the verge of being formed. Heise focuses as much on the technical condition of the scene as on its performative assembly. Over and over again, he provides takes of other recording devices: a guy with headphones and a microphone, amateur and professional photographers with cameras, a television camera from the West elevated on a small scaffold. But most significantly, we see another cameraman in the crowd, reaching a Sony video camera above his head and panning it nearly 360 degrees. This moment reminds the spectator that Heise's dynamic, fragmentary representation of the revolutionary unrest forfeits any totalizing view of history. Following some hollow promises by Krenz for reform, the crowd sings "The Internationale"—"No faith have we in prince or peer. Our own right hand the chains must shiver. Chains of hatred, greed and fear"— bringing the local sequence of self-directed reorganization from below to a close, at least for the moment.

The significance of releasing this dissonant revolutionary recording from the archive cannot be overstated. In contrast to the normalized national memory, these recollected images and sounds resituate the uprising in 1989 across time and space, placing it in relation to a trajectory of progressive nineteenth- and twentieth-century social movements. Preserved on VHS tape, the spontaneous chanting of the anthem—harkening back to the Paris Commune in 1871 and various socialist, Communist, and anarchist movements since then—was widespread in the streets of the GDR during the unrest in the fall of 1989. The chants "Liberté, Egalité, Fraternité" could be heard intermittently across the country, transporting the aspirations of the

French Revolution two hundred years earlier into the East German protests. Eyewitnesses also recall that crowds assembled in Leipzig's churches were moved to strike up the civil rights song "We Shall Overcome."[33] Arguably, during those weeks, East Germans drew on a familiar repertoire to come together in their shared resistance to the calcified, orthodox GDR state in the streets of Leipzig, Plauen, and Berlin. In this transitory, newly constituted public space, they articulated their demands through songs popularized by the official canon of the socialist internationalist movement. This audible repertoire is either persistently left out in the hegemonic post-1989 memory, emphasizing a normalized narrative of the so-called Peaceful Revolution, or it is dismissed as an awkward if not embarrassing placeholder for a naïve democratic imaginary in literary renditions of the uprising by East German authors. In Heise's *Material*, however, these revolutionary chants belong as much to a distant past as to an opening up of the world in 1989. Re-circulated, these songs may even carry future promises. The archival montage of old, repurposed footage recovers the spiritual and political lessons that have been lost or distorted during the past twenty or thirty years and re-moves these impulses of collective solidarity in '89–90 into the space of the present.

Cultural historians such as Paul Betts have recently drawn our attention to the inheritance of the French Revolution in the pictorial archive of Leipzig's street demonstrations during the fall of 1989. In a brilliant reading of Wolfgang Schneider's photo collection *Demontagebuch* (Diary of Monday Demonstrations/Book of a Dismantling), he uncovers revolutionary poses that echo the iconic painting "Liberty Leading the People" (1830) by Eugène Delacroix, which reflects the revolutionary events of that year, harking back to 1789. Committed to an elegiac reading of history, Betts ultimately interprets these scenes as inflected by nostalgia for a youthful revolutionary fervor that soon subsided.[34] In my view, however, the emphasis on forward mobility as a bodily, political practice is most striking in *Material*. Of course, "movement" carries two basic meanings: bodily mobility and political organization. In order to do something together, bodies have to comport themselves in (spatial, temporal, sensible) fields or zones of proximity so that people are close enough to hear, see, or sense what each is doing and saying. Affect theorists have made this point clear in recent years. I believe that Heise's archival montage provides invaluable insight into the historical potentiality of reorganizing society in '89–90 that goes beyond the fiction of a lost "third way" (between socialism and capitalism). In contrast to the hegemonic, national, and neoliberal narrative, the prospective archeology of '89–90 animated by *Material* orients the viewer toward the possibility of radical democratic change, which surges forth in ways that "[claim] and [alter] the attention of the world for some more enduring possibility of livable life for all."[35] According to thinkers such as Judith Butler, such collective action toward more sustaining conditions of livability is the final aim of politics.

Few commentators have remarked on the political significance of the interspliced footage that Heise filmed in a prison outside Berlin. I argue that this recovered material from a carceral space—furthest on the periphery of the social, the visible, the imaginary realm—allows us to recast the unidirectional narrative of 1989 (always already heading toward unification) anew. Like all segments, this footage is recirculated as unseen or lost archival fragments in *Material*. This archival effect is produced and further enhanced by intercutting the black-and-white VHS footage of interviews with prison inmates and guards from '89 with exterior scenes of the Brandenburg prison, showing its high-security architecture (that is, fences, walls, cell blocks, the shutting of massive iron gates), shot later on 35mm and in color. As Tobias Ebbrecht-Hartmann astutely points out, even the artist's earliest films took an interest in outcasts and petty criminality at the margins of society. Shelved works, such as Heise's student thesis, *Why a Film about These People*, already registered that prisons were a reality excluded from the state's official self-image. As an archeological project, this early film, like other works by the artist the GDR censors had canceled, contained images and sounds which could "bear witness for the future, a way of life not shown in the East German media."[36] Carrying this point further, I suggest that the uncovered prison footage recorded by Heise in 1989–90 offers a particularly incisive example of such archival futurity with regard to the radically democratic conditions of the East German uprising for our present times.

Here my focus will be on the significance of uncommon solidarities formed in the disintegration of the GDR. The primal scene in the official visual and sound archive of the Peaceful Revolution originated in Leipzig's mass demonstration on October 9, 1989, where seventy thousand demonstrators chanted "We are the people" for the first time, and the rallying call soon cascaded across the country. Notably, none of the protest clips collected in *Material* make the now reified slogan of 1989 "Wir sind das Volk" (We are the people) audible. As such, the sequence in the Brandenburg prison raises similar questions to those raised by the SED Party rally about participation in the performative constitution of public spheres amid revolutionary unrest. In an unearthed segment from December of 1989, Heise takes us into an austere meeting room at the prison, where twenty correctional staff members have assembled around a long industrial table. One after another, employees appear at the head of the table and speak. Most turn to the peril of their work in potentially violent conditions (a revolt had recently broken out) and their fear of being mistaken for pawns of the SED regime. The next sequence shows tightly framed interviews with prisoners, presumably in a separate space, who echo some of these concerns, if for different reasons. The rarely seen black-and-white footage of interviews with people at the societal margins, working and living inside prisons, indicates a desire to find, as several of them put it, "a public out there."

When asked how it was possible to arrange these incredible recordings, Heise explains that the prison employees mistook him for the television media they had been waiting for now that the GDR state was coming apart. The results are interview segments in which various officers, educators, and correctional staff of different ranks, as well as men incarcerated for murder and other serious crimes, express their "appreciation for being recognized and heard." When the black-and-white sequence starts with a miniature model of a prison (shot in color on 35mm), these personal accounts also become slightly denaturalized. Although Heise undoubtedly plays with analogies between the late GDR and a carceral space, what is more interesting is how the segment dwells on the ways in which diverse, interrelated publics could be constructed across differentiated realms of society. In a paradoxical reversal, the correctional staff and inmates collaborate in imagining the prison itself as a model of nonviolence. Reading audibly from a newly written text, the voice-over of a correctional administrator (Lieutenant Colonel Jahn) notes with alarm and consternation that in the last few days and hours, "people have been taking the law in their own hands and using violence throughout the German Democratic Republic." Therefore, all detainees must stay calm: "The hope is this will set an additional example for all of public life in the country to seek nonviolent solutions." At the same time, the prisoners show that they wear handmade armbands with the slogan "No Violence" on their prison uniforms. Similar bands were worn by members of the citizens' movements during public assemblies in the early fall of 1989. In this political imaginary, the boundary between the outside world and the prison becomes permeable, underscoring that as the GDR became undone, popular self-constitution was based on a "set of fragile, changeable associations: forms of mobilization, collective action, public opinion, and symbolic protest."[37] This call for nonviolence from the prison also exposes, in exemplary form, the perpetual volatility of unrest during this year.

Throughout this book, I have argued that only if we account for the volatility of the historical shift can we also gauge the magnitude of forms of cooperation and solidarity that emerged in '89–90 in a tensional field. The various citizens' organizations renewed urgent calls for nonviolence and violence-free democracy all the way into early 1990. Amid an acutely destabilized and shifting political sphere, signaled by Heise's prison sequence,

FIGURE 4.5. Inmate at Brandenburg-Görden Prison, interviewed by Thomas Heise. Still from *Material* (2009), directed by Thomas Heise.

FIGURE 4.6. "No Violence" armband. Still from *Material* (2009), directed by Thomas Heise.

an increasingly polarized and chaotic atmosphere was unleashed, for instance, in the streets of Leipzig (as I discussed in more detail in chapter 2). Even after the Wall fell, the Monday demonstrations in the city three hours south of the prison featured in *Material* continued all autumn to mobilize a hundred thousand citizens each week in front of the Opera House on Karl-Marx-Platz.[38] As the power of the SED-led city government deteriorated, a megaphone controlled by the activist group New Forum was placed there on the steps accessible to all citizens—*ganz offiziell frei* (officially free). Initially, the spontaneous speeches were broadcast over the city radio in twenty locations on the downtown ring road. Soon after, the megaphone was hoisted on the balcony of the opera above the giant square. Documents of eyewitnesses collected by the Archive of the Citizens' Movement Leipzig make the aggressive, increasingly nationalist (*deutschnationale*) climate audible that began to haunt the rallies by the end of 1989. Hackling, political positioning, and rumored manhunts of so-called red socks (leftists) or "foreigners" and non-white people, according to a sociological poll, had countless participants in the rallies afraid of violent escalation.[39] On December 18, two hundred thousand inhabitants took to the street again to reassert nonviolence. Holding candles, they proceeded silently around the ring road in the dark of the night with no speeches, slogans, or banners. In contrast to this volatile unmooring, the hegemonic post-1989 memory discourse remains invested in the narrative of October 9, 1989, as the decisive peaceful turning point.

Lost Treasure of the Revolution

With all this in mind, the media-archeological discoveries in Heise's '89–90 montage are truly astonishing. The film's archival futurity reveals the people's variegated, disruptive desires to participate in imaginative political processes, to actually "have a say." Rather than far-reaching social unrest and self-organizing in the late GDR, the loops of dominant mediatized images of the *Wende* prefer to imagine East Germans in a sea of West German flags. One of the most iconic images shows the inhabitants of Dresden clamoring for the attention of the FRG chancellor as 1989 draws to a close. However, we can only understand the true force of Heise's provisional history if we also uncover how the GDR became a laboratory for radical, participatory democracy. Intermittently, activists and ordinary citizens moved into the space left open by the eroding power of the SED regime and took on civil and political responsibilities. This lost treasure of the '89 revolution is perpetually on the verge of disappearing, even in Heise's extraordinary archival montage.

In early 1990, local grassroots organizing was far from abolished. East Germans did not only come together to tear down a defunct dictatorial system: they also experimented with a new alternative order of self-governing. These improvisations brought them into conflict with both the lingering forces of the old GDR regime and the "new" managerial strategies of the Western system. Digging further into the Archive of the Citizens' Movement in Leipzig, we discover previously unheard stories about the remarkable communal council systems where ordinary citizens came together to manage public affairs. These include archival evidence of the widespread efforts to sustainably self-organize in a country thrown ever further into upheaval. In December, the Central Roundtable assembled for the first time in East Berlin, bringing together oppositional citizens' organizations and new political parties with cadres of the SED whose power was diminishing. In addition, regional roundtables formed in the GDR's fifteen state districts (*Bezirke*).[40] Thousands of independent councils and roundtables sprang up all over the country in workplaces, universities, prisons, hospitals, the military, and factories during the fall of 1989.[41] But the roundtable was not only a practice and an instrument of control; it was also a political idea.

Anticipating the plural democratic movements that would lead to the eventual collapse of socialist (totalitarian) East Europe, Hannah Arendt lauded such alternative council systems as examples of freedom in action. She praised their potential for an entirely new form of government, where citizens' active participation in politics during the revolutions would continue to develop even after the uprising itself was over.[42] For our polarized times, the potentiality of this "treasure of the revolution" is particularly relevant. Of the countless archival, official, and alternative records I have sifted through in the past years, the photographer Andreas Rost most succinctly explains the radical, participatory origin and promise of the local council system. Recalling his participation in the citizens' movement, he explains:

> I had been in opposition circles in the GDR since I was fourteen or fifteen years old. Initially a lot in Dresden in the Weinbergskirche, there were prayers for peace from 1982, I wore the symbol "Swords to Plowshares" or was active in environmental groups. From September 1989 I kept in touch between the New Forum in Leipzig and the New Forum in Berlin. At that time, I studied in Leipzig but lived in Berlin. At the end of all this, as it turned out, I became a member of the "Roundtable" of the city of Leipzig [in December 1990]. This was an amazing experience because the SED people had given up and were unable to do anything useful. From the "roundtable" we organized city politics—I'll say "gas, water, shit" like a plumber—we organized the garbage collection, etc. . . . I had the im-

pression that the West Germans were so politically trained that they had already been able to use the term democracy cynically or operationally. But with us it was always about the matter radically, so much so that we could even come to an understanding with our enemies. We sat at the "roundtable" with people who wanted to put us in jail a few weeks beforehand. That was a fine philosophical exercise.[43]

The East German photographer and activist also remarked that no one had asked him about this exceptional political intervention into established governing protocols in thirty years. Fortunately, from the unsorted paper files of speeches, pamphlets, and typewritten meeting notes in the Archive of the Citizens' Movement Leipzig, it's possible to reimagine the sheer range of unfinished agendas put into play by organizing groups that participated in the management of public things. In 1990, a handful of local archivists rescued the discarded documents and stored them temporarily in a damp church basement on the city's outskirts; over the next decades, some of the archival holdings, albeit poorly preserved and perennially underfunded, were digitized. I'm still stunned that it appears merely incidental whether or not a dormant paper (or digital file) in the archive is displaced, obliterated, or catapulted to the status of historical record. It is merely by chance if the micro-temporality of a file takes on a mnemonic form (during one of my visits, the outdated IBM computer giving access to some of the files crashed altogether). What can be gleaned from the archival remnants is a sense of improvisation and urgency in the ad hoc governing of the city in 1990: already the material traces of the roundtable documents indicate disarray, for example, series of addendums, scratched-out plans, edited address lists, scribbled-over names and information, handwritten notes. Beginning in early 1990, many radically divergent civil initiatives, political parties, and thematic working committees gathered in the House of Democracy in the Bernhard Göring Strasse, abandoned by the old SED administration.[44] The co-moderator Friedrich Magirius urged the participants to "quickly become more competent in organizing the public affairs of the city" amid the accelerated breakdown of the GDR.[45] Yet there existed hardly any templates, even if the roundtable picked up on the participatory democratic practices and goals of the fall of 1989.[46]

In this improvised space, being seen and heard by others constituted a new reality, in Arendt's sense, where a public formed in the presence of others as a political (and decidedly agonistic) act.[47] In fact, the vast field of divergent participating forces in Leipzig's roundtable should be traced here to illustrate this astonishing project of local self-government. From the Christian Democratic Party to the grassroots organization Democracy

Now, and from the SED successor party PDS to the neoconservative DSU, old and new parties were constituting the roundtable alongside the city's interim mayor. A host of citizen organizations that had emerged in the late GDR and fall of 1989, such as the community-based New Forum and the Initiative for Peace and Human Rights, also assembled in this radically democratic forum. The provisional governing body involved coalitions including the Socialists, the Alliance of the Left, the Student Council of the Karl-Marx University, the Association of People with Disabilities, the Association of Gay and Lesbians, the Advocacy Group for the Environment Ökolöwe, the Free German Trade Union Federation, the Workers' Councils, the League for Children, City Council Representatives (now only in advisory function), the Leipzig's Citizens Committee, and those rapidly forming new democratic associations representing soldiers, retirees, women, or small businesses, and so forth. Like the prison staff and inmates in Heise's lost footage, the citizens' groups that formed in the fall of 1989 especially understood the significance of the media. They submitted a proposal to the roundtable in March of 1990 to establish an independent, nonpartisan television station, the *Leipzig International Kanal X*. Calling for broad participation, the activists envisioned that "the production studio and broadcasting station would serve as an experiential and experimental field where all people can learn the engagement with the public medium of television."[48] They did not yet anticipate (or defied the reality) that the restructuring of the GDR's local and national media outlets was already underway and determined by neoliberal interests.[49]

As East German society began rapidly disintegrating, the council's focus also shifted. Under the poignant slogan "What should I watch out for if my company no longer needs me?" the Committee for Work and Social Matters at the citizens' roundtable started communal workshops, warning that "structural changes, legal uncertainty, and layoffs are imminent." A report urged for free legal counseling for citizens about labor law protection (still based on the GDR labor law of 1977) at the district court and union offices. The recordkeeper scribbled a note on the protocol reproduced on carbon paper: "Commission should make this public xxx (newspapers)."[50] Other initiatives of the roundtable aimed to prevent and control the sale of public property and rental apartments to droves of Western investors who had begun to overrun the city.[51] In the margins of a pamphlet, someone wrote with a pencil, "Organize town hall meetings!"[52] As I write this passage, the digital file of the half-faded brochure hovers on my laptop screen as though this alternative historical strand of the council systems—the treasure of the revolution—threatens to erase itself. Needless to say, the dynamics of media archeology, memory, and the archive relevant to Heise's '89–90 provisional history also come into play here. These spontaneously arising local councils have been widely forgotten in collective memory and have gone largely unnoticed by historians (a fate 1989 shares with other modern revolutions).[53] Even if scholars do not agree on the political implications of the unification process—political scientists scrutinize the administrative and economic shifts with seeming objectivity, while cultural studies scholars stress the power asymmetries—in hindsight, it often appears as though the transfer of the GDR to the FRG in 1990 occurred in relatively linear, direct, and orderly fashion. Instead, in this memorial space of Leipzig's Archive of the Citizens' Movement, it becomes clear that an entire city was mobilizing, first against the SED regime and then to gain a foothold in the tectonic shifts toward market democracy and capitalism. As in Heise's media-archeological project of '89–90, the different constellations and heterogeneous forms in which people came together to manage the city's public affairs are noteworthy.

Perhaps the civil and political mobilization across the disintegrating GDR, and the ad hoc council system in particular, appear today like "a sort of fantastic utopia"—a utopia that came true for a fleeting moment to show, as it were, "the hopelessly romantic yearnings of the people, who apparently did not yet know the true facts of life."[54] Yet, in these assemblies of working groups in neighborhoods, town halls, and districts, the "sentiment of the people" was formed in the first place during that interval year. This grassroots formation is, in my view, the most significant exceptional revolutionary experience erased from the official record.

Transitional Parliament: Interval Footage

Over time, the inevitability of history simply established itself as truth. According to the official narrative, the Western order was so compelling that East Germans could not pass up a vote for it. After "the first and last free parliamentary election in the history of the GDR" was held on March 18, 1990, a governing body was constituted under a conservative majority, led by the Christian Democratic Party. The domination of the election campaigns by the Western parties, and especially the CDU, was noted across a broad spectrum. Unexpectedly, the center-left forces had lost.[55] Historians often remark that the results of the national elections had indeed been an absolute bombshell.[56] A prominent filmmaker recalled the shock among activists: "We thought we had enough support in the population to make it possible for us to work toward a different model, an alternative model to the West German society. . . . the break came on March 18 . . . when we learned to shed the illusion that the citizens' movements are also the people."[57] In a clear shift of tone from these radically democratic beginnings, the honorary president of the newly elected Volkskammer (literally, people's chamber) concluded his inaugural speech in early April with the nationalist pledge, "God, protect our united Fatherland."[58] Other elected officials echoed this call for unification, noting that neighboring countries, Europe, and the world were watching on.

Yet, together with Heise's media-archeological archive, a series of rediscovered black-and-white photographs by East German artist Andreas Rost can expose a different memory strand. This visual archive reveals that even after the election the people were not as univocally reaching for the Western order as the official post-unification memory often suggests. Popular sovereignty certainly translated into elected power with the vote, but it also retained the power to challenge and even delegitimize those representative forms of parliamentary governance. Arendt calls this lingering spirit of resistance the "reserve power of revolution."[59] In spring 1990, Rost documented the newly surging demonstrations, this time against a perceived abuse of Western power, when tens of thousands of people gathered in Leipzig and other cities across the GDR to call out the unfavorable conditions of the currency union (1:3), rumored to come in July of 1990. The protests coincided with the first session of the Volkskammer on April 5, 1990. Delving into the newspaper archive, we uncover a *Neue Deutschland* headline alongside fuzzy protest images: "Demonstrators in the GDR: A New Start with Electoral Fraud? Not with Us?" Reporters anticipated that East Germany would "become the poorhouse of the FRG" if citizens did not organize against the coming "exploitation by the FRG state and corporations from the West."[60] In June, the *Hannoverische Allgemeine Zeitung* warned that "strikes in the GDR are becoming an incalculable burden for Bonn."[61] Across the triumphal endpoint of history, marked by unification, one could draw a line from these strikes in 1990 to the sit-ins and hunger strikes of workers at the coal mine in Bischofferode, Thuringia, in July of 1993.[62] Collective memory has forgotten that East Germans reconvened in the streets in the spring and summer of 1990 to protest against the neoliberal dismantling of the GDR and to pressure the East German parliament to negotiate an acceptable transition to market capitalism. Like Heise's ad hoc VHS recordings, Rost's stunning black-and-white pictures are schooled in the East German documentary film and photography tradition of social observation—a precise way of looking, coupled with a sense of responsibility for the rendered subjects—and are shot from within the crowd.[63] For nearly thirty years, the negatives reportedly lay dormant in the artist's archive and were recirculated in Jan Wenzel's collection *Uncovering the Year*

1990.[64] Like Heise's *Material,* their afterlife has gone unrecognized until now. Taken together, these recirculated works by Eastern German artists disrupt and reorganize the field of the visible. Their intervention into the archive can be read as a gesture of alternative knowledge or counter-memory, which harbors historical potentiality.[65]

TRANSFORMING THE VISIBLE GIVEN

In hindsight, we can establish alongside other records that the recovered and recirculated parliamentary footage in *Material* is from the thirty-seventh (nearly the last and, at seventeen hours, the longest) session of the Volkskammer, on September 28, 1990. Here the legacy of the Stasi was at stake. A lengthy debate ensued about whether the names of Stasi collaborators in the parliament should be released to the assembly as a whole and possibly to the public.[66] Much of the political wrangle revolved around whether the television cameras recording the parliamentary session should be permitted. The undirected ways in which Heise intersplices the eventually aborted broadcast as interval amplifies that the session itself is about the negotiation of public participatory power and spectatorship performed by the parliamentary body. If we shift for a moment to the official, hegemonic archive, we can see the aim of the filmmaker's inquiry. Since the tenth Volkskammer had formed after the March 1990 election, all parliamentary sessions were directly broadcast on East German television. The official record states that the parliamentarians decided on the "fundamental questions of State politics." They did so "in the full light of the public," affirming the (normalized) relation between visual participation and political transparency.[67] The public perceptibility of governmental procedures is itself viewed as evidence for democratic victory, in contrast to the dictatorial GDR.

However, Heise's film challenges any positivist notion of democracy, unmasking the ideological illusions of autonomy and self-presence at work in all modern politics. Conceptual documentary is, of course, an artistic form, but it can also be read as a political declaration in Rancière's sense, where the status quo of seemingly self-evident ideas is disrupted.[68] *Material* is as much "an arrangement of words, a montage of gestures, an occupation of spaces"—the material—as it is a reflection on how competencies, bodies, roles, and spaces are arranged in and produced by the communal, public, and political spheres. Following the series of black-and-white VHS footage of grassroots assemblies, the Volkskammer segment is upgraded to a faded, flickering color. The parliamentary session also appears to be recorded from a television set with a video camera, marking it in its differentiated materiality even more as an archival record. Importantly, Heise's shaky

FIGURE 4.7. Taped 37th session of the last GDR Volkskammer, September 29, 1990. Still from *Material* (2009), directed by Thomas Heise.

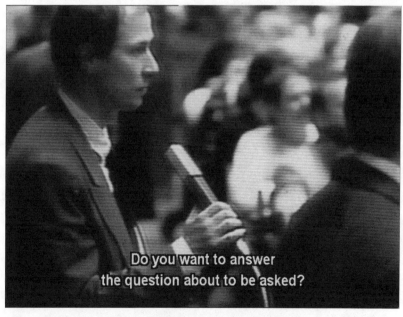

FIGURE 4.8. Parliamentarian steps to the microphone at the 37th session of the last GDR Volkskammer, September 29, 1990. Still from *Material* (2009), directed by Thomas Heise.

video camera alters the original broadcast by scanning extreme close-ups of a tense pair of hands, speaking faces, tired eyes, and waiting mics as though to index the historical making of representational democracy even in the most mundane of gestures. Here, Heise's interval segment interrogates the play of limits—of the sayable, seeable, knowable—in the performance of representational democracy. At the same time, official memory (including a post-1989 *Spiegel-TV* portrayal of this session) perpetuates the illusion of democratic self-presence in the West.[69] In a memoir essay, the New Forum civil rights activist Jochen Lässig lamented that the freedom of speech achieved through embodied action in the street was certainly relevant but that, ultimately, the political decisions about where the country was going were to be made in government backrooms.[70] Accordingly, Heise cuts from the aborted parliament broadcast to empty seats on a public transit bus, as though to signal the performative vacancy of the "we, the people." An empty windowpane with diffuse exterior reflections serves as a screen in the recess of the visual field.

On the most superficial level, this excavated footage of a parliamentary body in withdrawal—this interspliced broadcast of a twenty-five-minute segment in Heise's film—appears to critique the relationship between so-called representative or parliamentary democracy, media, and publics. In *Specters of Marx*, written in the immediate aftermath of the collapse of Eastern Europe, Derrida formulated one of the most scathing critiques of the dysfunction of Western democracies (that is, the electoral representativity), related, among other things, to socioeconomic distortions. He interlinked this critique with an analysis of the techno-tele-media apparatus, that is, the rhythms of information and communication forming a force field of unevenly distributed power. Likewise, Heise's mediated and remediated "parliament interval" deconstructs the topographical presumption "that there is a *place*, and thus an identifiable and stabilizable body for public speech, the public thing, or the public cause."[71] Film scholar Simon Rothöhler stresses the importance that the multiply repurposed footage of the Volkskammer television broadcast is the only one *not* originally shot by Heise (or his cameramen). (Recall that the session was taped off the television via a handheld video camera). They are images of images, reflecting a ghostly glare.[72] The sequence thus enacts a distancing and marks a closing down of direct-participatory possibilities achieved in the streets.

However, I want to challenge this view. What I find fascinating about Heise's 2009 film is that from within the temporality of this parliamentary broadcast (set in September 1990), the post-historic moment in which Derrida writes had not yet arrived. In that sense, these unrehearsed scenes are also dislodged from that teleological continuum. The retaped sequence reads like a historical interval nearing its end—unseen, as it were, until digitally recovered by *Material*. The improvised debates, the shaky camera, the stalling, and the perplexed look of the speakers at the microphone all contribute to our perception that history is not quite foreclosed. The disorientation among the people presiding over the assembly who have not quite yet turned into professional politicians gives this scene an indeterminate sense. We see a former civil rights activist (an unnamed Marianne Birthler) who is consternated at the decision to move into a closed session. The segment of this unfinished footage can be read as a trace or echo of the long-forgotten improvised, if not radically democratic, debates about the dissolution of the Stasi surveillance apparatus in the transitional GDR parliament.[73] The parliamentary disputes were interrelated with local, extra-parliamentary street protests, hunger strikes, occupation of Stasi district offices, and signature petitions in Berlin, Dresden, and Leipzig, in September 1990, regarding the fate of the Stasi files. Here, the Stasi issue became a litmus test for the democratic success of the peaceful revolution.

In the spring of 1990, Bärbel Bohley, founder of the New Forum and peace movement activist, made this point. How else, she asked, "can we get the lies and the heteronomy out of our public life? Unsparing accountability is the point of departure for responsible political action."[74] The historian Anne Sa'adah astutely notes that in 1989–90, the activists had aimed to build a civil society from the ground up rather than through a representative democracy with top-down party competition. For civil rights groups, a democratic culture of "trust and transparency" could only be achieved by disclosing the various networks of Stasi collaborators. As a result of contested debate and against the resistance of GDR mainstream parties and the West German government, Alliance '90 even temporarily succeeded in amending the Unity Treaty so that the Stasi archive would be preserved as a "memorial" and become accessible as an act of justice for the victims of the GDR. A few activist representatives, a tiny minority, had troubled the narrative of historical inevitability.

Yet, in light of this troubling, the performative effect produced by Heise's "found" (tele-optical) interval segment in *Material* can also be read as more elegiac. Devoid of context, the parliamentary scene ends on a fade-out to black, nearly mid-sentence. It appears that the first and last government body democratically elected by East Germans decides to disclose who the "Stasi spies among them" are before abolishing itself.[75] Another broken line in the memory of '89–90. No one remembers today that the GDR's transitional parliament was just a few weeks earlier on the brink of an emergency shutdown—nine ministers threatened to resign over the haste toward unification. In June, the Volkskammer had signed off on the legal constitution of the Trust Agency (Treuhand), which would end up privatizing nearly all GDR industries (disregarding the initial idea of giving East Germans shares in the companies). But when the deputies had only three weeks to review fifteen thousand clauses in the proposed Unification Treaty and to approve it, there was intermittent resistance. However, in the morning hours of a special session on August 22, 1990, a vote was forced, and the GDR's immediate accession to the FRG was ratified. On the audio recordings stored at the official radio archive of the FRG's public television channel, we hear the voice of the chamber's president, Sabine Bergmann-Pohl (CDU): "Ladies and gentlemen, I think this is a historic event. We certainly did not make the decision easy for ourselves, but we made it today on our responsibility before the citizens of the GDR due to their will to vote."[76] The parliamentarians decided to dissolve the East German state. The futures of people who would lose their livelihoods in the GDR's total dismantling and transformation (*Umbau*) were absent from these discussions.[77] (Arendt had it right when she cautions that the adage "all power resides in the people" is only true on election day. The fact that the word "revolution" originally meant restoration may be more than a mere oddity of semantics).[78]

Rather than developing a sustained critique of how the GDR parliament "turned itself into a solemn corpse" (Jens Reich, Alliance '90), the former activists of the peace and citizens' movement who served as parliament deputies focused on the exposure of informants and the dismantling of the Stasi. Otherwise, empty-handed, the activist found this confessional logic turned into the fragile legacy of the revolution. Arguably, the dreams of the citizens' movement were in the process of being mangled. All that would be left of these dreams by 1991 was the dubious wholesale public access to every secret file that existed about East Germans. One year after unification, the FRG government gave the people the Stasi Records Agency (albeit not on the terms the East German activists had demanded).

To my mind, then, what Heise's *Material* performs most palpably is this: it disrupts the regimes of the visible that established themselves in the post-1989, post–Cold War era as part of a larger configuration of domination and subjection (see also chapter 1). The media-archival memory project takes up modes of artistic and political representation to open up the landscape of the possible. Whether ending in success or disaster, people who went through such irruptive change as '89–90—who had risked a new beginning or participated in it against their inclination and expectation— will not easily forget that feeling. Even within the improvised transitional parliament, there was reportedly a playful sense, shared across the aisles, of shock that ordinary people had become deputies and even cabinet ministers.[79] Rather than using the term "democracy" cynically or operationally, radically democratic spaces in Heise's *Material* are constituted through myriad forms of self-organizing from below, inside and outside parliamentary bodies. Even by October 1990, when all was over, Jens Reich from Alliance '90 urged, "I don't want to leave Politics. We must find new ways of bringing like-minded people together for effective action."[80] This call for collective and adaptive organizing is where the greatest potential lies for uncovering a provisional history of the late GDR. Heise's *Material* stores the unfinalizable, heterogenous energies that circulated in the streets, communities, and transitional parliamentary body of an unmoored society for future encounters.

JAMMED (1992) / MATERIAL (2009)

Thomas Heise's media-archeological *Material* begins with a film remnant of abandoned children playing in an urban wasteland in Halle. They drag leftover pieces across scree to build a bridge into an uncertain future. The interspliced parliament interval also recalls, for a faint second, the children's industrious voices. Heise lets them echo over an edit seam at the beginning of the retaped Volkskammer session. The empty bus scene following this parliamentary montage cuts to the last, longer segment in the compilation, which was taken at a film screening of Heise's 1992 film *Jammed: Let's Get Moving*, a documentary about right-wing youth in Halle-Neustadt in the early 1990s. The screening also took place in 1992, at a Halle-Neustadt neighborhood center, where a confrontation between leftist antifascists and neo-Nazi skinheads escalated into violence. The recovered footage of the event was shot in Beta SP color, initially an analog format with digital modes following later, designed for professional TV recordings. Amid the polarization of the extreme Left and the Far Right, Heise himself appears for a second as though to embody a neutral position. Shot in Saxony-Anhalt, this local crisis echoes the alarming atmosphere across East Germany in the early 1990s. As the film projector keeps running, we see forlorn images of moving trains.[81] Off-screen, we also hear the mother of one of the skinhead teenagers featured in the documentary. After the fall of the Berlin Wall, she left for the West, presumably leaving her son behind in hopes of giving him a better future. *Jammed* records how working-class youth struggled with mass unemployment, petty criminality, and societal abandonment in the aftermath of unification. A staggering one-third of the former GDR's working population faced unemployment after the *Wende*.

However, for a brief moment at the screening, the chaos in the community center also draws new lines, where the defiant youth stop fighting each other and confront the perplexed audience of culturally aware, liberal leftists. Just three years earlier, they had been active in the GDR's oppositional peace and human rights groups or the citizens' movement that formed in the space of churches and eventually ignited the Peaceful Revolution. While windows smash and beer bottles fly, one exasperated instigator yells at the older intellectual folks, "You are even more stupid than us, you just talk and talk and talk, we can't talk to you . . . DOVES OF PEACE . . . what does that produce? . . . it stinks horribly of PEACE in here." Unwittingly, this critique echoes Heiner Müller's provocative argument about the failure of the East German revolution.

In the 1992 essay "At the Shores of the Barbarians" ("Die Küste der Barbaren"), the dissident playwright went so far as to argue that the '89 revolution was defanged by the pacifist tradition of the Protestant Church and the overwhelming public focus on the Stasi. Both had eclipsed the historic rise and expansion of the global, geopolitical system of capital. Once more, the open question transmitted by the emancipatory inheritance of the French Revolution—the struggle for liberty *and* equality—had not been answered, he argued. On the right-wing youth mobilization at the onset of the post-1989 neoliberal era, Müller only laconically commented: "From Leipzig, the city of heroes, to terrors of Rostock. Wounds cry out for wounds: The oppressed potential for violence, no revolution/emancipations without violence against the oppressors, vents itself in the attacks against those weaker: asylum seekers and poverty-stricken foreigners, the poor against the poorest. Not a finger is laid on a single property shark, regardless of what nation they come from."[82] In a similar vein, looking back on 1989, the filmmaker Konrad Weiss, who was one of the early initiators of the civil rights movement Democracy Now, contemplates the vexed, if not complicit, role of peacefulness in the revolutionary process. He, in fact, regretted the collaboration with the SED in the roundtables: "If we had been radical," he concluded, "then we would have taken on the *Macht* [power] in the fall of 1989; that's when power lay in the street . . . if the civil rights movements had understood power that autumn and seized the governing body, then history would have been different." He added, "I don't know, however, if it would have remained nonviolent."[83] In contrast, *Material*'s 1992 archival footage exposes how violence erupted in the right-wing peripheries post-unification. The liberal culture workers who had organized the screening of *Jammed* are enraged that Heise's cameraman (Sebastian Richter) is capturing this escalation on tape—they castigate the filmmakers as voyeuristic war journalists, citing the conflict in Bosnia-Herzegovina. In a variation on Heise's concern with disrupting the "visible given," the culture workers press the filmmaker's team to shut off the camera: "There is nothing to see here." These leftover images of fractures in the revolutionary aftermath are still waiting to be found when we try to make sense of the rise of the right-wing Alternative for Germany (AfD) in the East today. I shall return to this subject in the next and last chapter of this book.

Coda: Protest Memory

On October 3, 1990, with the official unification of Germany, the GDR ceased to be. "The tragedy began not when the liberation of the country as a whole ruined, almost automatically, the small hidden islands of freedom that were doomed anyhow, but when it turned out that there was no mind to inherit and to question, to think about and to remember. . . . [W]ithout this thinking completion after the act, without the articulation accomplished by remembrance," Arendt states, "there simply is no story left that could be told."[84] Surely, leftists such as the East German playwright Volker Braun foresaw that Germany's reunification and its politics of closure would give rise to a new era of conformity. Echoing Arendt, he lamented that "our job-less [*arbeitslos*] souls will soon remember a future, an old shared cause, that no longer has any name."[85] But even conservative commentators, who had supported German reunification, were now forced to face their own obsolescence when the GDR's constitutional and legal structure disappeared. In a 2020 interview, Herbert Schirmer (CDU), the minister of culture in the GDR's last parliament, recalled that he became unemployed on the day of unification: "After October 3, you were gone as if nothing had occurred."[86] When people need to arrange themselves in and with a new order, there are no usable frameworks to remember the world that is falling apart. In that odd in-between period, that interval, it is not apparent how to gather ideas that could make sense of the complexity and specificity that great historical ruptures demand.

However, at the same time, Arendt may have been too pessimistic. By concluding this chapter, let me indicate that the boundaries imposed by conceptions of historical breaks such as 1989 can restrain our imagination and split us off from the past. In that sense, it is not surprising that scholars in the last two decades have reconsidered their methodologies in disciplines such as literature and architecture, cultural studies, and media studies. As Thomas Elsaesser astutely points out, the discourse of rupture and epistemic breaks has often been supplanted with the "softer" ones of intertextuality and remediation, of emulation, pastiche, re-montage, and appropriation.[87] Drawing on these influences, I have attempted to grasp an element of indeterminacy in the relationships between collective memory and visual and archival production. My term of choice, however, is Rancière's "art of the possible," which he put forward around 2008 to counter post-historical interdictions; the term is thus more political than the postmodern theories of remediation are, I believe. For him, an artistic intervention can be political by "modifying the visible, the ways of perceiving and expressing it, of experiencing it as tolerable or intolerable."[88] In this vein, I hope to have shown how a reading of '89–90 as provisional, as unfinished history open to contest (as all histories are, of course), can be productive.

The conflation of 1989 with Western freedom in today's collective memory is a grave distortion. An eyewitness renders the forgotten radical openness best: "The year 1990 was the freest in the history of East Germany. Everything seemed to be possible, to become. Society awoke to a colorful, shrill, casual life. The old authorities disappeared . . . everywhere uncertainty and departure. Not only were the previous authorities gone—but there were also no new ones that could have represented a state that anyone would have taken seriously. There was a pulsating life in the cities that we had only seen in art films."[89] In other words, the particularity of '89–90 and its relevance today lie in the nascent and spontaneous, performative constitution of political publics. This chapter has shown there is no stable, originary point of the revolutionary event. Rather than linear, foreclosed, or normative interpretations of 1989, an understanding of the historical interval can reveal ideas in the midst of "being born, getting stirred up, disappearing, and reappearing."[90] Recalling '89–90 can serve as a potential screen for ongoing, self-critical questioning of today's Germany and the fragile state of democracy in our current polarized times more broadly.

Moreover, a media-archeological approach can draw attention to the dormancy of this historical potentiality, calling attention to the otherwise mute, the unseen and unheard—that is, to the conditions that produce the limits of archival and collective memory. While this approach is admittedly less objective than some, no academic account is fully so; this one can initiate multidirectional circulations of different kinds of archival media: photographs, films, pamphlets, audio recordings, TV news footage, letters, bureaucratic protocols, and so forth. Left behind in the wake of a historical rupture as minor categories, these materials cannot be as easily absorbed into a neoliberal trajectory. They allow us to read the established, dominant archive "against the grain" to locate misplaced memories of protest and self-organized publics. This minor, nonnormative approach, however, may also have limits. Working in transnational contexts, scholars have stressed in recent years that narratives and images of social movements in the public realm can help collective action by providing symbolic material from the past.[91] Although I support this idea, and it guides my thinking in this book, we cannot ignore that protest memories, especially in the official sphere, are also reifiable (an argument I took up in chapter 1).

Finally, and most importantly, films can function as archives, temporal spaces for remembering and forgetting, and artistic sites where tossed footage is stored. Thomas Heise knew that the older analog recordings about the late GDR, whether on video or film, would soon become unviewable without digitization. The filmmaker ends his 2009 art documentary *Material* with what is most probably the only 35mm film footage of the Republic Palace (the seat of the GDR state and transitional parliament) being torn down. By 2008, the building was destroyed after spectacular and lengthy attempts to decontaminate the structure from asbestos had turned it into a ruin. While plenty of digital material exists of the Palace's dismantling, Heise believes that his segment is the only material of this kind that will survive even a hundred years in the future. What remains turns into what stays and thus into salient questions about archival care and our relation to these dislocated, reassembled images.

In this final scene, after nearly three hours of discontinuous footage capturing the self-constituting performance of the people in the streets, prisons, and communal and parliamentary spaces before and long after the fall of the Wall, the documentary shifts in tone. From the interior of the giant skeletal structure of the Republic Palace, the camera captures an isolated group of workers in the distance. Their identities are concealed by decontamination suits while they tend to mountains of toxic debris. The images are suspended, as it were, in a "dumpf rauschende Raum" (dull murmuring expanse), an industrial soundscape that has become Heise's signature to render catastrophic utopian temporality as space somewhere in the trajectory of Benjamin's angel of history.[92] Decontextualized, we do not know if we are watching the past or images of a hazardous future. Refusing to provide a finished product, the film opens itself to differing views and interpretations. But *Material* also provides the means to counter the dominant narrative, as its preserved and recirculated materials stand in open contradiction to the generally remembered images of the Fall of the Wall on public television, the so-called *Wende*, and the historically inevitable unification. The artist's philosophy is that documentary film may last longer than any state in which it is made. In an accompanying essay, "Archeology Is about Digging," Heise writes that "this film depends on the reality of possibility, such as it could be found in the utopian images from that era [1989–90]. It is about the audience and the stage, about up and down, the first words spoken after a long silence, and the silence that returns after that brief moment of freedom."[93]

FIGURE 4.9. "Wir waren das Volk" (We were the people). Banner covering the House of the Teachers, Alexanderplatz, Berlin, 1999. On the occasion of the tenth anniversary of the Peaceful Revolution in the GDR. Photograph by W. Kölbel. IMAGO / snapshot.

In the fall of 1999, ten years after the civil unrest—or the Peaceful Revolution—organizers of a memorial initiative draped a massive banner over the former East German Teacher's House at Berlin's Alexanderplatz. It read, "We were the people" ("Wir waren das Volk").[94] Although the banner had multiple meanings (that is, we were a repressed people in the GDR and are citizens now, or we became the people in 1989), the photographer Andreas Rost captured the public square in an austere, sobering image, as though the people had taken off and vanished. In fact, the black-and-white photograph renders the vast urban space of Alexanderplatz deserted while a police patrol car in the foreground of the visual field looks on.[95] It is as if a hollow space marks the constitution of the people—"like a chalk outline at the scene of a crime." Rather than the ideological illusions of autonomy and self-presence at work in all modern (liberal) politics, to my eye, Rost's photograph, echoing *Material*, recalls that "the people" as a political category needs to be understood as a mixed scene to be staged and interpreted. Political theorists such as Bruno Bosteels, Jacques Rancière, and Étienne Balibar remind us that there is no "people" before the act by which a people becomes a people in the first place. Moreover, even afterward, the people are never one or homogenous but many, plural, and internally divided. Wherever "the people" show up, however fragile and fleeting this inscription may be, a sphere of appearance of the *demos* is created; an element of the *kratos*, the power of the people, exists.[96] However, as the empty Alexanderplatz in Rost's photograph renders so compellingly, the problem is in extending the sphere of this appearance, in sustaining its potential. Given the elusiveness inherent in categories such as "the people" (serving as a name here for the political process that produces its own subject), it is difficult to grasp how this appearance of the power of the people can be sustained and maximized in a process that has no end. Today, it could not be more evident that protests and popular uprisings can and do occur on both the political left and the far right. Long forgotten is that the people in the streets of East Germany identified with the seemingly egalitarian and emancipatory invocation of "We are the people." Long forgotten is also that they constituted themselves as political agents in various improvisational ways. Protest memory is mediated: it may be imperceptible, go underground, or even dissipate, but it remains to be reactivated.

[CHAPTER FIVE]

Futures of Hope

As I finish writing this book, in the fall of 2022, the planet is in peril to a degree we have not witnessed before. The world faces existential threats in the forms of climate change, overpopulation, global pandemics, and the depletion of natural resources. With little prospect for a livable future ahead of us, why should we look back? And why return to resonant and residual leftist ideals in particular, as I have done throughout these pages? After all, the massive failure of utopian thought was marked not only by the collapse of Cold War Eastern Europe. Following a brief interval, an opening in 1989, a more radically democratic inflection of these ideals in Germany also failed and was derailed once more during the early revolutionary fall. Obviously, there are no easy answers about how to proceed at this moment of unprecedented crises. Yet, amid the possibly irreversible climate catastrophe, the current state of hyper-inequality, and the reign of surveillance capitalism, mass protests are again on the rise. Thousands have taken to the streets in Chile, Bolivia, Hong Kong, France, and Spain in the past years alone. Sometimes deliberately, often unknowingly, these mobilizations of outrage and hope harness scripts of earlier revolutions, and that is of course true on the left and the right.

When the Berlin Wall fell, in 1989, and Eastern European socialism evaporated into thin air, the "end of history" was declared. Although scholars backed away from this assertion over time, it overshadowed the understanding of an entire era, eclipsing any sense of futurity until it slipped away. Even those who lived through it were under its spell: socialist state leaders had witnessed themselves fading into obsolescence in 1989, and the activists of the grassroots social movements that initiated the revolution appeared soon to forget their radically democratic agendas. Fast-forward to three decades later: progressive candidates have won major platforms in the United States and are mounting a challenge against nativist populism in a post-truth era. Then again, the current upsurge of right-wing populists across Western and Eastern Europe and the United States echoes nation-

200

alist movements of the early twentieth century. Thirty years after the collapse of socialism in Eastern Europe, we cannot help but observe that the hegemony of neoliberalism is in crisis. Capitalist democracy itself appears to be on trial, and even its most ardent proponents have begun to question the idea of the West as normative telos of contemporary history.[1] As grievances fill the streets and the World Wide Web—and as crowds across the globe, struggling for bandwidth, shout louder and louder—where are the unlocked, overlooked reservoirs of hope? In an age of ethical and ecological devastation, a stance of counterfactual hope is directed toward an improved future that transcends our current ability to understand it.[2] Those who have such hope still lack the appropriate concepts to make sense of what is to come and yet they submit to that openness.

In this book, I have made the case that the transitional period of 1989–90 is worth our attention. I have foregrounded the role of 1989 as an open-ended archive for the future—a memory space—that can perpetually supply, move, and re-move unfulfilled revolutionary potentialities engaged in structural change. After all, far from being over, or fixed in textbooks, the energies and impulses of events move through time. I have amplified the contingency of 1989 and challenged the dominant narrative that Germany's reunification inevitably had to unfold as the absorption of the GDR into the FRG. My focus has been on memorial and artistic practices that engage with "1989" as an inventive, heterotopian space across time. Here, the play of differences, inherent in the performance of "We, the people," continues to open itself up to vital displacement and transformation. More specifically, what I have brought into view is the radically (non)violent grassroots collaboration of hundreds of thousands of East Germans who came together, provisionally, *despite* the variegated visions of a better life they held and *despite* the vastly different forms of political subjectivity they inhabited.

Gathering the vibrant optimism of that lawless time and letting it shine onto the precarious terrains of our present, I have made a case that the anticipatory logic of hope can be radical. That hope turns into a potent possibility when performative, often incommensurable, and fragile forms of collective action are involved. In October of 1989, two activists appeared amid a crowd gathered at Karl Marx Square in front of the Leipzig Opera and secretly unfurled an illegal banner that read, "We will LIVE tomorrow how we protest today!" ("So wie wir heute demonstrieren werden wir morgen LEBEN!"). Facing police roundup, East Germans took to the streets and acted in concert, making themselves vulnerable but also demanding and giving political and spatial organization to their clandestine ideas. They petitioned not only to the police but also to the world to register what was happening in their country. They formed themselves into images to be transmitted and projected to all who watched.[3] We need to remember not only that these protesters cast themselves forward into an unknowable future but that their collective chants of "We are the people" ("Wir sind das Volk") also moved beyond the borders of a closed-in country to affect their contemporaries in Eastern Europe.[4] While current focus centers on the right-wing rise in Eastern Europe today, my hope is that future scholars will shed more light on the transnational interconnectedness of the progressive, activist movements in Czechoslovakia, Poland, Hungary, the GDR, China, and the USSR around 1989, while also tracking whether and how these movements entered a global archive of social mobilizations through forms of cultural memory.[5]

Even anecdotally, it is clear that Leipzig's protest images, cascading across East Germany and Eastern Europe, became crucial for the self-constitution of ordinary people as political subjects. These images became mobile, so to speak, and prompted people elsewhere to act. On November 17, 1989, the largest demonstration occurred in Prague since 1968, with fifteen thousand people demanding the end of a one-party state and the institution of a new system under the leadership of Václav Havel and the signatories of Charter 77. While the crowd was violently dispersed—by police with tear gas, riot batons, dogs, trucks, and tanks—the citizens there had reportedly mobilized in part because they had seen news and images of the demonstrations in Leipzig on television in the weeks before.[6] That same November day, when the revolutionary crisis erupted in Prague, a crowd of fifty thousand people also protested, for the first time, in Bulgaria, urging for a newly elected parliament, plurality, and a democracy without party dictatorship.

A few months earlier, citizens of the GDR had reportedly seen the images on (Western) television of the violent crushing of the Chinese student uprising in Beijing's Tiananmen Square.[7] These scenes of state brutality unfolding in China fueled East Germans' anxiety about the specter of impending violence—a storyline, we saw, that has reached nearly mythical proportions in collective memory today. Long forgotten is that this historical turning point also led East Germans to renegotiate the official dogma of international solidarity that had been in place since the 1960s. Through troubling imagery, relational bonds between East Germans and these distant protesters against authoritarian rule were formed. The ethical and political impulses of earlier state-orchestrated solidarity movements were not dead. Rather, they were alive and intermingling with, even intermittently encouraging, the democratically oriented civil uprisings in the countries of the Soviet empire. In the late twentieth century, today's infinite news streams and archives of social media had not yet come into existence, and thus, the collaborative mass gatherings that ripped through Eastern Europe in 1989 were soon eclipsed by the victory of the West. They were forced into the shadows of oblivion.

Moreover, in the early 1990s, at a moment of post–Cold War capitalist triumphalism, a historical revision took place that had profound effects on a global collective memory. Among other things, emerging intellectual disciplines erased the in-betweenness of Eastern Europe in the twentieth century, as a region situated between the colonial and anti-colonial, Western and non-Western worlds. This liminality had in fact defined a long-standing history of Eastern European global interconnections, according to historians Paul Betts and James Mark. However, new post–Cold War approaches placed "dictatorship, planning and illiberalism on one side, and western liberal multi-party democracy, markets and civil society on the other" in order to gauge the success of countries emerging from authoritarian rule. Consequently, "an interest in connections between Eastern Europe, Latin America, and African countries which had often turned to socialist or non-capitalist modernization during postwar decolonization was now replaced by a flattened, unidirectional 'from the west to the rest' model."[8] Betts and Mark further note that for the next two decades, this strategy served to repress not only the complex, contested nature and multiple forms of world-making (of which globalization is only one) but also the East's rich history of migration and international engagement. This erasure was successful until the 2008 crisis of finance capitalism put the Western model into question and cast doubt on the notion that the westernization of the Eastern European region was an inevitability.

Now, thirty years later, the Iron Curtain may be gone, but Europe's East and West are more divided than ever.[9] Right-wing nationalist movements in Poland, the Czech Republic, Slovakia, and Hungary have firmly established themselves in national governments and the European Union. The inroads made by radical right-wing parties in Eastern European countries appear to challenge the liberal cosmopolitan establishments that have fostered the global neoliberal turn over the past decades. Yet in effect, these right-wing nationalist movements present no substantial challenge to the current political and economic system. As Cristian Cercel succinctly states, they are much more part of it than their agendas claim.[10] In Germany, too, in the long aftermath of the fall of the Wall, the conservative, right-wing Alternative for Germany (AfD) rose to become the second majority party in three Eastern states: Brandenburg, Saxony, and Thuringia. As a recipient of the prestigious Leibniz Prize, awarded by the federally funded German Research Foundation (DFG), put it in 2019, "The AfD dominates in the area of the former GDR."[11] The use of Cold War language nearly thirty years after the country's unification in the highest and most visible institutional arenas suggests a causal link between the end of twentieth-century socialism and the rise of right-wing movements. Instead of being readily accepted, however, this link should be critically investigated. After all, the AfD has performed as counter-public space for the East, creating a supply of alternative narratives that, regardless of how dubious they are, have succeeded in challenging culturally dominant assumptions. Whether on the left or the far right, the claim to exclusion from the hegemonic sphere is central to counter-publicity.[12] In any case, the AfD is perceived as the shameful legacy of the so-called *Wende* (the turn in 1989).

How on earth did we get here? How was it possible for a nationalist, xenophobic imaginary to take hold amid a population that had collaboratively mobilized to challenge a state sovereign three decades earlier in the streets of Leipzig, Dresden, Karl-Marx-Stadt, and Berlin?[13] Jacques Derrida wrote that the historical event of 1989–90 carried with it an "excess of disjointure." When living in a "time out of joint," he noted, "it is easy to go from disadjusted to unjust," from the logic of rights to the logic of vengeance.[14] The year 1989 marked a sea change, a point at which grand narratives collapsed—narratives that had sustained utopian thinking and trust in the future since the onset of modernity, as Andreas Huyssen and, more recently, Enzo Traverso have argued. Once Eastern European state socialism disappeared, a "collective state of depression" arose.[15] And indeed, in Germany, the critical Left sank into such a morose state of failure and defeat that it was no longer able to transport the enduring relevance of its radical, plural aspirations, which were absorbed (displaced, stunted, submerged), if not taken hostage, during the revolutionary fall in 1989. To be clear, all revolutionary movements will eventually take down their avant-garde, and soon the horizon of expectation, briefly visible, disappears. People cannot live forever in an uninterrupted state of high tension and intense activity, as political theorist Slavoj Žižek has noted. And, arguably, the agent of popular pressure is always only a minority.[16] As we saw, the East German oppositional, basic-democratic movements formed in the church were propelled into a kind of social laboratory by the popular uprising in 1989. These provisional, alternative sovereignties consisted of many civic and political currents. After unification, a few activists obtained high offices in the new neoliberal order (for example, Joachim Gauck, Marianne Birthler, Roland Jahn, and Wolfgang Thierse), but most sank into unemployment and anonymity. Only a handful of former opposition leaders, such as Bärbel Bohley and Katja Havemann, vocalized their sense of defeat regarding the so-called peaceful revolution in the public realm. When historical shifts sidelined them, they refused participation in the governing bodies of the

FRG and ended up tending to the inheritance of the dissident movements surveilled by the Stasi. The critique of capitalism that informed their agenda in the fall of '89 had disappeared.

But the downfall of activists such as Christa Wolf, Volker Braun, or Heiner Müller—all of whom emerged from the cultural elite in the GDR—was remarkably swift. This acute crisis led to left-wing melancholia, if not the death of the Left, creating an ideational vacuum across the public sphere in Germany that persisted for nearly the next three decades.[17] Of course, variably, the idea of 1989 turned into a myth for endings (history, socialism, equality, etc.) and beginnings (civil society, democracy, a market economy, etc.)—a myth that came to occupy that imaginary open space of the revolutionary fall.

During the 2000s, leftist impulses began to reassemble in the margins of post-unification society and internationally. Ultimately, however, the neoliberal discourse of "There is no alternative" (TINA) sank Germany so successfully into the logic of a perpetual now that the right-wing movement began to claim the public space of political alternatives. While masking their own continued investment in a free-market approach, the elites of the AfD (mainly from the West) managed to galvanize populist resentments through a Germany-first approach. Paradoxically, this coup was staged, at least in part, through the appropriative, cross-wired recall of the fundamental democratic impulses of 1989. Abusing the unresolved memory of that transitional year, the AfD ran its advertising campaign in 2019 under the motto "Wende 2.0," repurposing slogans such as "Finish the peaceful revolution at the polls" ("Beende die friedliche Revolution im Wahllokal") or "Take your country back" ("Hol dir dein Land zurück").[18] The party's nationalist agenda gained momentum, especially in the aftermath of Germany's so-called refugee crisis in 2015, through the savvy use of well-organized networks and social media, as the memory scholar Wulf Kantsteiner has pointed out.[19] The conflict between disgruntled East Germans and the perceived political establishment was certainly fueled, however, by leading politicians (in most cases from the West) who misrecognized the complex historical conditions of the PEGIDA protests and contributed to framing East Germans as Others. The Green Party's Cem Özdemir's used *Mischpoke* (a term that derives from the Yiddish word for "family" but that has disdainful connotations in German) to describe the agitated crowds spewing anti-immigration, xenophobic, racist language—other high-ranking politicians called them "regrettable for Germany" (Maas, SPD) and people with "hatred in their hearts" (Merkel, CDU).[20] Since the 2010s, anti-statist sentiments have continued to spread across the Eastern federal states.

One of the conclusions I want to advance is that we need to pay more attention to how people—who are simply employees, heads of households, spouses, and so on, with individual lives—suddenly coalesce into a collective force and become a *Volk*, in the ethnic, nationalist sense, or become *the people* claiming sovereign self-rule, performing the community as negotiated and differentiated *Gemeinschaft*.[21] Memory scholars need to have an eye on the multiscalar circulation of narratives, images, and manifestos related to the protest pasts and precarious presents these collective enactments fabricate, produce, or elide in the name of better futures. In Eastern Germany, this kind of "strange magic whereby the whole becomes more than the sum of its parts" seems to have receded at the moment, or, in any case, has shifted most legibly to the right.[22] My aim in this final chapter, therefore, is to explore provisional thoughts on current alternatives to a binary, competitive imaginary. Notably, it is temporary migrant archives that have performed the most significant labor of reconfiguring 1989 as a collaborative *and* differentiated mnemonic space.[23] Refracting history, 1989 emerges once more as a rupture, a non-nonviolent event.

Exhibits such as the Turkish-German collaboration *BİZİM BERLİN 89/90* (Our Berlin 89/90, 2018) not only offer livable translocal alternatives to the "paranoid nationalism" that has arisen as society's hopes for a better future "shrink."[24] They also powerfully pick up and propel forward the "new revolutionary vernacular" that people who are displaced, discriminated, and marginalized may already share worldwide today. Developing a global consciousness, this new intersectional vernacular arises outside traditional Marxist frames, as Susan Buck-Morss recently argued. Twenty years after her landmark book *Dreamworld and Catastrophe*, the post-Soviet scholar affirmed that the expected leftist course of history—focusing on universalizing notions of modernization, progress, class, and internationalism—has inevitably failed.[25] To be clear, I am not advocating for an uncritical return to Marxist notions of universalism. The utopian social project of the GDR emphasized universality at the risk of ignoring its own racism.[26] Communists deemed class to be the medium that dissolves all other differences. Thus, racial discrimination was always located elsewhere, where the fascism still alive in Western capitalist imperialism reproduced it.[27] But I join scholars who have examined the ambivalent legacies of race discourse under the conditions of state socialism and who are less quick to dismiss the possibility of reopening the archives of that era to recover strands of an internationalist, even intersectional imaginary, post-1989.[28]

At the same time, I submit that such returns do not suffice at this current moment of (post)democratic illiberalism. We have to free our imagination from history, to a certain degree, and disclose new forms of arranging intersubjective relations and society. Instead, I offer the political notion of post-migrant allyship as an alternative, accounting for racialized *and* economic forms of dispossession. For, arguably, at this juncture of historical reckoning, the particularities of race discourse, gender, and concerns for the planet's survivability inspire vital revolutionary forces to take to the streets. And yet, I conclude, these new radical, often intersectional forms of organizing, which shatter any linear notion of historical time, also need to be augmented with visions of shared things and infrastructures, or what critical thinkers such as Bonnie Honig, drawing on Hannah Arendt, have called public commons. Actions of sharing compel us to reorient our perspectives and to imagine relations that are different from any instrumental form of exchange, economic or symbolic, in a highly polarized world that clings to the ideal of incessant growth.

Alternative Solidarities

Given that scholars today recast the Velvet Revolutions in Central Europe as carrying within them the seeds of illiberalism, reimagining 1989–90 as an intersectional and transcultural memory space may be the most provocative instruction this book can offer. While historians recently questioned 1989 as a lens for historical periodization, suggesting even that it might be disbanded to create new narratives for the FRG, let us investigate the cesura one final time by turning to the post-1989 controversy around the East German migrant status. Once larger dynamics of disenfranchisement come into view, long-accepted national frameworks and narratives can be rearranged; seemingly disparate legacies may be connected into new transnational and international *noeuds de mémoire* (nodes of memory).[29]

After 1989, the hegemonic language of Eastern Europe's liberation and integration implied a perpetual reminder that former East Germans should remember the authoritarian state from which they had been rescued by the West. In a previous chapter we saw how (self)stigmatization and shame experienced by East Germans often exacerbated the nearly imperceptible process by which the collapse of their biographies and collective networks became less and less accessible. The social and economic forms of dispossession to which East Germans had been (unevenly) subjected since the *Wende* were no longer legible in the dominant public sphere. However, in May 2018, the left-leaning German newspaper *taz* published an interview with Naika Foroutan, a professor of integration studies and sociology at Humboldt University, under the headline "East Germans Are Migrants Too" ("Ostdeutsche sind auch Migranten"). Although critical attempts to interrelate the differential histories of East Germans and Germans with migration backgrounds in neoliberal post-1989 Germany were not entirely new, Foroutan's position as a (West) German Iranian scholar with a research focus on postmigration society enabled the controversial thesis to gain traction.[30] Foroutan received support but also faced considerable backlash. The meaning of the term "migration" has changed in recent years—shifting from a focus on voluntary, legal mobility to forced moves across borders, involving refugees, asylum seekers, and undocumented immigrants exposed to hyper-precarity.[31] This shift in focus put further pressure on Foroutan's argument. In the long aftermath of 1989, the controversy pivoted on the question of which (im)mobilities can legitimately come into view.

Based on empirical research and a multiyear interview project, Foroutan concluded that the experiences East Germans have had since the fall of the Wall and those of migrants are not dissimilar. Be it displacement, discrimination, or the search for identity, migrants and East Germans, she argues, shared experiences of marginalization in a post-migrant society.[32] Other scholars and memoirists have elaborated the transgenerational effects of East German displacement, and the reorientations of p(ost)-migrants in contemporary Germany.[33] Among migrants, Foroutan's study centered on "Muslim communities" because the official discourse of the last decade, she states, had focused on them and, at the same time, "Muslims" formed the political frame of reference for the negative behavior (that is, PEGIDA) of the East Germans.[34] Since the influx of laborers into the FRG in the 1960s, the Turkish-German population comprises the country's largest migrant group, followed most recently by (among non-European foreign nationals) immigrants from Syria and other Middle Eastern countries, in addition to regions in South Asia and Africa. Scholars in German transnational studies have convincingly argued that discourses about these distinct migrant groups, and the variable conditions of their flight or transmobility, have impacted the racialized dynamic of the post-1989 European imaginary. In the contested unification process, the designation of Turkish and Kurdish migrants first and foremost as Muslim positioned them as the internal Other to secure Europe's own sense of cohesion, according to Yasemin Yildiz. This shift toward religion as the preeminent category dividing democratic cosmopolitans from those crippled by authoritarian mentalities, Katrin Sieg explains, aided the cultural integration of (secular) East Germans.[35] Yet those multiple jagged lines of othering appear less relevant for Foroutan's study.[36] While migrants left their country, East Germans "were abandoned by their country," according to her provocative thesis. Needless to say, the experience of crossing geopolitical borders is indeed not shared by these groups (which in themselves are heterogenous and unstable, and whose "'ethnic labeling'" has to be performed, to use Zafer Şenocak's formulation).[37] However, the notion, put forth by memory scholars, that migration involves the negotiation of "unscripted new linkages"[38] proves to be productive for our final considerations of an alternative, affiliative post-1989 memory.

As expected, the debate over Foroutan's thesis raised important concerns about the differential practices by which conditions of citizenship and forms of national identity are limited and constituted.[39] Anetta Kahane, for instance, the director of the Amadeu Antonio Foundation, an organization devoted to activism against anti-Semitism, rejected Foroutan's finding in shocked disbelief. She recalled the attacks on visible minorities, such as Vietnamese and Mozambican labor migrants, by radicalized East German men in the early 1990s (cheered on by ordinary citizens). Indeed, these abhorrent events haunt (East) Germany's collective memory today, giving Kahane's outrage and argument further legitimacy.[40] In recent years, a body of artistic works in film, theater, and radio on these pogroms has emerged, allowing for the transmission of (post)migrant perspectives on that memory.[41] Echoing Kahane, the managing editor of *Zeit Online*, Sasan Abdi-Herrle, admonished those supporters of Foroutan's study who conjectured that racism among East Germans might be explained by the stigmatization they experienced in the unification process.[42] Kahane pointed to the legacy of an inadequate memory politics surrounding the Nazi era and the Shoah in the GDR—as well as the colonialism of the Second Reich—and, to a certain extent, East Germans' own *Wende* experience. She argued that xenophobia and racism were already pervasive in the GDR (an argument that is supported by a number of studies).[43] Abdi-Herrle, however, referred to a younger cohort of Germans with multiple (post)historical experiences, who were more concerned with the future than with explaining current problems exclusively by looking to the past.

Despite this considerable public criticism, Foroutan's legitimacy as the lead researcher of the project "Postmigration Germany" ("Deutschland Postmigrantisch") at Humboldt University propelled the discussion forward. The differentiated yet ultimately supportive responses of Germans with (post)migration backgrounds, such as journalist Ferda Ataman, then at the influential weekly liberal magazine *Der Spiegel*, helped sustain the intersectional conversation in spaces online.[44] Panels were organized in select places across Berlin during the summer of 2018. At the same time, far-right protests escalated in Chemnitz and an upsurge of right-wing nationalist movements swept across Eastern and Western Europe. Inadvertently and for a brief time, the publicly staged debate provided an entirely new set of frameworks—alternative to the nation—and multiple strands of memory by which to make sense of the long aftermath of 1989. Animated within the transcultural particularities of Germany—and, more specifically, Berlin—these public gatherings also intersected with the emergence of larger transnational, translocal solidarities. People began to assemble across the globe in a decidedly *post*-post-utopian moment.

Paradoxically, perhaps—or out of good sense—other public figures who (like Kahane) grew up in the East, such as social scientist Thomas Ahbe, approached the controversial territory of comparative East German/migrant study more carefully. Jana Hensel, author of the international bestseller *Zonenkinder* (*After the Wall*, 2004) and a voice of the so-called *Wende* generation in the East, ultimately embraced Foroutan's suggestion to shift the public and academic understanding of the postcolonial, transnational, or diasporic in a post-1989 context, so that it encompasses post-socialist histories as well. Whereas Foroutan's critics were alarmed by the risk of appropriation and pointed out that East Germans are not physically identifiable as targets of racial hatred in the public sphere, Hensel turned (in)visibility itself into a central category and liminal space, around which the differential comparisons of minority groups should be examined.[45] In many ways, it is precisely the invisibility of East Germans, she argued, the illegibility of their status as marginalized and second class that is responsible for the success of the AfD and its racist, xenophobic, nativist platform. In the absence of conventional frameworks of race or ethnicity to conjure attention or differentiated solidarities, right-wing discourse fills the vacuum. Others point to the absence of class-based conceptions, arising from the downfall of the Soviet Bloc. Filmmaker Alexander Kluge and critic Slavoj Žižek examine the accelerated effects of post-human capitalism in recent years that have eroded the last vestiges of class consciousness (rather than being a member of the working class, they argue, one has to become a self-entrepreneur).[46] In this line of thinking, it is because traditional Marxist conceptions of class (or social vision) have been discredited, fallen out of the memory dynamics, or are simply no longer operational in a postindustrial, post-production era that East Germans have turned to other means of expression to occupy space and for their grievances to take place.

From that perspective, the broad base of AfD supporters may not necessarily be xenophobic (though I do not deny that "there are people who feel perfectly at home with those reactionary values," to recall Chantal Mouffe). Instead, their protest votes for a right-wing party render the real and imagined dispossession of Easterners audible in a neoliberal political arena that has erased their concerns and moved on without them.[47] Over time, protest votes establish their own normalcy, undergirding systems of power that are racist, sexist, ableist, and so forth.

Before it is too late, then, the slogan "We are the people" should be examined as a dislodged cipher of precarity that may be flexible enough to enable coalitional change. After all, "the people" is an empty signifier, which makes populism a powerful ideological tool for very different constituencies and demands.[48] In 1990, Turkish Germans and (post)migrants took to the streets to protest their marginalization, a condition exacerbated by the national regimes of the *Wende*. They carried signs reading, "We are also the people" ("Wir sind auch das Volk"), challenging the slipperiness between the people's power and the *Volk*. The claim to basic-democratic self-rule voiced by East Germans during the revolutionary fall had morphed into a national, ethnically based imaginary. Nearly thirty years later, the defiant slogan of the 1989 uprising echoed as the nationalist, right-wing sentiment "We are the *Volk*" ("Wir sind das *Volk*") in the Saxon city of Chemnitz. What would it take for members of this class to see that they are—economically, at least, and to a certain extent socially—in similarly precarious positions to some of the migrant groups they reject? To start, I argue that it takes differently organized, pluralizing narratives of 1989. In many ways, this kind of mnemonic labor—returning to 1989—involves a decentering, disjunctive, multidirectional approach, of which Germany (and German memory studies) still needs more today. A small exhibit at the Berlin City Museum (Märkische Museum) in 2018—which worked on multiple local, national, and transnational scales—stands at the forefront of such shifting memory politics.

BİZİM BERLİN 89/90

It is often smaller city museums that can undertake dynamic, multivocal public interventions. In the summer of 2018, an exhibit at the Berlin City Museum served as a temporary archival space where the rifts and reorientations of 1989 could be recirculated. Here, at the periphery of the capital's official museum circuit, a Turkish-German curatorial team organized the show *BİZİM BERLİN 89/90* (Our Berlin 89/90), which featured thirty-five large-scale photographs by the Istanbul artist Ergun Çağatay (1937–2018), who had visited East and West Berlin in early 1990 to report on the second generation of Turkish immigrants. According to the exhibit's promotional material, "the Wall incidentally fell, and he found a city in upheaval." But what Çağatay ended up capturing, the curators write, were not scenes of turmoil and crisis but, rather, "the everyday life of Turkish Berliners": a group of women on their way to prayer in a backyard mosque, passing the graffitied, Western side of the Berlin Wall; a multigenerational family gathering in front of their fruit-and-vegetable shop in West Berlin; a crowded flea market where immigrants sold Wall pieces and Soviet memorabilia. The curators wanted to show that the changes defining Germany's history during that transitional year have slipped into the realms of the unseen, hinted at only by small objects and subtle gestures. This approach is reminiscent of photographic theories where images become the "eye of history" and are able to traverse time. The porousness of temporality is indeed played up by the exhibition's layout. Çağatay's large-scale photographs (most of them in exquisite color) were hung on modular, rust-red wall installations arranged across the bare gallery spaces of the historic 1908 museum building. Even transnational memory practices must be instantiated locally, in specific places at particular times, as Susannah Radstone and others have argued.[49]

However, the curators did not just conceive of BİZİM BERLİN 89/90 to document the everyday life of Turkish Berliners; they also sought "to close a gap in the story of Berlin's recent history, in which the Turkish perspective on the fall of the Berlin Wall and Germany's reunification has been missing."[50] In *Beyond the Mother Tongue* (2012), literary scholar Yasemin Yildiz describes the impact of the radical rupture of 1989 on the Turkish-German population. She speaks of "claiming German, disjunctively," to account for the emergence of new social movements among Turkish-German (post) migrants in the early 1990s, whose "claims to belonging, however, were constantly rebuffed by a majority society in the process of rethinking Germanness across the East-West divide."[51] Historian Julia Wolrab observed the contemporary relevance of this constellation, noting that BİZİM BERLİN 89/90 functions as a "visual history," where the past is traced through images. "The pictures do not only speak for themselves," she writes, "they migrate from the past to the present and in this way become the subject of the current discourse about 'Heimat(en),' identity, and belonging."[52]

Taking on this highly localized and transcultural project, thirty years after the fall of the Wall, the curators of BİZİM BERLİN 89/90 grappled with the role of cultural institutions in shaping collective and national memory. They self-reflexively engaged with questions of who and what are visible and what dynamic forces shape those conditions. Who sets the topical agenda and decides on curatorial strategies? What forms of mediation can support the mobility of narratives beyond traditional state-supported settings? The outcome was a show that explores the new possibilities opening up in 1989–90, when Turkish businesspeople began to gain a foothold in East Berlin, alongside the numerous challenges and existential, racial threats West Berlin's Turkish inhabitants faced after the fall of the Berlin Wall. In a room adjacent to the main exhibit space, audio recordings of interviews were set up to play on a loop, documenting the fights between the Boys 36, a Turkish youth gang (also in one of Çağatay's images), and neo-Nazis in East Berlin.

What I find most striking, however, about Çağatay's '89–90 photographs is that precisely here—in this minor, peripheral archive, as in Foroutan's research on postmigration society—we find traces of a relational, even cohabitational thinking associated with Turkish-German and East German self-assertions during that transitional year. We are also reminded that affects produced by bodily proximity across multiple, more *or* less asymmetrical relations are embedded in racialized and gendered politics.[53] Arguably, these pictures catalog spaces in the work sphere. They are more indexical than spectral. Re-disseminated thirty years later, these ethnographic images put new imaginative possibilities into motion. By interlinking Turkish-German and East German histories of production, labor, and education, they accrue new meanings in the present. Let us focus on three of the photographs in the 1989–90 series.[54] One shows two employees of a Turkish wholesaler in West Berlin operating a green delivery van. They might also be the co-proprietors of this Turkish Tempelhof fruit-and-vegetable business.[55] The van, sporting a Mercedes star and the colorful logo FRUTA, is shown at the entrance of the GDR factory VEB Messelektronik. It appears these men are newcomers. They are smiling as they pose for the photographer. One of them is casually leaning out of the car. At the same time, the

FIGURE 5.1. Immigrants' first enterprise in East Berlin, 1989–1990. Photograph by Ergun Çağatay, from his series on second-generation Turks in Germany, in the exhibit *BİZİM BERLİN 89/90* (Our Berlin 89/90), Berlin City Museum, 2018. © Fotoarchiv Ruhr Museum / Stadtmuseum Berlin / Stiftung Historische Museen Hamburg.

other, older one stands upright, possibly performing what the political scientist Nevim Çil calls the limited upwardly mobile economic agency of the first generation of Turkish migrants, who, even after twenty or thirty years of living in Germany, were considered "outsiders."[56] The shot stretches into the empty opening of the factory's multiple inner courtyards, which are typical for the old working-class districts in Berlin, lending this moment a sense of unknowable opportunity. This openness is aided by the relatively unobstructed specular relation between the Turkish photographer and the Turkish-German Berliners in the frame, who look directly into the camera.

Two other images take the viewer inside public institutions in East Berlin: one captures a communal gathering in a cafeteria at Humboldt University, where students, faculty, and staff have lined up to pick up a lunchtime kebab from one of the West Berlin–Turkish vendors. Çağatay's gaze falls on the exchange between the vendor and one of the thousands of students from Angola, Ethiopia, Ghana, Chile, Zimbabwe, or Vietnam who came via international exchange programs to the GDR between 1954 and 1989.[57] Neither seems aware of the camera. In a gesture of a shared offering, their hands may nearly touch. In the wake of East Germany's involvement in African national and anti-colonial movements, the number of international students who arrived in the GDR increased after the 1960s. Alongside educational opportunities, students recall integrating into collective networks and forming personal friendships. They also recount being marginalized and exposed to everyday racism despite the centrality of international solidarity to East German self-understanding and despite being honored as political guests.[58] This unsettled history is conjured inadvertently, perhaps, in the image by the presence of those East Germans in the cafeteria, on the faculty and staff, and among other students, who (given the space and their habitus) may have supported the GDR's solidarity movements. An older East German employee is captured in the recess of the visual field, his affect withdrawn, his gaze dispersed as though he contemplates some hardship. The image's deep focalization triangulates the different tales of displacement amid the shifts in '89. In Çağatay's snapshot, the multidirectional forces of Turkish migration, anti-imperial liberation, and postcolonial struggle also come into play. (A history accounting for these interrelations across the permeable border between the GDR and FRG still needs to be written.) A third photograph shows the interior of a dining hall at the VEB Messelektronik factory. Here too, in this austere communal space, we find Turkish-German vendors in the middle of setting up crates of fruit and produce, under a makeshift poster of a flower bouquet. Although their work uniforms suggest a difference in status, both men appear as though they are trying out new roles. At the same time, the factory employees, mostly

FIGURE 5.2. Kebab sale at the Humboldt-Universität Berlin (Säulenmensa), Berlin, 1989–1990. Photograph by Ergun Çağatay, from his series on second-generation Turks in Germany, in the exhibit *BİZİM BERLİN 89/90* (Our Berlin 89/90), Berlin City Museum, 2018. © Fotoarchiv Ruhr Museum / Stadtmuseum Berlin / Stiftung Historische Museen Hamburg.

FIGURE 5.3. Selling fruit in the canteen, Berlin, 1989–1990. Photograph by Ergun Çağatay, from his series on second-generation Turks in Germany, in the exhibit *BİZİM BERLİN 89/90* (Our Berlin 89/90), Berlin City Museum, 2018. © Fotoarchiv Ruhr Museum / Stadtmuseum Berlin / Stiftung Historische Museen Hamburg.

women, gathered on the other side of the canteen—self-consciously—look on. The image of Humboldt University and that of the dining hall in the state-owned factory are among the few in the exhibit that are shot in black and white. As memory images, they appear to have fallen out of time.

Comparing these rarely seen '89–90 images, we must also remember that from within their original temporality, these differential transcultural encounters occur in a free-falling historical time-space—months before the unification would be finally sealed in October of 1990. Months before GDR laws, communal organization, and educational structures would be dismantled, and the comprehensive demolition and privatization of GDR industries would take place. Yet the body politic was already in the process of disappearing, and the citizens of the soon-to-be-former GDR were becoming, as it were, displaced, "unhoused." The lives of tens of thousands of international students and contract workers were ever further upended. Collective life in the GDR depended on the very existence of a work sphere, communal spaces, labor, and so forth. At a second take, we cannot help but notice how these images, taken by a photographer from Istanbul, put spaces of the collective life in the GDR—now being undone—in contact with multiple legacies of transnational migration, anti-colonial struggle, and leftist protest (the collection also includes images of dilapidated buildings in the Turkish-German neighborhood of Kreuzberg that have been graffitied with leftist political slogans). There is, of course, a nearly forgotten leftist legacy of the East German and Turkish alliance, embodied, for instance, by the work of Emine Sevgi Özdamar. What I wish to emphasize here, however, is how the Berlin City Museum provides a significant, if marginal, site where memory dynamics disclose political possibilities that are otherwise overlooked in the public sphere. While the exhibit recirculates memories of the everyday lives of Turkish Berliners that had been missing from the national narrative of 1989, it also relaunches other residual memories that had been blocked or marginalized, or had simply lost momentum, such as socialist narratives of internationalist and transnational solidarity, or, more broadly, what Astrid Erll calls "hopeful memories of multi-cultural co-existence."[59] Since such a notion of multiculturalism can become a normative fiction, and I am sure Erll is aware of that risk, I want to test a different vocabulary and trace the possibilities in Çağatay's transcultural images of sharing as a political act.

POLITICS OF CONVIVIALITY

Needless to say, orientations toward shared concerns will sometimes feed commitments to spontaneous self-organizing and amiability, and sometimes not. Here the exhibit's focus on the affective and material valence of food, and on related embodied performances, plays a central role. Curiously, all images of East Berlin in Çağatay's series involve the delivery of produce, bread, or meat. On the surface, of course, one could read this pattern as evidence of systemic conditions in the postwar FRG, in which Turkish migrants of the first and second generations had built networks and entered changing economies. (After Turkish immigrants came to Germany in the 1970s, many encountered problems becoming self-employed due to immigration laws. Eventually, in the 1980s, the number of small businesses, especially in the food distribution trade, rose.)[60] But I want to advance a different reading—one more attuned to the transitional, shifting grounds during the collapse of the GDR—in an attempt to re-move, release, as it were, the unfulfilled intersectional potentialities of 1989.

Possibly because we know the GDR disintegrated, one has the distinct sense in viewing these photographs that members of the Turkish-German community—small-business owners and vendors—were organizing meals for an East German population on the brink of transition. Çağatay's photographs were taken in the first weeks and months after the mass uprisings of GDR citizens and the fall of the Wall. "The GDR in spring," writes a West German newspaper in early May of 1990, "sometimes gives the impression that it is a country that has lost a war and not won a revolution."[61] A radical unmooring of existing structures set effects in motion that were significant yet often impacted the everyday lives of Berlin's populations—including Turkish Germans, East and West Germans, migrants, and international students from the Global South—in different ways. (What does not rupture into the images are particularities of the exposed displacements and racism experienced by Jewish Germans, (post)migrants, BIPoCs, and contract workers from Vietnam and elsewhere in '89–90, which have been examined by Peggy Piesche, Angelika Nguyen, and other activist artists and scholars.)[62] To my mind, Çağatay's images suggest that when moving through catastrophe—or, in any case, upheaval—work, food, and conviviality remain available for reestablishing rituals in collectively shared spaces. Notably, the long tables moved into the public cafeterias and dining halls serve as points of orientation, so to speak, as new social and economic arrangements have to be worked out in a broken-open historical terrain. Hannah Arendt describes the human need for durability and the capacity of things to anchor us. Tables, in particular, derive their meanings as stable objects from the food served on them. Those who arrange themselves around tables can be related or separated simultaneously. Like every in-between, the public realm "gathers us together and yet prevents our falling over each other," as it were.[63] In scenes like this one, concern for a shifting world can converge with concern for others.

Suppose my readings here are indeed productive. In that case, it cannot be emphasized enough that these food exchanges in communal spaces between East Berliners and Turkish Berliners unlock a radical complementary tale to, if not a reversal of, established post-1989 tropes. In the collective memory, these conventional narratives stretch from the centrality of racial violence and anti-immigrant attacks in East Germany in the early 1990s to the widespread perception of the AfD voter today. The images' attention to food remains vital and can help unsettle this narrative. In *Public Things*, political theorist Bonnie Honig points out that "food carries meanings and promises beyond what can be apprehended in one (desolate) moment. The food may be a thinned-out shadow of itself, as it were, or it might signpost an enriching future . . . Do we take up its invitation?"[64] Food and shared meals can provide space to think through modes of conviviality and differential care.

We sometimes forget that throughout modern history, from the Paris Commune onward, conviviality, not just struggle, has been central to celebrating leftist traditions and communal life. Conviviality is an essential feature of revolutionary practice. In her seminal 2018 essay "Futures of Hope," memory scholar Ann Rigney reminds us that "embodied communities" at a local level have long formed a counterpart to large-scale imagined communities. The importance of conviviality to these movements illustrates the pleasure of politics. At such moments of combining embodied co-presence with the sense of being part of a transnational community, she writes, social harmony is not just an abstract ideal but a lived experience.[65] I am less interested in the idea of social harmony, even if I understand what Rigney is getting at here. But what her thinking and mine indeed share is a desire to recuperate spaces for a memory of transnational activism beyond the traumatic. The exchanges between the photographic subjects in Çağatay's '89–90 images (between GDR workers, university faculty, students from postcolonial African nations, and Turkish-German vendors) are situated in heterogenous histories of social struggle, alterity, and dispossession. Yet I am also drawn to the affective relations these images animate. To my eye, rather than enactments of social harmony, these scenes dramatize— wordlessly—common, if unequal, encounters, which involve provisional agreement and proximity, even touch, but also a sense of fear and halting. We need only reconsider the uncertain, even obstinate, look given by one of the East German female workers at the VEB Messelektronik factory. She is displaced from the group and captured by Çağatay's gaze, as though to mark a *punctum* in the fleeting photographic scene, compelling viewers to contemplate how gendered and racialized relations of (in)visibility are formed. Being attentive to such a pause may turn out to be indispensable for exploring the ways in which we "come to see difference differently," past the typical and stereotypical and beyond historically established logics of knowing. In that sense, Çağatay's mnemonic archive, his ethnographic photographic work, explores the limits of a nonhierarchical relationality between East Germans, Turkish Germans, migrants, international delegates from postcolonial African countries, and so forth (conceived here not as self-identical, mimetic categories, which would reproduce exclusion, but as unstable subjectivities, whose meanings need to be performed.)

Afterlives of 1968/1989

We cannot attempt to reclaim 1989, at least partially, as a potential cross- and intersectional space of political conviviality without considering the long aftermath of the global 1960s. Let us take a brief detour to ascertain some narrative boundaries between these different yet interwoven historical legacies. Radically hopeful archives, such as *BİZİM BERLİN 89/90* at the Berlin City Museum, need to be interconnected with other minor local archives harking back to transnational mobility in the second half of the twentieth century. Such interconnection will create spaces for activist memorial networks in the shifting public sphere. In order to resituate 1989 in closer proximity to the historical trajectory of the global 1960s (rather than, say, the national memorial date of 1953), we must allow different Cold War migration waves associated with the liberal West and the socialist East to intersect. In 2018, the Archive of the Citizens' Movement in Leipzig organized a much-overlooked photographic traveling exhibit under the title *Decreed Solidarity—Dealing with "Foreigners" in the GDR* (*Verordnete Solidarität— der Umgang mit "Fremden" in der DDR*). In response to the GDR's engagement with national liberation movements and anti-imperialist struggle, tens of thousands came as contract laborers, students, trainees, or political emigrants from Angola, Mozambique, Chile, Vietnam, and other countries to work and live in the GDR during the 1970s and 1980s. These migration streams were imbricated in the global politics and shifting geopolitical aspirations of the socialist order in the long postwar era.[66] Largely forgotten today in collective memory is also that workers and students moved to the GDR with their own ideas of how to carve out a future in a foreign country. They were not passive in their dealings with East Germans or their state. Despite a culture of surveillance and often draconian restrictions of movement imposed on workers, the people who entered these transcontinental flows recall a certain sense of agency in the new society, as the 2020 interview-based, multimedia web documentary *Minds of Their Own: Mi-*

grants in the GDR (Eigensinn im Bruderland) shows.[67] Similarly, the 2018 traveling exhibit attempted to unearth such historical ambiguities and unheard, often ambivalent narratives. According to the local archivists in Leipzig, the show explored encounters between East Germans and people from the Global South, nearly three decades after the fall of the Wall. Instead of following established narratives about the Cold War era, the archive sought to explore the complex tension between internationalism, xenophobia, and unaddressed racism in the GDR since the 1960s and to open this history up to debates over the transnational and local meanings of solidarity.[68] Yet, despite being designed for widespread educational use by school and public institutions, the exhibit received very little public attention. Why has this remarkable minor archive of (failed) potentiality found no public resonance?

There are local reasons, including the dominance of the AfD in Eastern states such as Saxony, discussed above, and the normative connection between East Germans and xenophobia that has pervaded the public sphere. It takes imagination and critical courage to challenge these assumptions, while the exhibit also provides no ready-made pedagogies. Moreover, the East's anti-imperial engagements have been long dismissed as mere cynical propaganda or painted as caricature in Germany's collective memory.[69] Only three decades after the fall of the Wall did a meaningful shift toward a rediscovery of this ambiguous internationalist history take place. In the peripheral art and museum sphere, activist curators began to consider a kind of transcontinental "worldmaking after internationalism," or what I call a new form of intersectional memory politics.[70] But the enduring oversight of the Soviet East in scholarship on the global 1960s is also telling. Although an extensive literature has sprung up in the past decade that rehabilitates the political dimension of the global 1960s, this literature is almost exclusively concerned with the relationship between countries of the Global South and the West.[71] In this work on the West, the traditional association of the 1960s with softer conceptions of generation has given way in recent years to multi-sited research with a politicized focus on the emergence of worker alliances, anti-racist struggles, and transnational collectivity, as well as on the resilience of entrenched structures and polarizations.[72] However, the rich political histories of the 1960s in the socialist East are submerged. After 1989, Eastern Europe was erased from the global history of the 1960s or relegated to an auxiliary plotline. Historians of (post)socialism may have unwittingly contributed to this trend by focusing on consumption and Communist lifestyle (for example, tourism, television entertainment, sports) rather than decolonial politics or solidarity networks that since the 1960s had ensured "a certain limited multiracial mobility."[73] This fallible world-making model closed down when state socialism collapsed and Europe reimagined itself as racially bordered continent that supported only white European freedom of movement.

Arguably now, by way of rethinking the anti-colonial movements in countries of Africa and, to a certain extent, Asia and Latin America, the internalist paradigm has resurfaced in post-socialist and postcolonial studies. In 2019, anthropologist Kristen Ghodsee published a fascinating account that recovers the lost history of activism by Eastern European and African women in the 1970s, focused on Bulgaria and Zambia.[74] In Vietnam, according to Christina Schwenkel's impressive study, narratives about genuine efforts of the East German population to provide aid and cooperate with the Vietnamese population also continue to linger below the government level. At the same time, this history has been displaced officially by linking Vietnam's binational relations to the FRG.[75] And a new generation of political scientists, such as Adom Getachew, have brought the decolonial movements in Africa, including those from Ghana, Ethiopia, Liberia, and the West Indies, into view as internationalist rather than nationalist projects. In *World Making after Empire* (2019), Getachew stresses that for anti-colonial intellectuals and Black Atlantic thinkers, decolonization was a reordering of the world that sought to create a domination-free, postimperial, and egalitarian international order.[76] In *Socialism Goes Global*, under the heading "Forgotten History," Betts and Mark retrieve layers of these connections. With the rise of fascism in the 1930s, they write, "many anticolonial leaders and intellectuals—from Nehru to W. E. B. Du Bois to Aimé Césaire—encouraged the Soviets and Eastern Europeans to view their experiences of both liberation from and violence at the hands of empires as part of a shared historical experience that connected the 'other Europe' to non-European worlds."[77] Likewise, official Communist histories in the postwar era, and especially since the 1960s and 1970s, urged citizens to see how their struggle from the periphery against a capitalist world order connected to the liberation movements against collapsing Western European empires in Africa and Asia. More of these shifting connections have to be drawn into the memory maps that demonstrate how (post-)1960s liberatory activities cross-pollinated among people of different political systems, ideological projects, and continents.

More of these intersecting pasts have to be made legible in their afterlives. Their storylines have to be assembled into contiguous global anti-capitalist protest memories and animated as such. This shift in perspective would allow us also to see how some of the radically democratic and international anti-imperial impulses were alive in the GDR of 1989. Recall the demand of the New Forum's founding manifesto: "Participation in world trade should not lead to the exploitation of economically weaker countries." The oppositional movements and dissident spaces in the GDR, including punk music, church youth groups, and so-called third-world initiatives, were often inextricably linked to the legacies of the population's protests in 1968.[78] The idea of democratic socialism, harking back to the Prague Spring and its violent suppression, recirculated in the manifestos of some of the citizens' movements. In chapter 2, we saw that various activist and church groups since the 1980s organized around the issues of peace, human rights, and women's struggles. They also focused on third-world solidarities and antiracist work in the GDR.[79] One of the first of these groups to challenge the GDR internally was the well-known Leipzig group Hope Nicaragua (Hoffnung Nikaragua), founded in 1981. While the anti-capitalist commitment of these initiatives initially seemed compatible with the SED dogmatics, a number of groups became increasingly critical of the state. They counted the GDR's obsession with an accelerated modernity among the "causes for the economic imbalance in the world and therefore took critical positions toward the ideologically inflated, official declarations of solidarity."[80] In other words, anti-colonial solidaric feelings could become politically disruptive. This work, as Betts and Mark argue, provided exemplars and languages of critique that could be "turned against domestic authoritarianism, the seeming abandonment of revolution by consumerist Eastern European regimes,"[81] or indeed against the imperialism of the Soviet Union itself.

FIGURE 5.4. Demonstration against xenophobia, Berlin, April 24, 1990. Photograph credit Deutsches Bundesarchiv, Bild 183-1990-0424-035 / Oberst, Klaus / CC-BY-SA 3.0.

It is important to note that these political impulses continued to echo in the unmoored GDR of '89–90. In late fall of 1989, activists of the citizens' movements, together with government officials, formed a Working Group on Foreigners' Issues (Arbeitsgruppe "Ausländerfragen") at the Central Roundtable in Berlin (Anetta Kahane was a member). Multiple working groups in other cities and districts across the GDR were set up as well. In their proposal for a future GDR constitution (which was never realized) the activists stated, "The participants of the roundtable oppose xenophobia and neo-Nazism with all determination and strongly condemn the desecration of Soviet memorials and cemeteries. We regard solidaric behavior toward all foreign fellow citizens as an essential criterion for the credibility of the renewal process of the GDR." In conjunction with proposals for new legal protection and equality for migrants, they stated, "This is about active solidarity also *within* the GDR. There must be an effective practice of confronting any kind of racism and hostility toward foreigners."[82] The collapse of the GDR threw into chaos and uncertainty the lives of tens of thousands of workers and students who had come through the solidarity agreements ratified by the now dying state.[83] The transitional fora attempted to address this crisis on a global and structural scale. In February of 1990, a roundtable dedicated to rethinking relations with the Global South (*Entwicklungspolitischer Runder Tisch*) was organized by citizens who had been active in the dissident church spaces in the GDR. They drew on the earlier thematic roundtables for ecology, youth, and women's politics. In the post-unification neoliberal era, alternative narratives about the marches of thousands of East Germans protesting against xenophobia and demanding equality in 1990 in Berlin (with participants from both parts of the city), Leipzig, Schwerin, and Plauen have disappeared from public memory. Likewise, the new, restrictive "Act on Foreigners" ratified by West Germany's government in July of 1990 seems to be rarely recalled. (The xenophobic rhetoric of the West German media and the political discourse of the 1980s played a key role in preparing the tightening of asylum legislation.) Instead, as I have shown in this book, Germany's public and collective memory is invested in a national turn to democracy that liberated the Cold War East. Therefore, we need new epistemological frameworks and narratives to craft different memories of '89 in the afterlife of the 1960s. Exhibitions such as *BİZİM BERLİN 89/90* help resituate the contemporary mobilization for social justice in a longer historical arc that considers the interconnected geographies associated with the Western, non-Western, and formerly socialist worlds, reorienting perspectives of past and present struggles. To draw on Arjun Appadurai's hopeful formulation, such images help foster an understanding of how the imagination functions as a significant social force in the contemporary world, supplying alternative prescriptions for identity, cohabitation, and solidarity.

Finally, and most importantly, it will be clear by now that the concept of an affiliative post-1989 memory that undergirds my reading is not used in any teleological sense—suggesting a perpetual widening of the frameworks of memory within some homogeneously conceived (national) space. Çağatay's works enable different configurations of memory. By bringing Turkish Germans, (post)migrants, and East Germans into contact, these images help recirculate forgotten knowledge about the early post-unification period. Across that time and space, these photographs of provisional transcultural conviviality in East Berlin dining halls reach us in the present. They are propelled out of that brief interval of transformational possibility in the wreckage of 1989. Recirculating three decades later, they supply openended imaginaries for communal and transcultural forms of existence. In doing so, they re-move and relaunch the arrested trajectory not taken. These images reanimate "the before"—if there is such a thing (the before of unification, unfettered capitalism, unleashed racism). As Derrida reminded us in *Specters of Marx*, what comes before us, before any present, also comes from the future or as future: as the very coming of the event.[84] Freeing this time-space from a seemingly inevitable course toward the end of history, these images give artistic form to hopeful temporalities and affects. The exhibit at the Berlin City Museum articulates memory on local, national, and transnational scales. Cutting through time, Çağatay's '89–90 images transport radical hope. Ernst Bloch once described hope as "the still undischarged future of the past."[85] In this book, I have emphasized the capacity of future archives to accrue the unfulfilled impulses of political subjects who acted in concert, however fleetingly. This dynamic is at play in Çağatay's snapshots, which render Turkish-German (post)migrants, students from the Global South, and GDR workers, staff, and academics, encountering one another in spaces of East Germany's (still) state-owned factories and public universities. Together, these images release an unwritten, ultimately unlived—and, thus, possible—history, which opens time to new interpretations that are acutely relevant today.

Commons

It is true that we may be living through another interregnum, where, to borrow from Nancy Fraser, "the old is dying, and the new cannot be born."[86] Neoliberal capitalism very well may not die a natural death. Moving toward the final pages of this book, let me propose, taking my cue from Foroutan and Çağatay, that we need to be more inventive and work through, if not suspend, normalized ideological polarizations to challenge the existing order. The controversy around Foroutan's thesis that "East Germans are migrants too" gave rise to several virtual and public platforms, where she and her interlocutors explored how dialogue can be politicized and used as a tool across various marginalized—and in many ways asymmetrically positioned—groups (including those considered racist or right-wing). Through exchanges like these, the differences between multiple communities embedded in uneven relations of power and with their own particular histories of dispossession and resistance can become legible. Foroutan said that "solidarity" (*Solidarität*) is a beautiful word but implies a power hierarchy in which one introduces oneself to another. Rather than relying on solidarity, she prefers the term strategic "alliance" (*Allianz*); only then can we "stand side by side" (*nebeneinander*).[87] Although I admire Foroutan's argument, I am less convinced that the language of alliance can be recuperated, from the ruins of Eastern Europe, for the contemporary moment of heightened crisis and internationalist, translocal organizing. To my ear, what reverberates here is still the Cold War rhetoric of international relations and cultural diplomacy.[88] Political theorists also often question the viability of alliance altogether. They fear—rightly, in my view—that the concept is undergirded by an idea of a unitary subject (a notion that itself serves as a form of power) and that alliances can be appropriated for the "politics of recognition," among other things.[89] My term of choice, then, is "allyship," which echoes a host of old and new ways to name the kind of uneven relations where mutual dependency coexists with friction and violence. Allyship—a form of alliance that sheds that paradigm's stable, strategic, geopolitical connotations—is thus more suitable for the complex cross- and intersectional political collaborations needed for our polarized times.[90]

In closing *Remembering 1989*, I want to return to the idea of sharing. The exhibit *BİZİM BERLİN 89/90* and Çağatay's images augment visions of an alliance, or allyship, by pointing to the material conditions that are conducive to the emergence of intersectional and collective living. Nationalists and right-wing populists certainly know how to bind disparate people into communities through collective things, such as symbols, flags, hats, and songs. These transcultural snapshots of '89–90 East Berlin, however, linger in intimate social encounters and communal structures, such as dining halls, state factories, libraries, and universities. They emphasize the integrative powers of these encounters outside or, in any case, at the limits of economies of private property and systems of exchange. Sharing is typically associated with the intimate, private sphere, with the home rather than with the "exterior world of work and the market." But here, in these photographs, the sharing of space and, in particular, food is reworked as a pleasurable political and intimate practice. Notably, through dynamic cultural memory work, this exhibit also offers possibilities for a commons. Notions of the commons vary, but most seem to agree that the commons is a realm where resources should not be alienated for market use but should, for the most part, remain non-propertied, available to all, and people-owned.[91]

The collapse of socialism in Eastern Europe unleashed the forces of neoliberal capitalism. For nearly three decades, Germany's public culture lacked any viable frameworks in which the teleological national narrative of a Peaceful Revolution leading to an ultimately triumphant unification and the victory of market democracy could be substantively questioned. Elsewhere I have shown how Marxist critiques of capital espoused by East German writers such as Christa Wolf were delegitimized. In the absence of such frames, hardly any noteworthy discussions of property relations as foundational to capitalism—and, thus, to the absorption of the East by the West—occurred in the public sphere. Any discontinuous histories of the decollectivization of the GDR would have broken the thread of transcendental teleology. Around the thirtieth anniversary of the fall of the Wall, a tentative shift took place in the official, ritualized discourse. But didn't the disparities between East and West, let alone the rise of the right-wing movement in the East, already appear incontrovertible?[92] More than three decades had to pass for Germany's governmental sphere to officially reevaluate the unification process, even in the most minimal sense. Recent analogies in the German press between the catastrophic impact of the COVID-19 pandemic and the postwar collapse in 1945 attest once more to the absence of the rupture in 1989 in dominant, collective memory.

At the highest symbolic level, thirty years after the *Wende*, however, the tone also began to change. Amid the push from the right-wing AfD, the government rediscovered the legacy of 1989. At the State's ceremony commemorating the thirtieth anniversary of Germany's unification, Germany's president publicly pledged to foster a memory culture wherein East Germans "receive respect" not only "for their historic fight for freedom and democracy" but also for "the subsequent social and economic challenges they lived through"[93] This pledge certainly marked a discursive shift from previous decades, in which the Cold War axiom of the GDR as a dictatorial "illegitimate state" (*Unrechtsstaat*) had remained central. The memory of the GDR as illegitimate was instrumentalized throughout the past three decades, all the way to the contested state elections in Thuringia in 2019, when the conservative Christian Democratic Union (CDU) refused to form a coalition with the Linke (seen as the successor party to the SED), even if doing so meant risking an increased influence of the right-wing AfD. In the end, however, the official call for "recognizing" the relative setbacks experienced by East Germans once more obfuscated the political dimension of the radically democratic uprising in 1989. Since this shift in official memory politics, the failures in the 1990s have been attributed to the excess rather than the structural deficits of neoliberal capitalism. The effects of deindustrialization disproportionally (but not only) felt in the East have been partially acknowledged by politicians to prop up, some skeptics argue, the dying neoliberal project and market-conforming democracy. Likewise, the urgent call made in 1990 by the late Black German activist May Ayim for forming alliances between all those who do not tolerate racism and anti-Semitism has not been answered. Her vision of discussions in Germany that would change lives and connections in ways that an "uninterrupted equitable collaboration with immigrants and Black Germans would become an indisputable given and analysis of racism a permanent undertaking" remains as of yet unfulfilled.[94] While Black Lives Matter protests have emerged, the project of forging allyship across the socially constructed and guarded boundaries of race and nationality is, for the most part, still upended.

However, we have also arrived at an anti-capitalist moment. We witness the return of the political after years in a post-political era. In the long arch of the neoliberal era, post-socialism eventually steered toward post-democracy. In *In the Ruins of Neoliberalism*, Wendy Brown writes that the nation, family, property, and the traditions reproducing racial and gender privilege, mortally wounded by deindustrialization, have been reduced to affective remains. To date, these remains have been activated chiefly by the Right, prompting Brown to ask anew, "What kind of left political critique and vision might reach and transform them?"[95] The British writer Timothy Garton Ash is known for his personal history *The File*, a chronicle of Stasi surveillance in the GDR. In 2019 he examined the extensive right-wing fallout of 1989 in Eastern Europe today and asked whether it is "time for a new liberation"[96] He answered in the negative, praising the achievements of the liberal revolutions three decades prior and the stabilizing centrality of private forms of ownership on which the progress of market-driven democracy rests. However, one lesson of 1989 is that liberal and progressive visions must find a new language that resonates with people who otherwise attach their binding powers and future hopes to the *Volk*. According to Chantal Mouffe, this vocabulary needs to orient those aggrieved on the left and right toward egalitarian objectives and a common adversary: the oligarchy.[97] There are indeed limits to the logic of sharing.

Throughout this book, I have made a case for reading the interval of '89–90 as an "archive of the future," as a space in time where the unfinalizable impulses of a radically democratic imaginary can be located, recalled, and released—where we can grasp that a more satisfactory form of democracy "remains to come." Mouffe clarifies the ideas of radical democracy for the age of post-democracy, arguing that radical and plural democracy does not constitute a revolutionary break and does not imply a total refoundation (after all, current movements do not call for socialism). True forms of democracy are achieved from within, through an immanent critique and agonistic struggle. Therefore, Mouffe advocates for a radicalization of existing democratic institutions, which will result in the principles of liberty *and* equality becoming effective, based on widespread consultation. Most importantly, in our hyper-polarized times, agonistic politics assumes the adversary is to be engaged rather than an enemy. Harking back to the inheritance of 1989, I want to underscore that representative democracy ultimately relies on power hierarchies, where elected leaders often implement policies that privilege their narrow interests. In the (late) neoliberal era, they variably facilitate the increasing power of large corporations to fashion law and policy for their own ends. In a democracy that *remains to come*, to echo Derrida, power should be redistributed on the model of the wheel. In his vision for scholar-activists of color, John Streamas writes that the spokes of a wheel are all equally important, "as answerable to the hub as the hub must be to them."[98] Taking up this metaphor of horizontal redistribution, the myriad roundtables in East Germany in 1989 certainly actualized such radically democratic practice. While the wheel is an imperfect alternative model for democratic sovereignty—it may enable false equivalencies and obfuscate how each participant is differently situated—it still holds promise for a diversely reorganized and more equitable society. The metaphorical rotation of the wheel, the round, the circle—turning into zero, a gap—also holds a space for indeterminacy, without which the force of "the people" is not thinkable, as I have shown in this book.

After lingering in the blind spot of history, for thirty years, the unfulfilled impulses of the 1989 political and ecological movements are newly at stake. The collaborative and highly volatile attempts of hundreds of thousands of activists and ordinary citizens in the upended GDR to build a grassroots democracy out of a revolutionary uprising could not be more urgent. In their not fully realized forms, ideas for a collective and affiliative living—the commons, public things and shared space, sustainable environments, social justice, and economic redistribution—have found new hosts, and radically democratic, translocal revolutions may be waiting once more in the wings. A younger generation of activists, such as Fridays for Future protesters, are showing up around the globe to sound the alarm. Their concern for the planet's rapidly changing biophysical realities is sometimes dismissed as a kind of lifestyle choice, just as youth movements' dissent was in 1968. As the planetary emergency deepens, however, these protests in the midst of massively proliferating environmental wake-up calls need to be taken seriously, and they need to be interconnected to a range of pressing social issues, including continuing discrimination against women, people of color, and LGBTQ+ individuals; soaring economic inequality; and the rise of the far-right movement. In addition, these protests must be undergirded with a host of critical theories and transition histories that provide insight into the dynamics by which societies become undone and the processes through which real democracies can be reimagined and rebuilt. Indeed, what is needed is not only a breaking down of incalcitrant structures; as Lauren Berlant reminds us in her final book, *On the Inconvenience of Other People*, we also need visions for world-making and for creating a new common sense. At the intersection of scholarship and activism, calls have emerged for disrupting the conditions of a hyper-capitalist status quo whose fetishization of growth, if unaddressed, threatens to devour the planet. How can late neoliberal, post-democratic societies be transformed? We would do well to remember that in the fall of 1989, in the GDR, there was no poster, no slogan, no chant for privatization, and no demand to abolish the right to work (or to reinvent entrepreneurial labor under the most precarious and hyper-competitive conditions). Why can freedom and democracy not coexist with greater social ownership of the means of production, where workers, communities, and the state gain control from the ground up and where profits and concerns are seen as shared and dealt with collaboratively?

In May 2019, the multilocal campaign of *Die Vielen* (The Many), an emerging movement of civil self-organizing among regional groups in the cultural sphere, held a culminating assembly at the Volksbühne theater in the former downtown district of East Berlin. Under the mandate "Glänzende Demonstrationen—Unite and Shine" (Brilliant Demonstrations—Unite and Shine), the movement mobilized against the rise of right-wing extremist parties and in support of a Europe of many. The declaration stated, "For us, safe escape routes, solidarity, and an open society belong together with the right to freely participate in the community's cultural life, to enjoy the arts." In front of an enthusiastic crowd, East German writer Ingo Schulze ended his speech at the assembly with the following remarks: "Almost thirty years ago, I witnessed how to put aside a system that seemed prepared for any emergency, but whose language and thinking were so crusted that it could no longer perceive and respond to reality. Anyone who has learned once that the world can be changed considers this a second time possible. In this sense: we are the people! We are the people!"[99]

[CODA]

Unbound in the Open

This contemporary summoning of a revolutionary spirit brings us full circle to the burial transport of the Marx-Engels sculptures in East Berlin, which I invoked at the beginning of this book. Rather than a relic, Marxism's ideals come into view anew not only as ghost, secret, and inheritance but also as a debt and call to responsibility.[1] The reader recalls the displaced figures of Marx and Engels traversing Sibylle Bergemann's melancholic photographic landscapes in the mid-1980s, before the fall of the Berlin Wall and the demise of Eastern Europe. Appearing in Heiner Müller's book *A Specter Departs from Europe* (*Ein Gespenst verlässt Europa*) in 1990, the shrouded scenes signaled trauma and grief over the historical crimes committed under the sign of Marxism, as well as over the seemingly irreversible loss of socialist utopia. Imperceptibly, this loss lingered on, resisting and defying disappearance in the fashion of a spectral thing. This form of double mourning, while banished in the post-unification era, did not cease to exist.[2] Instead, these scattered energies continued to settle in liminal spaces of Germany's official memorial landscapes and were reanimated in minor literary, memorial, and cinematic archives. At last, amid the 2019 anniversary celebrations, Jürgen Böttcher's 2001 art documentary *Konzert im Freien* (Open-Air Concert), which focused on the legacies of the sculptures, was rescreened to the public in Berlin and across North America and Europe to international audiences.[3] Years after Bergemann had rendered the assembly of the Marx-Engels memorial as an elegiac act, Böttcher's film transmitted multiple temporalities of the site's pre- and post-1989 pasts into a "space of the open."

Truth always begins by naming the void, "by voicing the poem of the abandoned place," French scholar, activist, and author of *The Communist Hypothesis* Alain Badiou instructs us.[4] At the vacant center of history, the camera in Böttcher's film swirls around the memorial remnants on the circular plaza, over and over in 360-degree loops. In front of the cored-out, dilapidated Palace of the Republic, Marx and Engels may appear, as in

Bergemann's series, undead, like ghosts in the night. (The palace housed the 1989–90 transitional parliament and was demolished a decade and a half later.) And yet the spherical sounds of the jazz performers in front of the memorial enliven the space, turning the modern, radical thinkers of the nineteenth and twentieth centuries once more into witnesses of possibility. For a second, the vibrant, dissonant music stops and opens into an expansive, soundless interval, a gap in which past, present, and future temporalities come to a standstill. Boundless, we listen to planetary history, or earth, and earth may listen back and hear us. This auditory and visual gap permeates our present temporality with a life-sustaining element. After all, what is celebrated here is not so much what did happen; rather, to paraphrase Deleuze and Guattari, the Marx-Engels memorial space remediated in the documentary confides to the ear of the future what could happen. The incandescent drums of the jazz ensemble pick up, growing into a menacing, ceaseless call to action.[5]

In the ruins of neoliberalism and faced with ecological disaster, it may not be apparent whether the best is (indeed) yet to come or whether utopian visions of progress and greater social equality will always be already over, perpetually reabsorbed into the existing hegemonic order. And yet energies of revolutions that could have been and still might lie ahead hurdle across time and space. The catastrophic turmoil and large-scale protests around the globe today may suggest that we are entering a new phase, a postcapitalist age, where new conditions of livability and a new sense of a shared world are established, and where modes of resistance that advocate for radical social equality seek also to re-envision an inhabitable world that does not have humans at its center.

Revolutions may not survive their victories. As we have seen in this book, their partial, fleeting victories often do not take hold long enough to enter the variegated passages of cultural memory. My hope is that in exploring the radical rupture and historical cesura of 1989, the reader has also come to understand that even if a revolution is abbreviated, derailed, or fails, we cannot judge the event by its outcomes. But in the end, perhaps, the problem is less one of debating the criteria by which we can judge history than it is one of defining our ideas of what it means to judge in the first place. As Deleuze and Guattari remind us, "the success of revolutions resides in itself, and precisely in the vibrations, clinches, and openings it gave to the people in the moment of its making. This occurrence in itself composes a viable monument that is always in the process of becoming and can be activated in the present. The victory of a revolution is actually immanent and consists in the new bonds it installs between people, even if these bonds last no longer than the revolution's melted material and quickly give way to division and betrayal."[6] This transitoriness was certainly true for the multitudes of new and alternative solidarities that briefly formed in 1989. Thus, it is even more important today to reclaim that inheritance of concerted action. Recall that inheritance is never a given, it is always a task; it "remains before us," temporally (albeit not chronologically) and spatially.

The arresting silence in Böttcher's film *Konzert im Freien* cuts into linear perceptions of history and allows broken and unformed dreams to echo into our planetary present. A sonic opening such as this quiet interval, or pause, can be a gift. I began this book by suggesting that the gap (between past and future) is a symptom of rupture, erasure, or even willful neglect. But it is also the unbound space that allows us to gather ourselves, show up with others, and commit to figuring things out. In 2003, the Indian author and political activist Arundhati Roy wrote that "another world is not only possible, she is on her way. On a quiet day, I can hear her breathing." How long this vision remains viable, only the future knows.

Acknowledgments

Remembering 1989 recalls the collaborative energies of the citizens' uprising in East Germany and is interwoven with the many exchanges I've had with colleagues, friends, and students in the last decade about this transitional year. I am deeply grateful to Marc Silberman, Katrin Sieg, and Harriet Murav for supporting this project at every stage of its development. I want to thank Florence Vatan, Sabine Groß, Sonja E. Klocke, Stefan Soldovieri, Stephen Brockmann, Sabine Hake, Hunter Bivens, and participants in workshops at the University of Wisconsin–Madison for their invaluable input over the years. I also thank my colleagues and friends in the Initiative in Holocaust, Genocide, and Memory Studies at the University of Illinois at Urbana-Champaign (UIUC), especially Brett Kaplan, Michael Rothberg, and Peter Fritzsche, for their generous contributions and ideas that early on helped shape this project on 1989 future-oriented memory. At UIUC, I'm also indebted to Mark Steinberg, Maria Todorova, Zsuzsa Gille, John Randolph, Stephanie Hilger, Carl Niekerk, Laurie Johnson, Yasemin Yildiz, and Emanuel Rota for helpful conversations along the way.

I was lucky to be part of a smart and fun writing group. I want to thank my fellow GLOWers, Lilya Kaganovsky, Justine Murison, and Brett Kaplan (again), for reading nearly all of the manuscript in its various stages. Your sharp and generous minds have made each chapter better with every iteration. A special thanks to Antoinette Burton and Tamara Chaplin for their brilliant insights when I was too narrowly focused on Germany, and to Behrooz Ghamari-Tabrizi for nudging me to revisit 1989 when it had slipped into the distant past.

This book benefited from sustained research funding. I am grateful for support from various institutions, including the Center for Advanced Study, the College of Liberal Arts and Sciences, the Illinois Program for Research in the Humanities, and the European Union Center, all at UIUC. A Mellon-funded New Horizons Summer Faculty Fellowship allowed me to circle back into the archives in Germany. This book would not exist in its current form without unwavering support and feedback from my colleagues in the Office of the Vice Chancellor for Research and Innovation, including Maria Gillombardo, Craig M. Koslofsky, Shelley Weinberg, Gabriel Solis, and the late Nancy Abelmann. I would also like to express my gratitude to colleagues at institutions such as the University of California, Los Angeles; the University of Otago; Arcadia University's College of Global Studies, London Center; the University of Toronto; the University of Torino; the Chicago Film Seminar; and Southern Illinois University for providing opportunities to test out early ideas of the book.

Remembering 1989 evolved through teaching graduate seminars on "Protest Memory" and "Revolutionary Archives." I want to thank the graduate students in these seminars for their curiosity and original thought. Their perspectives on the contemporary world were instrumental in connecting the events of 1989 to today's social movements. My doctoral students, including Molly Markin, the late Jessica Wienhold, Lauren Hansen, Regine Criser, John Slattery, and Basil Agu, have opened my mind to generational and transnational perspectives on 1989.

My deepest thanks to friends, compatriots, and student-scholars in the Education Justice Project. You showed me the importance of community and the power of grassroots work, even if it moves at a glacial pace compared to revolutionary uprising. To Chris Higgins for his enthusiasm and friendship as we collaborated on building a Learning Publics Initiative at the University of Illinois.

I also want to express my deep appreciation for the thoughtful and incisive anonymous readers' reports I received from the University of Chicago Press, which greatly improved the manuscript. My heartfelt thank you goes to the press's editorial director, Alan Thomas, for believing in the project, to Mary Al-Sayed for our fruitful conversations, and also to Randy Petilos, Jessica Wilson, Elizabeth Ellingboe, and the staff at the press for seeing the book through production. An earlier version of chapter 3 on "Possible Archives" benefited from the rigorous editorial feedback of Carrie Collenberg-González, Martin P. Sheehan, and the anonymous readers. Jeff Castle, Ryan Allen, and Ellis Light improved the manuscript with their acute observations every step of the way. I also thank Nick Goodell for his stellar work during his Illinois Program for Research in the Humanities New Horizons Research Assistantship.

In Europe, I thank the dedicated staff at the Archive of the Citizens' Movement Leipzig e.V. for helping to retrieve archival files on-site and online during the COVID-19 pandemic. The archivists at the Marx Memorial Library and Workers School, London, revived my confidence in the transnational legacies of the GDR. I also thank the many other archives and museums, including the Stasi Records Agency, the Robert Havemann Foundation e.V./Archiv of the GDR Opposition, the Bundesarchiv (BArch), the Berlin Wall Foundation, and the Nikolaikirche, as well as Mischa Kuball, Milla and Partner, the Ostkreuz Foto Agency/Sibylle Bergemann Estate, and the Märkische Museum in Berlin, for their generous responses to my inquiries.

I would like to thank my lifelong friends in the field, nearby and far, whose passion for the inheritance of the GDR and 1989 has woven its way into this book: Mila Ganeva, Susanne Rinner, Cecilia Novero, and Katie Trumpener. I thank Constance Furey for her humor and brilliant mind and our shared daily writing practice for nearly a decade. Angie Marsh, Andrea Federle-Bucsi, and Miriam Sierig for keeping me level-headed. And, when the past eluded me, or my own recollection of 1989 intruded, I could rely on my family and friends in Germany for continued conversation about the late GDR, especially Ulrike Stengel, Katrin Schreiner, and Annedore Hänel, and, in the early stages, when I was planning out the twentieth-anniversary conference, Gabriele Gysi, Eva Grünstein-Neuman, and Grit Schorch. They all contributed to discussions about whether and how the event should be remembered.

Finally, thank you, Dietrich, for your unflagging support and deep insight, for your belief in me and this project. This book is dedicated to my parents. My mother's humor and resilience throughout the post-1989 transformations have been life-giving. My father's companionship during the visits to memorial sites across Eastern Germany will stay with me, always.

An earlier version of chapter 3 was originally published as "Possible Archives: Encountering a Surveillance Photo in *Karl Marx City* (2016)," in *Moving Frames: Photography in German Cinema*, ed. Carrie Collenberg-Gonzalez and Martin P. Sheehan (New York: Berghahn, 2022), 210–30.

Notes

INTRODUCTION

1. Ziegler, *Der Hass auf den Westen*, cited in Schulze, *Unsere schönen neuen Kleider*, 69. Unless otherwise marked, all translations from German are mine.

2. Traverso, *Left-Wing Melancholia*, 2–4, 20.

3. This point is noted in Cercel, "Whither Politics, Whither Memory?," 1–15.

4. Sonnevend, *Stories without Borders*, 48.

5. Hoare, "Let's Please Stop Crediting Ronald Reagan for the Fall of the Berlin Wall."

6. For this exercise, Wikipedia provides the most widely accessible information on Germany: s.v. "German Reunification," last edited October 3, 2023, https://en.wikipedia .org/wiki/German_reunification.

7. Derrida, *Specters of Marx*, 65.

8. Serge Schmemann's piece "East Germans Let Largest Protest Proceed in Peace" appeared on the front page of the *New York Times* on October 10, 1989. The state newspaper *Neues Deutschland* speaks of violence-prone rowdies and criminals who provoked the GDR police forces; the paper attacks the media in the West for spreading rumors that GDR police forces caused any deaths (ADN, "Proteste von BRD-Medien entschieden zurückgewiesen," *Neues Deutschland*, October 11, 1989, 2). On October 22, 1989, a West German weekly published an interview with the East German author Christoph Hein, who warned of the risk of further violence ("Die DDR ist nicht China," *Der Spiegel*, October 22, 1989, 43).

9. Müller, *Glaube wenig, hinterfrage alles, denke selbst*, 89.

10. Dan Morgan, "Protesters Ransack Offices of E. German Secret Police," *Washington Post*, January 16, 1990.

11. Kohl, *Erinnerungen 1982–1990*, 1020–28; and "Helmut Kohl's Welcome in Dresden (December 19, 1989)," One Germany in Europe (1989–2009), accessed May 12, 2022, https://ghdi.ghi-dc.org/sub_document.cfm?document_id=2889. Kohl used the iconic phrase of "flourishing landscapes" in his television address on July 1, 1990, the day the currency union took effect.

12. US State Department, "2+4 Talks and the Reunification of Germany 1990," Archive of the US Department of State, accessed January 22, 2022, https://2001-2009 .state.gov/r/pa/ho/time/pcw/108224.htm.

13. US State Department, "2+4 Talks"; Horst Teltschik, the chancellor's chief of staff, had already corresponded with the Communist Party of the Soviet Union to gauge how far the FRG could go at this point regarding Germany's unification (Wolf, "Das Zehn-Punkte-Programm Helmut Kohls," 91–92). The historian Mary Elise Sarotte also debunks the myth that NATO expansion had nothing to do with German reunification and that it never came up before the Clinton era. Instead, she shows that the US and West German leaders were in fact thinking about NATO expansion to Eastern Europe as early as February 1990; see *1989: The Struggle to Create Post–Cold War Europe*, 216–19.

14. Robert Pear, "Upheaval in the East; Kohl Arrives in U.S. for Talks on Europe's Future," *New York Times*, February 25, 1990.

15. This process was legally possible because the FRG's *Grundgesetz* (Basic Law) was conceived under the Allies as a placeholder that would remain in effect until unification, which, in 1949, was presumed to be imminent. The event in 1990 is called "reunification" (*Wiedervereinigung*) in official language, implying a return to an older state before division. When referring to official discourse, I reproduce this term in this book. Alternatively, I use the term "unification" to signal that the division of Germany was a consequence of Nazi Germany and the Second World War.

16. Kowalczuk, "Revolution in Germany," 33.

17. Buck-Morss, *Revolution Today*, 5–22. For a longer historical and planetary arc in which to analyze the neoliberal project, see Ghosh, *Nutmeg's Curse*. Ghosh underscores the significance of 1989 for promoting the ideologies and practices of settler colonialism, in neoliberal disguise, by the most powerful countries in the world. The 1989 Washington Consensus implemented a set of market-oriented policies for improving economic performances in Latin American and African countries (167). On colonial and postcolonial structures operating in the neoliberal project, see also Bangstad and Nilsen, "Thoughts on the Planetary."

18. Ther, *Europe since 1989*; Ghodsee and Orenstein, *Taking Stock of Shock*. Late Soviet socialism is examined by Alexei Yurchak in *Everything Was Forever, until It Was No More*. For the distinct conditions of neoliberal transformation in Eastern European countries, see Shevchenko, *Crisis and the Everyday in Postsocialist Moscow*; Oushakine, *Patriotism of Despair*; Ghodsee, *Lost in Transition*; Fehérváry, *Politics in Color and Concrete*, 31–33.

19. See Todorova and Gille, eds., *Post-Communist Nostalgia*; Bernhard and Kubik, eds., *Twenty Years after Communism*; Norris, ed., *Museums of Communism*.

20. For a detailed account of how thought cultivated in Soviet–East European contexts slipped away in the early 1990s, see Buck-Morss, *Dreamworld and Catastrophe*, 227–63.

21. Ash, "Time for a New Liberation."

22. On the protest banner reading "Long Live the Prague Spring" (Es lebe der Prager Frühling) amid the demonstrators in Leipzig in October 1989, see Schneider, ed., *Leipziger Demontagebuch*, 93.

23. Ross, *May '68 and Its Afterlives*, 19n2.

24. Kenney, *Carnival of Revolution*, 9; Ash, *Magic Lantern*. Although Kenney and Ash have become canonical, there is a rich body of historical studies on 1989 in Eastern European and global contexts, including Lawson, Armbruster, and Cox, eds., *Global*

1989; Mark et al., *1989: A Global History of Eastern Europe*. Earlier historical studies can be found in Tismaneanu, ed., *Revolutions of 1989*; Florath, ed., *Das Revolutionsjahr 1989*.

25. This case is carefully argued by Anne Sa'adah in *Germany's Second Chance*. Other scholars emphasize that the GDR's civic leaders were out of touch with the population (see Betts, "1989 at Thirty") or that the "dissident elite" alienated the population with their anti-capitalist aspirations (see Richardson-Little, *Human Rights Dictatorship*). In their own accounts, East German activists such as Frank Richter and Daniela Dahn stress the populist "national redirection" of the revolution, sealed by the heavily Western-funded "first free elections" in the GDR. See Richter, *Hört endlich zu*, 35; and Dahn, *Der Schnee von gestern ist die Sintflut von heute*.

26. Arendt, "Preface: The Gap between Past and Future," 3–15.

27. See, for instance, these excellent accounts: Tröger, *Pressefrühling und Profit*; Pritchard, *Reconstructing Education*, 69; Steding, *GDR Literature in German Curricula and Textbooks*, esp. 5. As a central component of public education, the Leipzig Forum of Contemporary History (Zeitgeschichtliches Forum, ZGF) was established in 1999. The museum belongs to the House of History Foundation of the Federal Republic of Germany (Stiftung Haus der Geschichte der Bundesrepublik Deutschland) alongside the House of History (Haus der Geschichte) Bonn, which opened in 1994. The ZGF is commonly described as the eastern counterpart to the Bonn original in whose foundation Chancellor Helmut Kohl was a major driving force (Berdahl, "Expressions of Experience and Experiences of Expression," 158). It features a permanent exhibit entitled "Our History: Dictatorship and Democracy after 1945."

28. "Bericht der Enquete-Kommission 'Aufarbeitung von Geschichte und Folgen der SED-Diktatur in Deutschland' gemäß Beschluß des Deutschen Bundestages vom 12. März 1992 und vom 20. Mai 1992—Drucksachen 12/7820, 12/2230, 12/2597," Deutscher Bundestag, Drucksache 12/7820.

29. Cooke, *Representing East Germany since Unification*, 12, 37.

30. Here it is instructive to reread the essay by Helmut Schmidt (SPD), then West Germany's chancellor, on the state of world affairs in times of crisis ("Policy of Reliable Partnership").

31. Eley, "Unease of History," 176.

32. I analyze this phenomenon in *Film and Memory in East Germany*, 203–16. In literature, 1989 forms a present absence in, for instance, Ruge, *In Zeiten des abnehmenden Lichts* (2011); Wolf, *Stadt der Engel oder The Overcoat of Dr. Freud* (2010); Seiler, *Kruso* (2014); and Erpenbeck, *Gehen, Ging, Gegangen* (2015). Novels such as Seiler's *Stern 111* (2020) and Erpenbeck's *Kairos* (2021) indicate a return to 1989. Earlier literary accounts of 1989 include Loest, *Nikolaikirche* (1995); and Brussig, *Wie es leuchtet* (2004).

33. Arendt, *On Revolution*, 114; referenced in Butler, *Notes on a Performative Theory of Assembly*, 46.

34. Letter, October 15, 1989, ABL/doku 004.027.007; letter, October 16, 1989, ABL/doku 004.027.010; letter, October 17, 1989, ABL/ doku 004.027.012. The letter by Lutz L. ends with "But now deeds must follow!" and is signed with a pledge "for peace and a new more human socialism." See also "Complaint," October 15, 1989, ABL/doku 004.027.006; and "Declaration of Intent by Nursing and Medical Staff at the Poliklinik Leipzig Südwest," October 12, 1989, ABL/doku 004.027.004. All documents with the

designation ABL/doku in this book are from the Archive of the Leipzig Citizens' Movement (Archiv der Bürgerbewegung Leipzig e.V.).

35. Arendt, "Preface: The Gap between Past and Future," 4. The discourse of being without masks circulated in '89; see Zwahr, *Ende einer Selbstzerstörung*, 8, 17; Neues Forum Leipzig, *Jetzt oder nie—Demokratie!*, 26. Unsurprisingly, Derrida complicates the notion of a masked self (*Specters of Marx*, 8).

36. On how historical events turn into global myths, see Sonnevend, *Stories without Borders*.

37. Magnus and Cullenberg, "Editors' Introduction," in Derrida, *Specters of Marx*, vii; Derrida, *Specters of Marx*, 46, 67; Fukuyama, *End of History and the Last Man*.

38. Brown, *In the Ruins of Neoliberalism*.

39. See, for example, Björn Menzel, "Die 70,000 Santftmutigen von Leipzig," *Die Zeit*, October 9, 2014; Joachim Gauck, "25th Anniversary German Unity" (speech given on October 3, 2015, in Frankfurt/Main); *Der Weg zur deutschen Einheit*, 7–30.

40. Dahn, *Der Schnee von gestern ist die Sintflut von heute*, 13–14.

41. On these various terms, see Arendt, *On Revolution*, 30–31; Kristeva, *Revolt, She Said*.

42. On the work of the Independent Commission for the Investigation of Police Abuses, October 7 and 8, see Wolf, *Umbrüche und Wendezeiten*, 60–70.

43. Schulze, *Neue Leben*, 497–99, 515; Schulze, *New Lives*, 356, 368.

44. Butler, *Force of Nonviolence*, esp. 5–15.

45. When I speak in this book of '89–90 as an interregnum, where life was virtually free and anarchic, I wish to recapture a sense of open-endedness from within the temporality of this historical moment, regardless of the outcomes—Germany's unification and the victory of the Western order—that ensued. In using the term "anarchy," I do not refer to a lawless state of disorder. After all, the nonviolent dimension of 1989 is one of the most admirable aspects of the opposition movement, and also a guiding principle that operated within a particular sphere of activity (i.e., as a shared rule). The voluntary citizens' organizations that assembled on the margins of GDR control in the autumn of 1989 were extremely peaceful and self-organized. And there were certainly provisional rules in place to govern these new social forms: Whose turn was it to speak? For how long would they get to speak? What I wish to highlight is the point where anarchy—the abolishing of hierarchical government *and* the reorganization of society on a voluntary, cooperative basis, without recourse to force or compulsion—meets society's civil or political sphere. The memory of '89–90 uncovered in this book straddles this very dynamic of alternatives: from a historical rupture in which disorder and mobility coexist there could emerge, on the one hand, an imperial, capitalist, or neofascist takeover or, on the other, the freedom to embody forms of cooperation and solidarity. See also Links, Nitsche, and Taffelt, eds., *Das wunderbare Jahr der Anarchie*.

46. Schell, "Introduction," in Arendt, *On Revolution*, xxii. Arendt generally rejected the cause of the poor as revolutionary project and revered the American revolution of 1776, aimed at political representation and freedom. See Arendt, "Freedom to Be Free."

47. On the (usually very brief) period of time when this kind of seizure of power is possible, see Žižek, *Relevance of the Communist Manifesto*, 52.

NOTES TO PAGES 16–20 › 241

48. Using the term "political happiness," I refer to the force of concerted action—in the form of public appearance, with freedom in action—in Arendt's sense; I also consider "the anxieties and the excitements of relationality [. . .] precisely at [such] moments of unknowingness" (Butler and Athanasiou, *Dispossession*, 92–93).

49. This body of work includes Sewell, *Logics of History*; Wagner-Pacifici, *What Is an Event?*; Horvath, Thomassen, and Wydra, eds., *Breaking Boundaries*.

50. The information in this section is drawn from Kowalczuk, *Endspiel*, 435–43, 469–74, 491–500. Patricia C. Sutcliffe's English translation of the book, under the title *Endgame*, is now available.

51. See Weil's excellent study *Verhandelte Demokratisierung*.

52. See Lässig, "Zeitzeuge," in Beier and Schwabe, *"Wir haben nur die Strasse,"* 216.

53. These and more founding documents and statements are discussed and cited in Dahn, *Der Schnee von gestern ist die Sintflut von heute*, 20–23.

54. See Sabrow, "'1989' und die Rolle der Gewalt in Ostdeutschland," esp. 10, 28–30; Gieseke, "Der entkräftete Tschekismus," esp. 71–74; Sabrow, ed., *1989 und die Rolle der Gewalt*. The publication resulted from a lecture series organized by the Center for Contemporary History (Zentrum für Zeithistorische Forschung, ZFF) Potsdam in 2009, and was sponsored by the Federal Foundation for the Reappraisal of the SED Dictatorship (Bundesstiftung zur Aufarbeitung der SED-Diktatur).

55. See Derrida, *Specters of Marx*, 67, also 46.

56. Some early examples of these works include Meuschel, *Legitimation und Parteiherrschaft in der DDR*; Niethammer, ed., *Der gesäuberte Antifaschismus*; Fulbrook, *Anatomy of a Dictatorship* and *People's State*; Sabrow, *Das Diktat des Konsenses*; Knabe, *Die Täter sind unter uns*. For a more culturally inflected account, see Jarausch, ed., *After Unity*. In some cases, the same historians rediscovered the contentious history of 1989; see, e.g., Sabrow, Siebeneichner, and Weiß, *1989: Eine Epochenzäsur*.

57. On the role of scholarly discourse in the production of hegemony ("dominant discourse"), see Derrida, *Specters of Marx*, 65–67. For this dynamic in the discipline of history after 1989 in Germany, see Weaver, *Rethinking Academic Politics in (Re)unified Germany and the United States*, esp. 4–5. Varying perspectives are provided in Fair-Schulz and Kessler, eds., *East German Historians since Unification*.

58. Dale, Review of *1989 und die Rolle der Gewalt*, 506.

59. There is a large body of scholarship on the memory and re-memorialization of the GDR. See, for instance, Bach, *What Remains*; Scribner, *Requiem for Communism*. See also Huyssen, *Twilight Memories*, esp. chapters 2 and 3; Cooke, *Representing East Germany since Unification*; Arnold de Simine, ed., *Memory Traces*; Saunders, *Memorializing the GDR*. In contrast to my argument, Anna Saunders considers "the ever-present narrative of 1989" (95). See also Novero, ed., *Imperfect Recall*. Scholarship on the culture of modernity in the GDR commonly concludes with remarks on 1989 or the memory of the GDR. See, for instance, Betts and Peance, eds., *Socialist Modern*; Betts, *Within Walls*; Rubin, *Amnesiopolis*.

60. This point is also noted by Jan Wenzel in *Das Jahr 1990 Freilegen*. Excellent (post-)1989 accounts emerged in theater and visual studies: see Naughton, *That Was the Wild East*; Cornish, *Performing Unification*. On the memory of the Monday demonstra-

tions, see Jessen, "Montagsdemonstrationen." As this book went into press, Stephen Brockmann's compelling account *The Freest Country in the World* was published.

61. Santner, *On the Psychotheology of Everyday Life*, 127.

62. Derrida, *Specters of Marx*, 20.

63. Boym, *Another Freedom*; Jameson, "Marx and Montage"; Badiou, *Communist Hypothesis*; Douzinas and Žižek, eds., *Idea of Communism*; Carnevale and Kelsey, with Rancière, "Art of the Possible."

64. See Frank Biess's review of *Germany since 1945*.

65. Betts, "1989 at Thirty"; Allen, "Against the 1989–1990 Ending Myth." For 1989 as a periodization beyond Eurochronology, see Coopan, "World Literature after 1989."

66. Rancière, *Disagreement*, 123, cited in Santner, *On the Psychotheology of Everyday Life*, 127.

67. Maier, *Dissolution*; Dale, *East German Revolution of 1989*; Sarotte, *Collapse*; Pfaff, *Exit Voice Dynamics and the Collapse of East Germany*; Hell, *Post-Fascist Fantasies*, 251–56; Pinkert, *Film and Memory in East Germany*; Lewis, "Analyzing the Trauma of German Unification."

68. Glaeser, *Political Epistemics*; Sa'adah, *Germany's Second Chance*.

69. Boyer, "Ostalgie and the Politics of the Future in Eastern Germany"; Berdahl, *Where the World Ends*.

70. I discuss this state of affairs in more detail in "Toward a Critical Reparative Practice in Post 1989 Literature."

71. Kowalczuk also states that much of the English-language literature fails to recognize the actual situation of the East German opposition, referring to Joppke, *East German Dissidents and the Revolution of 1989*, and the works of Mary Fulbrook ("Revolution in Germany," 22n23). But, as mentioned above, there are important studies by sociologists, anthropologists, and US-based historians, for instance, to consider. For a document-rich German-language history, see Bahrmann, *Finale*.

72. Brown, *Undoing the Demos*, 44; Stoler, *Interior Frontiers*, 275.

73. For a post-1989 historicization of this conflict, see Nycz, *Memory Politics in the Shadow of the New Cold War*.

74. This safeguarding of democracy against critique could be witnessed in the controversy around Georgio Agamben's 2021 book *Where Are We Now? The Epidemic as Politics*.

75. This observation brings to mind Benjamin's comment that revolutions are not, as Marx thought, the locomotives of history; instead, they indicate the desire of the train's passengers to reach for an "emergency brake"; see "Paralipomena to 'On the Concept of History,'" 402. I owe the notion of *pause* to my colleague Behrooz Ghamari.

76. Arendt uses a parable by Franz Kafka to illustrate this point; see "Preface: The Gap between Past and Future," 7.

77. This relative absence can be observed in important works, such as Rigney, "Remembering Hope"; Wüstenberg and Sierp, eds., *Agency in Transnational Memory Politics*. For an excellent analysis of memory work across boundaries between Eastern and Western Europe, see Jones, *Towards a Collaborative Memory*.

NOTES TO PAGES 25–28 › 243

78. On the cooptation of memory studies by concepts too closely aligned with neoliberal vocabulary, see Kantsteiner, "Migration, Racism, and Memory," 613. The continued relevance of power is noted in Bond, Craps, and Vermeulen, eds., *Memory Unbound*, 21; see also Rothberg, "Interview: Multidirectional Memory in Focus." Rey Chow foregrounds dynamics of force, dominance, submission, and antagonism across medial forms in *Entanglements, or Transmedial Thinking about Capture*.

79. On the interrelated dynamics of hegemonic and counter-hegemonic forces, see Gramsci, *Selections from the Prison Notebooks*; Butler, *Notes on a Performative Theory of Assembly*, 29, 36; Warner, *Publics and Counterpublics*, 63. On the "social performance" of memory, see Erll and Rigney, eds., *Mediation, Remediation, and the Dynamic of Cultural Memory*, 9.

80. Derrida, *Archive Fever*. I owe this succinct formulation to Lisa Blackman's discussion of data circulation (*Haunted Data*, 25–27, 166–68).

81. For key works, see Taylor, *Archive and the Repertoire*; Cvetkovich, *Archive of Feelings*; Stoler, *Along the Archival Grain*; Assmann, *Formen des Vergessens*, 36–38; Azoulay, *Potential History*.

82. For the archival turn in German studies, see Osborne, ed., *Archive and Memory in German Literature and Visual Culture*; Brandt and Glajar, eds., "Politics of the Archive"; Orich, "Archival Resistance"; Powell, *Films of Konrad Wolf*.

83. The term "anarchival" is used to refer to a surplus value of the archive (Striegl and Emerson, "Anarchive as Technique in the Media Archeology Lab"), to the violence of the archive (Huang, "Dwelling on the 'Anarchival'"), and to art's critical and self-reflexive exploration of practices such as classifying, collecting, and attributing (Lauf and Schäfer, curs., "anarchive").

84. Deleuze and Guattari, *Kafka*.

85. Derrida, *Athens, Still Remains*, 39. In *Archive Fever*, Derrida calls on photographic images, in particular, to delineate his notion of an "archive of the future" (70).

86. Derrida, *Archive Fever*, 36.

87. Foucault, "Historical *a priori* and the Archive (1969)," 28. In contrast to my own argument, some memory scholars believe that Derrida's and Foucault's formulations of the archive have become less relevant in the digital age; see Erll, *Memory in Culture*, 51.

88. Derrida, *Archive Fever*, 70.

89. Derrida, "Free Wheel," 8–9. Derrida addresses this notion of the "future remaining to come" in various works with respect to Marxism, the archive, and democracy.

90. Foster, "Archival Impulse (2004)."

91. Boym, *Future of Nostalgia*; Eshel, *Futurity*; Kazanjian, *Brink of Freedom*; Azoulay, *Potential History*. See also Jedlowski, "Memories of the Future." For a turn toward futurity in German studies, see Adelson and Fore, eds., "Futurity Now"; Adelson, *Cosmic Miniatures and the Future Sense*; Marc Silberman, ed., *Back to the Future*.

92. My work intersects with the "connective turn" in memory studies, and especially with the scholarship on the relation of digital media, archives, and forms of control. See, for instance, Hoskins, ed. *Digital Memory Studies*.

93. Buck-Morss, *Revolution Today*, 86–87.

94. On the relationality of images, see Azoulay, *Civil Contract of Photography*, 85;

Silverman, *Miracle of Analogy*, 87; Campt, *Listening to Images*. For memory and transcultural activism, see Altınay et al., eds., *Women Mobilizing Memory*; Taylor, *¡Presente!*. For a focus on mediation and protests, see Zamponi, *Social Movements, Memory and Media*; McGarry et al., eds., *Aesthetics of Global Protest*; Rigney and Smits, eds., *Visual Memory of Protest*.

95. Arendt, "Preface: The Gap between Past and Future," 13, 9.

96. Agamben, *State of Exception*. See also Dahn, *Schnee*. Here 1989–90 is described as a "completely exceptional situation," where "everything went haywire" (70). On the fear that further chaos would break out in the winter of '89, see also the dissident activist Ulrike Poppe in Weil, *Verhandelte Demokratisierung*, 52.

97. Arendt, "Preface: The Gap between Past and Future," 5. Also Arendt, *On Revolution*, esp. chapter 6.

98. Ziemer and Jackisch, "Volksfest," 125. The piece stresses the leaderless revolt and invokes a radically democratic, leftist legacy by referencing the deaths of Karl Liebknecht and Rosa Luxemburg in 1919. On the return of lethargy after the revolution and the eagerness for stability, see Arendt, *On Revolution*, 229, 31.

CHAPTER ONE

1. Baudrillard, "Anorexic Ruins," 67.

2. Brown, *Walled States, Waning Sovereignty*, 26.

3. Benjamin, "Work of Art in the Age of Mechanical Reproduction," 239–41.

4. On advertisement and false comprehensibility, see Adorno, *Minima Moralia*, 140.

5. On the memory of 1953, see my essay "Public Memory Underground."

6. Till, *New Berlin*, 204.

7. Huyssen, "Voids of Berlin." Notably, this gaze is one authorized in the West. In this otherwise invaluable essay, the normative Western gaze is also inscribed. Huyssen refers to the "gaze we all remember, the gaze from the primitive elevated wooden (later metal) platform erected near the Wall west of Potsdamer Platz to allow Western visitors to take a long look eastward across the death strip as emblem of communist totalitarianism" (64).

8. I draw inspiration here from Phillips, ed., *Framing Public Memory*, 4–6.

9. On mediated publics, see Warner, *Publics and Counterpublics*, esp. 68, 117. Warner, in turn, moves beyond Jürgen Habermas's influential account, which attends to structures of mediation but relies on an idealized notion of persuasion; see *Structural Transformation of the Public Sphere*.

10. Conventionally, social memory is linked to group identity (family, religion, profession, nation), whereas collective memory refers to the supply of shared knowledge and experiences relevant to the group and is shaped by social frameworks (Halbwachs). For more detailed elaborations of these two categories, see Erll, *Memory in Culture*, 14–16.

11. Arendt, *Human Condition*, 50, also 198–99.

12. Ther, *Europe since 1989*, 10, 26. For a succinct analysis of this economic transformation in Eastern Europe in the early 1990s, see Buck-Morss, *Dreamworld and Catastrophe*, 263–70.

13. For the Wall's material dismantling, see Sälter, "Das Verschwinden der Berliner Mauer."

14. Sarotte, *1989: The Struggle to Create Post–Cold War Europe*, 216, 218.

15. The actual transfer occurred more gradually; between 1989 and 1999 Berlin was a porous city that "embodied both euphoria and anxiety of transition" (Boym, *Future of Nostalgia*, 175). On transformational processes in early unified Berlin, see Ward, *Urban Memory and Visual Culture in Berlin*, 141–70; Hochmuth, *At the Edge of the Wall*, 279–303.

16. This point is noted by Traverso, *Left-Wing Melancholia*, 15, 57; See also Art, "Making Room for November 9, 1989?"

17. Chronister and Koepenick, "Introduction," 1. Drawing on Wendy Brown, the authors trace the emergence of neoliberal thought, emphasizing its Austro-German roots. While the tenets originated from the work of the Freiburg School at the end of World War II, the interventions of the Chicago School of Economics during the 1950s and the economic politics of Margaret Thatcher and Ronald Reagan in the late 1970s and 1980s consolidated neoliberal thought into a relentless economization of all aspects of life (1).

18. Chronister and Koepenick, "Introduction," 1.

19. For this argument, see Cooke, *Representing East Germany*, 6–7. On the reach of neoliberalism in post-1989 Eastern German society, see Chronister, *Domestic Disputes*, 1–19.

20. For the use of the notion *Unrechtsstaat* (illegitimate or unlawful state) in the early 1990s, see Sendler, "Die DDR ein Unrechtsstaat—ja oder nein?" The term "SED-Unrechts-Regime" (illegitimate SED regime)—a somewhat different term, but with the same meaning—was written into the law of the unification treaty (*Einheitsvertrag*) (2). The term *Unrechtsstaat* began to circulate in a parliamentary debate about the SED state in 1992, where the PDS argued it was used as an ideological battle term to demonize the GDR and to equate it with a Nazi-fascist state (1). The discourse of *Unrechtsstaat* (or approximate terminology) was first used in the postwar FRG regarding the Nazi state. The term referred to a state in which the law was used arbitrarily by those in power, leading to a perversion of the law (3). The meaning that established itself regarding the GDR was that the GDR itself was an illegitimate state. For the 1992 report of the government-appointed Enquete Commission, which classified the GDR as a "totalitarian system," see this book's introduction.

21. Betts and Mark, eds., *Socialism Goes Global*, 7.

22. Cercel, "Whither Politics, Whither Memory?," 15.

23. Berman, "Introduction," 3. On the pervasiveness of "warnings about the evil of totalitarianism" among historians of Eastern Europe who argued that post-1989 former Soviet bloc countries were liberated from Soviet despotism and returned to their real "European home," see also Betts and Mark, *Socialism Goes Global*, 6.

24. Glaeser, *Divided in Unity*, 283.

25. Cooke, *Representing East Germany*, 28.

26. Cercel, "Whither Politics, Whither Memory?," 7.

27. In 2010, *Alternativlosigkeit* (lack of alternatives) was voted as the *Unwort* (worst word) of the year.

28. Butler, *Notes on a Performative Theory of Assembly*, 14. On neoliberalism's de-democratizing effects, see Brown, *Undoing the Demos*, 50.

29. For Hildebrandt's project, see Frank, *Wall Memorials and Heritage*, 147–50.

30. Scholars have used various metaphors to examine this reappearance. Re-temporalizing and resiting the Wall are explored by Bach, *What Remains*, 137–69. On palimpsests, see Golden, "Following the Berlin Wall," 216–29. On the wall's material status and appropriation as a ruin, see Daniela Sandler, *Counterpreservation*, 229–30. Jürgen Böttcher's 1990 art documentary *Die Mauer* [The wall] provides a stunning meditation on the Wall and its (dis)appearance as architectural and historical object.

31. Flierl, *Gesamtkonzept zur Erinnerung an die Berliner Mauer*, esp. 12, 14–19. Notably, the city's comprehensive plan for the commemoration of the Wall did not mention the Peaceful Revolution; instead the motto read "Overcoming the Wall" (*Überwindung der Mauer*) (19). The experts consulted included Professor Dr. Konrad Jarausch, Professor Dr. Martin Sabrow, and Dr. Hans-Hermann Hertle (15). Flierl correctly points out that the "Comprehensive Plan" (2006) was not identical with the concept of the History Consortium "Reappraisal of the SED Dictatorship" (Geschichtsverbund zur Aufarbeitung der SED-Diktatur) (14); yet there existed close institutional connections in the official sphere of memory politics. The History Consortium was appointed by the federal government in 2005, under the leadership of Martin Sabrow, then director of the Potsdam Center for Contemporary History (Zentrum für Zeithistorische Forschung, ZFF). Konrad Jarausch served as one of the previous directors of the ZFF. Starting in 2005, the department of the Federal Government Commissioner for Culture and Media (Beauftragter der Bundesregierung für Kultur und Medien), which also appointed the History Consortium and oversaw the Stasi Records Agency (Behörde des Bundesbeauftragten für die Unterlagen des Staatssicherheitsdienstes der ehemaligen DDR) and the Federal Foundation for the Reappraisal of the SED Dictatorship (Bundesstiftung zur Aufarbeitung der SED-Diktatur). According to the website of the federal government, "this meant that the responsibilities for looking after the memorials and for the political reappraisal of the SED injustice (*Unrecht*) were bundled in one authority" ("Aufarbeitung der SED-Diktatur," *Die Bundesregierung*, August 8, 2007, https://www.bundesregierung.de/breg-de/aktuelles/aufarbeitung-der-sed-diktatur-476870).

32. Axel Klausmeier, "'In Order to Grasp Something, There Must Be Something to Grasp,'" 306. This document is one of the few that acknowledges a brief interval in '89–90 when it seemed possible that the "GDR would be able to assert itself as independent state" (304).

33. Klausmeier, "In Order to Grasp Something," 306.

34. Klausmeier, "In Order to Grasp Something," 306. This careful approach echoed local discussions in 1991, when politicians, citizens, and church leaders from Berlin-Mitte and Wedding argued whether the proposed preservation of Wall remnants would be too depressing for residents, reminding them of experienced injustice, or if the preservation would be welcome in its fragmentary form as a monument to the Wall's overcoming (Dolff-Bonekämper, "Denkmalschutz-Denkmalsetzung-Grenzmarkierung," 39–40).

35. Lehrer, Milton, and Patterson, eds., *Curating Difficult Knowledge*, esp. 179–80. At Bernauer Strasse, a first Documentation Center had opened in 1999. The Chapel of Reconciliation followed in 2000, the platform at the Documentation Center was added

NOTES TO PAGES 42–47 › 247

in 2002, and the Documentation Center reopened in 2014 with an expanded permanent exhibit.

36. Detjen, "Die Mauer," 264.

37. Take, for instance, the signature essay of the official catalogue for the exhibit at Bernauer Strasse, which is available at the Documentation Center to the more than one million visitors to the site each year and is translated into several languages. Devoid of any socialist imaginary, the GDR is featured in normative repetition as "wall regime" or "border-regime," and the Wall as "crime-site," "site of despotism and death, of suffering and grief" (Klausmeier, "Commemoration Needs a Place.")

38. On prosthesis, a "distorted substitute" where "a part of truth remains," see Derrida, *Archive Fever*, 88.

39. The concept of "Rückbindung der Toten," a reattachment to the dead for the production of social identity, is discussed by Jan Assmann in *Das kulturelle Gedächtnis, Schrift, Erinnerung, und politische Identität in frühen Hochkulturen*, 63; and cited in Flierl, *Gesamtkonzept zur Erinnerung an die Berliner Mauer*, 30. A series of mourning rituals were designed to uncover the victims' lives from anonymity: readings of the names of the dead, on weekdays at the Chapel of Reconciliation.

40. Official ceremonies are commonly staged in front of the memorial's functional inscription, which reads "Berlin Wall Monument in Commemoration of the Division of the City from August 13, 1961, to November 9, 1989 in Remembrance of the Victims of the Communist Tyranny. Established by the Federal Republic of Germany and the State of Berlin." For the "triumph of freedom," see also Klausmeier, "In Order to Grasp Something," 305.

41. Foster, "Archival Impulse (2004)," 145.

42. Libeskind, *Jewish Museum Berlin*. On the resonance of Holocaust memory for other injustices, see also Levy and Sznaider, *Holocaust and Memory in the Global Age*.

43. On this notion by Reinhart Koselleck, see Assmann, *Shadows of Trauma*, 1–6. For critical, less instrumentalized practices of multidirectional contacts with Holocaust memory in the German context, see Rothberg, "Multidirectional Memory in Migratory Settings," esp. 125.

44. Flierl, *Gesamtkonzept zur Erinnerung an die Berliner Mauer*, 19.

45. Bach, *What Remains*, 149.

46. On the double poetics of photographs, see Rancière, *Future of the Image*, 25, also 11–15.

47. Etkind, *Warped Mourning*, 11–12.

48. See Demke, "Mauerfotos in der DDR," 90–106.

49. Western cameras on August 15, 1961, were readily present, and an unrelenting fight over copyright and profits for the image ensued between different agencies and photographers. Conrad Schumann's identity was exposed by the worldwide circulation of the image (published in the *Bild-Zeitung*), reportedly leaving Schumann fearful throughout his life of being tracked down in the West by the Stasi. When he returned to his hometown after the Wall fell, some still rejected him as traitor. He committed suicide in 1998. The objectification of Schumann as photographic subject is enhanced by the fact that Leibing attributed the success of the image to his skill as derby pho-

tographer. Benjamin commented on sport snapshots' commodification, referring to Siegfried Kracauer. The "split second of exposure" determines publicity ("Little History of Photography," 514). On exploitation of images, see Azoulay, *Civil Contract of Photography*, 106.

50. Derrida, *Archive Fever*, 3.

51. The historian Frank Wolff goes as far as to use the term "Wall-Society" (*Mauergesellschaft*).

52. Here, it is worth rereading James J. Ward's essay "Remember When It Was the 'Antifascist Defense Wall?,'" esp. 21.

53. Traverso, *Left-Wing Melancholia*, 14–19.

54. This shift is examined, for instance, by Bauer and Hosek, eds., *Cultural Topographies of the New Berlin*, 7. For earlier accounts, see Ward, "Berlin, the Virtual Global City"; Huyssen, "Voids of Berlin," esp. 64. On the impact of neoliberal policies on the arts sector, see Woolf, *Institutional Theatrics*. See also Bach and Murawski, eds., *Re-Centring the City*.

55. This query expands on the question famously raised in 1968 by Henri Lefebvre and taken up by political geographers such as David Harvey; see Harvey's "Right to the City." For an insightful theorization of memory, space, and urban politics, see Karen E. Till, "Wounded Cities."

56. See, for instance, Bach, *What Remains*, 91–136; Staiger, "Cities, Citizenship, Contested Cultures"; Dieckmann, *Vom Schloss der Könige zum Forum der Republik*.

57. "Konzept der Bundesregierung zur Errichtung eines Freiheits-und Einheitsdenkmals in Berlin," in *Der Weg zum Denkmal für Freiheit und Einheit*, ed. Andreas H. Apelt (Schwalbach: Wochenschau Verlag, 2009), 169. (Based on the decree Bundestags-Drucksache 16/6925, November 9, 2007). The first cross-party (*überparteilich*) petition for the monument to the Bundestag, with support of the German National Foundation (Deutsche Nationalstiftung), was put forward in 2000 (Drucksache 14/3126) but did not find a majority.

58. See Eckhardt Barthel (SPD), "Plenarprotokoll, Deutscher Bundestag, 14/199," November 9, 2001, A-C.

59. "Initiative Denkmal Deutsche Einheit," in Apelt, *Der Weg zum Denkmal für Freiheit und Einheit*, 34–35. In 2000, the word "freedom" was added to "unity" in the monument's designation. Scholars have associated the Kohl era since the 1980s with efforts toward a so-called normalization of German identity and a new conservatism; see Olick, *Sins of the Fathers*, 322–42.

60. Mouffe, *For a Left Populism*, 56–57.

61. "Plenarprotokoll, Deutscher Bundestag, 16/124," November 9, 2007, 12967 B. In 2007, the Bundestag, in collaboration with the Deutsche Gesellschaft e.V., approved a design for the new memorial to be located at the *Schlossfreiheit*, the historic site where the Berlin Palace / Humboldt Forum would be rebuilt. Notably, this location was the site envisioned by Mausbach and others all along.

62. On the call for an enlightened patriotism by conservatives, see "Plenarprotokoll, Deutscher Bundestag, 14/199," November 9, 2001 (19511, D-19512, A). For the duality of joy and shame addressed by Wolfgang Thierse (SPD) and others, see "Plenarprotokoll, Deutscher Bundestag, 16/124," November 9, 2007 (12965, A-12967, A).

NOTES TO PAGES 52–56 › 249

63. Blei, "Monumental Problems."

64. Here, "past traumas are not allowed to register as traumatic in significantly different ways for different groups" (LaCapra, "Revisiting the Historians' Debate," 86). LaCapra refers to the conservative historians' debate in the 1980s. The debate itself diffused responsibility for the past by questioning the uniqueness of the Holocaust and the Nazi era with reference to Stalinist crimes. In the 2000s, one can no longer say that historical responsibility is denied, but discursive echoes are certainly palpable.

65. Mausbach, "Über Sinn und Ort eines nationalen Freiheits- und Einheitsdenkmals," 30.

66. "Gestaltungswettbewerb für ein Freiheits- und Einheitsdenkmal in Berlin—2010. Protokoll der Preisgerichtssitzung," Bundesrepublik Deutschland, represented by the Beauftragten der Bundesregierung für Kultur und Medien (BMK), Berlin, October 4, 2010, 18, https://www.freiheits-und-einheitsdenkmal.de/images/pdf/2010-protokollpreisgericht.pdf.

67. Volker Blech, "Interview with Sascha Waltz: 'Das Einheitsdenkmal ist keine Wippe,'" *Berliner Morgenpost*, August 14, 2011. The notion of sculpture as an expanded field is developed by Krauss, *Passages in Modern Sculpture*.

68. "Choreographin Sasha Waltz steigt aus Einheitsdenkmal aus," *Die Welt*, November 11, 2012.

69. McLuhan, "Medium is the Message (1964)," 399.

70. See Blei, "Monumental Problems." She refers to an interview with historian Cornelia Siebeck.

71. Dolff-Bonekämper, "Grosser Sockel."

72. Beuys, with von Bethmann et al., *What Is Money?*, 16–27 (the event was held in 1984 in Ulm). On the relation of freedom and equality in Beuys's thinking, see also the afterword by Ulrich Rösch (*What Is Money?* 69–89).

73. "Aktuelle Kamera," November 9, 1989 ("Bohley warned forces in the West to speculate about the property and land [*Grund und Boden*] in the GDR"), YouTube video, 29:47, at 17:00, https://www.youtube.com/watch?v=5kiqZhvQFZM. Jochen Lässig (New Forum), "Speech at the Montagsdemonstration: 13. November 1989," 73–74.

74. On form and visibility in the material world, see the chapter "The Surface of Design" in Rancière, *Future of the Image*, esp. 91. He also addresses commodification. I am intrigued by the perception of the monument as "occupiable memorial." See the post "Germany's National Monument to Freedom and Unity Breaks Ground in Berlin," *Designboom*, June 1, 2020, https://www.designboom.com/architecture/milla-partner-berlin-monument-freedom-unity-groundbreaking-06-01-2020/.

75. Judith Butler usefully points out that "We, the people" does not presuppose or make unity but enacts a set of debates about "who the people are and what they want." Speaking in one voice (i.e., "Wir sind ein Volk") invokes a kind of *Gleichschaltung* suggestive of fascist marches or military chants; see "'We, the People,'" 53.

76. For varying conceptions of democracy, see Brown, *Undoing the Demos*, 18–20. The post-Soviet scholar Susan Buck-Morss critiques the introduction of controlled

forms of democracy (and voting systems) after 1989 (*Dreamworld and Catastrophe*, 256).

77. Saunders, *Memorializing the GDR*, 268.

78. Warner, *Publics and Counterpublics*, 70. On a local level, Jenny Wüstenberg observes a similar dynamic, in which activist participation in post-unification memorial projects is frustrated, here regarding legacies of the SBZ/GDR in Potsdam; see *Civil Society and Memory in Postwar Germany*, 260.

79. Gunter Weissgerber (SPD), "Petition to the Bundestag, March 22, 2000," in *Leipziger Freiheits- und Einheitsdenkmal*, ed. Gunter Weissgerber, commissioned by the Foundation Peaceful Revolution Leipzig and the Archive of the Citizens' Movement Leipzig e.V. in 2014, ch. 1, p. 18, https://www.archiv-buergerbewegung.de/themen-sammlung/denkmal.

80. "Plenarprotokoll Bundestag, 16/124," November 9, 2007, 12963 D, 12969 D. See also "Plenarprotokoll Bundestag, 14/199," November 9, 2001, 19509 A. The Left Party criticized the managerial procedures in the so-called representational democracy by recalling the "birth of genuine democracy" at the roundtables in the GDR in 1989 (12963 D). Die Linke and the Green Party demanded broad public discussion, involving civil-rights activists who transformed the GDR at the time and who no longer see themselves represented by the political apparatus today (12964 B, also 12965 A).

81. Fraser, "Rethinking the Public Sphere," 77.

82. In 2017, even a conservative newspaper called the project an intellectual still-birth ("Totgeburt") promoted foremost by the cultural politicians of the CDU/CSU; see Sven Felix Kellerhoff, "Nun kommt die Wippe doch—das darf nicht wahr sein," *Die Welt*, February 14, 2017.

83. Mitchell, *What Do Pictures Want?*, 10, 250–51.

84. Arendt, "Preface: The Gap between Past and Future," 6. She states:

The history of revolutions—from the summer of 1776 in Philadelphia and the summer of 1789 in Paris to the autumn of 1956 in Budapest which politically spells out the innermost story of the modern age, could be told in parable form as the tale of an age-old treasure which, under the most varied circumstances, appears abruptly, unexpectedly, and disappears again, under different mysterious conditions, as though it were a fata morgana. There exist, indeed, many good reasons to believe that the treasure was never a reality but a mirage, that we deal with here not with anything substantial but with an apparition, and the best of these reasons is that the treasure thus far has remained nameless. (5)

85. Sieg, *Decolonizing German and European History at the Museum*.

86. See Nikolaus Bernau, "Das Humboldt-Forum ist nicht das Schloss," *Berliner Zeitung*, May 29, 2020, 12.

87. Arendt, "Preface: The Gap between Past and Future," 6.

88. The Robert Havemann Society e.V. was founded on November 19, 1990, as a political association of the New Forum in Berlin. The first advisory board included Bärbel Bohley, Katja Havemann, and Jens Reich. Robert Havemann, a physical chemist, was expelled from the SED and the Humboldt University of Berlin in 1963 and put under house arrest in 1976. He was one of the major dissidents in the GDR.

89. See Sa'adah, *Germany's Second Chance*, 76–77.

90. Such self-reflexive acts of meaning production are discussed in Butler, *Frames of War*, 6–9.

91. Bahrmann and Links, *Chronik der Wende 2*, 48–51. For the third-way variant, see Gysi and Modrow, eds., *Wir brauchen einen dritten Weg*. Modrow's ambivalent status between "traitor and political mediator" is examined in Bouma, *German Post-Socialist Memory Culture*, 246–53.

92. From a West German perspective, Horst Teltschik, a close advisor of Helmut Kohl, wrote on January 10, 1990, that, based on a new draft for the election on May 6, 1990, Modrow attempted to secure the power monopoly of the SED-PDS and to weaken the opposition (*329 Tage*, 103–4). The elections were moved to March 18, 1990.

93. In fact, substantial demographic support for the SED existed still by the end of 1989 (Schneider, *Leipziger Demontagebuch*, 173–76). According to a statistic published by the GDR Institute for Youth Research on January 4, 1990, 42 percent of the GDR population supported a confederacy between the FRG and GDR—that is, cooperation based on political independence (Wenzel, *Das Jahr 1990 Freilegen*, 27). However, in early 1990 the SED-PDS swiftly departed from the course of democratic socialism. For instance, only three days after the governmental address on January 11, Modrow and representatives of other parties and groups met with Edzard Reuter, the CEO of Daimler-Benz, where Minister for Economy Christa Luft (SED-PDS) declared her support for the social market economy (Bahrmann and Links, *Chronik der Wende 2*, 57–58). On February 1, in an unexpected turn of events, Modrow outlined the strategic paper "Deutschland einig Vaterland" (Germany, United Fatherland). The editorial staff of *Die andere Zeitung* reacted with acid disappointment and brandished it as a Communist-led retreat from socialism. The editorial statement rejected the "bourgeois democracy" of the FRG (with its own crisis) as an adequate political goal (Sa'adah, *Germany's Second Chance*, 83).

94. Gregor Gysi, "Interview with Alexander Kluge," in Wenzel, *Das Jahr 1990 Freilegen*, 91.

95. On photography's capacity to engage the limits of visibility, see Smith, *At the Edge of Sight*, esp. 8, 14–19. For the process of crafting new meanings, see Azoulay, *Civil Contract of Photography*, 420–21. For earlier work, see Alison Landsberg, who conceived of photography as a tool to retrain vision, where the contingency of reified "naturalized" structures of society can be recognized (*Prosthetic Memory*, 16).

96. See Bahrmann and Links, *Chronik der Wende 2*, 40–58. A selective list of events early that week alone provides a sense of the largely forgotten multiple agendas, plural sites, and variegated scales of protests across the GDR at the beginning of 1990. On January 7, ten thousand people formed a sixty-kilometer human chain between the GDR region Eichsfeld and the Werraland in the West; at an assembly of delegates in Leipzig, the New Forum (two hundred thousand members total) decided not to become a party and prevented possible splintering. On January 8, after a three-week pause, the Monday demonstrations started again in Leipzig, now changed and dominated by supporters of German unification with German flags; fifty thousand inhabitants of Karl-Marx-Stadt demonstrated for democratic participation in factories; five thousand protesters in New Brandenburg demanded transparency about the financial affairs of the SED-PDS; in Schwerin eight thousand people demonstrated against right-wing radicalism and the abuse of this situation by the SED-PDS, and so forth (40–58).

97. Sa'adah, *Germany's Second Chance*, 82. She concludes that, aside from the discomfort with party politics among the oppositional groups and citizens' movements, their skepticism toward the renewal of the SED-PDS, as well as increasing hostility toward socialism among the population, ultimately inhibited a durable coalition between the oppositional groups, the SED-PDS, and the SPD.

98. Laclau and Mouffe, *Hegemony and Socialist Strategy*. In basic terms, according to Laclau and Mouffe, liberal democracy tends to regulate differing opinions, whereas radical democracy is not only accepting of difference, dissent, and tension but dependent on it. For leftists such as the East German playwright Volker Braun, these radical possibilities were cut off with the election result in March 1990, and the politics of closure sealed with Germany's unification ("Erfahrungen der Freiheit," in *Wir befinden uns soweit wohl*, 57).

99. For this debate among feminist scholars, see Warner, *Publics and Counterpublics*, 58. Some scholars note that Arendt's concept of political organization in public space is somewhat antiquated (Warner, *Publics and Counterpublics*, 62), or naturalized (Butler, *Notes on a Performative Theory of Assembly*, 87). Butler moves beyond Arendt's notion of the public sphere (where primarily speech qualifies as paradigmatic political action) and focuses on politics as bodily enactment in space and on the limits that constitute publics.

100. Brown, *In the Ruins of Neoliberalism*, 9. Brown echoes Arendt's notion that "the space of appearance" (assembly) is by nature transient and that it disappears with the "arrest of the activities themselves." But "wherever people gather together, it is potentially there, but only potentially, not necessarily and not forever" and "never altogether loses its potential" (Arendt, *Human Condition*, 199–200).

101. Berdahl, *On the Social Life of Postsocialism*, 48–59. See also Boyer, "Ostalgie and the Politics of the Future in Eastern Germany"; Cooke, *Representing East Germany since Unification*; Bach, *What Remains*.

102. Cercel, "Whither Politics, Whither Memory?," 7.

103. For the first trend, see Harrison, *After the Berlin Wall*; for the latter, see chapter 5 of this book.

104. Butler, *Notes on a Performative Theory of Assembly*, 29, 36.

105. Foster, "Archival Impulse (2004)," 144.

106. For the controversial 2020 exhibit "Antifa—Myth and Truth," organized by the Peng! Collective at the art collection of the König-Albert Museum in Chemnitz, see Caspar Shaller, "Antifa ins Museum," *der Freitag* 34 (2020), https://www.freitag.de/autoren/caspar-shaller/antifa-ins-museum. In contrast, a nostalgic approach to antifascism within the East German Committee of Associations (OKV), a network of former Stasi officers and GDR officials, is examined in Bouma, *German Post-Socialist Memory Culture*, esp. 164–68. For a reevaluation of antifascist history in international contexts, see Traverso, "Intellectuals and Antifascism," 1–15.

107. See, for instance, the 2022 exhibit, "re.frau anders: Lesbian and Feminist Activism of the 1980s in East Berlin," held from July 1 to November 9, 2022, in the outdoor area at the former Wall watchtower at Schlesischer Busch, Berlin ("re. frau anders," *Watch*, 2022, https://thewatch-berlin.org/re-frau-anders). On legacies of anti-Semitism in the GDR, see Heitzer et al., eds., *After Auschwitz*.

108. See the nuanced account in Sheffer, *Burned Bridge*.

NOTES TO PAGES 72–78 › 253

INTERTEXT

1. Derrida complicates the relation between specter and spectator in *Specters of Marx*, 11.

2. On publics and spectatorship, see Hlavajova and Hoskote, eds., *Future Publics*, 11. For earlier work on acts of viewing and public memory, see Young, *Texture of Memory*, ix.

3. For the body of this work, see the introduction to this book.

4. For a brilliant counterpoint, see Trnka, "Suspended Time, Exile, and the Literature of Transnational Antifascism." The author offers an analysis of multidirectional antifascist memory in transnational contexts (42) and traces "the becoming contemporary of 1970s antifascism" (50).

5. This approach is exemplified by Könczöl and Meuschel, "Sacrilization of Politics in the GDR," 41.

6. Dillon, "Short History of Ruin," 14.

7. Etkind, *Warped Mourning*, 12.

8. Traverso, *Left-Wing Melancholia*, 19.

9. Konrad Schuller, "Die Heldenmutter hat keinen Blick für die Gräber der Gefallenen," *Frankfurter Allgemeine Zeitung* 34, February 10, 1998, 4.

10. On the controversy around the Lenin memorial, see Saunders, *Memorializing the GDR*, 65–72. For Soviet-era monuments, see Kuczyńska-Zonik, "Dissonant Heritage."

11. Lummer is quoted in "Danke, Gorbi. Russische Militärs bangen um 600 Ehrenmäler, die sie in Deutschland zurücklassen," *Der Spiegel* 9, February 28, 1993, 76.

12. Niethammer, ed., *Der gesäuberte Antifaschismus*; Meuschel, *Legitimation und Parteiherrschaft*. See also Hartewig, "Militarismus und Antifaschismus."

13. Courtney Glore Crimmins, "Reinterpreting the Soviet War Memorial in Berlin's Treptower Park after 1990," 57.

14. See the excellent essay by Kristine Nielsen, "Quid pro quo: Assessing the Value of Berlin's Thälmann Monument." Despite plans to remove it, the Ernst Thälmann monument (designed by Lev Kerbel and erected in the Prenzlauer Berg district of Berlin in 1986) is still at its original location today.

15. A complex transgenerational fictional account of this memory can be found in Christoph Hein's novel *Trutz*. The book deals with the pre-1989 suppression of Stalinist crimes and post-1989 hegemonic archival power over that history.

16. Crimmins, "Reinterpreting the Soviet War Memorial in Berlin's Treptower Park after 1990," 63.

17. On West Berlin Antifa groups, see Sontheimer and Wensierski, *Stadt der Revolte*, 396–98. For the statistics, see Bahrmann and Links, *Chronik der Wende* 2, 32. For a speculation that Stasi officers may have been behind the vandalism, see Wolle, *Die heile Welt der Diktatur, Alltag und Herrschaft in der DDR 1971–1989*, 333.

18. Wenzel, *Das Jahr 1990 Freilegen*, 17.

19. See Stangl, "Soviet War Memorial in Treptow, Berlin," 218 (citing Ladd, *Ghosts of Berlin*). According to Martin Kitchen, this rumor is not true. In fact, "the Soviets

graciously gave" valuable objects from the remains of the Chancellery to the British military; others ended up in the German Historical Museum in Berlin and at the Pentagon (Kitchen, *Speer*, 56).

20. See the account by the historian Götz Aly, "Befreiung 1945: Deutsche Ignoranz beleidigt Russland," *Berliner Zeitung*, April 21, 2020, 7.

21. Berman, "Introduction," 3.

22. In light of the shifting geopolitical present pointing once more toward conflict and polarity, Alexander Kluge's poetic-philosophical collection *Russia Container* (originally printed in German as *Russland-Kontainer* [Berlin: Suhrkamp, 2020]) is an important starting point for this work. Providing a longer temporal arch, Kluge meditates on the relationship between Russia and Germany as intrinsically linked by centuries-long histories of exchange and rejection. These short prose narratives are also characterized by an investment in "future-making under conditions of catastrophe," identified by Leslie Adelson as a recurring approach in Kluge's work (*Cosmic Miniatures and the Future Sense*, 27).

23. Tawada, "Pushkin Allee."

24. Şenocak, "Thoughts on May 8, 1995," 59. He further states, "History is far too seldom confronted with the present. . . . It is well known that the Federal Republic of Germany was not an uncomfortable place for many former Nazis. Many of them were able to continue their careers after brief reorientations. United Germany is that country in which four thousand to five thousand attacks and transgressions against 'foreigners' (*Fremde*) take place annually. The foreigners in Germany, most of whom have been at home here for a long time, barely bother to reflect on the history of the Germans" (59).

CHAPTER TWO

1. Augé, *Oblivion*, xi, 61–62, 89. I am paraphrasing in this opening section questions raised by James Young ("Foreword," in Augé, *Oblivion*, xi).

2. Pinkert, "Arrival," 1–14.

3. After 1989, three-quarters of GDR academics lost their jobs, while out of a total of 1,878 professors employed in the former East between 1994 and 1998, only 104 came from the East (Cooke, *Representing East Germany since Unification*, 3). On the transition, see also Lahusen, "Autobiography as Participation in the 'Master Narrative,'" 182–94.

4. Eisler and Geister, *Luxus Arbeit*.

5. Wenzel and König, *Zerrissene Gesellschaft*, 5.

6. The writer Christoph Hein dubbed Leipzig the GDR's "city of heroes" on November 4, 1989, at the mass assembly in Berlin.

7. Cahill, *Blessed Are the Peacemakers*.

8. Rancière, *Disagreement*, esp. 29, 63.

9. Zwahr, *Ende einer Selbstzerstörung*, 9. On Leipzig as "the true capital of the German Democratic Republic," see Meyer-Gosau, *Versuch eine Heimat zu finden*, 83–85.

10. Derrida, *Specters of Marx*, 64.

NOTES TO PAGES 83–88 › 255

11. Michael Warner's differentiated concept of the public proves useful: "The unity of the public is also ideological. . . . It depends on institutionalized forms of power to realize the agency attributed to the public; and it depends on a hierarchy of faculties that allows some faculties to count as public or general and others to be merely personal, private, or particular. Some publics, for these reasons, are more likely than others to stand in for *the* public, to frame their address as the universal discussion of the people" (*Publics and Counterpublics*, 117).

12. Erll, *Memory in Culture*, 28–29.

13. Assmann, *Shadows of Trauma*, 6.

14. See the umbrella organization Initiative Autumn '89—Departure to Democracy (Initiative Herbst '89—Aufbruch zur Demokratie), at https://www.herbst89.de/, accessed April 5, 2022.

15. Saunders, *Memorializing the GDR*, 256. Saunders provides an excellent, detailed overview of all realized and unrealized memorial projects in Leipzig between 1989 and 2014.

16. For more on the distinction between the French structuralist theories of Derrida and Foucault, who insist on a performative dimension of memory as dominance and power, and the tradition of Anglo-American studies and Marxist approaches to the study of nationalism (e.g., Hobsbawm, Anderson), see Erll, *Memory in Culture*, 50. On the politics of scales, see De Cesari and Rigney, eds. *Transnational Memory*, 19.

17. "Revolutionspflaster bleibt erhalten," *Leipziger Volkszeitung*, December 16, 2018. Since 2016 the cobblestones at the St. Nicholas Churchyard are under historic protection.

18. The idea of *Aufbruch* was ubiquitous in the fall of 1989. See the New Forum founding document "Departure '89" ("Aufbruch '89"), September 9, 1989, https:// www.hdg.de/lemo/bestand/objekt/dokument-aufbruch-89.html.

19. Neues Forum Leipzig, *Jetzt oder nie—Demokratie!*, 9. When the borders from Hungary to Austria opened on September 10, 1989, the New Forum pitched "staying in the GDR and the activities of political resistance" against "flight/emigration" (10). The notion of "voting with one's feet" is tied to a national Cold War imaginary. See also Naimark, "'Ich will hier raus.'"

20. "Einweisung der Genossen zur Besetzung der Nikolaikirche am 9. Oktober," in Beier and Schwabe, *"Wir haben nur die Strasse,"* 244–45. DVD included in book.

21. Zwahr, *Ende einer Selbstzerstörung*, 90–91.

22. Schedlinski, "die phase der *schönen revolution* ist vorbei," 340.

23. Kristin Ross tracks similar forms of dislocation (*May '68 and Its Afterlives*, 25). For detailed accounts of the various physical movements of people, groups, and bodies across the spaces of the city in October 1989, see Zwahr, *Ende einer Selbstzerstörung*, 86–90.

24. Saunders, *Memorializing the GDR*, 270.

25. "'We Are the People': Leipzig and the Peaceful Revolution," *Leipzig Region: Media Informationen* (originally at https://www.leipzig.travel/en/service/media/ media-information, accessed March 20, 2020; the post has since been taken down).

26. In contrast, consider Lutz Seiler's novel *Kruso*, where the chapter entitled "Keine Gewalt!" (No violence), set during the early fall of '89, is laced with language of violence, rupture, and force (364–76).

27. Huyssen, "Authentic Ruins," 52.

28. Butler, *Notes on a Performative Theory of Assembly*, 186–87. On the unprotected exposure of the demonstrators and the nonviolent character of the Peaceful Revolution, see also Stolpe, *Schwieriger Aufbruch*, 174. For a detailed account of how October 9, 1989, turned out to be nonviolent, see Qinna Shen, "Tiananmen Square, Leipzig, and the 'Chinese Solution.'"

29. Stötzner, *Über Klassik*. The quotations can be found at "Andreas Stötzner—Leipziger Grafiker, Signologe und Künstler," Hgb-lepizig.de, accessed September 9, 2019, https://www.hgb-leipzig.de/kunstorte/nk_stoetzner.html.

30. Cottin et al., *Leipziger Denkmale*, 2:50. Cited in Saunders, *Memorializing the GDR*, 274.

31. Hochmuth, *At the Edge of the Wall*, esp. 163–215.

32. Mitter and Wolle, eds., *"Ich liebe euch doch alle!,"* 128. Cited in Zwahr, *Ende einer Selbstzerstörung*, 20.

33. These tensions are captured in local accounts, especially with regard to the eve of the state's official celebration of the fortieth anniversary of the GDR, October 7, 1989 (Neues Forum Leipzig, *Jetzt oder nie—Demokratie!* 9). See also, Zwahr, *Ende einer Selbstzerstörung*, 61–78. This account speaks of "intended shock effects of military emergency forces" (64).

34. Such heroized characters are elaborated in Taylor, *Archive and the Repertoire*, 261.

35. For the resistance-stifling logic of labeling criticism as complaint, see Ahmed, *Complaint!* I thank John Slattery for this insight.

36. See *Friedensgebete in der Leipziger Nikolaikirche*.

37. Moldt, *Wunder gibt es immer wieder*. A link between the peace prayers and the peaceful revolution is stressed by the exhibit in Leipzig—"Eine Revolution, die aus der Kirche kam und vom Geist der Bergpredigt getragen wurde von vielen" (*Friedensgebete in der Leipziger Nikolaikirche*, 87). See also Schneider, *Leipziger Demontagebuch*, 13. Here the emphasis is on peacefulness (*Friedfertigkeit*), gentleness (*Sanftmut*), prayer (*Gebete*), and nonviolence (*Gewaltlosigkeit*).

38. This is noted by Betts and Mark, *Socialism Goes Global*, 8.

39. On the history of the symbol "swords to plowshares," see *Friedensgebete in der Leipziger Nikolaikirche*, 54–60. For the history of the pacifist movement in the GDR, see Kowalczuk, *Endspiel*, 206–8.

40. The historian Hartmut Zwahr added accounts of these escalations only in the 2014 edition of his local history. He marked these additions by blocking them in gray (*Ende einer Selbstzerstörung*, 21).

41. Kaden, "Von den Friedensgebeten ging alles aus."

42. *Offene Arbeit* was the term for work with nonconformist youth beginning in 1971, characterized by an anti-missionary approach, teamwork, basis-democratic decisions, cultural offerings of banned art, and training in case of arrests or Stasi recruitment.

NOTES TO PAGES 93–98 › 257

Groups existed across the country, including in Thuringia, Saxony, and Berlin (Kowalczuk, *Endspiel*, 205–6).

43. Führer, "Abend für den Frieden," in *Friedensgebete in der Leipziger Nikolaikirche*, 72.

44. "Staatliche Gesprächsnotiz," in *Freunde und Feinde*, 138–39, emphasis added.

45. "Interview with Beate Tischer," in *Friedensgebete in der Leipziger Nikolaikirche*, 140.

46. Führer, "Abend für den Frieden," in *Friedensgebete in der Leipziger Nikolaikirche*, 72.

47. "Erklärung zum Friedensgebet am 10.11.88," ABL/doku 002.003.005.

48. "Interview with Christoph Wonneberger," in *Friedensgebete in der Leipziger Nikolaikirche*, 143.

49. *Friedensgebete in der Leipziger Nikolaikirche*, 66. When Friedrich Magirius was awarded an honorary prize by the premier of North Rhine-Westphalia after the *Wende*, activists, including Frank Richter, protested that Magirius had not promoted social change and had suspended the peace prayers, and that someone like Christoph Wonneberger would be more suitable (ABL/doku 002.003.010).

50. See, for instance, a letter by the Evangelisch-Lutherisches Kirchenamt Landeskirchenamt Sachsens to a member of the "AK Unwelterziehung und Friedensschutz mit Kindern," January 31, 1989, ABL/doku 002.007.002.

51. Zwahr, *Ende einer Selbstzerstörung*, 62–64, 88–89.

52. Albrecht Kaul, "Macht der Gewaltlosigkeit. Christian Führer," 134.

53. "Interview with Beate Tischer," in *Friedensgebete in der Leipziger Nikolaikirche*, 140.

54. "Gabriele Schmidt, Schichtarbeiterin, protokolliert am 28. Oktober, 1989," in Neues Forum Leipzig, *Jetzt oder nie—Demokratie!*, 66–69. For still photographs of the police confrontation on October 7, see the 1989 documentary *Leipzig im Herbst* (Leipzig in the fall), by Andreas Voigt and Gerd Kroske.

55. For an eyewitness account of demonstrators held by police at the Agra Arena, see Szameit, "Lied von der Angst."

56. Even after October 9, 1989, calls for nonviolence persisted. The first petition of the New Forum published in the local press urged, "Wir rufen wiederum und eindringlich zur Gewaltslosigkeit auf. Wir distanzieren uns in aller Eindeutigkeit von Rechtsradikalen ebenso wie von antikommunistischen Tendenzen. Wir fordern zugleich keine Kriminalisierung der Demonstranten und Andersdenkenden, denn es schürt die Gewalt" ("Keine Kriminalisierung: Aufruf zur Gewaltlosigkeit und zum Dialog," *Union*, October 17, 1989, 6. Cited in Neues Forum Leipzig, *Jetzt oder nie—Demokratie!* 131).

57. Butler, *Force of Nonviolence*, 10, emphasis added.

58. Cited in Zwahr, *Ende einer Selbstzerstörung*, 93.

59. Kaden, "Von den Friedensgebeten ging alles aus," 105.

60. "Flugblatt mit Appell zur Gewaltlosigkeit am 9. Oktober 1989," *Friedensgebete in der Leipziger Nikolaikirche*, 85. In contrast, the slogan "We are the People" ("Wir sind das Volk") had emerged in the streets in confrontations with the police in order to sig-

nal that the demonstrators in the street were the people (*Volk*) the GDR state claimed to represent.

61. Butler points out that "nonviolent action is not simply a question of exercising the will to restrain oneself from acting out one's aggressive impulses; it is an active struggle with a cultivated form of constraint that takes corporeal and collective form" (*Force of Nonviolence*, 186).

62. Azoulay, *Civil Imagination*, 5, emphasis added.

63. Foucault, "Political Spirituality as the Will for Alterity," 129.

64. Arendt, *On Revolution*, 228.

65. Butler, *Force of Nonviolence*, 9.

66. Zwahr, *Ende einer Selbstzerstörung*, 78, also 9.

67. *Friedensgebete in der Leipziger Nikolaikirche*, 36.

68. *Friedensgebete in der Leipziger Nikolaikirche*, 30.

69. Stiftung Friedliche Revolution, accessed July 10, 2021, https://www.stiftung-fr.de/.

70. *Friedensgebete in der Leipziger Nikolaikirche*, 32.

71. Rectanus, "Refracted Memory," 42. See also Trigg, *Memory of Place*.

72. Sontag, *On Photography*, 180.

73. "Ausstellungsgestaltung 'Orte der Friedlichen Revolution,'" Studio Kw. Kommunikationsdesign, Frankfurt a.M., accessed February 14, 2021, https://www.studiokw .de/arbeitsfelder/ausstellungsgestaltung/ausstellungsgestaltung-orte-der-friedlichen -revolution/.

74. Foster, "Archival Impulse (2004)," 145.

75. "Permanent Pillar Exhibition," Runde-Ecke-Leipzig.de, accessed April 10, 2020, http://www.runde-ecke-leipzig.de/index.php?id=500&L=1. The Citizens' Committee (Bürgerkomitee Leipzig) is sponsored with resources from the federal government representative for culture and the media (Der Beauftragte der Bundesregierung für Kultur und Medien), the Saxony Memorials Foundation (Stiftung Sächsischer Gedenkstätten), the city of Leipzig, and the Leipzig Cultural Area (Kulturraum Leipziger Raum).

76. Such transnational connections are apparent in the archival legacies of the regional oppositional movements in Saxony. The Working Group of the Archives of Opposition and Resistance in Saxony (Arbeitskreis der Archive zu Opposition und Widerstand in Sachsen) includes the Archive of the Leipzig Citizens' Movement (Archiv der Bürgerbewegung Leipzig e.V.), the Grosshennersdorf Environmental Library (Umweltbibliothek), and the Martin Luther King Center for Nonviolence and Civil Courage in Werdau (Martin-Luther-King Zentrum für Gewaltfreiheit und Zivilcourage e.V. Werdau), founded in 1998 by members of the peace movement and advocates of conflict research in East and West Germany. Other centers exist in Atlanta, USA, and Havana, Cuba.

77. See Neubert, *Geschichte der Opposition in der DDR 1949–1989*, esp. 449 and 545–54.

78. *Universitätszeitung*, Karl-Marx-Universität Leipzig, December 15, 1989; *Der Spiegel* 43, no. 40, October 2, 1989, 29–30. Both cited in Zwahr, *Ende einer Selbstzerstörung*, 17n39 and 17n37. For industrial air pollution in the GDR, in the districts (*Bezirk*) of

Halle and Leipzig, see Welfens, *Umweltprobleme und Umweltpolitik in Mittel- und Osteuropa*, esp. 69.

79. Dietrich, "'Archiv zur Öffentlichkeitsarbeit und zu zivilem Ungehorsam,'" 11.

80. Uekötter, "Entangled Ecologies"; see also Eckert, *West Germany and the Iron Curtain*.

81. "Rat der Stadt Leipzig. Smog-Information," no. 56, December 1989, ABL/doku 004.002.001.

82. Bennett, *Vibrant Matters*, 55–60.

83. Siegert, "(Not) In Place," 282.

84. De Cesari and Rigney, eds., *Transnational Memory*, 9; Landsberg, *Prosthetic Memory*.

85. Butler, *Notes on a Performative Theory of Assembly*, 20. She cites Wolin, "Fugitive Democracy."

86. Here, I find the analogy of memory impulses to data useful. See Blackman, *Haunted Data*. Blackman develops a hauntological approach according to which data can accrue an afterlife—that is, data can be extracted, mapped, aggregated, condensed, measured, and translated, acquiring autonomies and agencies that extend and travel beyond the original event or transaction (xxi). Data can also disappear and dissipate. She asks what it might mean to live and learn to live with ghosts and to engage with a temporality beyond the living present.

87. The number that circulates is eight thousand, but it may have been lower, such as 3,100 police und several hundred combat forces (Zwahr, *Ende einer Selbstzerstörung*, 93n270).

88. Richter, *Afterness*, 152–53.

89. Richter, *Afterness*, 153.

90. See Bennett's discussion of Deleuze and Guattari's work on ontological frameworks of connectivity and the self-agentic power of assemblage (*Vibrant Matters*, 23–24).

91. Zwahr, *Ende einer Selbstzerstörung*, 90, 24n63; "Interview with Beate Tischer," in *Friedensgebete in der Leipziger Nikolaikirche*, 141; Voigt and Kroske, *Leipzig im Herst*.

92. Saunders, *Memorializing the GDR*, 275.

93. Butler, *Frames of War*, 6 (in reference to Foucault).

94. This language reproduces the discourse of the Bundestag debate. See the speech by Wolfgang Thierse (SPD) in the Bundestag, November 9, 2007, in "Plenarprotokoll 16/124," 12965 (B/D). See also "Künstlerischer Wettbewerb für ein Freiheits- und Einheitsdenkmal in Leipzig 2011. Internationaler, nichtoffener Wettbewerb mit vorgeschaltetem offenen Bewerbungsverfahren nach RPW 2008," Stadt Leipzig, represented by the Lord Mayor, October 9, 2011.

95. Taylor, *Archive and the Repertoire*, 28. For the post-1989 context, Azoulay's notion of a "uni-focal perspective concept" is also useful. Here multiple experiences are subsumed into a single, cohesive point of view (*Potential History*, 178–80).

96. For the history of the monument plans (2008–2014), see Weissgerber, *Leipziger Freiheits- und Einheitsdenkmal*, esp. ch. 2. In 2017, the project was taken up again.

97. Maritta Adam-Tkalec, "Interview mit Johannes Milla zum Einheitsdenkmal," *Berliner Zeitung*, July 30, 2018.

98. "Miley Frost: Sculptor," accessed July 27, 2020, http://mileyfrost.com/.

99. Derrida, *Given Time*, 30.

100. "Jetzt also doch: Wende-Denkmal von Miley Tucker-Frost soll aufgestellt werden," *Leipziger Volkszeitung*, February 25, 2019; Ralf Julke, "Bekommen die Leipziger jetzt doch noch das 'Pathos-Denkmal' aus den USA vor die Nase gesetzt?," *Leipziger Zeitung*, February 20, 2019.

101. Propp, *Morphology of the Folktale*, 20. Referenced in Taylor, *Archive and the Repertoire*, 55n3.

102. Taylor, *Archive and the Repertoire*, 82.

103. Traditionally, the festival has privileged the kind of superficial experience oriented toward instant gratification and quick consumption in the present—parameters German sociologists describe as characteristic for the *Erlebnisgesellschaft* (see Schulze, *Die Erlebnisgesellschaft*). This point was confirmed in 2019. At the thirtieth anniversary of the fall of the Wall, the organizers (and Lord Mayor Burkhard Jung, SPD) responded to the co-optation of 1989 by the AfD and announced the emphasis would henceforth be on the political dimension of "dialogue" and not on the eventification ("soll kein event werden"). See "Programm für Leipzigs Jubiläums-Lichtfest steht: Der Anspruch ist riesig," *Leipziger Volkszeitung*, August 29, 2019.

104. On the fundamentally political role of this process, see Huyssen, *Present Pasts*, 25–27.

105. Ingram, *Siting Futurity*.

106. Steiner, "Prepositions," 17n6.

107. See for instance Kuball, "Rettet die KMB/2013," 612.

108. Mischa Kuball, "public preposition," accessed September 11, 2019, http://www.public-preposition.net/projects/leipzig-i/.

109. Paver, "From Monuments to Installations," 253.

110. Skyba, Richter, and Schönfelder, eds., *Himmelweit gleich?*, 27.

111. Weibel, "Lichtpolitik/The Politics of Light," 267–71. The project involved fences, trusses, fog machines, lights, and white tarpaulins.

112. See Rosa, *Unverfügbarkeit* and *Uncontrollability of the World*.

113. On the philosophical and political role of light in "the era of post-Soviet dawn," see Sloterdijk, "Lichtung und Beleuchtung/Light and Illumination."

114. Honig, *Public Things*, 48.

115. Rosa, *Resonance*, 169; Schiermer, "Acceleration and Resonance," 5.

116. Ziemer and Jackisch, "Volksfest," 124.

117. Bennett, *Vibrant Matters*, 106.

118. Foucault, "Theatrum Philosophicum," 169–70. Cited in Bennett, *Vibrant Matters*, 57.

119. Schulze, *New Lives*, 314; Schulze, *Neue Leben*, 440.

120. Blackman, *Immaterial Bodies*, 26–53.

121. Neues Forum Leipzig, *Jetzt oder nie—Demokratie!* 69.

122. Weibel, "Lichtpolitik/The Politics of Light," 269.

123. For Kuball's interview, see the marketing trailer "Lichtfest Leipzig Künstlerstimmen," Leipzig Tourism and Marketing GmbH, 2014, YouTube video, 17:03, at 5:00–6:00, https://www.youtube.com/watch?v=OhF4ey4tvuU&t=352s.

124. Kuball's installation is part of an international trend wherein artists have used light temporarily as a memorial form to signal absence—often, however, in the context of violent events (e.g., *Tribute in Light* [2002], conceived by artists John Bennett, Gustavo Bonevardi, Richard Nash Gould, Julian LaVerdiere, and Paul Myoda, with lighting consultant Paul Marantz, to commemorate September 11, 2001).

125. For Rancière, the disruption of the police order is also a story of "the equality of speaking beings" (Bennett, *Vibrant Matters*, 105).

126. Arendt, *Human Condition*, 198. Cited in Butler, *Notes on a Performative Theory of Assembly*, 73, see also 154–57.

127. Braun, "Erfahrungen der Freiheit," in *Wir befinden uns soweit wohl*, 20.

128. Foster, "Archival Impulse (2004)," 144. Aleida Assmann refers to the internet more specifically as an archive of cultural memory (*Shadows of Trauma*, 2). Andreas Huyssen takes a critical approach to the relationship between new media, cyberspace, and memory (*Present Pasts*, 28). In contrast, Astrid Erll considers the liberatory archival capacities of digital spaces (*Memory in Culture*, 131–32).

129. Christian Führer, cited by Stiftung Friedliche Revolution, emphasis added, accessed July 12, 2021, https://www.stiftung-fr.de/. In this contemporary moment of protest, the foundation has changed its profile toward a more activist, international, human rights–based orientation.

130. Lear, *Radical Hope*, 41.

CHAPTER THREE

1. Buck-Morss, "Ephemeral Archives (2011)," 183.

2. When the Federal Republic of Germany (FRG) absorbed the German Democratic Republic (GDR) on October 3, 1990, the GDR's Ministry of State Security (Ministerium für Staatssicherheit) was officially dissolved. In December 1991, the Federal Commissioner for the Records of the State Security Service of the former German Democratic Republic (BStU), also known as the Stasi Records Agency, was established.

3. The "Concept for the Permanent Preservation of Stasi Records" was approved by the German Bundestag on September 26, 2019. See Bundesarchiv, "Überführung des Stasi-Unterlagen-Archivs in das Bundesarchiv," press release, October 1, 2019, https://www.bundesarchiv.de/DE/Content/Pressemitteilungen/ueberfuehrung-stasi -unterlagen.html.

4. Stasi Records Agency, *Access to Secrecy*, 7.

5. Müller, "Die Küste der Barbaren/1992," 347.

6. Cooke, "Watching the Stasi"; Hodgin, "'Screening the Stasi'"; Bathrick, "Memories and Fantasies about and by the Stasi." The writer Christoph Hein exposes the drama of authenticity around *The Lives of Others* in the anecdote "Mein Leben, leicht

überarbeitet," in *Gegenlauschangriff*, 102–6. Andreas Dresen's 2018 film *Gundermann* handles the Stasi issue with nuance and complexity.

7. A. O. Scott, "*Karl Marx City* Revisits the Everyday Terror of Dictatorship," *New York Times*, March 28, 2017.

8. Mayne, "Female Narration, Women's Cinema." See also Alter, *Projecting History*, esp. chapter 5.

9. For their early DVD artwork, see Epperlein and Tucker, dirs., *The Last Cowboy* (1998); Casad, "Rescreening Memory beyond the Wall," 335.

10. Foster, "Archival Impulse (2004)," 143.

11. On the archive as a storing and ordering place of the collective memory of a nation or people(s), see Brown and Davis-Brown, "Making of Memory."

12. Notably, the emergence of photography as modern technology itself has been inextricably bound up with the history of surveillance. See Sontag, *On Photography*, 5.

13. Campany, *Photography and Cinema*, 95–96; Pérez Ríu, "To Make You See." See also Guido and Lugon, eds., *Between Still and Moving Images*.

14. Derrida, *Archive Fever*, 70.

15. See Hirsch, *Family Frames*. For the use of visual media and national memory in various cultural contexts, see Shevchenko, ed., *Double Exposure*.

16. For touch as a privileged conduit to reality, see Olin, *Touching Photographs*, 7. For the tactile sensuality of archival manuscripts (here from pre-Revolutionary France), see Farge, *Allure of the Archives*. For a rethinking of touch in the context of current media technologies, see Ladewig and Schmidgen, "Symmetries of Touch," 3–23.

17. Assmann, *Formen des Vergessens*, 36–38. Assmann distinguishes between repressive or punitive forgetting, enacted by political archives, and "Verwahrensvergessen" (forgetting by preserving), which is enabled by historical archives that store information and objects that are no longer in active circulation. *Karl Marx City* challenges this distinction. Andreas Huyssen is skeptical regarding the reliability of digitalized archives as sites of preservation. He cites the difficulties faced by German authorities in decoding the "vast body of electronic records from the former East German state, a world that disappeared together with its Soviet-built mainframe computers and its East German office systems" (*Present Pasts*, 26).

18. Derrida, *Athens, Still Remains*, 43.

19. Derrida, *Archive Fever*, 3–4, 12, 18. For an alternative digital collection of memories by East Germans, see *Open Memory Box*, curated by Alberto Herskovits and Laurence McFalls. The online archive provides searchable access to 415 hours of home videos shot by 150 families in the GDR between 1947 and 1990 (https://open-memory-box.de/, accessed March 2, 2020). Under the rubric "Anti-Archive," the site also generates new sequences through the random automatization of existing film sequences.

20. Taylor, *Archive and the Repertoire*, 19. Taylor refers to the Greek etymology of *archive*, "a public building," a place where records are kept; from *arkhe*, it also means a beginning, the first place, the government.

21. On presumed notions of neutrality, see Azoulay, *Potential History*, esp. 42, 46.

22. For the centrality of the Stasi in Germany's post-1989 memory politics, see Cooke, *Representing East Germany since Unification*, 28. For West Germans' identifi-

cation of the Stasi with the secret police of the Nazi regime, the Gestapo, see Glaeser, *Divided in Unity*, 277.

23. Until 2021, when the BStU was absorbed into the German Federal Archives (Bundesarchiv) and the website redesigned, the slogan functioned as header. See also Federal Commissioner for the Records of the State Security Service of the former German Democratic Republic/Stasi Records Agency, August 2015, https://www .stasi-unterlagen-archiv.de/assets/bstu/en/Downloads/BStU-Image-EN_zur-Ansicht .pdf. The new website of the Stasi Records Archive emphasizes the documents' materiality. See the Federal Archives/Stasi Records Archive, accessed March 5, 2020, https:// www.stasi-unterlagen-archiv.de/en/.

24. Philip Olterman, "Stasi Files: Scanner Struggles to Stitch Together Surveillance State Scraps," *Guardian*, January 3, 2008.

25. On paper-based history, see Azoulay, *Potential History*, 169. This persistent focus of the German government on preserving the files is remarkable given that after the turbulent events of 1989 and the subsequent dissolution of the Stasi, many—including former GDR dissidents such as Stefan Heym and Friedrich Schorlemmer; official figures such as Manfred Stolpe; and Chancellor Helmut Kohl—initially advocated for the destruction of the files. The civil-rights activist Vera Wollenberger (née Lengsfeld), who was being surveilled by her husband (a fact revealed in 1992), warned that the files were a dangerous mixture of fact and fiction. The pervasive discourse at the time, however, maintained that those who wanted the files to be destroyed were those who were themselves implicated with the Stasi. As a result, the argument for making the files immediately accessible won out, although no critical analysis of the information released by the BStU ever took place. See Miller, *Narratives of Guilt and Compliance in Unified Germany*, 13. On polls among East Germans regarding the preservation of Stasi files, see Sa'adah, *Germany's Second Chance*, 227–28.

26. Azoulay, *Potential History*, 179.

27. Derrida, *Archive Fever*, 2.

28. For the hegemonic power of federal archives post-1989, see the case of Thomas Heise in chapter 4 of this book. For a fictionalized treatment of the hegemony of the Federal Archive of Lichterfelde (Bundesarchiv-Lichterfelde) and the Federal Foundation for the Reappraisal of the SED Dictatorship (Bundesstiftung zur Aufarbeitung der SED-Diktatur), see the prologue of Hein's novel *Trutz*. The epilogue of Seiler's novel *Kruso*, entitled "Missing Department (Edgar's Report)" (Abteilung Verschwunden [Edgars Bericht]), explores the power of the archive, including the BStU, to conceal and to enliven GDR pasts (esp. 450–52).

29. Benjamin, "Ausgraben und Erinnern," 400.

30. According to Sergej Eisenstein, a spherical dramaturgy creates a linkage of meanings in addition to storytelling. See also Alexander Kluge's monumental 2008 documentary *Nachrichten aus der ideologischen Antike: Marx-Eisenstein-Das Kapital* (News from ideological antiquity: Marx/Eisenstein/capital). The tension between surveillance, capture, and captivation by images is explored by Chow, *Entanglements*, esp. 2–7.

31. For a discussion of the double logic of remediation, which insists that there never was a past prior to mediation, see Erll and Rigney, eds., *Mediation, Remediation, and the Dynamic of Cultural Memory*, esp. 4.

32. Thierse, "Mut zur eigenen Geschichte: Lehren aus der Vergangenheit." See also the chapter "Tyranny and Intimacy: The Stasi and East German Society," in Betts, *Within Walls*, 21–50; Lewis, *State of Secrecy*.

33. For the distinction, see Silverman, *Miracle of Analogy*. The evidentiary mode is associated with technology, the index, the copy, and fixity and the disclosive mode with the world, interpretation, and the development of discontinuous meaning across time and space (7–11).

34. On touch and its privileged relation to indexicality, see Olin, *Touching Photographs*, 10–11. For C. S. Peirce's definition of the sign, and the distinction between index and icon in relation to memory work, see Hirsch, *Generation of Postmemory*, 36–37.

35. The relation of the haptic to other senses is discussed in Rushing, *Descended from Hercules*, 100. Contemporary film and media theory addresses a tension between the metaphorical and physical conception of the haptic. See Saether, "Touch/Space," 201–30.

36. On the camera as silencer, see Biguenet, *Silence*, 77–80.

37. The event was reported by the GDR press in reference to a "marauding mob" (Neues Forum Leipzig, *Jetzt oder nie—Demokratie!* 317). By October 5, the trains from Prague carrying more than eight thousand emigrants reached West Germany. More than six hundred emigrants arrived from Warsaw. Television images were broadcast around the world (Kowalczuk, "Revolution in Germany," 24–25).

38. Bahr, *Sieben Tage im Oktober*, esp. 43, 61. The train station swelled to twenty thousand people; the local head of the SED, Hans Modrow, ordered the deployment of soldiers; water cannons were used; the train station was partially destroyed; and unknown numbers of people were injured. Of the 1,300 people arrested by October 11, 428 were not released until December 1989 (Kowalczuk, "Revolution in Germany," 24–25).

39. Mulvey, *Death 24x a Second*, 56.

40. Bellour, "Pensive Spectator," cited in Campany, *Photography and Cinema*, 96.

41. Campany, *Photography and Cinema*, 96.

42. Sontag, *On Photography*; Barthes, *Camera Lucida*; Derrida, *Copy, Archive, Signature*.

43. Casad, "Rescreening Memory beyond the Wall."

44. Mulvey, *Death 24x a Second*, 19.

45. On the climate of hysteria, see Wolf, *Umbrüche und Wendezeiten*, 121. In May 1990, Ralf Hirsch, an opposition member wrongly accused of having worked as an IM, commented, "At the moment, there is nothing worse, either in the east or in the west, than the accusation of having worked for the Stasi. A robbery, even rape wouldn't cause the same uproar or prompt so much inquisitiveness" (cited in Sa'adah, *Germany's Second Chance*, 99).

46. "Der Lange Arm der Stasi: Verdacht gegen DDR-Abgeordnete," *Der Spiegel*, March 26, 1990, 13. Cited in Bathrick, "Memories and Fantasies about and by the Stasi," 223.

47. Starting in 2012, the BStU initiated a new research field, *Historische Denunzia-tionsforschung*, which considered the Stasi from a historical and comparative perspec-

NOTES TO PAGES 146–149 › 265

tive, especially in connection with the era of National Socialism. See Krätzner, ed., *Hinter vorgehaltener Hand*.

48. Former civil-rights activists petitioned against Gregor Gysi's keynote at the commemoration of the thirtieth anniversary of the Peaceful Revolution, held at the Peters Church (Peterskirche) ("Dank an Bürgerrechtler-Viel Beifall für Gysi," *Leipziger Volkszeitung*, October 9, 2019). Other controversies include Holger Friedrich, who purchased the *Berliner Zeitung* in 2019, shortly before his Stasi file as IM became public, and Manfred Stolpe, whose memorial in January 2020 high-ranking officials from the CDU-CSU declined to attend. See Stephan-Andreas Casdorff, "Die Achtlosigkeit der Westler: CDU and CSU mangelt es an Wertschätzung für Ostdeutschland," *Tagesspiegel*, January 23, 2020.

49. Miller, *Narratives of Guilt and Compliance in Unified Germany*, 2.

50. *Karl Marx City* shows excerpts from *The Lives of Others* (2006), which takes suicide in the GDR caused by the oppressive regime as a central subject. The historian Udo Grashoff has challenged this assumption ("Driven into Suicide by the East German Regime? Reflections on the Persistence of a Misleading Perception").

51. County College of Morris, "The Legacy Project: Petra Epperlein and Michael Tucker," November 29, 2017, YouTube video, 1:04:19, at 00:36:00, https://www .youtube.com/watch?v=6WutpyoUvwM&t=2169s.

52. Wolf Biermann, "Das wars. Klappe zu. Affe lebt," *Zeit Online*, March 2, 1990, https://www.zeit.de/1990/10/das-wars-klappe-zu-affe-lebt.

53. East German writer Angela Krauss associates her father's suicide with the aftermath of 1968 in *Die Gesamtliebe und die Einzelliebe* (46).

54. See Wolfgang Templin, "Ein Gespräch an historischem Ort," *Frankfurter Allgemeine Zeitung*, August 29, 1995, 8; Johannes Leithäuser, "Der Vorwurf heisst Verrat," *Frankfurter Allgemeine Zeitung*, September 16, 1995, 12; Christoph Dieckmann, "Die ruhmlosen Helden Ostdeutschlands," *Zeit Online*, January 3, 1997.

55. Osang, "Die verlorenen Revolutionäre." Osang notes that there is hardly any reference in Helmut Kohl's 1999 book *Ich wollte Deutschlands Einheit* to any of the leading figures of the civil rights movement (38).

56. In the post–Cold War climate of the 1990s, Joachim Gauck served as the Federal Commissioner of the Stasi Records Agency. Gauck—a staunch anti-Communist shaped by his father's horrific postwar internment in a Soviet gulag in Siberia—had emerged from the oppositional church movement as one of several co-founders of the New Forum in '89. Later, the Stasi Records Agency was headed by Marianne Birthler, a former activist of Alliance '90 who had also served in the GDR's transitional parliament, followed by Roland Jahn, whom the GDR had first imprisoned for his support of the Polish Solidarność movement and then expelled in 1983. Also, Vera Lengsfeld and Günter Nooke, who were members of Alliance '90 and the Green Party of the GDR respectively, left for the conservative CDU when Alliance '90 and the West German Green Party merged in 1993. Fueling a hegemonic memory politics, in 1998 Nooke joined the conservative lobbying group that promoted the national "Monument to Freedom and Unity" in Berlin and gave it legitimacy as a former civil-rights activist from the East despite the lack of popular support (see chapter 1). Symbolically significant, Angela Merkel became the chairperson of the CDU in 2000 (although she was

largely silent on her East German socialization, until a high-profile speech when she left office as chancellor in 2021).

57. Straub, "Der Suizid und 'die Wende' in der DDR, " 68.

58. Azoulay, *Civil Contract of Photography*, 86; Campt, *Listening to Images*, 25–26, 33; Campt et al., *Imaging Everyday Life*.

59. See Bluhm, *Zwischen Markt und Politik*, 59, 67–69. This transformation toward privatization was already on the agenda of the UrTreuhand-Anstalt (UrTHA), formed on March 1, 1990, under the Modrow government, but the earlier ordinance still attempted to secure shares for East Germans in the companies. Between December 1989 and June 1991, the number of employees in the tool-manufacturing industry was reduced by 40 percent (from around sixty thousand down to around twenty-four thousand). See Holland and Kuhlmann, eds., *Systemwandel und industrielle Innovation*, 91. For a detailed account of the sudden economic and cultural changes in the East post-1989, see Sa'adah, *Germany's Second Chance*, 222–25. Thirty years later, in 2019, the inequitable transformation process was taken up in a public exhibit on the Treuhand, organized by the Rosa Luxemburg Foundation (see Enkelmann, ed., *Schicksal Treuhand—Treuhand-Schicksale*).

60. For an excellent sociological analysis of how the collapse of socialism impacted women and their role in the work force, see Guenther, *Making Their Place*.

61. This collage of narratives includes Frank Capra's 1946 film *It's a Wonderful Life*. The film's main protagonist is contemplating suicide on Christmas Eve. The American actor Dean Reed, shown in the clip of a DEFA *Indianerfilm* at the beginning *Karl Marx City*, committed suicide in 1986 in East Berlin. See also *The Lives of Others* (2006).

62. The interpretations of suicide rates in the East post-1989 differ widely. Historian Ilko-Sascha Kowalczuk speaks of about fifty suicides of functionaries in the fall of 1989–90 and concludes that such suicides were rare (*Endspiel*, 438). Historian Udo Grasshoff notes an increase in suicides (by 10 percent) when the GDR collapsed. He notes, "Although women were more affected by unemployment in the East, they coped better with it." However, contrary to common belief, Grasshoff argues, suicides were not primarily committed by SED and Stasi officials; most suicides in the post-reunification period were committed by "normal people," who had suddenly lost their jobs and who, often rightly, feared they would never find another one. While the cultural shock of reunification disappears after 1991 from the national suicide statistics, Grasshoff points out that alcohol-related mortality among men from the East increased after 1991, in conjunction with a rise in unemployment, and has remained well above Western levels. See Wendt, "Das Sterben der Anderen." For an existentialist account of suicides after the collapse of the Soviet Union, see Alexijewitsch, *Im Banne des Todes*. Suicide in the aftermath of GDR's collapse is fictionalized in Andreas Kleinert's *Wege in die Nacht* (Paths in the night, 1999).

63. Kowalczuk, *Übernahme*, 14. The trauma and loss experienced by East Germans, and men in particular, after 1989 has returned in narratives of "sons" (born in the 1960s). See Wenzel, "Ein Jahr von langer Dauer (Nachwort)," 360. Notably, Ilko-Sascha Kowalczuk opens a book about the takeover of the East by the West with two stories of fathers of the postwar generation; see *Übernahme*, 9–13.

64. See Wiesenthal, "Post-Unification Dissatisfaction" *German Politics* 7, no. 2 (1998): 1–30. On polls taken between 1991 and 1996, indicating 47 percent of East

Germans said in their view West Germans treated East Germany as a colony (1991) and 72 percent of East Germans said that ex–East Germans were second-class citizens in the FRG, even if fewer than 17 percent of those counted themselves as "losers" in the unification process (1994); see Sa'adah, *Germany's Second Chance*, 222.

65. For the lasting economic and social devastation of eastern regions post-1989, see Milev, *Entkoppelte Gesellschaft-Ostdeutschland seit 1989/90*. Milev argues that there is to this day a public silence regarding the structural dispossession of East Germans since 1990. See also Milev, *Das Treuhand-Trauma*; Laabs, *Der Deutsche Goldrausch*.

66. Mulvey, *Death 24x a Second*, 56.

67. Photography's silence is addressed by Barthes, *Camera Lucida*. Jacques Rancière further elaborates the image and its relation to the sayable and visible (*Future of the Image*, 9–11).

68. Mitchell, *What Do Pictures Want?* 42.

69. A similar image of the interior of the Luxor-Palast is included in Reum and Geissler, eds., *Auferstanden aus Ruinen*, 35. For the making of such illegal banners in Leipzig, see Martin Jankowski's autobiographical novel *Rabet oder das Verschwinden einer Himmelsrichtung*, 155–58.

70. The role of theatres is discussed by Kowalczuk, *Endspiel*, 443, whose take I summarize here in English.

71. Reum and Geissler, *Auferstanden aus Ruinen*, 48, 27. Inside the theatre, the atmosphere was laden with risk and fear. When the illegal banner in the upper balcony was confiscated, presumably by the Stasi, voices arose from the audience, crying words like "pigs" and "traitors." In an effort to de-escalate the situation, a pediatrician, Dr. Günther Bartsch, appealed to the audience not to get provoked (Reum and Geissler, *Auferstanden aus Ruinen*, 35). Naturally, these sounds of unrest have been drained from the photograph Epperlein handles in the archive.

72. On the Stasi observation of oppositional groups in Karl-Marx-Stadt, see Zwahr, *Ende einer Selbstzerstörung*, 68. Official media reports on the protests reproduced the language of the Stasi. The violently dispersed local assemblies in the other cities on October 7, 1989, are recorded in Bahrmann and Links, eds., *Chronik der Wende*, 10.

73. Cited in Reum and Geissler, *Auferstanden aus Ruinen*, 48–49.

74. Butler, *Force of Nonviolence*, 21.

75. "Das Publikum erhob sich von den Plätzen und spendet minutentlangen Applaus—für alle Beteiligten ein unvergessliches Erlebnis" (Reum and Geissler, *Auferstanden aus Ruinen*, 48).

76. Glaeser, *Political Epistemics*, xxiv.

77. I draw the concept of performative indexicality from Olin, *Touching Photographs*, 18, 69.

78. Zuboff, *Age of Surveillance Capitalism*. See also Later, "Surveillance History and the History of New Media"; Grinberg, "Troubling Histories"; Leeds, "Snowden and the Cinema of Surveillance."

79. Silverman, *Miracle of Analogy*, 4, 37.

80. I take inspiration from Jacques Rancière, who suggests that critique of image consumption may be overdrawn and that spectators can learn to read images; see

Emancipated Spectator. For a historical approach to media literacy, see Higdon, *Anatomy of Fake News.*

81. Blatt, "Thinking Photography in Film," 182.

82. For critical approaches to hyperconnectivity, see Vaidhyanathan, *Anti-Social Media*; Hoskins and Tulloch, *Risk and Hyperconnectivity.*

83. Kyong Chun, "Enduring Ephemeral." For an early landmark essay in digital memory studies, see Hoskins, "Mediatisation of Memory."

84. Mitchell, *What Do Pictures Want?* 27.

CHAPTER FOUR

1. Heise's description of the opening scene (16 mm, color) can be found in *Spuren*, 39.

2. The metaphor of the wasteland is pervasive in East German films of the 1990s. See also Schreiber, *Östliche Landschaften* [Eastern Landscapes], 1991; Böttcher, *Die Mauer* [The Wall], 1990; Misselwitz, *Sperrmüll* [Bulky Trash], 1990; Foth, *Letztes aus der DaDaeR* [Latest from the Da-Da-R], 1990.

3. On the privatization of the GDR's DEFA film studio, see Hecht, "Der letzte Akt."

4. For a snapshot of how Western television and iconic media images dominated the public sphere in 1989–90, see Hoffmann, "Dokumentarische Gedächtnisräume 1989–90." See also Hecht, "Der letzte Akt," 240.

5. Schulze, *New Lives*, 315; *Neue Leben*, 441. For October 9, 1989, see Maier, *Dissolution*, 144; Bahrmann and Links, *Chronik der Wende*, 17–18.

6. Arendt, "Preface: The Gap between Past and Future," 9.

7. Gross, *Das letzte Jahr*, 29.

8. Lear, *Radical Hope*, 3.

9. Arendt, "Freedom to Be Free," 57.

10. Arendt, "Preface: The Gap between Past and Future," 9.

11. Elsaesser, "Media Archeology as Symptom," 183, 188. On media archeology's mistrust in historiography, reaching back to Michel Foucault, see Zielinski, *Variations on Media Thinking*, esp. chapter 2.

12. Zielinski, "Arqueología prospectiva." Heise himself uses the term *vorausschauende Archeologie* (prospective archeology), with respect to the State Film Documentation at the GDR Film Archive (Staatliche Filmdokumentation am Filmarchiv der DDR, SFD). The metaphorical link between utopia and archeology in a postcommunist age is deployed by Jameson, *Archaeologies of the Future*. On histories as leftovers turned into active forces, see Stoler, *Duress.*

13. Elsaesser, "Media Archeology as Symptom," 206.

14. Wenzel, *Das Jahr 1990 Freilegen.*

15. In 2020, the film toured in the United States, including screenings at the Anthology Film Archives in New York City. See Hoberman, "Living Memory."

16. The October 9, 1989, edition of the West German evening news *Tagesschau* included a segment covering the events around Gethsemane Church. The report spoke

NOTES TO PAGES 167–173 › 269

of two thousand demonstrators and arrests of more than a thousand people, and it showed brief footage.

17. The way in which the secretly taped VHS footage of the demonstrations on October 9, 1989, reached West German television are described in Wensierski, *Die unheimliche Leichtigkeit der Revolution*, 377–94. See also Grossmann, *Fernsehen, Revolution und das Ende der DDR*; Hesse, "Fernsehen und Revolution."

18. This notion is the credo of Beshty's colossal history of photography, *Picture Industry*, 28.

19. Thomas Heise, "Archäologie hat mit Graben zu tun" [Archeology is about Digging].

20. Zielinksi, "Arqueología prospectiva."

21. Zielinski, "Arqueología prospectiva." On media archeology and the role of specific technologies in shaping contemporary memory, see Ernst, *Digital Memory and the Archive*.

22. Barnert, ed., *Filme der Zukunft*, 9. The State Film Documentation at the GDR Film Archive (SFD) was dissolved in 1986; the DEFA Documentary Film Studio existed from 1986 to 1990.

23. Löser, "Radikale Ambivalenz," 13.

24. Heise, "Archäologie hat mit Graben zu tun."

25. Heise, "Archäologie hat mit Graben zu tun."

26. Hoffmann, "Dokumentarische Gedächtnisräume, 1989–90," 288. The films included Heise's *Imbiss Spezial* [Snack bar special] (1989); Denzler, Tschörtner, and Wintgen, *In Berlin 16.10.89–4.11.89* (1989); Berger-Fiedler, *Dresden Oktober '89* (1989); Voigt and Kroske, *Leipzig im Herbst* [Leipzig in the fall] (1989); the HFF film by Eichberg and Jung, *Aufbruch '89–Dresden* [Departure '89 –Dresden] (1989); and Tetzlaff, *Reports from a Peaceful Revolution: Report for Posterity (1990) and In Transition: Report of Hope (1991)*.

27. On GDR official and subversive film culture, see Fritzsche and Löser, eds., *Gegenbilder*, esp. 10–24. Notably, the Soviet model "Quarz," a Super-8 camera based on a Kodak cassette system, had to be wound up like a mechanical clock and therefore only allowed for a maximum of thirty seconds of uninterrupted filming (*Gegenbilder*, 17). For this reason alone, it did not lend itself to social documentation. On amateur photography clubs as state loyal, see Kuehn, *Caught*, 42. For a terrific examination of video art and the politics of vision in the late GDR, see Howes, *Moving Images on the Margins*.

28. Eichberg, "Interview by Thomas Heise—Regisseur."

29. Rothöhler, "Ihr seid Schauspieler?," 212–15.

30. See also "Appell Christa Wolfs an DDR-Bürger: Fassen Sie Vertrauen!" *Neues Deutschland* 264, November 9, 1989, 1. The petition was broadcast on the GDR evening news and signed by a wide range of dissidents, artists, and oppositional leaders representing five civic organizations (Wolf, *Umbrüche und Wendezeiten*, 80–81).

31. Eichberg, "Interview by Thomas Heise—Regisseur," 272–74.

32. Cornish, *Performing Unification*; Bach, *What Remains*, esp. 171–82. Regarding Heise's *Material*, see Rothöhler, "Ihr seid Schauspieler?"; Baecker, "Material (2009)."

33. The Internationale was circulated by different groups. On September 29, 1989, for example, eight to ten thousand church-affiliated demonstrators moved through East Berlin's streets singing the Internationale. The two hundredth anniversary of the French Revolution, in the summer of 1989, had already resulted in dissident responses by artists and art students in Leipzig (Zwahr, *Ende einder Selbstzerstörung*, 23, 41).

34. Betts, "Intimacy of Revolution," 266–67; Schneider, *Leipziger Demontagebuch*, 163.

35. Butler, "'We, the People,'" 62.

36. Ebbrecht-Hartmann, "Archives for the Future," 70–71.

37. Olson, "Conclusion," 107.

38. The demands included free elections (Schneider, *Leipziger Demontagebuch*, 64); free travel (67); justice and equality (*Gerechtigkeit*) instead of political elitism (78); the GDR belonging to the people (*Volk*) and not the SED (79); and references to the Prague Spring (92).

39. See "Aufruf der Initiative 'Prinzip Hoffnung,'" *Leipziger Volkszeitung*, December 16–17, 1989, in Beier and Schwabe, *"Wir haben nur die Strasse,"* 173; Lässig, "Zeitzeuge"; "Gotthard Weidel (Pfarrer) am 29. Januar 1990," in Beier and Schwabe, *"Wir haben nur die Strasse,"* 188–89. The visual records also show a shift by mid-December '89 toward a polarization between, on one side, supporters of reunification and the market model of the West, using national slogans, and, on the other, supporters of the SED or other social movements, aiming at a confederacy with the FRG, based on the independence of the GDR (Schneider, *Leipziger Demontagebuch*, 175–77).

40. See Weil, *Verhandelte Demokratisierung*. Weil challenges the conventional (hegemonic) argument that these council structures were an imposed instrument of power (*Herrschaftsinstrument*) in the tradition of SED politics, and underscores their participatory, democratic potential (14n5).

41. A list of spontaneous independent council groups formed in the late GDR, in '89–90, in schools, hospitals, prisons, universities, and the military, can be found at "Räte," DDR 1989/90, accessed December 2, 2020, https://www.ddr89.de/raete/inhalt_raete.html.

42. See Arendt, *On Revolution*, esp. 232, 254–56. The councils also connect 1989 to other modern revolutions, such as the French Revolution of 1789 (municipal bodies; spontaneously formed clubs and societies), Russia (1905 and 1917, Soviets), Germany (1918 and 1919, *Räte*) and Hungary (1956, council system). The fact that the councils "crossed all party lines" and that they were "the only political organs for people who belonged to no party" made them a remarkable, radically democratic, participatory space (255). "The councils," she states, "obviously, were spaces of freedom" (256). On participatory democracy, see also Lederman, *Hannah Arendt*, esp. 199–222.

43. Rost and Peters, "Pure Neugierde, pure Fassungslosigkeit." Unlike other roundtables on the district level, the Leipzig district roundtable was successful, advancing, for instance, the environmental agenda for the Opencast lignite mining area Cospuden by the New Forum, Ökolöwen, and other citizens' organizations in the spring of 1990 (Weil, *Verhandelte Demokratisierung*, 164–68).

44. After the city government dissolved itself in January of 1990, the local roundtable in Leipzig (formed in December of 1989) stepped into this space, remaining until

May 1990. For the roundtable's independent governing, see "Erklärung des Rates der Stadt, 26. 1. 1990," ABL/doku 004.002.018; "Vorschlag des Bürgerkomitees und von Vertretern der neuen demokratischen Kräfte am Runden Tisch der Stadt Leipzig zur Gewährleistung der Regierbarkeit der Stadt nach Auflösung der Stadtverordneten-versammlung, Januar 1990," ABL/doku 004.001.005; and "Entwurf. Satzung und Geschäftsordnung des Runden Tisches in der Stadt Leipzig, 8.1. 1990," ABL/doku 004.002.010. The Citizens Committee, with its own working groups, had to remain separate, but retained its voting rights within the roundtable (ABL/doku 004.001.005).

45. "Protokoll der Beratung des Runden Tisches, 28.3.1990," ABL/doku 004.001.210.

46. In Leipzig, in the fall of 1989, these practices included a series of public forums on Sundays, entitled "Dialogue at Karl-Marx-Platz" (Schneider, *Leipziger Demontage-buch*, 57); the call for student councils and for hegemony of the demonstrators (61); for access to Stasi files by the New Forum (69); for independent unions (76); and for public dialogue between the New Forum and Leipzig's mayor Bernd Seidel (77).

47. Arendt, *Human Condition*, 57–58. Arendt stresses the need for plurality of perspectives and difference of positions.

48. "Antrag an den Runden Tisch der Stadt Leipzig. Lokaler Fernsehsender Leipzig-International Kanal X, 21.3.1990," ABL/doku 004.001.018.

49. On the dismantling of the GDR press and media industry, see Tröger, *Presse-frühling und Profit*. Notably, it took thirty years for a slight shift to occur. In 2019, the *Berliner Zeitung* was bought by two former East Germans, who framed the paper as a contribution to an extra-parliamentary opposition. See Silke und Holger Friedrich, "Was wir wollen," editorial, *Berliner Zeitung*, November 8, 2019.

50. "Runder Tisch der Stadt Leipzig: Kommission Arbeit und Soziales" [undated], ABL/doku 004.001.002.

51. "Bürgerkomitee, Beschlussgrundlage für den Runden Tisch am 11.4.1990, 9.4.1990," ABL/doku 004.001.031; "Protokoll der Beratung des Runden Tisches, 28.3.1990," ABL/doku 004.001.210. The city aimed to retain State-owned property in municipal holdings.

52. "Erklärung des Rates der Stadt, Auflösung der Stadtverordnetenversammlung Januar 1990," ABL/doku 004.002.018.

53. Francesca Weil points to hegemonic knowledge regimes after 1989 that led to the forgetting and under-examination of the roundtables (*Verhandelte Demokratisierung*, 13).

54. Arendt, *On Revolution*, 255.

55. Günther Fleischmann, "Die Bergpredigt für de Maizière sehr hoher Massstab," *Neues Deutschland*, April 6, 1990, 3, 10; Bärbel Bohley (New Forum) castigated Western election interference and underlined her commitment to the utopian ideal that "something other than capitalism has to exist" (Bahrmann and Links, *Chronik der Wende 2*, 57). On the manipulation of public opinion in 1989–90, see Dahn and Mausfeld, *Tam-tam und Tabu*. However, conflict had also emerged within radically democratic groups, such as the New Forum, Democracy Now, and the Initiative of Peace and Human Rights over procedural matters and haste in forming the Alliance '90 for the election ("Erklärung zum vorgezogenen Bezirksdelegiertentreffen des Neuen Forum Leipzig mit dem Ziel der Festlegung von Kandidaten für die Volkskammer, 16.2.1990," ABL/doku 004.033.192). The emphasis on transparency and on basic-democratic processes

had turned the citizens' movement into a historical force. Yet ultimately it was those very ideals and practices, which required of all things time, that were obstacles in the rushed election process.

56. Kowalczuk, "Revolution in Germany," 30.

57. Konrad Weiss, "'Macht ist nichts Schlechtes an sich,'" interview, *Die Andere Zeitung*, November 14, 1990, 14.

58. See Fleischmann, "Bergpredigt."

59. Arendt, *On Revolution*, 229. Butler calls it an "anarchist" energy ("We, the People," 51).

60. "Demonstranten in der DDR: Neubeginn mit Wahlbetrug? Mit uns nicht?: Gewerkschaftler fordern 1:1," *Neues Deutschland*, April 6, 1990, 1. In the same issue, *Neues Deutschland* reports on the first session of the Volkskammer; see Günther Fleischmann and Uwe Stemmler, "Mit Dr. Sabine Pohl-Bergmann erstmals eine Volkskammerpräsidentin," *Neues Deutschland*, April 6, 1990, 1. The paper mentions the decision to form a commission to review potential Stasi implication of deputies.

61. "Streiks in der DDR werden für Bonn zur unkalkulierbaren Last," *Hannoversche Zeitung*, June 29, 1990. Cited in Kowalczuk, "Revolution in Germany," 35n80.

62. See Francine S. Kiefer, "Treuhand Nears End of Its Thankless Job," *Christian Science Monitor*, July 28, 1993.

63. The East German photographer Ute Mahler describes this socially precise style in Wenzel and König, *Zerrissene Gesellschaft*, 55. Alf Lüdtke discusses GDR photography's social observation in "Kein Entkommen? Bilder-Codes und eigensinniges Fotografieren: eine Nachlese," 227–36. On the tradition of precise social observation in DEFA film, see Löser, "Radikale Ambivalenz."

64. In 2019, the publisher Suhrkamp promoted Andreas Rost's photographs taken in Berlin, Leipzig, or Dresden in 1989–90 as images of events "that only few people know today" (Rost and Peters, "Pure Neugierde, pure Fassungslosigkeit"). Rost's photos appeared in a collaborative open-air exhibit entitled "In-Situ: Uncovering the Year 1990," at the 8th f/stop Festival for Photography in Leipzig: "Broken Bonds" ("Zerrissene Gesellschaft") (June 23 to July 1, 2018), and in Wenzel, *Das Jahr 1990 Freilegen*.

65. Hal Foster, "Archival Impulse (2004)," 145.

66. For a rich historical description of this session, see Sa'adah, *Germany's Second Chance*, 95–96.

67. The official record today can be found in "1989–1990 Wende-Zeiten," *Deutsches Rundfunkarchiv: Stiftung von ARD und Deutschlandradio*, accessed December 12, 2021, http://1989.dra.de/themendossiers/politik/volkskammer.

68. Carnevale and Kelsey, with Rancière, "Art of the Possible," 256–61. Here, it would be fruitful to read Heise's *Material* (2009) together with Alexander Kluge's colossal documentary montage *Nachrichten aus der ideologischen Antike: Marx-Eisenstein-Das Kapital* (News from ideological antiquity: Marx/Eisenstein/capital) (2008) in order to excavate "Western" and "Eastern" critical traditions.

69. In 1990, *Spiegel-TV* released a three-part VHS box set of materials shot by Western *Spiegel-TV* camera teams from the fall of 1989 to the winter of 1990. It is instructive how conservative-liberal public television reframes the aborted broadcast of the

NOTES TO PAGES 190–192 › 273

thirty-seventh GDR Volkskammer in this officially endorsed historical documentation one year after the absorption of the GDR by the West. Unsurprisingly, the *Spiegel-TV*'s documentary legitimizes the inevitable trajectory toward Western "freedom and democracy" by figuring the Stasi issue prominently. When the television cameras are requested to leave the parliamentary floor, the *Spiegel-TV* voice-over comments with sensationalist doom and gloom on the GDR Volkskammer's secrecy, and offers the following conclusion: "*a population, still inexperienced in matters of democracy*, was supposed to be spared this shock that the GDR spying state [*Schnüffelstaat*] could stay in the hands of the Stasi until the very end" (emphasis added). In the post–Cold War era, such tactics are how historical hegemony is spun across the air waves, transmitted through the most innocuous and seemingly plausible metaphors, until a normalized notion of history is metabolized. The enduring perception of the East German population as democracy-debilitated reaches all the way into discussions about the right-wing AfD (Alternative for Germany) today, thirty years later. Ironically, of course, as we see in this chapter, East Germans in '89 –90 practiced myriads of radically democratic actions. See "Protokoll einer deutschen Revolution: Teil 3, Die letzten Tage bis zur Einheit," *Spiegel-TV*, 1990, YouTube video, 1:33:12, at 00:31:00–00:36:00, https://www.youtube.com/watch?v=ZANWGxo4HkA.

70. Lässig, "Zeitzeuge," 217.

71. Derrida, *Specters of Marx*, 98–99.

72. Rothöhler, "Ihr seid Schauspieler?," 215 (the session is misdated here).

73. See Zwahr, *Ende einer Selbstzerstörung*, 175n467.

74. Bärbel Bohley, "Damit sich Geschichte nicht wiederholt: Keine Stasi-Mitarbeiter in die neue Volkskammer," *taz*, March 12, 1990, 10. Cited in Sa'adah, *Germany's Second Chance*, 67n21.

75. This language, harking back to the postwar era and Wolfgang Staudte's film *Murderers among Us* (*Die Mörder sind unter uns*, 1946), is used in Zwahr, *Ende einer Selbstzerstörung*, 16n33. Zwahr recounts the co-founder of the New Forum, Bärbel Bohley, calling the six million Stasi files "the gravest legacy (*Altlast*) in our history of the last forty years" ("Bürgerrechtler besetzen ehemalige Stasi Zentrale," *Sächsisches Tageblatt*, September 5, 1990).

76. "1989–1990 Wende-Zeiten," *Deutsches Rundfunkarchiv*. With the GDR's accession to the Federal Republic according to article 23 of the constitution ("Grundgesetz"), 104 of the 409 parliamentarians were sent to the all-German FRG Bundestag, which held its first session on October 4, 1989. There were small protests against unification across the country, including in Leipzig (Wenzel, *Das Jahr 1990 Freilegen*, 30).

77. Kowalczuk, *Übernahme*, 81. For an incisive discussion of the "economic and social subjugation of the former GDR by the FRG," see Cooke, *Representing East Germany since Unification*.

78. Arendt, *On Revolution*, 229.

79. Anja Reich and Sabine Rennefanz, "Herbert Schirmer, 'Nach dem 3. Oktober war man weg, als wäre nichts gewesen," interview podcast, *Berliner Zeitung*, September 27, 2020. See also Bundesstiftung Aufarbeitung, "Ministerbiografie: Herbert Schirmer," *Deutsche Einheit*, accessed November 5, 2021, https://deutsche-einheit-1990.de/ministerien/mfk/ministerbiografie.

80. Jens Reich, "Adieu Volkskammer," *Die Andere Zeitung*, October 10, 1990, 2. Cited in Sa'adah, *Germany's Second Chance*, 97.

81. For a snapshot of these polarizations, see the film review by Stephan Speicher, "Gewaltstau. Deutsche Szene: ein Dokumentarfilm im Widerstreit," *Frankfurter Allgemeine Zeitung*, November 27, 1992.

82. Müller, "Die Küste der Barbaren/1992," 345–48. This text is also used by Heise in *Heimat Is a Space in Time*.

83. Konrad Weiss, "Von 'Musterbürgern' und verpassten Chancen. Interview mit dem DDR-Bürgerrechtler und Regisseur Konrad Weiss (Demokratie Jetzt)," *Frankfurter Allgemeine Zeitung*, July 6, 1990. Cited in Zwahr, *Ende einer Selbstzerstörung*, 172; Konrad Weiss, "Der Runde Tisch und die Friedliche Revolution," *Publik Forum* 23, December 3, 1999.

84. Arendt, "Preface: The Gap between Past and Future," 6.

85. Braun, "Erfahrungen der Freiheit," in *Wir befinden uns soweit wohl*, 57.

86. Schirmer, "Nach dem 3. Oktober."

87. Elsaesser, "Media Archeology as Symptom," 187.

88. Rancière, "Art of the Possible," 259.

89. Kowalczuk, *Übernahme*, 50.

90. In 1978, Michel Foucault made this point with regard to a report from the Iranian Revolution. See Bremner, "Introduction to Michel Foucault's 'Political Spirituality as the Will for Alterity,'" 115.

91. This focus on visual culture and protests in the last decade is evident. See, for instance, Berger, *For All the World to See*; Cussons, *Protest!*; Griffing, *Power of Protest*; Noni, *Photography of Protest and Community*; Ferris, *I Am a Man*.

92. Heise elaborates this approach to history in the context of his multimedia installation "Entfernte Verwandte" [Distant Relatives] at the exhibit "Arbeit am Gedächtnis - Transforming Archives," Academy of the Arts, Berlin (2021).

93. Heise, "Archäologie hat mit Graben zu tun."

94. This commemorative event of the demonstration on November 4, 1989, was organized by the district of Berlin-Mitte, with support of the leftist Rosa Luxemburg Foundation (see "Programm: Wir waren das Volk," *UINIC*, accessed November 5, 2021, http://uinic.de/alex/programm.html).

95. For the photograph by Andreas Rost, see Rost and Peters, "Pure Neugierde, pure Fassungslosigkeit."

96. Adopting a theatrical interpretation of staging the people in politics is a matter of interpreting "the gap between a place where the *demos* exists and a place where it does not, where there are only populations, individuals, employers and employees, heads of households and spouses, and so on" (Rancière, *Disagreement*, 88). Cited in Bosteels, "Introduction: This People Which is Not One," 13. See also Balibar, *Equaliberty*, esp. 207.

CHAPTER FIVE

1. Frank Biess and Astrid Eckert make this point in "Introduction: Why Do We Need New Narratives for the History of the Federal Republic?," 2, 10.

NOTES TO PAGES 201–205 › 275

2. Lear, *Radical Hope*, esp. 103. On counterfactual hope under conditions of catastrophe, see also Adelson, *Cosmic Miniatures and the Future Sense*, 21, 27, 29.

3. This image appears on the back cover of Neues Forum Leipzig, *Jetzt oder nie—Demokratie!* The relation of visibility and translocal protest movements is taken up by Buck-Morss, *Revolution Today*, 79.

4. On October 3, 1989, the GDR government closed the borders to the ČSSR, de facto preventing anyone from leaving.

5. In 2010, a multinational exhibition compared the upheaval in 1989 across various Eastern European cities, seen from the perspective of a younger generation, twenty years later. See Skyba, Richter, and Schönfelder, eds., *Himmelweit gleich?*

6. Kurz, "Acht Wochen DDR Geschichte," 341.

7. Slobodian, ed., *Comrades of Color*, 10.

8. Betts and Mark, *Socialism Goes Global*, 8.

9. The international press noted the persistent division between East and West. See Anna Sauerbrey, "30 Years After Reunification, Germany Is Still Two Countries," *New York Times*, August 29, 2019; Bojan Pancevski, "The Iron Curtain Is Gone, but Europe's East and West Are Again Divided," *Wall Street Journal*, November 10, 2019.

10. Cercel, "Whither Politics, Whither Memory?," 7.

11. At the assembly of the Deutsche Forschungsgemeinschaft (DFG), held at the annual meeting of the German Studies Association (GSA) in Portland, Oregon, USA, in October 2019, Lutz Raphael delivered a keynote address "Von der Revolution zur Routine? 100 Jahre Demokratie in Deutschland." For activist resistance to the dominant Western perspective on the memory of the *Wende*, see Oberender, ed., *Occupy History*.

12. On the notion of counter-publicity (rather than antipublics) for the analysis of right-wing movements, see Reijven, Cho, Ross, and Dori-Hacohen, "Conspiracy, Religion, and the Public Sphere."

13. For a historical perspective, see Frei et al., *Zur Rechten Zeit*, esp. chapter 8. The authors usefully contextualize the rise of the AfD within Germany's postwar history in both East and West, where, if for different reasons (antifascism and the *Schlussstrich* debate), nationalist-conservative and right-wing undercurrents existed. See also the March 2020 special issue of *German Society and Politics* on "Responses to the Rise of the Alternative for Germany: The AfD's Origins in Comparative Perspective," edited by Sarah Wiliarty and Louise K. Davidson-Schmich.

14. Derrida, *Specters of Marx*, 26–27.

15. Huyssen, *Present Pasts*, 28–29; Traverso, *Left-Wing Melancholia*. Referenced in Rigney, "Remembering Hope," 369.

16. Žižek, *Relevance of the Communist Manifesto*, 54. In the collective memory, the number of East Germans who joined the demonstrations in the fall of 1989 may also be inflated. Overall, two million of the sixteen million GDR citizens participated, 7 percent in the larger cities and 18 percent in smaller towns (Frei et al., *Zur Rechten Zeit*, 187).

17. Richter, *Hört endlich zu*, 42. On the downfall of GDR intellectuals, see Geyer, ed., *Power of Intellectuals in Contemporary Germany*, esp. 11. For a contrasting argument, that Communism as an intellectual project extended across 1989, see Oushakine and Bradatan, eds., *In Marx's Shadow*.

18. Other slogans included "Become a Citizen Activist!" ("Werde Bürgerrechtler") and "Peaceful Revolution by Vote" ("Friedliche Revolution an der Wahlurne"). A group of activists involved in 1989 publicly protested against the appropriation of the *Wende* memory by the AfD. See Maria Fiedler, "Erklärung von DDR-Bürgerrechtlern. 'AfD missbraucht friedliche Revolution,'" *Tagesspiegel*, August 20, 2019. In contrast, other former dissidents, such as Vera Lengsfeld and Sigmar Faust, became supporters of the AfD.

19. Kantsteiner, "Migration, Racism, and Memory," 611. In 2015, Chancellor Angela Merkel temporarily lifted a European Union law (Dublin Regulation) requiring refugees to claim asylum in the first EU member state they enter, announcing, "We can do this" ("Wir schaffen das"). In 2015 and 2016, Germany accepted 1.3 million refugees. The AfD (Alternative for Germany) was founded in 2013, and PEGIDA (Patriotic Europeans against the Islamization of the West) was founded in 2014.

20. Richter, *Hört endlich zu*, 21.

21. Bosteels, "Introduction: This People Which Is Not One," 13, 16. Judith Butler also draws a useful distinction between surging multitudes—for example, collective action that resists expanding inequality and so forth—and other forms of congregating, such as racist, fascist, or violent anti-parliamentary mass movements ("'We, the People,'" 62).

22. Bosteels, "Introduction: This People Which Is Not One," 5.

23. Here my approach intersects with that of Rothberg and Yildiz, "Memory Citizenship," 34n12. The authors argue that migrant practices of memory are neither canonical nor comprehensively stored in official political or historical archives, but they do circulate widely, even if they are not recognized by national memory cultures.

24. Rigney, "Remembering Hope," 370.

25. Buck-Morss, *Revolution Today*, 38. For a reevaluation of Communist ideals and antifascist practices, see Ghodsee, *Left Side of History*.

26. See Slobodian, "Socialist Chromatism"; Piesche, "Black and German?" See also the documentary by Ines Johnson-Spain, *Becoming Black* (2019).

27. Mark, "Race," 221.

28. See, for example, Trnka, "Suspended Time, Exile, and the Literature of Transnational Antifascism"; Horakova, "Paradigms of Refuge." I developed a similar approach in "'Postcolonial Legacies.'"

29. Rothberg, "Multidirectional Memory in Migratory Settings." See also Creet and Kitzmann, eds., *Memory and Migration*.

30. Naika Foroutan, "Ostdeutsche sind auch Migranten," *taz*, May 13, 2018. Her work is based on two collaborative research projects, in which around eight thousand people were polled in 2014 and 2018–19, respectively. In contrast, the historian Frank Wolff stresses a reluctance in Germany to use the term "migration" for "co-ethnic movements," on grounds that "one is not a foreigner" (*Mauergesellschaft*, 74).

31. Brandt and Yildiz, *Tales that Touch*, 11.

32. According to Foroutan, the term "post-migrant" serves as a "subversive reference to the fluidity of culture and the transformation of collective identity, when something new is added and old things remain, where these forces exist alongside, merge or exclude one another, or are sorted in entirely new ways . . . a constant hybridization and

pluralization of societies" ("Was will eine Postmigrantische Gesellschaftsanalyse?," in Foroutan, Karakayali, and Spielhaus, eds., *Postmigrantische Perspektiven*, 269).

33. Haag, "Ein Blick auf die DDR-Transformation als Migration," 217–36. See also Nichelmann, *Nachwendekinder*; Schönian, *Ostbewusstsein*.

34. Foroutan and Hensel, *Gesellschaft der Anderen*, 97.

35. Yildiz, "Governing European Subjects," 75–77; Sieg, "Class of 1989," 166. Conceptions of the Turkish-German population as Other have been crucial to the self-imagination of the European Union as enlightenment project (Adelson, *Turkish Turn in Contemporary German Literature*, 6–7). For an argument that racialized practices are foundational to "imperial democracies," including the European Union, see Stoler, *Interior Frontiers*, 275.

36. In contrast, scholars in transnational German studies have stressed the need to articulate the workings of race and racialized thinking, in light of the officially sanctioned taboo on invoking race in the postwar, post-Holocaust period. See Chin, "Thinking Difference in Postwar Germany"; El-Tayeb, *European Others*. For post-1989 racial dynamics, see Yildiz, "Reading Racialization." See also Gezen, Layne, and Skolnik, eds., *Minority Discourse in Germany since 1990*; Florvil, *Mobilizing Black Germany*.

37. Rothberg, "Multidirectional Memory in Migratory Settings," 124. Matt Cornish also engages with misgivings about mimetic (sociological) conceptions of Turkish-German identities, rather than hybridizations (*Performing Unification*, 187–88).

38. Rothberg, "Multidirectional Memory in Migratory Settings," 133. Jenny Erpenbeck's 2015 novel *Gehen, Ging, Gegangen* fictionalizes the emergence of such unstable, productive linkages.

39. See Mandel, *Cosmopolitan Anxieties*. Mandel draws particular attention to the arrival of two million "ethnic Germans" from Eastern Europe and the former Soviet Union in the 1990s. Their legal status in Germany was superior to that of Turkish immigrants. This hierarchical relational dynamic applies even more to the legal integration, in 1990, of sixteen million East Germans into the FRG.

40. Anetta Kahane, "Nicht in die Falle tappen," *taz*, June 12, 2018.

41. A salient example is Burhan Qurbani's *Wir sind jung. Wir sind stark* [We are young. We are strong] (2014), an elegiac film set in Rostock-Lichtenhagen in 1992. See also Nguyen, *Bruderland ist abgebrannt* [Brotherland is burned down] (1991–92); Nguyen and Panagiotopoulos, *Das Sonnenblumenhaus* [Sunflower house] (2014); and Minh Thu Tran and Vanessa Vu's podcast series *Rice and Shine*, featuring an award-winning episode entitled "Hamburg 1980: Als der rechte Terror wieder aufflammte" [Hamburg 1980: When right-wing terror flared up again] (August 15, 2020) that complicates the national narrative of right-wing extremism emerging solely in the East (https://www.migration-lab.net/medien/rice-shine/).

42. Sasan Abdi-Herrle, "Der Luxus, unsichtbar sein können," *Die Zeit*, May 27, 2018. For controversial support of the East's devaluation argument, see Köpping, *Integriert erstmal uns*.

43. See Zatlin, "Scarcity and Resentment"; Mau, *Lütten-Klein*, 17n2. For a counterargument stressing forces in the *Wende* process, see Kowalczuk, "Revolution in Germany." Kowalczuk concludes that "the radical right-wing scene that began to emerge publicly in East Germany in late 1989 was not new, but it was henceforth able

to develop freely and received significant support from West Germany. The soil in the East may have been 'fertile.' At the same time, West German right-wing radicals helped to 'professionalize' the scene" (37). On right-wing shifts among the so-called *Wende* children, see Rennefanz, *Eisenkinder*.

44. Ferda Ataman, "Sind Ostdeutsche auch nur Migranten," *Der Spiegel*, May 19, 2018.

45. This position emerged in the early phase of the debate. See Hannah Bley, "Hausblog," *taz*, June 29, 2018, https://blogs.taz.de/hausblog/sind-ostdeutsche-auch-migranten; and Jana Hensel, "Willkommen im Club," *Zeit Online*, May 20, 2018. Key ideas of the debate are addressed and clarified in Foroutan and Hensel, *Gesellschaft der Anderen*, esp. 95–134.

46. Kluge, *Nachrichten aus der ideologischen Antike* [New from ideological antiquity], esp. part 3: "Paradoxe der Tauschgesellschaft" [The paradoxes of exchange society]. See also Žižek, *Relevance of the Communist Manifesto*, 24, 47.

47. For the argument that the AfD gained its votes from the Left Party (*Linke*) when the Left envisioned itself as party for all of Germany and not just the East, see Olsen, "Left Party and the AfD."

48. See Mudde and Kaltwasser, *Populism*, 9.

49. Radstone, "What Place Is This?"

50. Charlotte Wittenius, "*BİZİM BERLİN 89/90* im Märkischen Museum in Berlin. Mauerfall und Wiedervereinigung aus deutsch-türkischer Sicht," *Zeitgeschichte-online*, September 13, 2018, https://zeitgeschichte-online.de/geschichtskultur/bizim-berlin-8990-im-maerkischen-museum-berlin.

51. Yildiz, *Beyond the Mother Tongue*, 174. See also Adelson, "Back to the Future."

52. Wolrab, "BİZİM BERLİN 89/90."

53. These dynamics are explored by Maria Stehle and Beverly Weber in *Precarious Intimacies*.

54. The museum's website includes a video of the exhibit; see "BİZİM BERLİN 89/90: Photographs by Ergun Çağatay," accessed July 20, 2023, https://www.stadtmuseum.de/ausstellung/bizim-berlin-89-90, accessed July 20, 2023.

55. Çağatay visited several German cities from late March to early May 1990 as part of a project on work migration commissioned by the Paris-based agency Gamma, resulting in 3,500 photographs (Küçükyılmaz, "Wir Sind von Hier").

56. Nevim Çil, "Türkische Migranten und der Mauerfall," *Bundeszentrale für politische Bildung*, May 10, 2009, https://www.bpb.de/apuz/31988/tuerkische-migranten-und-der-mauerfall?p=all.

57. About seventy thousand students from 125 different countries studied in the GDR, half of whom came from socialist countries. In 1989, 1,200 international students from eighty countries were enrolled at Humboldt University of Berlin, which was 10 percent of the total number of students there (Mac Con Uladh, "Studium bei Freunden," 175). The person in the image could also be Afro East German; any fuller reading of the image must deal with these vexing meanings.

58. For a complex historiography, see Pugach, *African Students in East Germany, 1949–1975*, esp. 12, 17. For student accounts, see "Ausländer in der DDR—geholt, gekom-

men, gewollt?," *Ausländer in der DDR*, accessed May 2, 2022, https://www.auslaender
-in-der-ddr.com/home/studenten/. See also Hosek, *Sun, Sex, and Socialism*, esp. 75.

59. Erll, "Travelling Memory," cited in De Cesari and Rigney, eds., *Transnational Memory*, 11.

60. Blaschke and Ersoz, "Turkish Economy in West Berlin," 38–45.

61. Schneider, *Frühling im Herbst*, 142.

62. Piesche, "Leerstelle im Archiv"; Lierke and Perinelli, eds., *Erinnern Stören*. See also Piesche, ed., *Labor 89*.

63. Arendt, *Human Condition*, 52; Honig, *Public Things*, 39, 69–70. Arendt also uses the metaphor of a shared meal with regard to the lost treasure of the revolution and public happiness ("At every meal that we eat together, freedom is invited to sit down. The chair remains vacant, but the place is set," ["Preface: The Gap between Past and Future," 4]). See the introduction to this book.

64. Honig, *Public Things*, 70. Shared meals, provided by migrants living in West Germany to East Germans in 1989–90, are fictionalized in Lutz Seiler's novel *Stern 111* (158).

65. Rigney, "Remembering Hope," 377.

66. See the well-informed and nuanced account by former deacon and East German activist Hans-Joachim Döring, *'Es geht um unsere Existenz': Die Politik der DDR gegenüber der Dritten Welt am Beispiel von Mosambik und Äthiopien*. Döring situates the GDR's relation with the Global South in the party's and state leadership's "central trauma" in the postwar era. It is worth recalling that during this time the GDR suffered from a lack of official diplomatic relations with countries in the world at large, a state of affairs that was an effect of both the Cold War and the Hallstein Doctrine, applied by its West German political and economic rival into the 1960s (21–23).

67. Enzenbach, Kollath, and Oelkers, "Minds of Their Own" (Eigensinn im Bruderland). Some hundred thousand "foreigners" (sic) worked in the GDR (Kowalczuk, "Revolution in Germany," 33). For complex accounts about and by contract workers, see Beth, "Wir mussten die Schuld für unserer Land bezahlen"; Stefano and Serafin, "Vor und nach dem Mauerfall."

68. "Prescribed Solidarity—Handling 'Foreigners' in the GDR" (Verordnete Solidarität—der Umgang mit 'Fremden' in der DDR), Archiv Bürgerbewegung Leipzig e.V., accessed July 31, 2021, https://www.archiv-buergerbewegung.de/ausstellungen/plakat-ausstellungen/174-fremde-in-der-ddr. On *Alltagsrassismus* in the GDR, see O'Dea, "Lucia Engombe's and Stefanie-Lahya Aukongo's Autobiographical Accounts of *Solidaritätspolitik* and Life in the GDR as Namibian Children."

69. This is noted by Betts and Mark, *Socialism Goes Global*, 21.

70. In 2019, the exhibition *East Berlin: Half of the Capital* (*Ost-Berlin: Die halbe Hauptstadt*), at the Ephraim Palais, Berlin, included a complex engagement with histories of international solidarity and racism in the GDR. See also the exhibit *1 Million Roses for Angela Davis*, October 2020 to May 2021, Kunsthalle im Lipsiusbau, Dresden; *The Missed Seminar. After Eslanda Robeson. In Conversation with Steve McQueen's "End Credits,"* October 2022 to December 2022, Haus der Kulturen der Welt, Berlin. It is noteworthy that *The Missed Seminar* presents a "situated reading of transcontinental world-making practices that reveal and upset the continuities of the Cold War's ex-

treme binarism: an exhibition, conversations and an installation unfold a study towards a political imaginary today" (https://archiv.hkw.de/en/programm/projekte/2022/the_missed_seminar/start.php).

71. Ross, *May '68 and Its Afterlives*; Slobodian, *Foreign Front*; Rinner, *German Student Movement and the Literary Imagination*; Brown, *West Germany and the Global Sixties*; Mercer, *Student Revolt in 1968 in France, Italy, and West Germany*.

72. Chaplin and Mooney, eds., *Global 1960s*; Christiansen and Scarlett, eds., *Third World in the Global 1960s*.

73. This trend in (post)socialist research can be observed in Koenker and Gorsuch, *Socialist Sixties*. On limited multiracial mobility, see Mark, "Race," 250.

74. Ghodsee, *Second World, Second Sex*.

75. Schwenkel, *Building Socialism*. In Angola, on the other hand, narratives of Soviet and East German involvement with the Popular Movement for the Liberation of Angola appear virtually nonexistent (Vasco Martins, "Hegemony, Resistance, Gradations of Memory").

76. Getachew, *Worldmaking after Empire*.

77. Betts and Mark, *Socialism Goes Global*, 5.

78. See Seeck, *Begehren, anders zu sein*; Neubert, *Geschichte der Opposition in der DDR*, esp. 260, 455–57.

79. Witkowski, "Between Fighters and Beggars."

80. Neubert, *Geschichte der Opposition in der DDR*, 456, also 260.

81. Betts and Mark, *Socialism Goes Global*, 21.

82. "Runder Tisch der DDR. Arbeitsgruppe Ausländerfragen: Protokoll vom 2.1.1990, Berlin," p. 1. Cited in Almuth Berger, "Die ausländerpolitischen Vorstellungen des Runden Tisches und ihre gesellschaftliche Situiertheit" (PDF) and "Arbeitsgruppe Ausländerfragen des Runden Tisches" (PDF). Both PDFs are available at "Ausländer in der DDR—geholt, gekommen, gewollt?," *Ausländer in der DDR*, accessed May 23, 2022, https://www.auslaender-in-der-ddr.com/home/runder-tisch/.

83. After the fall of Wall, for instance, most GDR scholarship holders did not meet the criteria of Western law. For more on the legal vacuum and transition for students and contract workers, see Enzenbach, Kollath, and Oelkers, "Minds of Their Own."

84. Derrida, *Specters of Marx*, 33.

85. On Bloch, see Rigney, "Remembering Hope," 377.

86. See also Fraser, *Old Is Dying and the New Cannot Be Born*.

87. Foroutan, *Die postmigrantische Gesellschaft*, 197–203. See also the bilingual German-Turkish manifesto by Can Dündar, *Tut Was! Plädoyer für eine aktive Demokratie/ Bir şey yap! Aktif demokrasi için çagri*. He argues the division is not between Germans and German Turks but between those who support democracy and those who support fascism.

88. Rutter, "Unity and Conflict in the Socialist Scramble for Africa, 1960–1970."

89. On liberal politics of recognition, see Butler and Athanasiou, *Dispossession*, esp. 75–91.

90. I owe this insight to Katrin Sieg, a Europeanist and scholar of post-migration studies.

91. Notably, Honig argues for the significance of public things and the commons at a time when the energy of the Left in political theory tends to be anti-statist or anti-sovereigntist (*Public Things*, 85–97). On the distinction between a political theory of public things and the biopolitical notions of the commons by Hardt and Negri, see Honig, *Public Things*, esp. 91n9. On the failure of Communism and the need for the commons as a solution, see Žižek, *Relevance of the Communist Manifesto*, 56–57. Lauren Berlant describes the commons as a space to explore non-sovereign relationalities; see *On the Inconvenience of Other People*. On the concept of a common world, see Butler, *What World Is This?* See also Bangstad and Nilsen, "Thoughts on the Planetary."

92. See Oschmann, *Der Osten*. The differential effects of unification in 1990 are systemically perpetuated. East Germans constitute 17 percent of Germany's overall population. In 2019, only 2–4 percent of leading positions in politics, administration, economy, science, and culture were held by East Germans. Sixteen percent of all German citizens are dependent on social welfare, but in the states of the former East it is 22 percent (Kowalczuk, *Übernahme*, 17–18).

93. Frank Walter Steinmeier, "Rede beim Festakt zum Tag der Deutschen Einheit am 3. Oktober 2020 in Potsdam," Die Bundesregierung bulletin 107-2, October 12, 2020, https://www.bundesregierung.de/breg-de/service/bulletin/rede-von -bundespraesident-dr-frank-walter-steinmeier-1798176. See also Angela Merkel's last official speech, on October 3, 2021, in Halle/Saale. at the thirty-first anniversary of Germany's unification (Die Bundesregierung, https://www.bundesregierung.de/ breg-de/suche/rede-von-bundeskanzlerin-merkel-anlaesslich-des-festakts-zum-tag -der-deutschen-einheit-am-3-oktober-2021-in-halle-saale-1964938). In 2023, the federal government approved Halle/Saale, Saxony-Anhalt, as the seat for the "Future Center for German Unity and European Transformation."

94. Ayim, "The Year 1990."

95. Brown, *In the Ruins of Neoliberalism*, 187. See also Feldner, Vighi, and Žižek, eds., *States of Crisis and Post-Capitalist Scenarios*; Harvey, *Anti-Capitalist Chronicles*; Traverso, "Fascisms Old and New."

96. Ash, "Time for a New Liberation." See also Sławek Blich, "Little Luck for the Left in Central and Eastern Europe," *Dissent*, June 12, 2019.

97. Chantal Mouffe's notion of agonistic politics takes the conception of asymmetrical alliance or allyship further (*For a Left Populism*, 24, also 40, 93).

98. Streamas, "Vision for Scholar-Activists of Color," 7.

99. Ingo Schulze, "Demonstration—Unite and Shine," speech organized by Die Vielen and delivered May 19, 2019, in Berlin, in front of the Volksbühne.

CODA

1. Derrida, *Specters of Marx*, 114.

2. Etkind, *Warped Mourning*.

3. The film, released under the English title *A Place in Berlin* (2001), experienced a revival, including screenings at the Rosa-Luxemburg Foundation, Berlin, 2018; the

Wende-Museum in Culver City, California, USA, 2018; and the International Film Festival Viennale, Vienna, 2021.

4. Badiou, *Handbook of Inaesthetics*, 12, 55. Cited in Blume and Nicols, eds., *Capital*, 17n35.

5. On acoustic mobilization, see Morat, ed., *Sounds of Modern History*, 5.

6. Deleuze and Guattari, *What Is Philosophy?*, 176–77.

Bibliography

Adelson, Leslie A. "Back to the Future: Turkish Remembrances of the GDR and other Phantom Pasts." In *The Cultural After-Life of East Germany? New Transnational Perspectives,* edited by Leslie A. Adelson, 93–109. Washington, DC: American Institute for Contemporary German Studies, 2002.

———. *Cosmic Miniatures and the Future Sense: Alexander Kluge's 21st-Century Literary Experiments in German Culture and Narrative Form.* Berlin: De Gruyter, 2017.

———. *The Turkish Turn in Contemporary German Literature.* New York: Palgrave Macmillan, 2005.

Adelson, Leslie, and Devin Fore, eds. "Futurity Now." Special issue of *Germanic Review* 88, no. 3 (2013).

Adorno, Theodor. *Minima Moralia: Reflections on a Damaged Life.* London: Verso, 2005.

Agamben, Georgio. *State of Exception.* Chicago: University of Chicago Press, 2005.

———. *Where Are We Now? The Epidemic as Politics.* Lanham, MD: Rowman and Littlefield, 2021.

Ahmed, Sara. *Complaint!* Durham, NC: Duke University Press, 2021.

Alexijewitsch, Swetlana. *Im Banne des Todes.* Frankfurt: S. Fischer, 1993.

Allen, Jennifer. "Against the 1989–1990 Ending Myth." Special issue: "New Narratives for the History of the Federal Republic," edited by Frank Biess and Astrid M. Eckert. *Central European History* 52 (March 2019): 125–47.

Alter, Nora M. *Projecting History: German Nonfiction Cinema, 1967–2000.* Ann Arbor: University of Michigan Press, 2002.

Altınay, Ayşe Gül, María José Contreras, Marianne Hirsch, Jean Howard, Banu Karaca, and Alisa Solomon, eds. *Women Mobilizing Memory.* New York: Columbia University Press, 2019.

Apelt, Andreas H., ed. *Der Weg zum Denkmal für Freiheit und Einheit.* Schwalbach: Wochenschau Verlag, 2009.

Arendt, Hannah. "The Freedom to Be Free." *New England Review* 38, no. 2 (2017): 56–69.

———. *The Human Condition.* Chicago: University of Chicago Press, 1958.

———. *On Revolution.* Introduction by Jonathan Schell. New York: Penguin Books, 1963.

———. "Preface: The Gap between Past and Future." In *Between Past and Future: Eight Exercises in Political Thought,* 1–15. New York: Penguin Books, 1968.

Arnold de Simine, Silke, ed. *Memory Traces: 1989 and the Question of German Cultural Identity*. New York: Peter Lang, 2012.

Art, David. "Making Room for November 9, 1989? The Fall of the Berlin Wall in German Politics and Memory." In *Twenty Years after Communism: The Politics of Memory and Commemoration*, edited by Michael Bernhard and Jan Kubik, 195–212. Oxford: Oxford University Press, 2014.

Assmann, Aleida. *Formen des Vergessens*. Göttingen: Wallstein, 2016.

———. *Shadows of Trauma: Memory and the Politics of Postwar Identity*. New York: Fordham Press, 2016.

Assmann, Jan. *Das kulturelle Gedächtnis, Schrift, Erinnerung, und politische Identität in frühen Hochkulturen*. Munich: C. H. Beck, 1992.

Augé, Marc. *Oblivion*. Translated by Marjolijn De Jager. Minneapolis: University of Minnesota Press, 2004.

Ayim, May. "The Year 1990: Homeland and Unity from an Afro-German Perspective." In *Germany in Transit: Nation and Migration 1955–2005*, edited by Deniz Göktürk, David Gramling, and Anton Kaes, 126–29. Berkeley: University of California Press, 2006.

Azoulay, Ariella. *The Civil Contract of Photography*. New York: Zone Books, 2012.

———. *Civil Imagination: A Political Ontology of Photography*. London: Verso, 2015.

———. *Potential History: Unlearning Imperialism*. New York: Verso, 2019.

Bach, Jonathan. *What Remains: Everyday Encounters with the Socialist Past in Germany*. New York: Columbia University Press, 2017.

Bach, Jonathan, and Michał Murawski, eds. *Re-Centring the City: Global Mutations of Socialist Modernity*. London: UCL Press, 2020.

Badiou, Alain. *The Communist Hypothesis*. London: Verso, 2010.

———. *Handbook of Inaesthetics*. Translated by Alberto Toscano. Palo Alto, CA: Stanford University Press, 2005.

Baecker, Dirk. "Material (2009)." In *Über Thomas Heise*, edited by Matthias Dell and Simon Rothöhler, 104–12. Berlin: Vorwerk 8, 2014.

Bahr, Eckhart. *Sieben Tage im Oktober: Aufbruch in Dresden*. Leipzig: Forum Verlag, 1990.

Bahrmann, Hannes. *Finale: Das letzte Jahr der DDR*. Berlin: Links, 2019.

Bahrmann, Hannes, and Christoph Links, eds. *Chronik der Wende: Die DDR zwischen 7. Oktober 1989 und 18. März 1990*. Berlin: Christoph Links Verlag, 1994.

———. *Chronik der Wende 2: Stationen der Einheit. Die Letzten Monate der DDR*. Berlin: Christoph Links Verlag, 1995.

Balibar, Étienne. *Equaliberty: Political Essays*. Translated by James Ingram. Durham, NC: Duke University Press, 2014.

Bangstad, Sindre, and Tobjørn Tumyr Nilsen. "Thoughts on the Planetary: An Interview with Achille Mbembe." *New Frame*, February 13, 2019.

Barnert, Anne, ed. *Filme der Zukunft: Die Staatliche Filmdokumentation am Filmarchiv der DDR*. Berlin: Neofelis, 2015.

Barthes, Roland. *Camera Lucida: Reflections on Photography*. New York: Hill and Wang, 1980.

———. *Mythologies*. Translated by Annette Lavers. New York: Farrar, Straus and Giroux, 1972.

Bathrick, David. "Memories and Fantasies about and by the Stasi." In *Remembering the German Democratic Republic: Divided Memory in a United Germany*, edited by David Clarke and Ute Wölfel, 223–34. New York: Palgrave Macmillan, 2011.

Baudrillard, Jean. "The Anorexic Ruins." In *Ruins*, edited by Brian Dillon, 67. Cambridge, MA: MIT Press, 2011.

Bauer, Karin, and Jennifer Ruth Hosek, eds. *Cultural Topographies of the New Berlin*. New York: Berghahn Books, 2017.

Beier, Achim, and Uwe Schwabe, eds. *"Wir haben nur die Strasse": Die Reden auf den Leipziger Montagsdemonstrationen 1989/90. Eine Dokumentation*. Halle (Saale): Mitteldeutscher Verlag, 2016.

Bellour, Raymond. "The Pensive Spectator." *Wide Angle* 9, no. 1 (1987): 6–10.

Benjamin, Walter. "Ausgraben und Erinnern." In *Gesammelte Schriften*, vol. 4.1, edited by Rolf Tiedemann and Hermann Schweppenhäuser, 400–401. Frankfurt: Suhrkamp, 1972.

———. "Little History of Photography." In *Selected Writings*, vol. 2, *1927–1934*, edited by Michael W. Jennings, Howard Eiland, and Gary Smith, translated by Rodney Livingstone et al., 507–30. Cambridge, MA: Belknap Press of Harvard University, 1999.

———. "Paralipomena to 'On the Concept of History.'" In *Selected Writings*, vol. 4, *1938–1940*, edited by Michael W. Jennings and Howard Eiland, translated by Edmund Jephcott et al., 401–11. Cambridge, MA: Belknap Press of Harvard, 2006.

———. "The Work of Art in the Age of Mechanical Reproduction." In *Illuminations*, edited by Hannah Arendt, translated by Harry Zohn, 239–41. New York: Schocken Books, 2007.

Bennett, Jane. *Vibrant Matters: A Political Ecology of Things*. Durham, NC: Duke University Press, 2010.

Berdahl, Daphne. "Expressions of Experience and Experiences of Expressions: Museum Re-Presentations of GDR History." *Anthropology and Humanism* 30, no. 2 (2005): 156–70.

———. *On the Social Life of Postsocialism: Memory, Consumption, Germany*. Edited by Matti Bunzl. Bloomington: Indiana University Press, 2010.

———. *Where the World Ends: Re-Unification and Identity in the German Borderland*. Berkeley: University of California Press, 1999.

Berger, Maurice. *For All the World to See: Visual Culture and the Struggle for Civil Rights*. New Haven, CT: Yale University Press, 2011.

Berger-Fiedler, Róza, dir. *Dresden, Oktober '89*. Berlin: DEFA-Studio für Dokumentarfilme, 1989.

Berlant, Lauren. *On the Inconvenience of Other People*. Durham, NC: Duke University Press, 2022.

Berman, Russell. "Introduction." Special issue: "Germany after the Totalitarianisms: Part II." *Telos* 136 (Fall 2006): 3–9.

Bernhard, Michael, and Jan Kubik, eds. *Twenty Years after Communism: The Politics of Memory and Commemoration*. Oxford: Oxford University Press, 2014.

Beshty, Walead, ed. *Picture Industry: A Provisional History of the Technical Image*. Zurich: JRP/Ringier, 2018.

Beth, Uta. "Wir mussten die Schuld für unserer Land bezahlen: von Leben und Arbeit der vietnamesischen Vertragsarbeiterinnen." In *Das Begehren, anders zu sein: Politische und kulturelle Dissidenz von 68 bis zum Scheitern der DDR*, edited by Anne Seeck, 268–86. Münster: Unrast, 2012.

Betts, Paul. "1989 at Thirty: A Recast Legacy." *Past and Present* 244, no. 1 (August 2019): 271–305.

———. "The Intimacy of Revolution: 1989 in Pictures." In *The Ethics of Seeing: Photography and Twentieth-Century German History*, edited by Jennifer Evans, Paul Betts, and Stefan-Ludwig Hoffmann, 250–73. New York: Berghahn, 2018.

———. *Within Walls: Private Life in the German Democratic Republic.* Oxford: Oxford University Press, 2013.

Betts, Paul, and James Mark, eds. *Socialism Goes Global: The Soviet Union and Eastern Europe in the Age of Decolonisation.* Oxford: Oxford University Press, 2022.

Betts, Paul, and Katherine Peance, eds. *Socialist Modern: East German Everyday Culture and Politics.* Ann Arbor: University of Michigan Press, 2008.

Beuys, Joseph, with Johann Philipp, Hans Binswanger, Werner Ehrlicher, and Rainer Willert. *What Is Money? A Discussion.* Forest Row: Clairview, 2010.

Biess, Frank. Review of *Germany since 1945: Politics, Culture, and Society,* edited by Peter C. Caldwell and Karrin Hanshew. *German History* 37, no. 3 (September 2019): 445–47.

Biess, Frank, and Astrid M. Eckert. "Introduction: Why Do We Need New Narratives for the History of the Federal Republic?" *Central European History* 52, no. 1 (2019): 1–18.

Biguenet, John. *Silence.* New York: Bloomsbury, 2015.

Blackman, Lisa. *Haunted Data: Affect, Transmedia, Weird Science.* London: Bloomsbury Academic, 2019.

———. *Immaterial Bodies: Affect, Embodiment, Mediation.* New York: Sage Publications, 2013.

Blaschke, Jochen, and Ahmet Ersoz. "The Turkish Economy in West Berlin." *International Small Business Journal: Researching Entrepreneurship* 4, no. 3 (1986): 38–45.

Blatt, Ari J. "Thinking Photography in Film, or the Suspended Cinema of Agnès Varda and Jean Eustache." *French Forum* 36, nos. 2–3 (Spring/Fall 2011): 181–200.

Blech, Volker. "Interview with Sascha Waltz: 'Das Einheitsdenkmal ist keine Wippe.'" *Berliner Morgenpost,* August 14, 2011.

Blei, Daniela. "Monumental Problems: Freedom and Unity Come to Berlin." *Marginalia. Los Angeles Review of Books,* January 28, 2016.

Bluhm, Katharina. *Zwischen Markt und Politik: Probleme und Praxis von Unternehmenskooperation in der Transitökonomie.* Opladen: Leske und Budrich, 1990.

Blume, Eugen, and Catherine Nicols, eds. *Capital: Debt, Territory, Utopia.* Dortmund: Verlag Kettler, 2016.

Bond, Lucy, Stef Craps, and Pieter Vermeulen, eds. *Memory Unbound: Tracing the Dynamics of Memory Studies.* New York: Berghahn, 2017.

Bosteels, Bruno. "Introduction: This People Which Is Not One." In Alain Badiou, Pierre Bourdieu, Judith Butler, Georges Didi-Huberman, Sadri Khiari, and Jacques Rancière, *What Is a People,* translated by Jody Gladding, 21–32. New York: Columbia University Press, 2013.

Böttcher, Jürgen, dir. *Die Mauer* [The Wall]. Berlin: DEFA-Studio für Dokumentarfilme GmbH, 1991. 35mm.

———, dir. *Konzert im Freien* [A Place in Berlin]. Berlin: Ö-Filmproduktion Löprich und Schlösser GmbH, 2001. 35 mm (FAZ von DigiBeta), Dolby SR.

Bouma, Amieke. *German Post-Socialist Memory Culture: Epistemic Nostalgia.* Amsterdam: Amsterdam University Press, 2019.

Boyer, Dominic. "Ostalgie and the Politics of the Future in Eastern Germany." *Public Culture* 18, no. 2 (2006): 361–81.

Boym, Svetlana. *Another Freedom: The Alternative History of an Idea*. Chicago: University of Chicago Press, 2012.

———. *The Future of Nostalgia*. New York: Basic Books, 2001.

Brandt, Bettina, and Valentina Glajar, eds. Special issue: "Politics of the Archive." *Seminar: A Journal of Germanic Studies* 53, no. 3 (September 2017).

Brandt, Bettina, and Yasemin Yildiz, eds. *Tales that Touch: Migration, Translation, and Temporality in Twentieth- and Twenty-First-Century German Literature and Culture*. Berlin: De Gruyter 2022.

Braun, Volker. *Wir befinden uns soweit wohl: Wir sind erst einmal am Ende*. Frankfurt: Suhrkamp, 1998.

Brockmann, Stephen. *The Freest Country in the World: East Germany's Final Year in Culture and Memory*. Rochester, NY: Camden House, 2023.

Brown, Richard Harvey, and Beth Davis-Brown. "The Making of Memory: The Politics of Archives, Libraries and Museums in the Construction of National Consciousness." *History of the Human Sciences* 11, no. 4 (1998): 17–32.

Brown, Timothy Scott. *West Germany and the Global Sixties: The Anti-Authoritarian Revolt, 1962–1978*. Cambridge: Cambridge University Press, 2015.

Brown, Wendy. *In the Ruins of Neoliberalism: The Rise of Anti-Democratic Politics in the West*. New York: Columbia University Press, 2019.

———. *Undoing the Demos: Neoliberalism's Stealth Revolution*. New York: Zone Books, 2015.

———. *Walled States, Waning Sovereignty*. New York: Zone Books, 2014.

Brussig, Thomas. *Wie es leuchtet*. Frankfurt: Fischer, 2004.

Buck-Morss, Susan. *Dreamworld and Catastrophe: The Passing of Mass Utopia in East and West*. Cambridge, MA: MIT Press, 2000.

———. "Ephemeral Archives (2011)." In *Destruction*, edited by Sven Spieker, 183–84. London/Cambridge, MA: Whitechapel Gallery/MIT Press, 2017.

———. *Revolution Today*. Chicago: Haymarket Books, 2019.

Bundesstiftung Aufarbeitung. "Ministerbiografie: Herbert Schirmer." *Deutsche Einheit*, accessed November 5, 2021. https://deutsche-einheit-1990.de/ministerien/mfk/ministerbiografie.

Butler, Judith. *The Force of Nonviolence*. London: Verso, 2020.

———. *Frames of War*. London: Verso, 2009.

———. *Notes on a Performative Theory of Assembly*. Cambridge, MA: Harvard University Press, 2015.

———. "'We, the People': Thoughts on Freedom of Assembly." In Alain Badiou, Pierre Bourdieu, Judith Butler, Georges Didi-Huberman, Sadri Khiari, and Jacques Rancière, *What Is a People?*, translated by Jody Gladding, 49–64. New York: Columbia University Press, 2013.

———. *What World Is This? A Pandemic Phenomenology*. New York: Columbia University Press, 2022.

Butler, Judith, and Athena Athanasiou. *Dispossession: The Performative in the Political*. Cambridge: Polity, 2013.

Cahill, Lisa. *Blessed Are the Peacemakers: Pacifism, Just War, and Peacebuilding*. Minneapolis, MN: Fortress Press, 2019.

Caldwell, Peter C., and Karrin Hanshew, eds. *Germany since 1945: Politics, Culture, and Society*. London: Bloomsbury Academic, 2018.

Caldwell, Peter C., and Robert Shandley, eds. *German Unification: Expectations and Outcomes*. London: Palgrave, 2011.

Campany, David. *Photography and Cinema*. London: Reaktion Books, 2008.

Campt, Tina. *Listening to Images*. Durham, NC: Duke University Press, 2017.

Campt, Tina, Brian Wallis, Marianne Hirsch, and Gil Hochberg, eds. *Imaging Everyday Life: Engagements with Vernacular Photography*. New York: Steidl/Walther Collection, 2020.

Carnevale, Fulvia, and John Kelsey, in conversation with Jacques Rancière. "Art of the Possible." *Artforum International* 45, no. 7 (March 2007): 256–61.

Casad, Madeleine. "Rescreening Memory beyond the Wall." *Germanic Review: Literature, Culture, Theory* 88, no. 3 (1999): 320–38.

Cercel, Cristian. "Whither Politics, Whither Memory?" *Modern Languages Open* 1 (2020): 1–15.

Chaplin, Tamara, and Jadwiga E. Pieper Mooney, eds. *The Global 1960s: Convention, Contest, and Counterculture*. London: Routledge, 2017.

Chin, Rita. "Thinking Difference in Postwar Germany: Some Epistemological Obstacles around 'Race.'" In *Migration, Memory, and Diversity: Germany from 1945 to the Present*, edited by Cornelia Wilhelm, 206–29. New York: Berghahn, 2016.

Chow, Rey. *Entanglements, or Transmedial Thinking about Capture*. Durham, NC: Duke University Press, 2012.

Christiansen, Samantha, and Zachary A. Scarlett, eds. *The Third World in the Global 1960s*. New York: Berghahn, 2012.

Chronister, Necia. *Domestic Disputes: Examining Discourses of Home and Property in the Former East Germany*. Berlin: De Gruyter, 2021.

Chronister, Necia, and Lutz Koepenick. "Introduction." Special issue: "On 24/7: Neoliberalism and the Undoing of Time." *Studies in Twentieth and Twenty-First Century Literature* 40, no. 2 (2016): 1–10.

Çil, Nevim. "Türkische Migranten und der Mauerfall." Berlin: Bundeszentrale für politische Bildung, 2009.

Conze, Eckart, ed. *Die demokratische Revolution 1989 in der DDR*. Cologne: Böhlau, 2009.

Cooke, Paul. *Representing East Germany since Unification: From Colonization to Nostalgia*. Oxford: Berg, 2005.

———. "Watching the Stasi: Authenticity, *Ostalgie* and History in Florian Henckel von Donnersmarck's *The Lives of Others* (2006)." In *New Directions in German Cinema*, edited by Paul Cooke and Chris Homewood, 111–27. London: I. B. Tauris, 2011.

Coopan, Vilashini. "World Literature after 1989: Revolutions in Motion." In *The Cambridge History of World Literature*, edited by Debjani Ganguly, 180–98. Cambridge: Cambridge University Press, 2021.

Cornish, Matt. *Performing Unification: History and Nation of Theater after 1989*. Ann Arbor: University of Michigan Press, 2017.

Cottin, Markus, Karl-Heinz Kretzschmar, Dieter Kürschner, and Ilona Petzold. *Leipziger Denkmale*. Vol. 2. Beucha: Sax Verlag, 2009.

Creet, Julia, and Andreas Kitzmann, eds. *Memory and Migration: Multidisciplinary Approaches to Memory Studies*. Toronto: University of Toronto Press, 2011.

Crimmins, Courtney Glore. "Reinterpreting the Soviet War Memorial in Berlin's Treptower Park after 1990." In *Remembering the German Democratic Republic: Divided*

Memory in a United Germany, edited by David Clarke and Ute Wölfel, 54–63. New York: Palgrave Macmillan, 2011.

Cussons, Thomas. *Protest! 65 Years of Rebellion in Photographs*. London: Andre Deutsch, 2011.

Cvetkovich, Ann. *An Archive of Feelings: Trauma, Sexuality and Lesbian Cultures*. Durham, NC: Duke University Press, 2003.

Dahn, Daniela. *Der Schnee von gestern ist die Sintflut von Heute*. Hamburg: Rowohlt, 2019.

Dahn, Daniela, and Peter Mausfeld. *Tamtam und Tabu: Die Einheit, drei Jahrzehnte ohne Bewährung*. Frankfurt: Westend, 2020.

Dale, Gareth. *The East German Revolution of 1989*. Manchester: Manchester University Press, 2007.

———. Review of *1989 und die Rolle der Gewalt*, edited by Martin Sabrow. *English Historical Review* 130, no. 543 (April 2015): 504–6.

De Cesari, Chiara, and Ann Rigney, eds. *Transnational Memory: Circulation, Articulation, Scales*. Berlin: De Gruyter, 2013.

Deleuze, Gilles, and Felix Guattari. *Kafka: Toward a Minor Literature*. Translated by Dana Polan. Minneapolis: University of Minnesota Press, 1986.

———. *What Is Philosophy?* Translated by Hugh Tomlinson and Graham Burchell III. New York: Columbia University Press, 1994.

Demke, Elena. "Mauerfotos in der DDR: Inszenierung, Tabus, Kontexte." In *Die DDR im Bild: Zum Gebrauch der Fotografie im anderen deutschen Staat*, edited by Karin Hartewig and Alf Lüdtke, 90–106. Göttingen: Wallstein, 2004.

Der Weg zur deutschen Einheit: Dossier. Berlin: Deutscher Bundestag, 2020. Denzler, Jochen, Petra Tschörtner, and Hans Wintgen, dirs. *In Berlin 16.10.89 – 4.11. 89*. Berlin: DEFA-Studio für Dokumentarfilme, 1989/1990.

Derrida, Jacques. *Archive Fever: A Freudian Impression*. Translated by Eric Prenowitz. Chicago: University of Chicago Press, 1995.

———. *Athens, Still Remains: The Photographs of Jean-François Bonhomme*. Translated by Pascale-Anne Brault and Michael Naas. New York: Fordham University Press, 2010.

———. *Copy, Archive, Signature: A Conversation on Photography*. Translated by Jeff Fort. Stanford, CA: Stanford University Press, 2010.

———. "The Free Wheel." In *Rogues: Two Essays in Reason*, translated by Pascale-Anne Brault and Michael Naas, 6–18. Stanford, CA: Stanford University Press, 2005.

———. *Given Time: I. Counterfeit Money*. Translated by Peggy Kamuf. Chicago: University of Chicago Press, 1992.

———. *Specters of Marx: The State of Debt, the Work of Mourning and the New International*. Translated by Peggy Kamuf. Introduction by Bernd Magnus and Stephen Cullenberg. London: Routledge, 1994.

Detjen, Marion. "Die Mauer." In *Erinnerungsorte der DDR*, edited by Martin Sabrow, 253–66. Munich: C. H. Beck, 2009.

Didi-Huberman, Georges. *The Eye of History: When Images Take Positions*. Translated by Shane B. Lillis. Boston, MA: MIT Press, 2018.

Dieckmann, Friedrich. *Vom Schloss der Könige zum Forum der Republik: Zum Problem der architektonischen Wiederaufführung*. Berlin: Theater der Zeit, 2015.

Dietrich, Christian, "'Archiv zur Öffentlichkeitsarbeit und zu zivilem Ungehorsam'— wie alles begann." In *Was uns bewegt(e): Festschrift zum 30-jährigen Jubiläum*, edited by Archiv der Bürgerbewegung Leipzig e.V., 11–12. Leipzig: Archiv der Bürgerbewegung, 2020.

Dillon, Brian. "A Short History of Ruin." In *Ruins*, edited by Brian Dillon, 10–14. Cambridge, MA: MIT Press, 2011.

Dolff-Bonekämper, Gabi. "Denkmalschutz-Denkmalsetzung-Grenzmarkierung: Erinnerungsarbeit an der Berliner Mauer." In *Markierung des Mauerverlaufs [in Berlin]: Hearing am 14. Juni 1995 Dokumentation*, edited by Senatsverwaltung für Bau-und Wohnungswesen Berlin, Abt. Städtebau und Architektur-Kunst im Stadtraum-Berlin, 39–40. Berlin: Senatsverwaltung, 1995.

———. "Grosser Sockel: Das Projekt in Berlin ist eine Premiere in der Denkmalpolitik der Nachkriegszeit. Es bleibt eine anspruchsvolle Aufgabe." *Das Parlament*, no. 19–20 (May 8, 2017).

Döring, Hans-Joachim. *"Es geht um unsere Existenz": Die Politik der DDR gegenüber der Dritten Welt am Beispiel von Mosambik und Äthiopien*. Berlin: Ch. Links Verlag, 1999.

Douzinas, Costas, and Slavoj Žižek, eds. *The Idea of Communism*. New York: Verso, 2010.

Dresen, Andreas, dir. *Gundermann*. Produced by Pandora Filmproduktion, Kineo Filmproduktion, Rundfunk Berlin-Brandenburg (RBB), Kinoinitiative Leuchtstoff, Arte. Aschaffenburg: Pandora Film Distribution, 2018.

Dündar, Can. *Tut Was! Plädoyer für eine aktive Demokratie/ Bir şey yap! Aktif demokrasi için çagri*. Hamburg: Hoffmann und Campe, 2018.

Ebbrecht-Hartmann, Tobias. "Archives for the Future: Thomas Heise's Visual Archeology." *Imaginations* 8, no. 1 (2017): 64–77.

Eckert, Astrid M. *West Germany and the Iron Curtain: Environment, Economy, and Culture in the Borderlands*. Oxford: Oxford University Press, 2019.

Eichberg, Thomas. "Interview by Thomas Heise—Regisseur: Arbeit in Feindesland. Interview (2012)." In *Filme der Zukunft: Die Staatliche Filmdokumentation am Filmarchiv der DDR*, edited by Anne Barnert, 255–78. Berlin: Neofelis, 2015.

Eichberg, Thomas, and René Jung, dirs. *Aufbruch '89–Dresden* [Departure '89 –Dresden]. Potsdam Babelsberg: Hochschule für Film und Fernsehen, 1989.

"Einweisung der Genossen zur Besetzung der Nikolaikirche am 9. Oktober." In *"Wir haben nur die Strasse": Die Reden auf den Leipzig Montagsdemonstrationen 1989/90-Eine Dokumentation*, edited by Achim Beier and Uwe Schwabe, 244-45. Halle (Saale): Mitteldeutscher Verlag, 2016. DVD included in book.

Eisler, Christiane, and Silke Geister. *Luxus Arbeit*. Berlin: Schüren, 1992.

Eley, Geoff. "The Unease of History: Settling Accounts with the East German Past." *History Workshop Journal* 57, no. 1 (Spring 2004): 175–201.

Elsaesser, Thomas. "Media Archeology as Symptom." *New Review of Film and Television Studies* 14, no. 2 (2016): 181–215.

El-Tayeb, Fatima. *European Others: Queering Ethnicity in Postnational Europe*. Minneapolis: University of Minnesota Press, 2011.

Enkelmann, Dagmar, ed. *Schicksal Treuhand—Treuhand-Schicksale: Begleitbuch zur gleichnamigen Ausstellung*. Berlin: Rosa-Luxemburg Stiftung, 2019.

Enzenbach, Isabel, Mai-Phuong Kollath, and Julia Oelkers. "Minds of Their Own: Migrants in the GDR" (Eigensinn im Bruderland). *Bruderland*, accessed November 3, 2022. https://bruderland.de/en.

Epperlein, Petra, and Michael Tucker, dirs. *Karl Marx City*. Produced by Petra Epperlein and Michael Tucker (pepper & bones). New York: Bond/360, 2017.

BIBLIOGRAPHY › 291

———. *The Last Cowboy*, dirs. Produced by Petra Epperlein and Michael Tucker (nomad). Betacam SP, color. DVD-ROM. 1998.

Erll, Astrid. *Memory in Culture*. Translated by Sara B. Young. New York: Palgrave Macmillan, 2011.

———. "Travelling Memory." Special issue: "Transcultural Memory," edited by Rick Crownshaw. *Parallax* 17, no. 4 (2011): 4–18.

Erll, Astrid, and Ann Rigney, eds. *Mediation, Remediation, and the Dynamics of Cultural Memory*. Berlin: De Gruyter, 2009.

Ernst, Wolfgang. *Digital Memory and the Archive*. Edited and with an introduction by Jussi Parikka. Minneapolis: University of Minnesota Press, 2013.

Erpenbeck, Jenny. *Gehen, Ging, Gegangen*. Munich: Penguin Verlag, 2015.

———. *Kairos*. Munich: Penguin Verlag, 2021.

Eshel, Amir. *Futurity: Contemporary Literature and the Quest for the Past*. Chicago: University of Chicago Press, 2013.

Etkind, Alexander. *Warped Mourning: Stories of the Undead in the Land of the Unburied*. Stanford, CA: Stanford University Press, 2013.

Fair-Schulz, Axel, and Mario Kessler, eds. *East German Historians since Unification: A Discipline Transformed*. New York: Suny Press, 2017.

Farge, Arlette. *The Allure of the Archives*. New Haven, CT: Yale University Press, 1989.

Fehérváry, Krisztina. *Politics in Color and Concrete: Socialist Materialities in the Middle Class in Hungary*. Bloomington: Indiana University Press, 2013.

Feldner, Heiko, Fabio Vighi, and Slavoj Žižek, eds. *States of Crisis and Post-Capitalist Scenarios*. London: Routledge, 2014.

Ferris, William R. *I Am a Man: Photographs of the Civil Rights Movement, 1960–1970*. Foreword by Lonnie G. Bunch. Jackson: University of Mississippi Press, 2021.

Flierl, Thomas. *Gesamtkonzept zur Erinnerung an die Berliner Mauer: Dokumentation, Information und Gedenken*. Berlin: City of Berlin, 2006.

Florath, Bernd, ed. *Das Revolutionsjahr 1989: Die Demokratische Revolution in Osteuropa als Transnationale Zäsur*. Göttingen: Vandenhoeck and Ruprecht, 2011.

———. *Selbstzeugnisse von Opposition und Widerstand in der DDR 1961 bis 1990: Ein archivübergreifendes Bestandsverzeichnis*. Berlin: Basis Druck, 2007.

Florvil, Tiffany N. *Mobilizing Black Germany: Afro-German Women and the Making of a Transnational Movement*. Champaign: University of Illinois, 2021.

Florvil, Tiffany N., and Vanessa D. Plumly, eds. *Rethinking Black German Studies: Approaches, Interventions and Histories*. Berlin: Peter Lang, 2018.

Foroutan, Naika. *Die Postmigrantische Gesellschaft: Ein Versprechen der Pluralen Demokratie*. Bielefeld: Transcript, 2019.

Foroutan, Naika, and Jana Hensel. *Die Gesellschaft der Anderen*. Berlin: Aufbau, 2020.

Foroutan, Naika, Juliane Karakayali, and Riem Spielhaus, eds. *Postmigrantische Perspektiven: Ordnungssysteme, Repräsentationen, Kritik*. Frankfurt: Campus Verlag, 2018.

Foster, Hal. "An Archival Impulse (2004)." In *The Archive*, edited by Charles Merewether, 143–48. Cambridge, MA: MIT Press, 2006.

Foth, Jörg, dir. *Letztes aus der DaDaeR* [Latest from the Da-Da-R]. Potsdam, Babelsberg: DEFA Studio Babelsberg/Künstlerische Gruppe "DaDaeR," 1990.

Foucault, Michel. *The Archeology of Knowledge and the Discourse on Language*. New York: Vintage, 1969.

———. "The Historical *a priori* and the Archive (1969)." In *The Archive*, edited by Charles Merewether, 26–30. Cambridge, MA: MIT Press, 2006.

———. "Political Spirituality as the Will for Alterity: An Interview with the *Nouvel Observateur* (1979)." Translated by Sabina Vaccarino Bremne. *Critical Inquiry* 47, no. 1 (Autumn 2020): 121–34.

———. "Theatrum Philosophicum." In *Language, Counter-Memory, Practice: Selected Essays and Interviews*, edited by Donald F. Bouchard, 165–98. Ithaca, NY: Cornell University Press, 1977.

Frank, Sybille. *Wall Memorials and Heritage: The Heritage Industry of Berlin's Checkpoint Charlie*. London: Routledge, 2018.

Fraser, Nancy. *The Old Is Dying and the New Cannot Be Born: From Progressive Neoliberalism to Trump and Beyond*. New York: Verso, 2019.

———. "Rethinking the Public Sphere: A Contribution to the Critique of Actually Existing Democracy." *Social Text* 25–26 (1990): 56–80.

Frei, Norbert, Christina Morina, Franka Maubach, and Maik Tändler. *Zur Rechten Zeit: Wider die Rückkehr des Nationalismus*. Berlin: Ullstein Verlag, 2019.

Friedensgebete in der Leipziger Nikolaikirche: Gottesdienst im Alltag der Welt. Begleitbuch zur Dauerausstellung in der Südkapelle. Leipzig: Evangelisch-Lutherische Kirchgemeinde St. Nikolai, 2017.

Fritzsche, Karin, and Claus Löser, eds. *Gegenbilder: Filmische Subversion in der DDR, 1976–1989. Texte, Bilder, Daten*. Berlin: Janus Press, 1996.

Führer, Christian. "Abend für den Frieden: 11.11.1988, St. Nikolai." In *Friedensgebete in der Leipziger Nikolaikirche: Gottesdienst im Alltag der Welt. Begleitbuch zur Dauerausstellung in der Südkapelle*, 72. Leipzig: Evangelisch-Lutherische Kirchgemeinde St. Nikolai, 2017.

Fukuyama, Francis. *The End of History and the Last Man*. New York: Free Press, 1992.

Fulbrook. Mary. *Anatomy of a Dictatorship*. Oxford: Oxford University Press, 1995.

———. *The People's State: East German Society from Hitler to Honecker*. New Haven, CT: Yale University Press, 2005.

Garton Ash, Timothy. *The Magic Lantern: The Revolution of '89 Witnessed in Warsaw, Budapest, Berlin, and Prague*. New York: Vintage, 1990.

———. "Time for a New Liberation." *New York Review of Books*, October 24, 2019.

Geissler, Steffen, and Monika Reum, eds. *Auferstanden aus Ruinen . . . und wie weiter? Chronik der Wende in Karl-Marx Stadt/ Chemnitz 1989/90*. Chemnitz: Heimatland Sachsen, 1991.

Getachew, Adom. *Worldmaking after Empire: The Rise and Fall of Self-Determination*. Princeton, NJ: Princeton University Press, 2019.

Geyer, Michael, ed. *The Power of Intellectuals in Contemporary Germany*. Chicago: University of Chicago Press, 2001.

Gezen, Ela, Priscilla Layne, and Jonathan Skolnik, eds. *Minority Discourse in Germany since 1990*. Berlin: De Gruyter, 2022.

Ghodsee, Kristen. *The Left Side of History: World War II and the Unfulfilled Promise of Communism in Eastern Europe*. Durham, NC: Duke University Press, 2015.

———. *Lost in Transition: Ethnographies of Everyday Life after Communism*. Durham, NC: Duke University Press, 2011.

———. *Second World, Second Sex: Socialist Women's Activism and Global Solidarity during the Cold War*. Durham, NC: Duke University Press, 2019.

Ghodsee, Kristen, and Mitchell A. Orenstein. *Taking Stock of Shock: Social Consequences of the 1989 Revolutions*. Oxford: Oxford University Press, 2021.

Ghosh, Amitav. *The Nutmeg's Curse: Parables for a Planet in Crisis*. Chicago: University of Chicago Press, 2021.

Gieseke, Jens. "Der entkräftete Tschekismus. Das MfS und seine ausgebliebene Niederschlagung der Konterrevolution 1989/90." In *1989 und die Rolle der Gewalt*, edited by Martin Sabrow, 56–81. Göttingen: Wallstein, 2012.

Glaeser, Andreas. *Divided in Unity: Identity, Germany, and the Police*. Chicago: University of Chicago Press, 2000.

———. *Political Epistemics: The Secret Police, the Opposition, and the End of East German Socialism*. Chicago: University of Chicago Press, 2011.

Golden, Elizabeth. "Following the Berlin Wall." In *Terrain Vague: Interstices at the Edge of the Pale*, edited by Patrick Barron and Manuela Mariani, 216–29. London: Routledge, 2013.

Gramsci, Antonio. *Selections from the Prison Notebooks*. New York: International Publishers, 1971.

Grashoff, Udo. "Driven into Suicide by the East German Regime? Reflections on the Persistence of a Misleading Perception." *Central European History* 52 (2019): 310–32.

Griffing, Brenda. *The Power of Protest: A Visual History of the 50 Biggest Social Justice Movements that Changed the World*. Naperville, IL: Sourcebooks, 2018.

Grinberg, Daniel. "Troubling Histories: Re-Viewing Documentary Production and Surveillance through the Freedom of Information Act." *Media, War and Conflict* 12, no. 3 (September 2019): 331–53.

Gross, Martin. *Das letzte Jahr: Aufzeichnungen aus einem ungültigen Land*. Leipzig: Spector, 2020.

Grossmann, Thomas. *Fernsehen, Revolution und das Ende der DDR*. Göttingen: Wallstein, 2015.

Guenther, Katja M. *Making Their Place: Feminism after Socialism in Eastern Germany*. Stanford, CA: Stanford University Press, 2010.

Gysi, Gregor, and Hans Modrow, eds. *Wir brauchen einen dritten Weg*. Hamburg: Konkret, 1990.

Haag, Hanna. "Ein Blick auf die DDR-Transformation als Migration." In *Vergangene Vertrautheit: Soziale Gedächtnisse des Ankommens, Aufnehmens und Abweisens*, edited by Oliver Dimbath, Anja Kinzler, and Meyer Katinka, 217–36. Wiesbaden: Springer VS, 2019.

Habermas, Jürgen. *Structural Transformation of the Public Sphere: An Inquiry into a Category of the Bourgeois Society*. Translated by Thomas Burger. With assistance of Frederick Lawrence. Cambridge, MA: MIT Press, 1991.

Harrison, Hope M. *After the Berlin Wall: Memory and Making of the New Germany, 1989 to the Present*. New York: Cambridge University Press, 2019.

Hartewig, Karin. "Militarismus und Antifaschismus: Die Wehrmacht im Kollektiven Gedächtnis der DDR." In *Der Krieg in der Nachkriegszeit: der Zweite Weltkrieg in Politik und Gesellschaft der Bundesrepublik*, edited by Michael Th. Greven and Oliver von Wrochem, 237–54. Opladen: Leske and Budrich, 2000.

Harvey, David. *The Anti-Capitalist Chronicles*. London: Pluto Press, 2020.

———. "The Right to the City." *New Left Review* 53 (September/October 2008).

Hecht, Arno. *Der Ostdeutsche–ein Fehlgriff der sozialen Evolution? Oder eine Gegenwart ohne Zukunft*. Berlin: Edition Wortmeldung, 2006.

Hecht, Heidemarie. "Der letzte Akt." In *Schwarzweiss und in Farbe: DEFA Dokumentarfilm. 1946–1992*, edited by Günter Jordan and Ralf Schenk, 235–70. Berlin: Filmmuseum Potsdam/Jovis, 1996.

Hein, Christoph. *Gegenlauschangriff: Ankedoten aus dem letzten deutsch-deutschen Kriege*. Berlin: Suhrkamp, 2019.

———. *Trutz*. Berlin: Suhrkamp, 2017.

Heise, Thomas, "Archäologie hat mit Graben zu tun" [Archaeology Is about Digging]. Munich: Filmmuseum, 2009. DVD brochure.

———. dir. *Heimat ist ein Raum aus Zeit* [Heimat Is a Space in Time]. Leipzig, Vienna: Ma.Ja.De Filmproduktion, Navigator Film, with ZDF/3sat, 2019.

———, dir. *Imbiss Spezial* [Snack bar special]. Berlin: DEFA-Studio für Dokumentarfilme, 1990.

———, dir. *Material*. Ma.Ja.De Filmproduktion, ZDF/Arte, 2009. Munich: Filmmuseum, 2019. 2 DVDs.

———. *Spuren: Eine Archäologie der realen Existenz*. Berlin: Vorwerk, 2010.

Heitzer, Enrico, Anetta Kahane, Martin Jander, and Patrice G. Poutrus, eds. *After Auschwitz: The Difficult Legacies of the GDR*. New York: Berghahn Books, 2021.

Hell, Julia. *Post-Fascist Fantasies: Psychoanalysis, History, and the Literature of East Germany*. Durham, NC: Duke University Press, 1997.

Hensel, Jana. *Zonenkinder* [After the Wall]. Hamburg: Rowohlt, 2004.

Hesse. Kurt R. "Fernsehen und Revolution: Zum Einfluss der Westmedien auf die politische Wende in der DDR." *Rundfunk und Fernsehen* 38 (1990): 328–42.

Heym, Stefan, and Werner Heiduczek, eds. *Die Sanfte Revolution*. Leipzig: Gustav Kiepenheuer Verlag, 1990.

Higdon, Nolan. *The Anatomy of Fake News: A Critical News Literacy Education*. Berkeley: University of California Press, 2020.

Hirsch, Marianne. *Family Frames: Photography, Narrative, and Postmemory*. Cambridge, MA: Harvard University Press, 1997.

———. *The Generation of Postmemory: Writing and Visual Culture after the Holocaust*. New York: Columbia University Press, 2012.

Hlavajova, Maria, and Ranjit Hoskote, eds. *Future Publics (The Rest Can and Should Be Done by the People): A Critical Reader in Contemporary Art*. Amsterdam: BAK, 2015.

Hoare, Liam. "Let's Please Stop Crediting Ronald Reagan for the Fall of the Berlin Wall." *Atlantic*, September 20, 2012.

Hoberman, J. "Living Memory." *Film Comment* (March–April 2020): 54–57.

Hochmuth, Hanno. *At the Edge of the Wall: Public and Private Spheres in Divided Berlin*. New York: Berghahn, 2021.

Hodgin, Nick. "'Screening the Stasi': The Politics of Representation in Postunification Film." In *The GDR Remembered: Representations of the East German State since 1989*, edited by Nick Hodgin and Caroline Pearce, 78–84. Rochester, NY: Camden House, 2011.

Hoffmann, Hilde. "Dokumentarische Gedächtnisräume 1989–90." In *Erinnern Vergessen: Das Visuelle Gedächtnis des Dokumentarfilms*, edited by Tobias Ebbrecht, Hilde Hoffmann, and Jörg Schweinitz, 286–303. Marburg: Schüren Verlag, 2009.

Holland, Doris, and Stefan Kuhlmann, eds. *Systemwandel und industrielle Innovation: Studien zum technologischen und industriellen Umbruch in den neuen Bundesländern*. Heidelberg: Physica Verlag, 1995.

Honig, Bonnie. *Public Things: Democracy in Disrepair*. New York: Fordham, 2017.

Horakova, Anna. "Paradigms of Refuge: Reimagining GDR Legacy and International Solidarity in Jenny Erpenbeck's *Gehen, Ging, Gegangen*." *Transit* 122, no. 2 (2020): 70–89.

Horvath, Agnes, Bjørn Thomassen, and Harald Wydra, eds. *Breaking Boundaries: Varieties of Liminality*. New York: Berghahn, 2015.

Hosek, Jennifer R. *Sun, Sex, and Socialism: Cuba in the German Imaginary*. Toronto: University of Toronto Press, 2012.

Hoskins, Andrew, ed. *Digital Memory Studies: Media Pasts in Transition*. London: Routledge, 2017.

———. "Mediatisation of Memory." In *Save as . . . Digital Memories*, edited by Joanne Garde-Hansen, Andrew Hoskins, and Anna Reading, 27–43. New York: Palgrave MacMillan, 2009.

Hoskins, Andrew, and John Tulloch. *Risk and Hyperconnectivity: Media and Memories of Neoliberalism*. Oxford: Oxford University Press, 2016.

Howes, Seth. *Moving Images on the Margins: Experimental Film in Late Socialist East Germany*. Rochester, NY: Camden House, 2019.

Huang, Carolin. "Dwelling on the 'Anarchival': Archives as Indexes of Loss and Absence." *Archival Science* 20 (2020): 263–77.

Hui Kyong Chun, Wendy. "The Enduring Ephemeral, or the Future Is a Memory." *Critical Inquiry* 35, no. 1 (Autumn 2008): 148–71.

Huyssen, Andreas. "Authentic Ruins." In *Ruins*, edited by Brian Dillon, 52–54. Cambridge, MA: MIT Press, 2011.

———. *Present Pasts: Urban Palimpsests and the Politics of Memory*. Stanford, CA: Stanford University Press, 2003.

———. *Twilight Memories: Marking Time in the Culture of Amnesia*. New York: Routledge, 1995.

———. "The Voids of Berlin." In *Present Pasts: Urban Palimpsests and the Politics of Memory*, 64. Stanford, CA: Stanford University Press, 2003.

Ingram, Susan. *Siting Futurity: The "Feel Good" Tactical Radicalism of Contemporary Culture in and around Vienna*. Santa Barbara, CA: Punctum Books, 2021.

"Initiative Denkmal Deutsche Einheit." In *Der Weg zum Denkmal für Freiheit und Einheit*, edited by Andreas H. Apelt, 34–35. Schwalbach: Wochenschau Verlag, 2009.

Jameson, Fredric. *Archaeologies of the Future: The Desire Called Utopia and Other Science Fictions*. London: Verso, 2005.

———. "Marx and Montage." *New Left Review* 58 (July/August 2009): 109–17.

Jankowski, Martin. *Rabet oder das Verschwinden einer Himmelsrichtung*. Wambach: via verbis verlag, 1999.

Jarausch, Konrad, ed. *After Unity: Reconfiguring German Identities*. New York: Berghahn, 1997.

Jedlowski, Paolo. "Memories of the Future." In *International Handbook of Memory Studies*, edited by Anna Lisa Tota and Trever Hagen, 121–30. London: Routledge, 2019.

Jessen, Ralph. "Montagsdemonstrationen." In *Erinnerungsorte der DDR*, edited by Martin Sabrow, 304–9. Munich: C. H. Beck, 2009.

Johnson-Spain, Ines, dir. *Becoming Black*. Berlin: Kobalt Productions, 2019.

Jones, Sara. *Towards a Collaborative Memory: German Memory Work in a Transnational Context*. New York: Berghahn, 2022.

Joppke, Christian. *East German Dissidents and the Revolution of 1989: Social Movement in a Leninist Regime*. New York: New York University Press, 1995.

Kaden, Klaus. "Von den Friedensgebeten ging alles aus." In *Die Sanfte Revolution*, edited by Stefan Heym and Werner Heiduczek, 101–5. Leipzig: Gustav Kiepenheuer Verlag, 1990.

Kantsteiner, Wulf. "Migration, Racism, and Memory." *Memory Studies* 12, no. 6 (2019): 611–16.

Kaul, Albrecht. "Macht der Gewaltlosigkeit: Christian Führer." In *Wegen Gefährdung des sozialistischen Friedens: Bewegende Schicksale von Christen in der DDR*, 131–40. Gießen: Brunnen, 2014.

Kazanjian, David. *The Brink of Freedom: Improvising Life in the Nineteenth-Century Atlantic*. Durham, NC: Duke University Press, 2016.

Kenney, Padraic. *A Carnival of Revolution: Central Europe 1989*. Princeton, NJ: Princeton University Press, 2002.

Kitchen, Martin. *Speer: Hitler's Architect*. New Haven, CT: Yale University Press, 2015.

Klausmeier, Axel. "Commemoration Needs a Place." In *The Berlin Wall*, edited by Axel Klausmeier and Anna von Arnim-Rosenthal, 7–10. Berlin: Links Verlag, 2015.

———. "'In Order to Grasp Something, There Must Be Something to Grasp,' or: The Remnants of the Berlin Wall as Objects of Monument Preservation." In *The Berlin Wall*, edited by Axel Klausmeier and Anna von Arnim-Rosenthal, 304–7. Berlin: Links Verlag, 2015.

Kleinert, in Andreas, dir. *Wege in die Nacht* [Paths in the night]. 35 mm, black & white. Berlin, Germany: Film-Board Berlin-Brandenburg (FBB), Studio Babelsberg Independents, Ö-Filmproduktion, 1999.

Kluge, Alexander, dir. *Nachrichten aus der ideologischen Antike: Marx-Eisenstein-Das Kapital* [News from ideological antiquity: Marx/Eisenstein/capital]. Berlin: Suhrkamp, 2008. 3 DVDs.

———. *Russia Container*. In collaboration with Thomas Combrink. Translated by Alexander Booth. London: Seagull Books, 2022.

Knabe, Hubertus. *Die Täter sind unter uns: Über das Schönreden der SED-Diktatur*. Berlin: Propyläen, 2007.

Koenker, Diane P., and Anne E. Gorsuch, eds. *The Socialist Sixties: Crossing Borders in the Second World*. Bloomington: Indiana University Press, 2013.

Kohl, Helmut. *Erinnerungen 1982–1990*. Munich: Droemer, 2005.

———. *Ich wollte Deutschlands Einheit*. Berlin: Propyläen, 1999.

Könczöl, Barbara, and Sigrid Meuschel. "Sacrilization of Politics in the GDR." *Telos* 136 (Fall 2006): 26–58.

Köpping, Petra. *Integriert erstmal uns: Eine Streitschrift für den Osten*. Berlin: Christoph Links Verlag, 2018.

"Konzept der Bundesregierung zur Errichtung eines Freiheits-und Einheitsdenkmals in Berlin." In *Der Weg zum Denkmal für Freiheit und Einheit*, edited by Andreas H. Apelt, 169–73. Schwalbach: Wochenschau Verlag, 2009.

Kowalczuk, Ilko-Sascha. *Die Übernahme: Wie Ostdeutschland Teil der Bundesrepublik wurde*. Munich: C. H. Beck, 2019.

———. *Endgame: The 1989 Revolution in East Germany*. Translated by Patricia C. Sutcliffe. New York: Berghahn, 2022.

———. *Endspiel: Die Revolution von 1989 in der DDR*. Munich: C. H. Beck, 2015.

———. "The Revolution in Germany: The End of the SED Dictatorship, East German Society, and Reunification." In *German Reunification: A Multinational History*, edited by Frédéric Bozo, Andreas Rödder, and Mary Elise Sarotte, 15–42. London: Routledge, 2016.

Krätzner, Anita, ed. *Hinter vorgehaltener Hand: Studien zur historischen Denunziationsforschung*. Göttingen: Vandenhoeck and Ruprecht, 2015.

Krauss, Angela. *Gesamtliebe und die Einzelliebe: Frankfurter Poetikvorlesungen*. Frankfurt: Suhrkamp, 2004.

Krauss, Rosalind. *Passages in Modern Sculpture*. Cambridge, MA: MIT Press, 1981.

Kristeva, Julia. *Revolt, She Said*. Los Angeles: semiotexte, 2002.

Kuball, Mischa. "Rettet die KMB/2013." In *Global Activism: Art and Conflict in the 21st Century*, edited by Peter Weibel, 612–13. Cambridge, MA: MIT Press, 2015.

Küçükyılmaz, Meltem. "Wir Sind von Hier: Türkisch-Deutsches Leben 1990. Fotografien von Ergun Çağatay." In *Türkisch-Deutsche Studien: Jahrbuch 2020*, edited by Şeyda Ozil, Michael Hofmann, Jens Peter Laut, Yasemin Dayıoğlu-Yücel, Cornelia Zierau, and Didem Uca, 137–40. Göttingen: Universitätsverlag Göttingen, 2022.

Kuczyńska-Zonik, Aleksandra. "Dissonant Heritage: Soviet Monuments in Eastern and Central Europe." In *Historical Memory of Central and East European Communism*, edited by Agnieszka Mrozik and Stanislav Holubec, 101–21. London: Routledge, 2018.

Kuehn, Karl Gernot. *Caught: The Art of Photography in the German Democratic Republic*. Berkeley: University of California Press, 1997.

Kurz, Josef. "Acht Wochen DDR Geschichte: Eine Chronik vom 25.9. bis 18.11.89 im Spiegel zentraler DDR-Medien." In Neues Forum Leipzig, *Jetzt oder nie—Demokratie! Leipziger Herbst '89*, 313–42. Leipzig: Forum Verlag, 1989.

Laabs, Dirk. *Der Deutsche Goldrausch: Die Wahre Geschichte der Treuhand*. Munich: Pantheon, 2012.

LaCapra, Dominick. "Revisiting the Historians' Debate: Mourning and Genocide." *History and Memory* 9, nos. 1–2 (1997): 80–112.

Laclau, Ernesto, and Chantal Mouffe. *Hegemony and Socialist Strategy: Toward a Radical Democratic Politics*. London: Verso, 2014. Originally published 1985.

Ladd, Brian. *The Ghosts of Berlin: Confronting German History in the Urban Landscape*. Chicago: University of Chicago Press, 1997.

Ladewig, Rebekka, and Henning Schmidgen. "Symmetries of Touch: Reconsidering Tactility in the Age of Ubiquitous Computing." *Body and Society* special issue 28, nos. 1–2 (March–June 2022): 3–23.

Lahusen, Christiane. "Autobiography as Participation in the 'Master Narrative': GDR Academics after Unification." In *Remembering the German Democratic Republic: Divided Memory in a United Germany*, edited by David Clarke and Ute Wölfel, 182–94. New York: Palgrave, 2011.

Landsberg, Alison. *Prosthetic Memory: The Transformation of American Remembrance in the Age of Mass Culture*. New York: Columbia University Press, 2004.

Lässig, Jochen. "Speech at the Montagsdemonstration: 13. November 1989." In *"Wir haben nur die Strasse": Die Reden auf den Leipzig Montagsdemonstrationen 1989/90-Eine Dokumentation*, edited by Achim Beier and Uwe Schwabe, 73–74. Halle (Saale): Mitteldeutscher Verlag, 2016.

———. "Zeitzeuge." In *"Wir haben nur die Strasse": Die Reden auf den Leipzig Montagsdemonstrationen 1989/90-Eine Dokumentation*, edited by Achim Beier and Uwe Schwabe, 214–17. Halle (Saale): Mitteldeutscher Verlag, 2016.

Later, Josh. "Surveillance History and the History of New Media: An Evidential Paradigm." *New Media and Society* 14, no. 4 (2011): 586–82.

Lauf, Vera, and Julia Schäfer, curs. "anarchive." Exhibit at the Galerie für Zeitgenössische Kunst Leipzig, March 9–June 23, 2019. https://gfzk.de/2019/deanarchive/.

Laurent, Guido, and Oliver Lugon, eds. *Between Still and Moving Images: Photography and Cinema in the 20th Century*. New Barnet: John Libbey Publishing, 2012.

Lawson, George, Chris Armbruster, and Michael Cox, eds. *The Global 1989: Continuity and Change in World Politics*. Cambridge: Cambridge University Press, 2019.

Lear, Jonathan. *Radical Hope: Ethics in the Face of Cultural Devastation*. Cambridge, MA: Harvard University Press, 2008.

Lederman, Shmuel. *Hannah Arendt and Participatory Democracy: A People's Utopia*. London: Palgrave, 2019.

Leeds, David. "Snowden and the Cinema of Surveillance." *Harvard Political Review*, October 1, 2016.

Lehrer, Erica, Cynthia E. Milton, and Monica Patterson, eds. *Curating Difficult Knowledge: Violent Pasts in Public Places*. New York: Palgrave, 2011.

Leonhard, Nina, and Uwe Krähnke. "Ankommen im ehemaligen Feindesland." In *Vergangene Vertrautheit: Soziale Gedächtnisse des Ankommens, Aufnehmens und Abweisens*, edited by Oliver Dimbath, Anja Kinzler, and Katinka Meyer, 237–63. Wiesbaden: Springer VS, 2019.

Levy, Daniel, and Natan Sznaider. *The Holocaust and Memory in the Global Age*. Translated by Assenka Oksiloff. Philadelphia, PA: Temple University Press, 2006.

Lewis, Alison. "Analyzing the Trauma of German Unification." *New German Critique* 64 (Winter 1995): 135–59.

———. *A State of Secrecy: STASI Informers and the Culture of Surveillance*. Dulles, VA: Potomac Books, 2021.

Libeskind, Daniel. *Jewish Museum Berlin*. New York: Prestel, 1999.

Liedtke, Ulf. "Seelsorge im Strafvollzug." Leipzig Initiative of Peace and Human Rights. *Studienmaterial* 2 (April 1990).

Lierke, Lydia, and Massimo Perinelli, eds. *Erinnern Stören: der Mauerfall aus migrantischer und jüdischer Perspektive*. Berlin: Verbrecher Verlag, 2020.

Lindner, Bernd. *Die Demokratische Revolution in der DDR 1989/90*. Berlin: Bundeszentrale für Politische Bildung, 1998.

Links, Christoph, Sybille Nitsche, and Antje Taffelt, eds. *Das wunderbare Jahr der Anarchie: Von der Kraft des Zivilen Ungehorsams 1989/90*. Berlin: Christoph Links, 2004.

Loest, Erich. *Nikolaikirche*. Berlin: dtv, 1995.

Löser, Claus. "Radikale Ambivalenz: Thomas Heise, ein Porträt." *film-dienst* 56, no. 24 (November 18, 2003): 12–14.

Lüdtke, Alf. "Kein Entkommen? Bilder-Codes und eigensinniges Fotografieren: eine Nachlese." In *Die DDR im Bild: Zum Gebrauch der Fotografie im anderen deutschen Staat*, edited by Karin Hartewig and Alf Lüdtke, 227–36. Göttingen: Wallstein, 2004.

Mac Con Uladh, Damian. "Studium bei Freunden: Ausländische Studierende in der DDR bis 1970." In *Ankunft. Alltag. Ausreise. Migration und interkulturelle Begegnung in der DDR Gesellschaft*, edited by Christian Th. Müller and Patrice G. Poutrus, 75–220. Cologne: Böhlau, 2005.

Maier, Charles. *Dissolution: The Crisis of Communism and the End of East Germany*. Princeton, NJ: Princeton University Press, 1997.

Mandel, Ruth. *Cosmopolitan Anxieties: Turkish Challenges to Citizenship and Belonging in Germany*. Durham, NC: Duke University Press, 2008.

Mark, James, Bogdan C. Iacob, Tobias Rupprecht, and Ljubica Spaskovska. *1989: A Global History of Eastern Europe*. Cambridge: Cambridge University Press, 2019.

———. "Race." In *Socialism Goes Global: The Soviet Union and Eastern Europe in the Age of Decolonisation*, edited by Paul Betts and James Mark, 221–54. Oxford: Oxford University Press, 2022.

Martins, Vasco. "Hegemony, Resistance, Gradations of Memory: The Politics of Remembering Angola's Liberation Struggle." *History and Memory* 33, no. 2 (Fall/Winter 2021): 80–106.

Mau, Steffen. *Lütten-Klein: Leben in der Ostdeutschen Transformationsgesellschaft.* Frankfurt: Suhrkamp, 2019.

Mausbach, Florian. "Über Sinn und Ort eines nationalen Freiheits-und Einheitsdenkmals." In *Der Weg zum Denkmal für Freiheit und Einheit,* edited by Andreas H. Apelt, 12–30. Schwalbach: Wochenschau Verlag, 2009.

Mayne, Judith. "Female Narration, Women's Cinema: Helke Sander's *The All-Round Reduced Personality/Redupers.*" *New German Critique* 24–25 (Autumn 1981–Winter 1982): 155–71.

McGarry, Aidan, Itir Erhart, Hande Eslen-Ziya, Olu Jenzen, and Umut Korkut, eds. *The Aesthetics of Global Protest: Visual Culture and Communication.* Amsterdam: Amsterdam University Press, 2019.

McIsaac, Peter M., and Gabriele Mueller, eds. *Exhibiting the German Past: Museums, Films, and Musealization.* Toronto: University of Toronto Press, 2015.

McLuhan, Marshall. "The Medium is the Message (1964)." In *Picture Industry: A Provisional History of the Technical Image 1844–2018,* edited by Walead Beshty, 397–99. Zurich: JRP/Ringier, 2018.

Mercer, Ben. *Student Revolt in 1968 in France, Italy, and West Germany.* Cambridge: Cambridge University Press, 2021.

Meuschel, Sigrid. *Legitimation und Parteiherrschaft in der DDR.* Frankfurt: Suhrkamp, 1992.

Meyer-Gosau, Frauke. *Versuch eine Heimat zu finden: Uwe Johnson.* Munich: H. C. Beck, 2014.

Milev, Yana. *Das Treuhand-Trauma: Die Spätfolgen der Übernahme.* Berlin: Das Neue Berlin, 2020.

———. *Entkoppelte Gesellschaft-Ostdeutschland seit 1989/90: Band 3: Exil.* Frankfurt: Peter Lang, 2020.

Miller, Barbara. *Narratives of Guilt and Compliance in Unified Germany: Stasi Informers and Their Impact on Society.* New York: Routledge, 1999.

Misselwitz, Helke, dir. *Sperrmüll* [Bulky Trash]. Berlin: DEFA-Studio für Dokumentarfilme GmbH, 1990. 35 mm.

Mitchell, W. J. T. *What Do Pictures Want? The Lives and Loves of Images.* Chicago: University of Chicago Press, 2005.

Mitter, Armin, and Stefan Wolle, eds. *"Ich liebe euch doch alle!" Befehle und Lageberichte des MfS. Januar-November 1989.* Berlin: Elefanten Press, 1990.

Moldt, Dirk. *Wunder gibt es immer wieder: Das Chaos ist aufgebraucht, es war die schönste Zeit. Fragmente zur Geschichte der Offenen Arbeit Berlin und der Kirche von Unten.* Berlin: Eigenverlag Kirche von Unten, 1997.

Morat, Daniel, ed. *Sounds of Modern History: Auditory Cultures in 19th- and 20th-Century Europe.* New York: Berghahn, 2014.

Mouffe, Chantal. *For a Left Populism.* London: Verso, 2019.

Mudde, Cas, and Cristóbal Rovira Kaltwasser. *Populism: A Very Short Introduction.* Oxford: Oxford University Press, 2017.

Müller, Albrecht. *Glaube wenig, hinterfrage alles, denke selbst: wie man Manipulationen durchschaut.* Frankfurt: Westend, 2019.

Müller, Heiner. "Die Küste der Barbaren/1992." In *Für alle reicht es nicht: Texte zum Kapitalismus*, 345–48. Suhrkamp: Berlin, 2017.

Mulvey, Laura. *Death 24x a Second: Stillness and the Moving Image*. London: Reaktion Books, 2006.

Naimark, Norman. "'Ich will hier raus': Emigration and the Collapse of the German Democratic Republic." In *Eastern Europe in Revolution*, edited by Ivo Banac, 72–95. Ithaca, NY: Cornell University Press, 1992.

Naughton, Leonie. *That Was the Wild East: Film Culture, Unification, and the New Germany*. Ann Arbor: University of Michigan Press, 2002.

Negt, Oskar, and Alexander Kluge. *Public Sphere of Experience: Analysis of the Bourgeois and Proletarian Public Sphere*. London: Verso, 2016.

Neubert, Erhart. *Geschichte der Opposition in der DDR 1949–1989*. Berlin: Links Verlag, 1997.

Neues Forum Leipzig. *Jetzt oder nie—Demokratie! Leipziger Herbst '89*. Leipzig: Forum Verlag, 1989.

Nguyen, Angelika, dir. *Bruderland ist abgebrannt* [Brotherland is burned down]. Germany: 1991–92.

Nguyen, Dan Thy, and Iraklis Panagiotopoulos, *Das Sonnenblumenhaus* [Sunflower house]. Play premiered in Hamburg, at the Museum für Völkerkunde, 2014.

Nichelmann, Johannes. *Nachwendekinder: die DDR, unsere Eltern und das grosse Schweigen*. Berlin: Ullstein, 2019.

Nielsen, Kristine. "Quid pro quo: Assessing the Value of Berlin's Thälmann Monument." In *Art Outside the Lines: New Perspectives on GDR Art Culture*, edited by Elaine Kelly and Amy Wlodarski, 63–89. Leiden: Brill, 2011.

Niethammer, Lutz, ed. *Der gesäuberte Antifaschismus: die SED und die roten Kapos von Buchenwald*. Berlin: Akademie Verlag, 1994.

Noni, Stacey. *Photography of Protest and Community: The Radical Collectives of the 1970s*. London: Lund Humphries, 2020.

Norris, Stephen M., ed. *Museums of Communism: New Memory Sites in Central and Eastern Europe*. Bloomington: Indiana University Press, 2020.

Novero, Cecilia, ed. *Imperfect Recall: Re-Collecting the GDR*. Otago German Studies vol. 30. Dunedin: University of Otago, 2020.

Nycz, Grzegorz. *Memory Politics in the Shadow of the New Cold War*. Berlin: De Gruyter Oldenbourg, 2021.

Oberender, Thomas, ed. *Occupy History, Gespräche im Palast der Republik 13 Jahre nach seinem Verschwinden: Ausstellungskatalog Palast der Republik*. König: Walther, 2019.

O'Dea, Meghan. "Lucia Engombe's and Stefanie-Lahya Aukongo's Autobiographical Accounts of *Solidaritätspolitik* and Life in the GDR as Namibian Children." In *Rethinking Black German Studies: Approaches, Interventions and Histories*, edited by Tiffany N. Florvil and Vanessa D. Plumly, 105–34. Berlin: Peter Lang, 2018.

Olick, Jeffrey K. *The Sins of the Fathers: Germany, Memory, Method*. Chicago: University of Chicago Press, 2016.

Olin, Margaret. *Touching Photographs*. Chicago: University of Chicago Press, 2012.

Olsen, Jonathan. "The Left Party and the AfD: Populist Competitors in East Germany." *German Politics and Society* 126, no. 1 (Spring 2018): 70–83.

Olson, Kevin. "Conclusion: Fragile Collectivities, Imagined Sovereignties." In Alain Badiou, Pierre Bourdieu, Judith Butler, Georges Didi-Huberman, Sadri Khiari, and

Jacques Rancière, *What Is a People?* translated by Jody Gladding, 107–32. New York: Columbia University Press, 2013.

Orich, Annika. "Archival Resistance: Reading the New Right." Special issue: "Responses to the Rise of the Alternative for Germany: Societal and Party-Political Reactions to the AfD and its Policy Positions." *German Society and Politics* 38, no. 2 (June 2020): 1–34.

Osang, Alexander. "Die verlorenen Revolutionäre: Eine Herbstreise." In *Ankunft in der Mitte: Reportagen und Porträts*, 36–60. Berlin: Christoph Links Verlag, 1999.

Osborne, Dora, ed. *Archive and Memory in German Literature and Visual Culture*. Rochester, NY: Camden House, 2015.

Oschmann, Dirk. *Der Osten: eine Westdeutsche Erfindung. Wie die Konstruktion des Ostens unsere Gesellschaft spaltet*. Berlin: Ullstein, 2023.

Qurbani, Burhan, dir. *Wir sind jung. Wir sind stark* [We are young. We are strong]. Berlin: UFA GmbH, 2014.

Oushakine, Serguei Alex. *The Patriotism of Despair: Nation, War, and Loss in Russia*. Ithaca, NY: Cornell University Press, 2009.

Oushakine, Serguei Alex, and Costica Bradatan, eds. *In Marx's Shadow: Knowledge, Power, and Intellectuals in Eastern Europe and Russia*. Lanham, MD: Lexington Books, 2010.

Paver, Chloe. "From Monuments to Installations: Aspects of Memorialization in Historical Exhibitions about the National Socialist Era." In *Memorialization in Germany since 1945*, edited by Bill Niven and Chloe Paver, 253–64. London: Palgrave Macmillan, 2010.

Pérez Ríu, Carmen. "To Make You See: Photography as Intermedial Resource in Theatre and Film Adaptation (*Closer* and *The Winter Guest*)." *Adaptation* 8, no. 2 (2015): 176–91.

Pfaff, Steven. *Exit Voice Dynamics and the Collapse of East Germany: The Crisis of Leninism and the Revolution of 1989*. Durham, NC: Duke University Press, 2006.

Phillips, Kendall R., ed. *Framing Public Memory*. Tuscaloosa: University of Alabama Press, 2004.

Piesche, Peggy. "Black and German? East German Adolescents before 1989: A Retrospective View of a Non-Existent Issue in the GDR." In *The Cultural After-Life of East Germany? New Transnational Perspectives*, edited by Leslie A. Adelson, 60–93. Washington, DC: American Institute for Contemporary German Studies, 2002.

———, ed. *Labor 89: Intersektionale Bewegungsgeschichte*n aus West und Ost*. Berlin: Yılmaz-Günay, 2020.

———. "Leerstelle im Archiv." In *Wildes wiederholen, material von unten: Dissidente Geschichten zwischen DDR und pOstdeutschland#1*, edited by Elske Rosenfeld and Suza Husse, 139–48. Berlin: Archive Books, 2019.

Pinkert, Anke. "Arrival: A Postcommunist Émigré in the Prairies." In *Imperfect Recall: Re-Collecting the GDR*, edited by Cecilia Novero, 1–14. German Studies vol. 30. Dunedin: University of Otago, 2020.

———. *Film and Memory in East Germany*. Bloomington: Indiana University Press, 2008.

———. "'Postcolonial Legacies': The Rhetoric of Race in the East/West German National Identity Debate of the Late 1990s." Special issue: "Translating within and across Cultures." *M/MLA* 35, no. 2 (2002): 13–33.

———. "Public Memory Underground: Photographs of Protest in Uwe Johnson's *The Third Book about Achim* (1967)." *CoSMo: Comparative Studies in Modernism* 13, no. 2 (Winter 2018): 207–19.

———. "Toward a Critical Reparative Practice in Post 1989 Literature: Christa Wolf's *City of Angels.*" In *Memory and Postwar Memorials: Confronting the Violence of the Past*, edited by Marc Silberman and Florence Vatan, 177–96. New York: Palgrave McMillan, 2013.

Powell, Larson. *The Films of Konrad Wolf: Archive of the Revolution.* Rochester, NY: Camden House, 2020.

Pritchard, Rosalind M. O. *Reconstructing Education: East German Schools and Universities after Unification.* New York: Berghahn, 1999.

Propp, V. *Morphology of the Folktale.* Translated by Laurence Scott. Austin: University of Texas Press, 1988.

Pugach, Sara. *African Students in East Germany.* Ann Arbor: University of Michigan Press, 2022.

Radstone, Susannah. "What Place Is This? Transcultural Memory and the Locations of Memory Studies." Special issue: "Transcultural Memory," edited by Rick Crownshaw. *Parallax* 17, no. 4 (2011): 109–23.

Rancière, Jacques. *Disagreement: Politics and Philosophy.* Translated by Julie Rose. Minneapolis: University of Minnesota Press, 1999.

———. *The Emancipated Spectator.* Translated by Gregory Elliott. London: Verso, 2011.

———. *The Future of the Image.* Translated by Gregory Elliott. London: Verso, 2007.

Rectanus, Mark W. "Refracted Memory: Museums, Film, and Visual Culture in Urban Space." In *Exhibiting the German Past: Museums, Films, and Musealization*, edited by Peter M. McIsaac and Gabriele Mueller, 42–62. Toronto: University of Toronto Press, 2015.

Reich, Anja, and Sabine Rennefanz. "Herbert Schirmer, 'Nach dem 3. Oktober war man weg, als wäre nichts gewesen.'" Interview podcast, *Berliner Zeitung*, September 27, 2020.

Reijven, Menno H., Sarah Cho, Matthew Ross, and Gonen Dori-Hacohen. "Conspiracy, Religion, and the Public Sphere: The Discourse of Far-Right Counterpublics in the U.S. and South Korea." *International Journal of Communication* 14 (2020): 5331–50.

Rennefanz, Sabine. *Eisenkinder: Die stille Wut der Wendegeneration.* Munich: Luchterhand, 2013.

Richardson-Little, Ned. *The Human Rights Dictatorship: Socialism, Global Solidarity and Revolution in East Germany.* Cambridge: Cambridge University Press, 2020.

Richter, Frank. *Hört endlich zu: Weil Demokratie Auseinandersetzung bedeutet.* Berlin: Ullstein, 2018.

Richter, Gerhard. *Afterness: Figures of Following in Modern Thought and Aesthetics.* New York: Columbia University Press, 2011.

Rigney, Ann. "Remembering Hope: Transnational Activism beyond the Traumatic." *Memory Studies* 11, no. 3 (2018): 368–80.

Rigney, Ann, and Thomas Smits, eds. *The Visual Memory of Protest.* Amsterdam: Amsterdam University Press, 2023.

Rinner, Susanne. *The German Student Movement and the Literary Imagination: Transnational Memories of Protest and Dissent.* New York: Berghahn, 2013.

Rosa, Hartmut. *Resonance: A Sociology of Our Relationship to the World*. Cambridge: Polity Press, 2019.

———. *The Uncontrollability of the World*. New York: Polity, 2020.

———. *Unverfügbarkeit*. Wien: Residenz Verlag, 2019.

Rösch, Ulrich. "Afterword." In Joseph Beuys, with Johann Philipp, Hans Binswanger, Werner Ehrlicher, and Rainer Willert, *What Is Money? A Discussion*, 69–89. Forest Row: Clairview, 2010.

Ross, Kristin. *May '68 and Its Afterlives*. Chicago: University of Chicago Press, 2002.

Rost, Andreas, and Nina Peters. "Pure Neugierde, pure Fassungslosigkeit." *Logbuch Suhrkamp*, November 9, 2019. https://www.logbuch-suhrkamp.de/andreas-rost/pure-neugierde-pure-fassungslosigkeit/.

Rothberg, Michael. "Interview: Multidirectional Memory in Focus." *Observing Memories* 3 (December 2019): 28–33.

———. "Multidirectional Memory in Migratory Settings: The Case of Post-Holocaust Germany." In *Transnational Memory: Circulation, Articulation, Scales*, edited by Chiara De Cesari and Ann Rigney, 123–45. Berlin: De Gruyter, 2013.

Rothberg, Michael, and Yasmin Yildiz. "Memory Citizenship: Migrant Archives of Holocaust Remembrance in Contemporary Germany." *Parallax* 17, no. 4 (2011): 32–48.

Rothöhler, Simon. "'Ihr seid Schauspieler? Die Wende als revolutionäre Theaterprobe in Thomas Heise's *Material*." *Die andere Szene: Theaterarbeit und Theaterproben im Dokumentarfilm* 91 (2014): 211–23.

Rubin, Eli. *Amnesiopolis: Modernity, Space, and Memory in East Germany*. Oxford: Oxford University Press, 2016.

Ruge, Eugen. *In Zeiten des abnehmenden Lichts*. Hamburg: Rowohlt, 2011.

Rushing, Robert. *Descended from Hercules: Biopolitics and the Muscled Male Body on Screen*. Bloomington: Indiana University Press, 2016.

Rutter, Nick. "Unity and Conflict in the Socialist Scramble for Africa, 1960–1970." In *The Global 1960s: Convention, Contest, and Counterculture*, edited by Tamara Chaplin and Jadwiga E. Pieper Mooney, 33–51. London: Routledge, 2017.

Sa'adah, Anne. *Germany's Second Chance: Trust, Justice, and Democratization*. Cambridge, MA: Harvard University Press, 1998.

Sabrow, Martin, ed. *1989 und die Rolle der Gewalt*. Göttingen: Wallstein Verlag, 2012.

———. "'1989' und die Rolle der Gewalt in Ostdeutschland." In *1989 und die Rolle der Gewalt*, edited by Martin Sabrow, 9–31. Göttingen: Wallstein, 2012.

———. *Das Diktat des Konsenses: Geschichtswissenschaft in der DDR 1949–1969*. Berlin: De Gruyter, 2001.

———, ed. *Erinnerungsorte der DDR*. Munich: C. H. Beck, 2009.

Sabrow, Martin, Tilmann Siebeneichner, and Peter Ulrich Weiß, eds. *1989: Eine Epochenzäsur*. Göttingen: Wallstein, 2021.

Saether, Susanne Ø. "Touch/Space: The Haptic in 21st-Century Video Art." In *Screen Space Reconfigured*, edited by Susanne Ø. Saether and Synne T. Bull, 2013. Amsterdam: Amsterdam University Press, 2020.

Sälter, Gerhard. "Das Verschwinden der Berliner Mauer." In *Revolution und Vereinigung 1989/90: als in Deutschland die Realität die Fantasie überholte*, edited by Klaus-Dietmar Henke, 353–62. Munich: dtv, 1990.

Sandler, Daniela. *Counterpreservation: Architectural Decay in Berlin since 1989*. Ithaca, NY: Cornell University Press, 2016.

Santner, Eric. *On the Psychotheology of Everyday Life: Reflections on Freud and Rosen-zweig*. Chicago: University of Chicago Press, 2001.

Sarotte, Mary Elise. *The Collapse: The Accidental Opening of the Berlin Wall*. Basic Books, 2015.

———. *1989: The Struggle to Create Post–Cold War Europe*. Princeton, NJ: Princeton University Press, 2009.

Saunders, Anna. *Memorializing the GDR: Monuments and Memory after 1989*. New York: Berghahn, 2018.

Schedlinski, Rainer. "Die phase der *schönen revolution* ist vorbei." In *Die Sanfte Revolution*, edited by Stefan Heym and Werner Heiduczek, 339–45. Leipzig: Gustav Kiepenheuer Verlag, 1990.

Schiermer, Bjørn. "Acceleration and Resonance: An Interview with Hartmut Rosa." E-Special: Four Generations of Critical Theory in *Acta Sociologica*, 2018.

Schmidt, Helmut. "A Policy of Reliable Partnership." *Foreign Affairs* 59, no. 4 (Spring 1981): 743–55.

Schneider, Rolf. *Frühling im Herbst: Notizen zum Untergang der DDR*. Göttingen: Steidl Verlag, 1991.

Schneider, Wolfgang, ed. *Leipziger Demontagebuch*. Leipzig: Gustav Kiepenheuer, 1990.

Schönian, Valerie. *Ostbewusstsein: Warum Nachwendekinder für den Osten streiten und was das für die Deutsche Einheit bedeutet*. Munich: Piper, 2020.

Schreiber, Eduard, dir. *Östliche Landschaften* [Eastern Landscapes]. Berlin: DEFA-Studio für Dokumentarfilme GmbH, 1991. 35 mm.

Schulze, Gerhard. *Die Erlebnisgesellschaft: Kultursoziologie der Gegenwart*. Frankfurt: Campus, 1992.

Schulze, Ingo. *Neue Leben*. Munich: dtv, 2007.

———. *New Lives*. Translated by John E. Woods. New York: Alfred A. Knopf, 2008.

———. *Unsere schönen neuen Kleider: Gegen die marktkonforme Demokratie—für demokratische Märkte*. Munich: Hanser, 2012.

Schwenkel, Christina. *Building Socialism: The Afterlife of East German Architecture in Urban Vietnam*. Durham, NC: Duke University Press, 2020.

Scribner, Charity. *Requiem for Communism*. Cambridge, MA: MIT Press, 2003.

Seeck, Anne, ed. *Das Begehren, anders zu sein: politische und kulturelle Dissidenz von 68 bis zum Scheitern der DDR*. Münster: Unrast, 2012.

Seiler, Lutz. *Kruso*. Frankfurt: Suhrkamp, 2014.

———. *Stern 111*. Frankfurt: Suhrkamp, 2020.

Sendler, Horst. "Die DDR ein Unrechtsstaat—ja oder nein? Missverständnisse um 'Rechtsstaat' und 'Unrechtsstaat.'" *Zeitschrift für Rechtspolitik* 26, no. 1 (1993): 1–5.

Şenocak, Zafer. "Thoughts on May 8, 1995." In *Atlas of a Tropical Germany: Essays on Politics and Culture*, edited and translated by Leslie Adelson, 20–61. Lincoln: University of Nebraska Press, 2000.

Sewell, William, Jr. *Logics of History: Social Theory and Social Transformation*. Chicago: University of Chicago Press, 2005.

Sheffer, Edith. *Burned Bridge: How East and West Germans Made the Iron Curtain*. Oxford: Oxford University Press, 2011.

Shen, Qinna. "Tiananmen Square, Leipzig, and the 'Chinese Solution': Revisiting the *Wende* from an Asian-German Perspective." *German Studies Review* 42, no. 1 (2019): 37–55.

Shevchenko, Olga. *Crisis and the Everyday in Postsocialist Moscow*. Bloomington: Indiana University Press, 2009.

————, ed. *Double Exposure: Memory and Photography*. New York: Routledge, 2014.

Sieg, Katrin. "Class of 1989: Who Made Good and Who Dropped Out of German History? Postmigrant Documentary Theater in Berlin." In *The German Wall: Fallout in Europe*, edited by Marc Silberman, 165–86. New York: Palgrave Macmillan, 2011.

————. *Decolonizing German and European History at the Museum*. Ann Arbor: University of Michigan Press, 2022.

Siegert, Bernhard. "(Not) In Place: The Grid, or, Cultural Techniques of Ruling Spaces." In *Picture Industry: A Provisional History of the Technical Image 1844–2018*, edited by Walead Beshty, 282–93. New York: LUMA Bard, 2018.

Silberman, Marc, ed. *Back to the Future: Tradition and Innovation in German Studies*. Berlin: Peter Lang, 2018.

————, ed. *The German Wall: Fallout in Europe*. New York: Palgrave Macmillan, 2011.

Silverman, Kaja. *The Miracle of Analogy: The History of Photography, Part 1*. Stanford, CA: Stanford University Press, 2015.

Skyba, Peter, Sebastian Richter, and Stefan Schönfelder, eds. *Himmelweit gleich? Europa '89: 4 Ausstellungen in Dresden, Prag, Wrocław and Bratislava/Žilina*. Schwerin: Barens and Fuss, 2010.

Slobodian, Quinn, ed. *Comrades of Color: East Germany in the Cold War World*. New York: Berghahn, 2015.

————. *Foreign Front: Third World Politics in Sixties West Germany*. Durham, NC: Duke University Press, 2012.

————. "Socialist Chromatism: Race, Racism, and the Racial Rainbow in East Germany." In *Comrades of Color: East Germany in the Cold War World*, edited by Quinn Slobodian, 23–39. New York: Berghahn, 2015.

Sloterdijk, Peter. "Lichtung und Beleuchtung/Light and Illumination." In *Mischa Kuball . . . In Progress: Projekte/Projects 1980–2007*, edited by Florian Matzner, 15–34. Ostfildern: Hatje Cantz Verlag, 2007.

Smith, Shawn Michelle. *At the Edge of Sight: Photography and the Unseen*. Durham, NC: Duke University Press, 2013.

Sonnevend, Julia. *Stories without Borders: The Berlin Wall and the Making of a Global Iconic Event*. Oxford: Oxford University Press, 2016.

Sontag, Susan. *On Photography*. New York: Picador, Farrar, Strauss and Giroux, 1977.

Sontheimer, Michael, and Peter Wensierski. *Stadt der Revolte*. Berlin: Christoph Links Verlag, 2018.

"Staatliche Gesprächsnotiz: Auszug aus einer Information vom Rat des Bezirkes Leipzig, [Bereich] Kirchenfragen, über ein Gespräch am 18.08.1988 zwischen H. Reitmann und zwei Vertretern des Landeskirchenamtes vom 19.08.1988." In *Freunde und Feinde: Friedensgebete in Leipzig zwischen 1981 und dem 9. Oktober, 1989*, edited by Christian Dietrich and Uwe Schwabe, commissioned by the Archiv für Bürgerbewegung e.V., 138–39. Leipzig: Evangelische Verlagsanstalt, 1994.

Staiger, Ute. "Cities, Citizenship, Contested Cultures: Berlin's Palace of the Republic and the Politics of the Public Sphere." *Cultural Geographies* 16 (July 2009): 309–27.

Stangl, Paul. "The Soviet War Memorial in Treptow, Berlin." *Geographical Review* 93, no. 2 (April 2003): 213–36.

Stasi Records Agency. *Access to Secrecy: Exhibition on the Stasi Records Archive*. Berlin: BStU, 2021.

Staudte, Wolfgang. *Die Mörder sind unter uns* [Murderers among us]. Berlin and Potsdam-Babelsberg: DEFA, 1946.

Steding, Elizabeth Priester. *GDR Literature in German Curricula and Textbooks: Exploring the Legacy of GDR Authors, 1985-2015*. London: Palgrave Macmillan, 2023.

Stefano and Serafin. "Vor und nach dem Mauerfall: Mosambikanische Vertragsarbeiter erzählen." In *Das Begehren, anders zu sein: Politische und kulturelle Dissidenz von 68 bis zum Scheitern der DDR*, edited by Anne Seeck, 287–89. Münster: Unrast, 2012.

Stehle, Maria, and Beverly Weber. *Precarious Intimacies: The Politics of Touch in Contemporary Western European Cinema*. Evanston, IL: Northwestern University Press, 2020.

Steiner, Barbara. "Prepositions." In *Public Preposition*, edited by Vanessa Joan Müller, 16–19. Berlin: Distanz Verlag, 2015.

Stoler, Ann. *Along the Archival Grain: Epistemic Anxieties and Colonial Common Sense*. Princeton, NJ: Princeton University Press, 2008.

———. *Duress: Imperial Durabilities in Our Times*. Durham, NC: Duke University Press, 2016.

———. *Interior Frontiers: Essays on the Entrails of Inequality*. Oxford: Oxford University Press, 2022.

Stolpe, Manfred. *Schwieriger Aufbruch*. Berlin: Siedler, 1992.

Stötzner, Andreas. *Über Klassik: Reflexionen über Bauen und Gestalten*. Leipzig: Passage-Verlag, 1999.

Straub, Sibylle. "Der Suizid und 'die Wende' in der DDR: Zur Tragfähigkeit von Durkheim's Konzeption des (anomischen) Selbstmords am Beispiel Thüringens." *System Familie* 13 (2000): 59–69.

Streamas, John. "A Vision for Scholar-Activists of Color." *AAUP Journal of Academic Freedom* 10 (2019): 1–10.

Striegl, Libi, and Lori Emerson. "Anarchive as Technique in the Media Archeology Lab." *International Journal for Digital Humanities* 1 (2019): 59–70.

Szameit, Michael. "Lied von der Angst." In *Die Sanfte Revolution*, edited by Stefan Heym and Werner Heiduczek, 107–20. Leipzig: Gustav Kiepenheuer Verlag, 1990.

Tawada, Yoko. "Pushkin Allee." In *Three Streets*, translated by Margaret Mitsutani. New York: New Directions, 2022.

Taylor, Diana. *The Archive and the Repertoire: Performing Cultural Memory in the Americas*. Durham, NC: Duke University Press, 2003.

———. *¡Presente!: The Politics of Presence (Dissident Acts)*. Durham, NC: Duke University Press, 2020.

Teltschik, Horst. *329 Tage: Innenansichten der Einigung*. Munich: Siedler Verlag, 1991.

Tetzlaff, Kurt. *Reports from a Peaceful Revolution: Report for Posterity (1990) and In Transition: Report of Hope (1991)*. Amherst, MA: DEFA Film Library, 2022. 2 DVDs.

Ther, Phillip. *Europe since 1989: A History*. Princeton, NJ: Princeton University Press, 2016.

Thierse, Wolfgang. "Mut zur eigenen Geschichte: Lehren aus der Vergangenheit." In *Vergangenheitsbewältigung 1945 und 1989: Ein unmöglicher Vergleich? Eine Diskussion*, edited by Klaus Sühl, 19–36. Berlin: Volk und Welt, 1994.

Till, Karen E. *The New Berlin: Memory, Politics, Place*. Minneapolis: University of Minnesota Press, 2005.

———. "Wounded Cities: Memory-Work and Place-Based Ethics of Care." *Political Geography* 31 (2012): 3–14.

Tismaneanu, Vladimir, ed. *The Revolutions of 1989: Rewriting Histories*. London: Routledge, 1999.

Todorova, Maria, and Zsuzsa Gille, eds. *Post-Communist Nostalgia*. New York: Berghahn, 2010.

Tran, Minh Thu, and Vanessa Vu. "Hamburg 1980: Als der rechte Terror wieder aufflammte" [Hamburg 1980: When right-wing terror flared up again]. In *Rice and Shine*. Podcast. August 15, 2020. https://www.migration-lab.net/medien/rice-shine/.

Traverso, Enzo. "Fascisms Old and New." *Jacobin*, April 2, 2019.

———. "Intellectuals and Antifascism: For a Critical Historization." *New Politics* 9 (2004): 1–15.

———. *Left-Wing Melancholia: Marxism, History, and Memory*. New York: Columbia University Press, 2017.

Trigg, Dylan. *The Memory of Place: A Phenomenology of the Uncanny*. Athens: Ohio University Press, 2012.

Trnka, Jamie H. "Suspended Time, Exile, and the Literature of Transnational Antifascism: Parentheses and Postscripts." In *Tales that Touch: Migration, Translation, and Temporality in Twentieth- and Twenty-First-Century German Literature and Culture*, edited by Bettina Brandt and Yasemin Yildiz, 36–52. Berlin: De Gruyter, 2022.

Tröger, Mandy. *Pressefrühling und Profit: Wie westdeutche Verlage 1989/90 den Osten eroberten*. Cologne: Halem Verlag, 2019.

Tuchfeldt, Egon. "The Transformation of Economic Systems-The German Example." In *The Economics of German Unification*, edited by Achmed Ghanie Ghaussy and Wolf Schäfer, 36–52. London: Routledge, 1993.

Uekötter, Frank. "Entangled Ecologies: Outlines of a Green History of Two or More Germanys." In *A History Shared and Divided: East and West Germany since the 1970s*, edited by Frank Bösch, translated by Jennifer Walcoff Neuheiser, 147–90. New York: Berghahn, 2018.

Vaccarino Bremner, Sabina. "Introduction to Michel Foucault's 'Political Spirituality as the Will for Alterity.'" *Critical Inquiry* 47 (Autumn 2020): 115–20.

Vaidhyanathan, Siva. *Anti-Social Media: How Facebook Disconnects Us and Undermines Democracy*. Oxford: Oxford University Press, 2018.

Voigt, Andreas, and Gerd Kroske, dirs. *Leipzig im Herbst* [Leipzig in the fall]. Berlin: DEFA-Studio für Dokumentarfilme, 1989. 35mm.

Wagner-Pacifici, Robin. *What Is an Event?* Chicago: University of Chicago Press, 2017.

Ward, James J. "Remember When It Was the 'Antifascist Defense Wall'? The Use of History in the Battle for Public Memory and Public Space." In *The Berlin Wall: Representations and Perspectives*, edited by Ernst Schürer, Manfred Keune, and Philip Jenkins, 11–24. New York: Peter Lang, 1996.

Ward, Janet. "Berlin, the Virtual Global City." *Journal of Visual Culture* 3, no. 2 (2004): 239–56.

Ward, Simon. *Urban Memory and Visual Culture in Berlin: Framing the Asynchronous City 1957–2012*. Amsterdam: Amsterdam University Press, 2016.

Warner, Michael. *Publics and Counterpublics*. New York: Zone Books, 2005.

Weaver, John A. *Rethinking Academic Politics in (Re)unified Germany and the United States*. New York, Routledge, 2001.

Weibel, Peter, ed. *Global Activism: Art and Conflict in the 21st Century*. Cambridge, MA: MIT Press, 2015.

———. "Lichtpolitik/The Politics of Light." In *Mischa Kuball . . . In Progress: Projekte/ Projects 1980–2007*, edited by Florian Matzner, 267–71. Ostfildern: Hatje Cantz Verlag, 2007.

Weil, Francesca. *Verhandelte Demokratisierung: Die Runden Tische der Bezirke 1989/90 in der DDR.* Göttingen: V and R Unipress, 2011.

Weissgerber, Gunter, ed. *Leipziger Freiheits—und Einheitsdenkmal.* Leipzig: Leipzig Peaceful Revolution Foundation and Archive of the Citizens' Movement Leipzig e.V., 2014. https://www.archiv-buergerbewegung.de/themen-sammlung/denkmal.

Weissgerber, Gunter (SPD). "Petition to the Bundestag, March 22, 2000." In *Leipziger Freiheits- und Einheitsdenkmal*, edited by Gunter Weissgerber, 18. Leipzig: Leipzig Peaceful Revolution Foundation and Archive of the Citizens' Movement Leipzig e.V., 2014. https://www.archiv-buergerbewegung.de/themen-sammlung/denkmal.

Welfens, Maria J. *Umweltprobleme und Umweltpolitik in Mittel- und Osteuropa: Ökonomie, Ökologie und Systemwandel.* Heidelberg: Physica Verlag, 2013.

Wendt, Alexander. "Das Sterben der Anderen: Interview mit Udo Grashoff." *Focus Magazin* 19 (May 8, 2006): 51–53.

Wensierski, Peter. *Die unheimliche Leichtigkeit der Revolution: Wie eine Gruppe Leipziger die Revolution Wagte.* Munich: Deutsche Verlagsanstalt, 2017.

Wenzel, Jan, ed. *Das Jahr 1990 Freilegen: Mit 32 Geschichten von Alexander Kluge* [Uncovering the year 1990: with 32 stories by Alexander Kluge]. Leipzig: Spector Books, 2019.

———. "Ein Jahr von langer Dauer (Nachwort)." In Martin Gross, *Das letzte Jahr: Aufzeichnungen aus einem ungültigen Land*, 359–67. Leipzig: Spector, 2020.

Wenzel, Jan, and Anna König. *Zerrissene Gesellschaft: Remontage der Zeit.* Leipzig: Spector, 2018.

Wiesenthal, Helmut. "Post-Unification Dissatisfaction, or Why Are So Many East Germans Unhappy with the New Political System?" *German Politics* 7, no. 2 (1998): 1–30.

Wilhelm, Cornelia. "Epistemological Obstacles around 'Race.'" In *Migration, Memory, and Diversity: Germany from 1945 to the Present*, edited by Cornelia Wilhelm, 206–29. New York: Berghahn, 2016.

Wiliarty, Sarah, and Louise K. Davidson-Schmich, eds. "Introduction." Special issue: "Responses to the Rise of the Alternative for Germany: The AfD's Origins in Comparative Perspective." *German Society and Politics* 38, no. 1 (March 2020): 1–6.

Winkler, Anne. "Remembering and Historicizing Socialism: The Private and Amateur Musealization of East Germany's Everyday Life." In *Exhibiting the German Past: Museums, Films, and Musealization*, edited by Peter M. McIsaac and Gabriele Mueller, 100–122. Toronto: University of Toronto Press. 2015.

Witkowski, Gregory. "Between Fighters and Beggars: Socialist Philanthropy and the Imagery of Solidarity in East Germany." In *Comrades of Color: East Germany in the Cold War World*, edited by Quinn Slobodian, 73–94. New York: Berghahn, 2015.

Wittenius, Charlotte. "BİZİM BERLİN 89/90 im Märkischen Museum in Berlin. Mauerfall und Wiedervereinigung aus deutsch-türkischer Sicht." *Zeitgeschichte-online*, September 2018. https://zeitgeschichte-online.de/geschichtskultur/bizim-berlin-8990-im-maerkischen-museum-berlin.

Wolf, Christa. *City of Angels or, The Overcoat of Dr. Freud.* New York: Farrar, Straus and Giroux, 2013 (2010).

———. "Das Zehn-Punkte-Programm Helmut Kohls." In *Umbrüche und Wendezeiten*, 91–92. Berlin: Suhrkamp, 2019.

BIBLIOGRAPHY > 309

———. *Stadt der Engel oder The Overcoat of Dr. Freud*. Berlin: Suhrkamp, 2010.

———. *Umbrüche und Wendezeiten*. Berlin: Suhrkamp, 2019.

Wolff, Frank. *Die Mauergesellschaft: Kalter Krieg, Menschenrechte und die deutsch-deutsche Migration 1961–1989*. Berlin: Suhrkamp, 2019.

Wolin, Sheldon S. "Fugitive Democracy." *Constellations: An International Journal of Critical Democratic Theory* 1, no. 1 (1994): 11–25.

Wolle, Stefan. *Die heile Welt der Diktatur, Alltag und Herrschaft in der DDR 1971–1989*. Bonn: Schriftenreihe der Bundeszentrale für politische Bildung, 1998.

Wolrab, Julia. "BİZİM BERLİN 89/90. Fotografien von Ergun Çağatay im Märkischen Museum Berlin." *Visual History*, August 7, 2018. https://www.visual-history.de/2018/08/07/bizim-berlin-89-90/.

Woolf, Brandon. *Institutional Theatrics: Performing Arts Policy in Post-Wall Berlin*. Evanston, IL: Northwestern University Press, 2021.

Wüstenberg, Jenny. *Civil Society and Memory in Postwar Germany*. Cambridge: Cambridge University Press, 2017.

Wüstenberg, Jenny, and Aline Sierp, eds. *Agency in Transnational Memory Politics*. New York: Berghahn, 2020.

Yildiz, Yasemin. *Beyond the Mother Tongue: The Postmonolingual Condition*. New York: Fordham University Press, 2012.

———. "Governing European Subjects: Tolerance and Guilt in the Discourse of 'Muslim Women.'" *Cultural Critique* 77 (Winter 2011): 70–101.

———. "Reading Racialization: Yadé Kara's *Selam Berlin*." *German Studies Review* 46, no. 1 (2023): 97–115.

Young, James. "Foreword." In Marc Augé, *Oblivion*, translated by Marjolijn De Jager, vii–xii. Minneapolis: University of Minnesota Press, 2004.

———. *The Texture of Memory: Holocaust Memorials and Meanings*. New Haven, CT: Yale University Press, 1994.

Yurchak, Alexei. *Everything Was Forever, until It Was No More*. Princeton, NJ: Princeton University Press, 2005.

Zamponi, Lorenzo. *Social Movements, Memory and Media: Narrative in Action in the Italian and Spanish Student Movements*. London: Palgrave, 2018.

Zatlin, Jonathan. "Scarcity and Resentment: Economic Sources of Xenophobia in the GDR, 1971–1989." *Central European History* 40 (2007): 683–720.

Ziegler, Jean. *Der Hass auf den Westen: Wie sich die armen Völker gegen den wirtschaftlichen Weltkrieg wehren*. Munich: Goldman Verlag, 2011.

Zielinski, Siegfried. "Arqueología prospectiva." *H-ART: Revista de Historia, Teoría y Crítica de Arte*; *Bogata* 8 (January 2021): 217–43.

———. *Variations on Media Thinking*. Minneapolis: University of Minnesota Press, 2019.

Ziemer, Gudula, and Holger Jackisch. "Volksfest." In *Die Sanfte Revolution*, edited by Stefan Heym and Werner Heiduczek, 123–25. Leipzig: Gustav Kiepenheuer Verlag, 1990.

Žižek, Slavoj. *The Relevance of the Communist Manifesto*. Cambridge: Polity, 2019.

Zuboff, Soshana. *The Age of Surveillance Capitalism: The Fight for a Human Future at the Frontier of Power*. New York: Public Affairs, 2019.

Zwahr, Hartmut. *Ende einer Selbstzerstörung: Leipzig und die Revolution in der DDR*. Beucha: Sax Verlag, 2014. [1993].

Index

Note: Page numbers in italics refer to figures.

Abdi-Herrle, Sasan, 209
absence. *See* erasure; (in)visibility
Access to Secrecy exhibit (Stasi Records Agency), 129, 137
activist movements. *See* public protests
Adelson, Leslie, 254n22
AfD (Alternative for Germany), 57, 128, 203–4, 205, 210, 218, 226, 275n13, 276n19
Africa, anti-colonial movements in, 221
"afterness," 109, 111
Agamben, Georgio, 30
Ahbe, Thomas, 210
"AK Environment" *Basisgruppe*, 98
"AK Human Rights" *Basisgruppe*, 98
"AK Justice" *Basisgruppe*, 94, 98
Allen, Jennifer, 22
Allende, Salvador, 15
alliance, as concept, 225
Alliance for Germany, 6, 18, 149
Alliance '90/Green Party, 57, 148, 191, 250n80, 265n56
allyship, 207, 225, 227
Alternative Church Congress, 107
Alternative for Germany (AfD), 57, 128, 203–4, 205, 210, 218, 226, 275n13, 276n19
Altınay, Ayşe Gül, 28
Amadeu Antonio Foundation, 209
anarchic cooperation, 15, 240n45
anarchival, as concept, 26, 243n83
anti-colonial movements, 221–22
Appadurai, Arjun, 223

archival turn, 26
Archive of the Citizens' Movement Leipzig, 93, 94, 107, 182, 183, 258n76
archives: and aesthetics, 44; and archival turn, 26; and deconstructing temporalities, 168–69; digitalized, 184, 262n17, 262n19; hegemonic power over, 128, 136, 170–71, 192, 261n2, 263n23, 263n28; internet as, 124, 261n129; of oppositional movements in Saxony, 93, 94, 107, 258n76; preserving vs. discarding, 165, 263n25; spectrality of, 27, 132, 135–36, 138; violence of, 136–37, 160, 243n83. *See also* Stasi Records Agency (BStU)
archives of the future, as concept, 26–28, 131, 227–28
Arendt, Hannah, 18, 39, 109, 130, 207, 240n46; on citizens' councils, 183; on elections, 192; on freedom, 11, 12, 21, 58, 67, 195, 250n84; on political authority, 99; on public political space, 21, 67, 123, 184, 252nn99–100; on reality and appearance, 35; on reserve power of revolution, 187; on revolutionary treasure, 58, 59, 67, 279n63; on social anchoring, 217; on temporality, 22–23, 30, 165; on transmitting revolutionary histories, 9, 20, 59, 68, 164, 195
Ash, Timothy Garton, xiii, 9, 227
Assmann, Aleida, 26, 136, 261n128, 262n17
Ataman, Ferda, 209

Aufarbeitung (reappraisal), 148
Aufbruch discourse, 86, 255n18
Aufhebung discourse, 52
Augé, Marc, 80, 126
Ayim, May, 227
Azoulay, Ariella, 28, 59, 137, 149, 259n95

Bach, Jonathan, 45, 114, 173
Badel, Peter, 168
Badiou, Alain, 21, 230
Balibar, Étienne, 198
Barthes, Roland, 114, 143
Bartsch, Günther, 267n71
Bathrick, David, 145
Baudrillard, Jean, 31
Becker, Jurek, 127
Bellour, Raymond, 143–44
Benjamin, Walter, 31, 139, 197, 248n49
Bennett, John, 261n124
Berdahl, Daphne, 23, 68
Bergemann, Sibylle, xi–xii, 230
Bergmann-Pohl, Sabine, 192
Berlant, Lauren, 229, 281n91
Berlin Cathedral Church, 59
Berlin City Museum. See *BİZİM BERLİN 89/90* exhibit (Berlin City Museum)
Berlin memorials. See memorial politics, Berlin
Berlin Palace/Humboldt Forum, 51, 58, 59. See also Monument to Freedom and Unity, Berlin
Berlin Wall: absent presence of, 31–32; alternative perspectives of, 70–71, *71*; first private memorialization of, 40–41. See also Berlin Wall Memorial
Berlin Wall Foundation, 38, 41
Berlin Wall Memorial, 33–34, *43, 45, 48*, 129; debates on material form, 41–42, 246n34; Documentation Center, 49, 246–47n35, 247n37; freedom narrative, 47–50; function of, 42–43; performativity of, 43, 47, 247nn39–40; planning, 38, 41, 246n31; victimization narrative, 44–46
Bernauer Strasse site, 41. See also Berlin Wall Memorial
Betts, Paul, 22, 38, 178, 203, 221, 222
Beuys, Joseph, 55

Biermann, Wolf, 147–48
Biess, Frank, 22
Birthler, Marianne, 191, 204, 265n56
BİZİM BERLİN 89/90 exhibit (Berlin City Museum), 211–12, *213, 215*; and Eastern globalization context, 219–24; sharing dynamics in, 225–26; transcultural conviviality in, 213–19, 224
Blackman, Lisa, 259n86
Bloch, Ernst, 82
Bohley, Bärbel, 5, 55, 61, 148, 191, 204, 250n88, 271n55, 273n75
Bonevardi, Gustavo, 261n124
border crossing. See migration
Bosteels, Bruno, 198
Böttcher, Jürgen, *Konzert im Freien*, 230–31, 232
Boyer, Dominic, 23
Boym, Svetlana, 21–22, 28
Boys 36, 212
Brandenburg prison, 179–80
Braun, Volker, 124, 195, 205, 252n98
Broken Bonds: Remontage of Time (editorial newspaper), 125
Brown, Wendy, 24, 67, 227, 245n17, 252n100
BStU. See Stasi Records Agency (BStU)
Buck-Morss, Susan, 8, 28, 37, 127, 206, 249–50n76
Bundesarchiv (Federal Archives), 128, 170–71, 263n23, 263n28
Bush, George H. W., 6
Butler, Judith, 109; on collective action, 123, 179, 276n21; on nonviolence/violence, 15, 89, 97, 258n61; on public political space, 252n99; on "We, the people," 249n75

Çağatay, Ergun. See *BİZİM BERLİN 89/90* exhibit (Berlin City Museum)
Campany, David, 132, 144
Campt, Tina, 28, 149
capitalism and privatization, 7, 8, 37, 55, 150–51, 185, 192, 226, 266n59
Capra, Frank, 266n61
CDU (Christian Democratic Union), 6, 7, 57, 113, 147, 186, 226, 250n82

Ceaușescu, Nicolae, 14
Central Roundtable, 17, 18, 183, 223
Cercel, Cristian, 40, 203
China, demonstrations in, 98, 202
Christian Democratic Union (CDU), 6, 7, 57, 113, 147, 186, 226, 250n82
Chronister, Necia, 37
church: clergy-activist dynamics, 93–96, 98, 99; state surveillance of, 87–88, 89, 93, 95. *See also* peace prayer gatherings
Çil, Nevim, 214
Citizens' Committee Leipzig, 104–5, 108, 125, 258n75
citizens' movements. *See* public protests
City of Angels (Wolf), 174
civic seeing, 102
"civilization" discourse, 19
civil unrest. *See* public protests
classical architecture, 88
clergy-activist dynamics, 93–96, 98, 99
climate change activism, 228–29
collective guilt, 10, 130
collective memory, 35, 244n10
colonialism, and decolonization, 221–22
commemorative politics. *See* memorial politics, Berlin; memorial politics, Leipzig
commercialism, 116, 117, 125, 260n103
commons, the, 207, 226, 228, 281n91
communicative memory, as concept, 116
connective turn, 243n92
conviviality, transcultural, 213–19, 224
Cooke, Paul, 10, 39
cooptation, 149
Cornish, Matt, 173, 277n37
council systems and roundtables, 17, 183–86, 194, 223, 270nn40–44
counter-memory, 27, 68, 77, 131–32, 188
counter-publics, 77, 92, 126, 204, 275n12
Crimmins, Courtney Glore, 77
cultural memory, as concept, 116

Dahn, Daniela, 13–14, 239n25
Dale, Gareth, 19
data, afterlife of, 259n86
death, and memory, 146–47
De Cesari, Chiara, 109

decolonization, 221–22
Decreed Solidarity—Dealing with "Foreigners" in the GDR (traveling photographic exhibit), 219–20
DEFA film studio, 161, 170, 171, 269n22
Delacroix, Eugène, "Liberty Leading the People," 178
Deleuze, Gilles, 231–32
democracy: contemporary crisis of, 23–24, 203; vs. dictatorship and totalitarian label for GDR, 10, 13, 37, 38, 136, 156, 201, 245n20; and neoliberalism, 24, 67, 227; and othering, 79; participatory, 18, 66, 174, 183–84, 188, 190, 270n40, 270n42; radical, 66, 228, 252n98; and self-government efforts during '89–90 interval period, 182–86, 192–93, 194, 270nn40–44; teleological narrative of, 19, 49–50, 52, 56, 67
Democracy Now, 17, 194
Democratic Awakening, 17, 149
demonstrations. *See* public protests
Demontagebuch (Schneider), 178
Derrida, Jacques, 49, 243n85; on archives of the future, xiii, 26, 27, 132, 243n89; on capitalism, 82–83; on democracy, 190, 228; on inheritance, 18–19, 27; on mass media, 4; on politics of the archive, 136; on post-1989 mentality, 13, 204; on the spectral, 18, 27, 79, 132; on temporality, 21, 65, 224
Detjen, Marion, 42
Dieckmann, Friedrich, 51
digital culture, modern, 159–60
displacement. *See* migration
Döring, Hans-Joachim, 279n66
Dresen, Andreas, 262n6
Dündar, Can, 280n87
Durkheim, Émile, 149

Eastern Europe: in "civilization" discourse, 19; and globalization, 7–8, 203, 219–24; in Western historical framework, 8–9
Ebbrecht-Hartmann, Tobias, 179
economic decline and unemployment, 80, 149–52, 193, 266n59, 266n62

economic inequality, 15, 55, 221–22

Eisenman, Peter, 36

Eisenstein, Sergej, 263n30

election process and results, 6, 147, 186–87, 271–72n55, 273n76

Eley, Geoff, 11

Elsaesser, Thomas, 165, 195

emigration. *See* migration

energy, and resonance, 121–22

Enquete Commission, 10, 11

"Entfernte Verwandte" installation (Heise), 274n92

environmental movements, 106–7, 228–29

Epperlein, Petra, 129–30, 131. See also *Karl Marx City* (documentary film)

equality: economic inequality, 15, 55, 221–22; and freedom, ideal of, 49, 55, 156, 194, 228

erasure: and absent presence of the Wall, 31–32; of '89 disruptive dynamics in memorial politics, 88–89, 90, 99–100, 125, 126; of '89–90 interval period in memorial politics, 35, 37, 40, 43, 46–47, 49–50, 55–56, 77, 123; and punitive forgetting, 136, 262n17. *See also* (in)visibility; memory

Erll, Astrid, 216

Eshel, Amir, 28

Etkind, Alexander, 47, 75

European Union, 38–39, 203, 276n19, 277n35

Europe '89 exhibit, 120

Evangelical Church Berlin, 17, 18

exhibitions vs. memorials, 119–20

exit visas, 91, 94

Faust, Sigmar, 276n18

Federal Archives (Bundesarchiv), 128, 170–71, 263n23, 263n28

Federal Foundation for the Reappraisal of the SED Dictatorship, 52, 57, 69, 105, 157, 241n54, 246n31

Federal Government Commissioner for Culture and the Media, 67, 246n31

Federal Republic of Germany (FRG): and archival power, 128, 136, 170–71, 192, 261n2, 263n23, 263n28 (*see also*

Stasi Records Agency [BStU]); and collapse of the GDR, official history, 6–7; and discursive shift in memorial politics, 36–40 (*see also* memorial politics, Berlin); and superiority discourse, 10–11, 19, 39

film: and photographs, 132–33, 142, 143, 144, 159–60; and preservation, 168, 197; social observation tradition, 187; and technology, 169–70, 171, 172, 173, 269n27; underground scene, 171–72

film festival activism, 91–92

Fischer, Manfred, 41–42

Flierl, Thomas, 41, 45, 246n31

Flusser, Vilém, 118

Flying Universities, Poland, 106

food exchanges, 214–16, 217–18, 226

forgetting, punitive, 136, 262n17. *See also* erasure

Foroutan, Naika, 207–9, 213, 225, 276n30, 276–77n32

Foster, Hal, 27, 44, 69, 124, 131

Foucault, Michel, 27, 99, 121, 274n90

framing, in photography, 63

Fraser, Nancy, 57, 224

freedom: Arendt on, 11, 12, 21, 58, 67, 195, 250n84; and equality, ideal of, 49, 55, 156, 194, 228; in memorial discourse, 47–50

Freedom and Unity Monument, Leipzig: design proposals, 113–14, 115; opposition to, 115, 118; teleological narrative, 114. *See also* Monument to Freedom and Unity, Berlin

French Revolution, 177–78, 194

FRG. *See* Federal Republic of Germany (FRG)

Fridays for Future, 228

Friedrich, Holger, 265n48

Friedrich Wilhelm IV (king of Prussia), 58

Fuchs, Jürgen, 61

Führer, Christian, 93, 94, 95–96, 98, 101, 109, 125

Fukuyama, Francis, 13

Fulbrook, Mary, 241n56, 242n71

future archives, as concept, 26–28, 131, 227–28

future-oriented memory, 25–28, 69, 132

Gauck, Joachim, 204, 265n56

GDR and SED. *See* German Democratic Republic (GDR) and Socialist Unity Party (SED)

Georgia, revolution in, 14

German Democratic Republic (GDR) and Socialist Unity Party (SED): collapse of, official history, 4–9 (*see also* memorial politics, Leipzig; Peaceful Revolution); demonstrations against (*see* public protests; violence); dictatorship and totalitarian label, 10, 13, 37, 38, 136, 156, 245n20. *See also* Stasi and police force

Germania Tod in Berlin (Müller), 167, 171

German Lottery Foundation Berlin, 67

German Society e.V., 52, 248n61

Getachew, Adom, 221

Ghosh, Amitav, 8, 238n17

Glaeser, Andreas, 23, 39

Gorbachev, Mikhail, 3, 4, 64, 155, 163

Gould, Richard Nash, 261n124

Gramsci, Antonio, 243n79

Grashoff, Udo, 150, 265n50, 266n62

grassroots movements. *See* public protests

Green Party/Alliance '90, 57, 148, 191, 250n80, 265n56

Gross, Martin, 163

Grosshennersdorf Environmental Library, 258n76

Guattari, Félix, 231–32

guilt, collective, 10, 130

Gundermann (film), 262n6

Gysi, Gregor, 64, 148, 265n48

Habeck, Robert, 69

Habermas, Jürgen, 244n9

haptics and touch, 133, 137–38, 140–41, 147

Harrison, Hope, 252n103

Harvey, David, 248n55

Havel, Václav, 202

Havemann, Katja, 61, 148, 204, 250n88

Havemann, Robert, 250n88

hegemony and counter-hegemony: as framework, 25; Gramsci on, 243n79; limits of, 81–85, 103, 113. *See also* memorial politics, Berlin; memorial politics, Leipzig

Heimat Is a Space in Time (documentary film), 166–67

Hein, Christoph, 237n8, 254n6, 261n6; *Trutz*, 253n15, 263n28

Heise, Thomas: "Entfernte Verwandte" installation, 274n92; *Heimat Is a Space in Time*, 166–67; *The House*, 170, 171; *Jammed: Let's Get Moving*, 168, 193–94; *People's Police Force*, 170, 171; SFD/DEFA involvement, 161, 170–71, 172, 268n12; *Why a Film about These People*, 170, 179. See also *Material* (documentary film)

Hell, Julia, 23

Hempel, Johannes, 97–98

Henckel von Donnersmarck, Florian, *The Lives of Others*, 130, 146, 157–58, 261n6, 265n50

Hensel, Jana, 210

Herskovits, Alberto, 262n19

Hertle, Hans-Hermann, 246n31

Heym, Stefan, 5, 173, 263n25

Hildebrandt, Alexandra, 41

Hirsch, Marianne, 28

Hirsch, Ralf, 264n45

History Consortium, 246n31

Hochmuth, Hanno, 89

Holocaust memorials, 33, 36, 41, 44–45

Holzer, Jenny, 117

Honecker, Erich, 5

Honig, Bonnie, 120, 207, 218, 281n91

Hope Nicaragua, 222

House, The (documentary film), 170, 171

House of History Bonn, 239n27

House of History Foundation of the FRG, 239n27

Hovestädt, Dagmar, 137

Hummitzsch, Manfred, 89

Huyssen, Andreas, 204, 244n7, 262n17

immigration. *See* migration

inequality. *See* equality

Ingram, Susan, 117

inheritance, 18–19, 27

Initiative for Peace and Human Rights, 185

International Documentary and Short Film Week, Leipzig, 91–92 international student exchange programs, 214, 278n57

intersectional memory politics, 220

(in)visibility: and digital culture, 159, 160; of East Germans, 210; and integrative memorial design, 103; and public memory, 34, 60, 65, 72, 111–12, 132. *See also* erasure; spectrality

It's a Wonderful Life (film), 266n61

Ives, Charles, 168

Jackisch, Holger, 30, 121

Jahn, Roland, 204, 265n56

Jameson, Fredric, 21

Jammed: Let's Get Moving (documentary film), 168, 193–94

Jammer-Ossi label, 90

Jarausch, Konrad, 246n31

Jewish Museum, Berlin, 36, 44

Jung, Burkhard, 83, 113, 260n103

Kaden, Klaus, 93

Kahane, Anetta, 209, 223

Kantsteiner, Wulf, 205

Karl Marx City (documentary film), 129–33, *135, 138, 140, 141, 142, 143, 155*; alternative memory spaces in, 152–57, 158; archival evidentiary status in, 134, 137–38, 139–40, 143, 144; authenticity in, 142–44; and destabilization of hegemonic narratives, 140–42; digital culture commentary in, 159–60; and failure of the socialist vision, 147–49; memory-death dynamics in, 146–47, 153; photograph-film dynamics in, 142, 143, 144, 159–60; and post-1989 economic decline, 149–52; totalitarian framing in, 134–36, 139, 157

Kazanjian, David, 28

Kenney, Padraic, 9

Kerbel, Lev, 131, 151, 253n14

Kitchen, Martin, 253–54n19

Klausmeier, Axel, 41, 42

Kluge, Alexander, 64, 165, 210, 254n22; *Nachrichten aus der ideologischen Antike*, 272n68

Koepnick, Lutz, 37

Kohl, Helmut, 6, 19, 37, 52, 148,

237n11, 248n59, 263n25; *Ich wollte Deutschlands Einheit*, 265n55

König, Anna, 80

Konzert im Freien (documentary film), 230–31, 232

Koselleck, Reinhart, 37

Kowalczuk, Ilko-Sascha, 17, 23, 154, 242n71, 266n62, 266n63, 277–78n43

Kracauer, Siegfried, 248n49

Krauss, Werner, 82

Krenz, Egon, 5, 60, 175

Kroske, Gerd, 171

Kruso (Seiler), 256n26, 263n28

Kuball, Mischa: *Private Light/Public Light*, 124; *Solidarity Grid*, 124; *white space/ Critical Thinking Needs Time and Space*, 116–18, *118, 119*, 120–21, 122–24, *123*

LaCapra, Dominick, 53, 249n64

Laclau, Ernesto, 66, 252n98

Landsberg, Alison, 109, 251n95

language, power of, 114

Lässig, Jochen, 190

LaVerdiere, Julian, 261n124

"Leap into Freedom" (Leibing), 47–48, *48*, 49

Lear, Jonathan, 163

Lefebvre, Henri, 248n55

Left Party, 250n80

legacies of 1953, 49, 60, 63, 64, 173, 219

legacies of 1968, 8–9, 164

legacies of 1989. *See* archives; memorial politics, Berlin; memorial politics, Leipzig; Peaceful Revolution; provisional history; public protests

Leibing, Peter, "Leap into Freedom," 47–48, *48*, 49

Leipzig: communal council systems, 183–86, 270nn43–44, 271n46; disruptive dynamics of demonstrations in, 87–88, 99; factors for revolution in, 82; influence on Prague demonstrations, 202; in official history of '89, 81–82. *See also* memorial politics, Leipzig

Leipzig Forum of Contemporary History, 239n27

Leipzig Opposition, 94
Lengsfeld, Vera, 263n25, 265n56, 276n18
Lenin, Vladimir, 75
Lewis, Alison, 23
liberty. *See* freedom
"Liberty Leading the People"
    (Delacroix), 178
Libeskind, Daniel, 44
Liebknecht, Karl, 106, 244n98
Lieser, Helga, 67
Light Festival, Leipzig, 116, 117–18, 120,
    122–23, 260n103
light installations, 116–18, *118*, *119*, 120–21,
    122–24, *123*, 261n124
Linke Party, 56, 57, 226, 250n80
Lives of Others, The (film), 130, 146,
    157–58, 261n6, 265n50
Löser, Claus, 170
Luft, Christa, 251n93
Lummer, Heinrich, 75
Luxemburg, Rosa, 106, 176, 244n98
Luxor-Palast citizens' assembly, Karl-
    Marx-Stadt (October 7, 1989), 152,
    154–57, 267n71
Luxus Arbeit (photography series), 80

Maas, Heiko, 205
Magirius, Friedrich, 95, 257n49
Maier, Charles, 23
Maier, Hans, 82
Mandel, Ruth, 277n39
Marantz, Paul, 261n124
Mark, James, 38, 203, 221, 222
Marquardt, Fritz, 168, 171
Martin Luther King Center for
    Nonviolence and Civil Courage,
    Werdau, 258n76
Marx, Karl, 15, 242n75
Marx Engels Forum monument, xi, *xii*,
    230–31
Masur, Kurt, 163
Material (documentary film), 161–62,
    162, *175*, *176*, *181*, *189*; deconstructed
    temporalities in, 168–69;
    improvisational and open-ended
    dynamics in, 165, 172, 173, 174–77,
    178–79, 191; and *Jammed* screening,
    193–94; parliamentary footage in,

188–91, 193; Republic Palace
    footage in, 197; solidarity dynamics
    in, 179–82
materiality: in memorial discourse,
    41–42, 108, 110, 246n34; of
    photographs, 137–38, 140–41; and
    preservation, 168
Mausbach, Florian, 53
May '68 legacies, 8–9, 164
McFalls, Laurence, 262n19
McLuhan, Marshall, 54
media archeology, 164–65, 169
memorial politics, Berlin: absence of
    '89–90 interval period in, 35, 37,
    40, 43, 46–47, 49–50, 55–56, 77,
    123; activist approach, 68–70;
    counter-discursive sites, 72, 76,
    77–78; discursive shift in, 36–40;
    and entangled legacies, 37, 45,
    53, 71, 76–77, 79; freedom narrative,
    47–50; memorial topography,
    32–34, *32*; mourning dynamics,
    74–75, 78; peacefulness narrative,
    66–67; and professionalization, 42;
    public's resistance to hegemonic
    schemes, 56–58, 115, 250n80;
    teleological narrative, 49, 51–53,
    54–55, 56, 60, 67; victimization
    narrative, 39–40, 43, 44–46;
    visibility/invisibility dynamics,
    34, 60, 65, 72, 132. *See also specific
    memorials*
memorial politics, Leipzig, 82–85;
    absence of '89 disruptive dynamics,
    88–89, 90, 99–100, 125, 126; counter-
    discursive sites, 116–17, *118*, 121,
    123–24; peacefulness narrative, 86–87,
    88, 90, 100, 125–26; public's resistance
    to hegemonic schemes, 113, 115, 118;
    spirituality framing, 100–102; state
    oppression narrative, 108; teleological
    narrative, 90, 114; traumatic memory
    grids, 102–3, 108–9; visibility/
    invisibility dynamics, 111–12, 132. *See
    also specific memorials*
memorials vs. exhibitions, 119–20
Memorial to the Murdered Jews of
    Europe, 33, 36, 53

memory: collective, 35, 244n10; counter-hegemonic, 25, 68, 113, 115; death and, 146–47; future-oriented, 25–28, 69, 132; and media-archeological practices, 164–65, 169; mediated, 34, 65, 77–78, 109, 158, 199; refracted, 102; types of, 116. *See also* erasure; (in)visibility; memorial politics, Berlin; memorial politics, Leipzig; performativity; provisional history

memory of publics, as concept, 34, 68, 83

memory studies, as field, 25

Merkel, Angela, 7, 38, 149, 205, 265–66n56, 276n19

metal, symbolism of, 108, 110

Mielke, Erich, 89

migration: Eastern globalization context of, 219–24; migrant status of East Germans, 147, 207–11, 276n30, 276n32; out of East Germany, 84, 87, 91, 141–42, 255n19, 264nn37–38; refugee crisis (2015), 57, 205, 276n19; and transcultural conviviality, 213–19, 224

Milla and Partner (design agency), 53, 54, 55, 115

Minds of Their Own: Migrants in the GDR (documentary film), 219–20

Mitchell, W. J. T., 58, 154

Modrow, Hans, 64, 66, 251nn92–93, 264n38

Monument to Freedom and Unity, Berlin, 38; design proposals, 53–55, 54, 57, 248n61; Leipzig monument as counterproposal to, 113; opposition to, 56–58, 115, 250n80; teleological narrative, 51–53, 54–55, 56. *See also* Freedom and Unity Monument, Leipzig

Monument to the Peaceful Revolution, St. Nicholas Church, Leipzig, 85–89, 86, 126

Mouffe, Chantal, 66, 210, 227, 228, 252n98

Müller, Heiner, xi, 5, 130, 173, 194, 205; *Germania Tod in Berlin*, 167, 171; *A Specter Departs from Europe*, 230

Mulvey, Laura, 144

Murderers among Us (film), 273n75

Myoda, Paul, 261n124

Nachrichten aus der ideologischen Antike (documentary film), 272n68

national monument. *See* Monument to Freedom and Unity, Berlin

NATO, 238n13

Nazism and Third Reich, in memorial discourse, 33, 35, 36–37, 44–45, 46

neoclassical architecture, 88

neoliberalism: Brown on, 24, 67, 227; contemporary crisis of, 23–24, 201, 203, 227; and democracy, 24, 67, 227; memory shift in, 1–2, 40 (*see also* memorial politics, Berlin); and privatization/capitalism, 7, 8, 37, 55, 150–51, 185, 192, 226, 227, 266n59; shock therapy, 35; as term, 40; urban policies, 50

neo-Nazis/skinheads, 77, 193, 212

New Forum: citizen support for, 11–12; establishment of, xiv, 5; Karl-Marx-Stadt demonstrations, 155; Leipzig demonstrations, 87, 182, 257n56; objectives, 16, 17; post-1989 relevance, 148; and Robert Havemann Society, 61, 250n88; self-government efforts, 185

New Lives (Schulze), 14–15, 121–22, 150–51, 173–74

Nguyen, Angelika, 217

1984 (Orwell), 130

nonviolence, interdependence with violence, 95–99, 182, 258n61. *See also* violence

Nooke, Günter, 265n56

Nordbahnhof metro station, 44

Offene Arbeit (open work) ideology, 93, 256n42

Open Memory Box (online archive), 262n19

Orwell, George, *1984*, 130

Osang, Alexander, 265n55

Ostalgie (nostalgia for the East), 23, 68, 131, 164

Ottinger, Ulrike, 131

Özdamar, Emine Sevgi, 216

Özdemir, Cem, 205

INDEX > 319

pacifism, twofold definition of, 84
pamphlet distribution, 97, 98, 106
Party of Democratic Socialism (PDS), 38, 245n20
Paver, Chloe, 119
PDS (Party of Democratic Socialism), 38, 245n20
Peaceful Revolution: contemporary significance of, 23–24; official history of, 3–9, 13–14, 81–82; reframing, 25–29; scholarship on, 20–23. *See also* archives; memorial politics, Berlin; memorial politics, Leipzig; provisional history; public protests; violence
peace prayer gatherings: as phenomenon, 91, 92; radical fringe group dynamics, 92–95; solidarity dynamics, 97–99; spiritual framing in memorial politics, 100–102; state surveillance of, 87–88, 89, 95; street protests outside of, 95–97, 98, 162–63, 182
"Peace Prayers" exhibit, St. Nicholas Church, Leipzig, 90–91, 93, 94, 96, 100–102, *101*
PEGIDA, 57, 205, 208, 276n19
pensiveness, 143–44
"people, the," as signifier, 211. *See also* "We are the people" slogan
people's movements. *See* public protests
People's Police Force (documentary film), 170, 171
performativity: of memory, 25, 68, 83; in public demonstrations, 173–74, 177; of publics, 67, 83; in Wall memorials, 43, 47, 247nn39–40
Pfaff, Steven, 23
photographs: alternative memories stored in, 152, 154–57; epistemological narrowing with, 47–49; evidentiary status of, 132, 133, 144; evidentiary vs. disclosive modes of, 140, 264n33; and film, 132–33, 142, 143, 144, 159–60; framing, 63; institutional, 149; as intermedial spaces, 109–10, 132–33, 143–44; materiality of, 137–38, 140–41; as silent, 46, 141, 144, 154; social observation tradition, 187; spectrality

of, 46, 103, 132, 153; subjectification and commodification of, 247–48n49; teleological arrangement of, 49, 60; and temporality, 110, 152–53, 212; and traumatic memory, 102–3; and visibility, 65
Piesche, Peggy, 217, 276n26, 279n62
Pillar to the Peaceful Revolution, Berlin, *61, 62*; context missing from, 63–65; location, 34, 59; in memorial network, 59–60, 66–67; photographs selected for, 60, 63; and Robert Havemann Society, 59, 61–63
Pleiße pilgrimage (June 1989), 106
police force. *See* Stasi and police force
police order, disruption of, 21, 81–82, 87–88, 261n125
political, the, defined, 21
political happiness/joy, 1, 16, 30, 35, 67, 241n48
post-migrant, as term, 276–77n32
post-1989 memory. *See* archives; memorial politics, Berlin; memorial politics, Leipzig; memory; Peaceful Revolution; provisional history; public protests
potential history, 59. *See also* future archives, as concept
Prague, demonstrations in, 202
prayers for peace. *See* peace prayer gatherings
Prisoner, The, or: How I Planned to Kill Tony Blair (documentary film), 131
prisons, 129, 179–80
privatization and capitalism, 7, 8, 37, 55, 150–51, 185, 192, 226, 266n59
prospective archeology, 165, 268n12
protests. *See* public protests
provisional history: as artistic intervention, 195–96; as concept, 167–68; open-ended and unfulfilled potentiality in, 152, 156–57, 173, 176, 178–79, 196; vs. teleological narratives, 162, 165, 169, 172–73, 186
public memory, as concept, 34–35, 56, 116
public prepositions, 116, 117, 124

public protests: anarchic cooperation of, 15, 240n45; disruptive and dislocating force of, 81–82, 84, 87–88, 99, 124; and energetic resonance, 121–22; environmental movements, 106–7, 228–29; and failure of the socialist vision, 28, 148–49, 164, 194, 204–5, 251n93; film festival activism, 91–92; flexible mobility of, 123–24; and French revolutionary legacy, 177–78, 194; global influence of East German, 202–3; improvisational dynamics of, 165, 172, 174–77, 184, 192; 1953 uprising, 49, 60, 63, 64, 173, 219; open-ended and unfulfilled potentiality of, 152, 156–57, 173, 176, 178–79, 196; and performativity, 173–74, 177; pluralistic dynamics of, 65–66, 106, 251n96, 252nn97–98; prominence and growth of, 16–18; and self-government efforts, 182–86, 192–93, 194, 270nn40–44; solidarity dynamics, 97–99, 179–82, 185, 221–24; theaters as gathering places, 152, 154–57, 267n71; transience of, 109, 120–21. *See also* memorial politics, Berlin; memorial politics, Leipzig; peace prayer gatherings

publics: defined, 35; as mediated acts, 244n9; performative role, 83, 180; self-organized, 57, 60, 193, 196; unity of, 83, 255n11

public sphere: defined, 72, 244n9; and GDR, 92, 174; and late capitalist society, 57; and representational democracy, 168

punitive forgetting, 136, 262n17

Qurbani, Burhan, 277n41

racism and xenophobia, 205, 209, 210, 220–24, 277n39
radical democracy, 66, 228, 252n98
Radstone, Susannah, 212
Rancière, Jacques: on artistic intervention, 195–96; on critique of image consumption, 267n80; on "the people," 198, 274n96; on police order,

21, 81; on political possibility, 23, 121; on space of political dispute, 20, 35
Raphael, Lutz, 275n11
Reagan, Ronald, 3–4, 245n17
records. *See* archives; Stasi Records Agency (BStU)
refracted memory, 102
refugee crisis (2015), 57, 205, 276n19
Reich, Jens, 5, 192, 250n88
Reich Chancellery, 78
Reitmann, H., 93
Republic Palace (GDR), 34, 38, 50–51, 174, 197, 230–31
resistance movements. *See* public protests
resonance, relational field of, 121–22
reunification narrative. *See* Peaceful Revolution
Reuter, Edzard, 251n93
"Revolution and Fall of the Wall" exhibit, 38, 60
revolutionary protests. *See* public protests
Richter, Frank, 239n25, 257n49
Richter, Gerhard, 111
Richter, Sebastian, 168, 194
right-wing politics and extremism, 22, 23–24, 128, 193–94, 200–201, 203–4, 205, 209, 226, 277n41, 277–78n43
Rigney, Ann, 25, 109, 218
Robert Havemann Society, 59, 61–62, 66, 250n88
Romania, revolution in, 14
Rosa, Hartmut, 121, 122
Ross, Kristin, 9, 255n23
Rost, Andreas, 183–84, 187–88, 198, 272n64
Rothberg, Michael, 25, 276n23
Rothöhler, Simon, 172, 190
roundtables and council systems, 17, 183–86, 194, 223, 270nn40–44
Roy, Arundhati, 232
Russia: as imperial Other, 78–79; and Soviet War Memorial, 72–78

Sa'adah, Anne, 23, 66, 191, 239n25, 252n97
Sabrow, Martin, 246n31
samizdat, 106
Sanders, Helke, 131
Santner, Eric, 20, 22, 35

Sarotte, Mary Elise, 23, 36, 238n13
Saunders, Anna, 56–57, 83, 113–14, 255n15
Schabowski, Günter, 60
Schell, Jonathan, 15
Schirmer, Herbert, 195
Schmemann, Serge, 237n8
Schmidt, Gabriele, 96
Schmidt, Helmut, 239n30
Schneider, Wolfgang, *Demontagebuch*, 178
Schorlemmer, Friedrich, 263n25
Schulze, Ingo, 229; *New Lives*, 14–15, 121–22, 150–51, 173–74
Schumann, Conrad, 47, 247n49
Schütterle, Johanna, 137, 139
Sebald, W. G., 46
SED. *See* German Democratic Republic (GDR) and Socialist Unity Party (SED)
Seiler, Lutz, *Kruso*, 256n26, 263n28
Şenocak, Zafer, 79, 208–9, 254n24
SFD (State Film Documentation), 170, 268n12, 269n22
sharing, collective and public, 207, 225–26, 228, 279n63
Sieg, Katrin, 208, 250n85
silence, of photographs, 46, 141, 144, 154
Sites of the Peaceful Revolution, Berlin, 59–60. *See also* Pillar to the Peaceful Revolution, Berlin
Sites of the Peaceful Revolution, Leipzig, *104, 105, 110*; and Citizens' Committee, 104–5, 108, 258n75; events selected for, 106, 111; invisibility of, 111–12; materiality of, 108, 110; as traumatic memory grid, 102–3, 108–9; urban setting, 103–4
skinheads/neo-Nazis, 77, 193, 212
Slobodian, Quinn, 275n7, 276n26, 280n71
Socialist Unity Party. *See* German Democratic Republic (GDR) and Socialist Unity Party (SED)
social memory, 35, 244n10
social observation, photography and film tradition, 187
social sculpture, 55

socioeconomic inequality, 15, 55, 221–22
solidarity: and allyship, 207, 225, 227; in public protests, 97–99, 179–82, 185, 221–24; transcultural conviviality, 213–19, 224
Solidarity Grid (Kuball), 124
Sontag, Susan, 103
Soviet War Memorial, Berlin, 72–78
Spartacist Workers Party (SpAD), 77
Specter Departs from Europe, A (Müller), 230
spectrality: and afterlife of data, 259n86; of archives, 27, 132, 135–36, 138; and mourning, xi–xii, 74–75, 78, 230; of photographs, 46, 103, 132, 153; of postcommunist life, 151. *See also* (in)visibility
Speer, Albert, 78
Spiegel-TV, 190, 272–73n69
Stalin, Joseph, 74, 75
Stasi and police force: collaborator and informer allegations, 145–46, 264n45, 265n48; and collapse of GDR, official history, 5; and disruption of police order, 21, 81–82, 87–88, 261n125; legacy of, 61–63, 133–34, 145; opposition from within, 122; peace prayer gatherings, surveillance of, 87–88, 89, 95; violence of, 14–15, 95–97, 141–42, 167
Stasi Records Agency (BStU): *Access to Secrecy* exhibit, 129, 137; destabilization of hegemonic narratives in, 140–42; establishment of, 191, 192, 261n2; evidentiary status of, 134, 137–38, 139–40, 144; oversight of, 128, 246n31, 265n56; and preservation vs. destruction of files in, 263n25; reconstruction efforts, 137; records in, 129; research programs, 264–65n47; totalitarian framing, 134–37, 139, 157
State Film Documentation (SFD), 170, 268n12, 269n22
Staudte, Wolfgang, *Murderers among Us*, 273n75
Steiner, Barbara, 117

St. Lucas Church, 94
St. Nicholas Church: Monument to the Peaceful Revolution, 85–89, *86*, 126; peace prayer phenomenon, 91, 92; "Peace Prayers" exhibit, 90–91, 93, 94, 96, 100–102, *101*; peace prayer solidarity, 97–99; radical activists, 92–95; street protests outside of, 95–97, 98, 162–63, 182
Stoler, Ann, 24
Stolpe, Manfred, 263n25
Stötzner, Andreas, 85–86, 88, 89
Streamas, John, 228
student exchange programs, 214, 278n57
suicide, 146–47, 148, 149, 150, 151, 266n62

Tawada, Yoko, 79
Taylor, Diana, 28, 114, 136, 262n20
television broadcast medium, 188–91, 272–73n69
Telos (journal), 39
Teltschik, Horst, 238n13, 251n92
Thälmann, Ernst, 253n14
Thatcher, Margaret, 40, 245n17
theaters, activist gatherings in, 152, 154–57, 267n71
Thierse, Wolfgang, 139, 204
Third Reich and Nazism, in memorial discourse, 33, 35, 36–37, 44–45, 46
Tiananmen Square, 98, 202
Till, Karen, 33
TINA (There Is No Alternative) ideology, 40, 205
Tischer, Beate, 96
Tomski, Nikolai, 75
"Topography of Terror" exhibit, 33, 36
touch and haptics, 133, 137–38, 140–41, 147
traumatic memory grids, 102–3, 108–9
Traverso, Enzo, 2, 50, 204
Tribute in Light installation, 261n124
Trnka, Jamie H., 253n4
Trutz (Hein), 253n15, 263n28
Tschörtner, Petra, 171
Tucker, Michael, 129, 131. See also *Karl Marx City* (documentary film)
Tucker-Frost, Miley, 115
Turkish Germans, 208, 211–19, *213*, *215*, 224, 277n37, 277n39, 280n87

Uekötter, Frank, 107
Uncovering the Year 1990 (archival art object), 165–66, *166*, 167, 187–88
unemployment, 80, 149–52, 193, 266n59, 266n62
unification narrative. *See* Peaceful Revolution
universalism, 206
Unrechtsstaat (illegitimate state) label, 38, 148, 226, 245n20
uprisings. *See* public protests
urban space, installations integrated with, 59, 60, 103–4

Velvet Revolutions, xii, 8, 15, 99, 207
victimization narrative, 44–46
Vielen, Die, campaign, 229
Vietnam, anti-colonial movements in, 221
violence: of the archive, 136–37, 160, 243n83; of ideological and structural disruption, 21, 156; interdependence with nonviolence, 95–99, 182, 258n61; militant activist factions, 92–93; vs. "Peaceful Revolution" narrative, 5, 13–14, 237n8; police brutality, 14–15, 95–97, 141–42, 167, 202; and prisons, 180; racial, 209; right-wing, 23–24, 193–95
visas, exit, 91, 94
visibility. *See* erasure; (in)visibility
Voigt, Andreas, 171
Voigt, Peter, xi–xii

Wall. *See* Berlin Wall
Waltz, Sasha, 53–54, 58
Warner, Michael, 57, 244n9, 255n11
"We are the people" slogan, 22, 56–57, 179, 198–99, 202, 210–11, 229, 249n75, 257–58n60
Weber, Hasko, 156, 157
Weil, Francesca, 270n40, 271n53
Weiss, Konrad, 194
Wende (turn/change), 4. *See also* Peaceful Revolution
Wensierski, Peter, 69
Wenzel, Jan, 80; *Uncovering the Year 1990* (ed.), 165–66, *166*, 167, 187–88
Western gaze, 47, 70, 244n7

West Germany. *See* Federal Republic of Germany (FRG)

white space/ Critical Thinking Needs Time and Space (Kuball), 116–18, *118*, *119*, 120–21, 122–24, *123*

Why a Film about These People (documentary film), 170, 179

Wiener, Lawrence, 117

Wilcken, Dagmar, 67

Wilhelm I (German emperor), 54

Wilhelm-Leuschner-Platz, Leipzig, 113, 118

"Window of Remembrance," Berlin Wall Memorial, 45–46, *45*

Winnicott, D. W., 120

"Wir sind das Volk" slogan, 22, 56–57, 179, 198–99, 202, 210–11, 229, 249n75, 257–58n60

Wir sind jung. Wir sind stark (film), 277n41

Wolf, Christa, 5, 127, 173, 205, 226; *City of Angels*, 174

Wolrab, Julia, 212

Wonneberger, Christoph, 94, 95, 98, 257n49

Working Group of the Archives of Opposition and Resistance in Saxony, 258n76

Working Group on Foreigners' Issues, 223

Wüstenberg, Jenny, 250n78

xenophobia and racism, 205, 209, 210, 220–24, 277n39

Yildiz, Yasemin, 208, 212, 276n23

Yugoslav republics, revolution in, 14

Zetkin, Clara, 118

Ziegler, Jean, 2

Zielinski, Siegfried, 165, 169

Ziemer, Gudula, 30, 121

Žižek, Slavoj, xiv, 21, 204, 210

Zwahr, Hartmut, 82, 99, 256n40, 273n75